MADE IN CANADA LEADERSHIP.

JB JOSSEY-BASS™

MADE IN CANADA
LEADERSHIP.

WISDOM FROM THE NATION'S BEST AND BRIGHTEST ON LEADERSHIP PRACTICE AND DEVELOPMENT

AMAL HENEIN & FRANÇOISE MORISSETTE

John Wiley & Sons Canada, Ltd.

National Library of Canada Cataloguing in Publication Data

Henein, Amal, 1951-
  Made in Canada leadership : wisdom from the nation's best and brightest on leadership practice and development / Amal Henein, Françoise Morissette.

Includes bibliographical references and index.
ISBN 978-0-470-83943-0

  1. Leadership—Canada. I. Morissette, Françoise, 1949- II. Title.

HD57.7.H46 2007   658.4'0920971   C2007-901603-0

Production Credits
Cover design: Jason Vandenberg
Interior Text Design: Natalia Burobina
Wiley Bicentennial Logo: Richard J. Pacifico
Printer: Friesens

John Wiley & Sons Canada, Ltd.
6045 Freemont Blvd.
Mississauga, Ontario
L5R 4J3

Printed in Canada

1 2 3 4 5 FP 11 10 09 08 07

CONTENTS

Foreword by Mr. Alban D'Amours, President and CEO, Desjardins Group   *ix*

Acknowledgements   *xi*

Introduction   *1*

Part I—DEVELOPING COMPETENT LEADERS   **7**

Section A: What Is the Process?   **8**

Chapter 1   Leadership Essentials (4Ps): *What is leadership?*   9

Chapter 2   The Leadership Ride: *How does leadership feel to the leader?*   23

Chapter 3   The Leadership Garden: *Evolutionary steps towards leadership maturity*   41

Chapter 4   The 'Force' and the 'Blueprint': *Internal access routes to leadership*   57

Section B: How Can We Optimize the Process?   **76**

Chapter 5   Individual Leadership Strategy: *What individuals can do to facilitate their development*   77

Chapter 6   The Master and the Apprentice: *The best framework for leadership development*   95

Chapter 7   Program Architecture: *Optimal infrastructure for leadership development programs*   109

Chapter 8   Program Enhancement: *Program evolution and continuous improvement*   129

Part II—ENSURING A RELIABLE LEADERSHIP SUPPLY   **143**

Chapter 9   Organizational Leadership Strategies: *What organizations can do to enhance leadership capacity*   145

Chapter 10   Co-op Fundamentals: *Orientation to the co-op sector*   161

Chapter 11   Best Practices from the Co-op Sector: *Innovative solutions for all sectors*   175

Chapter 12   National Leadership Strategy: *What Canada can do to enhance its leadership capacity*   195

Part III—STRENGTHENING CANADIAN LEADERSHIP   **215**

Chapter 13   Our National Leadership Brand: *How we lead*   217

Chapter 14   The Scholar and the Warrior: *How we can improve our leadership impact and effectiveness*   241

Chapter 15   Public Leadership Issues: *How we can enhance leadership capacity in this important sector*   259
Chapter 16   Conclusion   287

Part IV—RESEARCH AND INTERVIEWEE INFORMATION   **301**
Appendix I   Research Process and Statistical Information   303
Appendix II   Leaders Interviewed   313
Appendix III Leadership Programs   333

Bibliography   341
Index   343

*This book is dedicated to all the leaders who made
a difference in Canada's history,
particularly these heroes of the war of 1812:
General Isaac Brock, Tecumseh,
Charles-Michel d'Irumberry de Salaberry and Laura Secord.
May their leadership and courage never be forgotten.*

Leadership allowed me to make a difference. If a thousand individuals each make a small difference, together, we make a huge difference. In the past, people fought for the advantages we enjoy today. We also have to do our part.

Johanna Maria Bates-Van der Zeijst
President, Johanna M. Bates Literary Consultants Inc.

FOREWORD

Since time immemorial, the success of any collective endeavour has depended largely on the strength and calibre of leaders. Driven by a vision and compelled to share it, leaders enable groups and individuals to surpass the limits of their current reality.

Today, we need a critical mass of leaders to overcome the challenges we face and to fulfill our collective ambitions. This book will stimulate our thought process by examining this important issue.

In order to benefit from the experience of established leaders, the authors interviewed remarkable individuals across Canada in a variety of sectors. They also consulted leadership development professionals in order to identify the best practices, that is, what is new, innovative, effective and inspiring in the field of leadership development across the country.

Moreover, they researched leadership practice and development in co-operatives, whose framework and operational model offer an original approach to community involvement and ownership. In Canada, this sector is flourishing, with four of every ten Canadians belonging to a co-operative. In Québec, due to the deep roots planted by Desjardins, the proportion is higher: seven out of ten people belong to a Desjardins financial services co-operative.

The authors were also interested in finding out more about the Canadian brand of leadership in order to leverage its distinctive attributes on the international scene and generally strengthen Canadian leadership.

THE MANY FACES OF LEADERSHIP

Integrating these various perspectives, this book takes into account all aspects of leadership development, in which individuals, organizations and societies all have a role to play, as they share a collective responsibility.

The book considers the means to awaken leadership potential and nurture the development of the competencies required for leadership. It also examines the ways people can contribute to the success of valued projects and the organizations that strive to implement them.

Moreover, it shows how organizations can create an environment that values leadership and is conducive to its emergence. Does this mean creating a supportive culture that allows experimentation and accepts the inevitable ensuing mistakes? Does it also mean implementing programs and infrastructures, thereby fostering leadership practice and development?

For example, our organization's founder, Alphonse Desjardins, exhibited a determined and inclusive leadership style when he implemented the caisse populaire model and enlisted associates. For all of us at Desjardins, he continues to be a great source of inspiration. Moreover, his leadership qualities enabled him to contribute to the creation of the first credit unions in other parts of Canada and the United States, where he is widely acknowledged as a pioneer of co-operative development. At Desjardins, we continue our founder's tradition by paying particular attention to the conditions required for leadership success, as we know that the growth and sustainability of our organization rely, for the most part, on our employees and leaders.

At the social level, the book examines how to broaden our collective awareness of the importance of leadership and how to foster its development. How can we raise the population's interest in this topic? What processes and systems can be put in place to identify potential leaders and support them adequately, thereby increasing our development prospects?

By encapsulating the experience and expertise of exceptional leaders and professional experts, this book presents a unique opportunity to explore leadership issues, identify leadership potential and enhance the growth of vibrant leadership in our organizations and communities.

Desjardins is proud to be associated with this stimulating initiative.

Happy reading,

Alban D'Amours
President and CEO
Desjardins Group

ACKNOWLEDGEMENTS

First, we want to thank all the leaders interviewed for generously sharing their time and wisdom. Many also opened doors to other respected leaders. Several cheered us on the sidelines and made useful suggestions to improve the project. Without them all, this book could not have become a reality. A list of interviewees is included in Appendix II.

Second, we want to thank the leadership development professionals who shared their experience and expertise. Your input shaped our thinking and opened our minds. Your passion for leadership development was nothing short of electrifying. A list of participating organizations is included in Appendix III.

Third, we want to thank the supporters who believed in the project from the start and never tired of lending a sympathetic ear or a helping hand, of providing a word of encouragement, and of recommending other leaders. Throughout, people found innovative ways to help, including: the neighbour who mowed the lawn to allow more writing time, the chiropractor who straightened the back strained by too many hours at the computer, the accountant who provided expert guidance, the ophthalmologist who healed the tired eyes, the massage therapist who released stiff muscles, the relatives who listened patiently to endless excited tales about our interviewees' accomplishments, the friends who provided home-cooked meals, the clients who expressed interest, the colleagues who acted as sounding boards, etc. Without you, we couldn't have made it.

Thank you, Michele Allan, Doug Alley, Sandra Arseneault, Catherine Bachand, Marie-Andrée Boivin, Pierre Boivin, Josée Bouchard, Marie-Joelle Brassard, Joanne Brown, Wendy Burton, John Christensen, Ian Cooper, Christiane Côté,

Paul Dolby, Keith Doxsee, Jean Dubois, Marie-Josée Duquette, Reginald Ellis, Martine Flibotte, Quintin Fox, Robert Frosi, Peter Gammell, Fabienne Girard, Madeleine Guimond, Christine Greco, Bob Harris, Brian Henry, Chris Henry, Carol Hunter, Vincent Johnston, Mandy Joseph, Brad Kates, Barbara Katz, Norma Kennedy, Doug Kirby, Gilberte Landry-Boivin, Stewart Lee, Susan Letson, Lois Dyer Mann, Michelle Martel, Jude Martineau, Robin Metcalfe, Hélène Morissette, Tanya Mruck, Lynne Nusyna, Brent Pederson, Robert Potvin, John Rankin, Diane Scheidler, Shelley Stevenson, Dan Steward, Heather Stride, Chris Temovsky, Allyson Thompson, Jacques Viens, Charles Vincent, Richard Wilson and Paul Zmiyiwsky.

Of course, we want to thank our talented and dedicated research assistants from the bottom of our hearts: Michel Plante and Chris Hutcheson. Your contribution, positive attitude, insights and professionalism inspired and touched us, particularly during hard times.

We would also like to express our deep appreciation to the organizations and their representatives who acted on faith and committed to sponsoring the project. In particular, we want to recognize the Desjardins Group (Micheline Paradis, Louise-Marie Brousseau and Isabelle Adams) and Enbridge Inc. (Bonnie Dianne DuPont and Daniel O'Grady) A number of other contributors have also offered to support us moving forward and we are thankful for their generosity.

This book would not have become a reality without the assistance of our publisher, John Wiley & Sons Canada. We would like to thank Karen Milner, Executive Editor, Michelle Bullard, substantive and copy editor, Pam Vokey, and the marketing and sales team: Meghan Brousseau, Leah Campbell, Stacey Clark, Terry Palmer and Lucas Wilk.

Amal Henein would like to thank her husband, Nabil, and their son, Marc, for their constant support, encouragement and unconditional love. Françoise Morissette would like to thank her colleagues at the Industrial Relations Centre of Queen's University for their assistance and support: Brenda Barker, Paul Juniper and Alan Morantz, as well as Bruno-Marie Béchard, Rector, Université de Sherbrooke, for his commitment and trust.

This book is based on aggregated data collected from interviewees, subsequently interpreted and modelled. We take full responsibility for any mistakes contained, and for any contentious conclusions.

A.H. & F.M.

INTRODUCTION

Leadership is like art: the artist sees beauty where another person only sees reality. Likewise, the leader sees energy. His job is to capture this energy and to use and channel it for the task at hand. It's a transformational process, akin to alchemy.
Antoni Cimolino
General Director, The Stratford Festival of Canada

THE CASE OF THE MISSING LEADERS

In recent years, much noise has been made in the media and elsewhere about a leadership 'crisis.' Apparently, a lack of leadership quality and quantity currently prevails: supply simply cannot meet present and future demand. A leadership deficit is indeed worrisome, because, more than any other factor, leadership affects the success or failure of an enterprise. Organizations and nations must have access to a steady pipeline of proficient leaders to achieve their goals and embrace the future with confidence.

Acknowledging there is a problem, however, is only the first step. We must move beyond denouncing and despairing, to finding solutions. This book is an attempt to propose viable alternatives for consideration.

Therefore, our research aimed to answer three fundamental questions:

- How can we develop competent leaders?
- How can we ensure Canada has a reliable supply of capable leaders?
- How can we strengthen Canadian leadership?

Research Overview

To explore these queries, we sought advice from the best and assembled a representative sample of 295 exceptional leaders from coast to coast in the following sectors: arts, business, community, co-operatives, public, and sports. These accomplished individuals shared what contributed to their own development, and made recommendations to expand national leadership capacity.

We believe that good leadership is required in all sectors, and that outstanding leaders can be found everywhere. Best practices exist in arts as well as in business, and considerable benefits can be derived from cross-sector pollination. Therefore, this book is intended for all leaders everywhere. Whether you are a corporation executive, a government official, a community activist, an athletic coach, a symphony conductor or a co-op officer, this book is for you. We hope it will facilitate a national dialogue between all parties interested in leadership excellence.

We also wanted the opinion of professionals and to this end, sought 66 experts involved with leadership development programs in community organizations, consulting firms, co-operatives, corporations, institutes, sport organizations, universities and youth programs. These specialists described best practices and provided insight on optimal program infrastructure. Through their observations, we examined the complexity and intricacies of leadership development and pieced together an appropriate blueprint. We trust that their knowledge and expertise will benefit all involved with leadership development in Canada.

Research began in the summer of 2004 and, from the start, proved a labour of love. From an aggregate perspective, approximately 84% of the leaders and organizations we approached agreed to participate. We were overwhelmed by the level of collaboration we received. In our minds, we visualized the project like a chain of people holding hands across a map of Canada.

Speaking to accomplished and passionate people from all over the country was a privilege and an inspiration. From the Atlantic to British Columbia, we encountered exceptional leaders and learned from every one of them. We are grateful to all for taking the time to share their wisdom with us. Of course, we could have interviewed different or additional people. However, we are confident that we assembled a representative sample of the Canadian landscape.

The book showcases models, practices and strategies based on the experience of exceptional leaders and organizations. The focus is on success stories and on what works, instead of failures and problems. Our goal is to inspire individuals and organizations to enhance leadership capacity and provide practical advice on how to do so.

We have used a number of quotes from interviewees to illustrate points, so you will hear the voices of many participants. You will find pearls of wisdom, profound sentiments and touching stories along the way. Our notes filled thousands of pages. We would have liked to quote more, but doing so would have resulted in at least four books. You will find on our website, www.leadership-canada.com, additional information. A list of leaders and programs is provided in Appendix II and III.

A NEW PARADIGM IS REQUIRED

Leadership is crucial to the success of any entity. A great leader can take an average group and bring it to excellence. A bad leader can ruin a great group. On a scale from 1 to 10, leadership is in the 8 to 10 range. Yet, we mostly leave leadership emergence and development to chance.

Decisive Success Factor

As Human Resources professionals, we have observed the powerful impact of leadership throughout our careers. When positive, people can soar to impossible heights; when negative, they plunge to unspeakable lows. Compare for instance, the impact of Churchill and Hitler during the Second World War. In our opinion, leadership is the single most important factor for the well-being and success of any organization. Like a rare gem, quality leadership is extremely precious.

When interviewees shared their admiration and appreciation for the significant leaders in their lives, we could feel the depth of their emotions over the phone lines. Talented Canadian performing artist Gregory Charles puts it well in his smash hit *I Put My Trust In You*: "I believe what you say is true, I have faith in what you do." Trust is the channel through which leadership flows, the glue that bonds leader and follower, the foundation that enables the relationship to last. Because of the high level of trust required, the leadership relationship, much like love, makes us vulnerable and is imbued with profound meaning.

Critical Mass

In order to ensure an abundant supply of capable leaders in all sectors of the economy, Canada must generate a critical leadership mass. This represents a huge paradigm shift from the hero who appears during a crisis, saves the day and sails into the sunset. Knights in shining armour are simply too few and far between to meet society's vast leadership needs. A more appropriate paradigm to today's reality is the Canadian geese flying in a V formation: birds taking turns at leading.

DEVELOPING COMPETENT LEADERS

Leadership development is a major enterprise, not a casual undertaking. Sending someone on a two-day training program simply won't do; time, caring and respect for the uniqueness of each individual are required.

The most appropriate model for leadership development is the apprenticeship system, because it combines theory, practice and coaching—blending art and science. Apprenticeship acknowledges that proficiency doesn't happen overnight but evolves progressively. It also recognizes the importance of the master-apprentice relationship, providing extensive exposure to role-modelling and mentoring.

Consequently, the best program configuration follows the apprenticeship model: development occurs from the inside out to foster self-discovery; practice and education reinforce each other, and growth is sustained through support and communities of practice.

ENSURING A RELIABLE LEADERSHIP SUPPLY

As baby boomers retire en masse, a vacuum is created. Organizations and society in general are looking for established leaders and for effective ways to prepare future leaders. Interviewees overwhelmingly agreed that producing larger quantities of capable leaders will require more comprehensive approaches and reaching out to youth in early years.

We require a national leadership strategy to make leadership a priority, to stress the importance of competence and the imperative to invest in this crucial resource. The strategy should include leadership education for all ages, mentoring for more people and the creation of a National Leadership Institute to oversee the implementation of the national leadership strategy.

STRENGTHENING CANADIAN LEADERSHIP

As the world gets smaller, interdependent and more complex, the importance of integrating various perspectives, achieving win-win solutions and collaborating with diverse people increases. In other words, in the global 21st century world, success will belong to the integrators, not the bullies. Canadians are uniquely positioned to succeed.

What is it about our leadership style that appeals on the international scene? "Our style is effective, a quiet exercise of leadership with no flash or ostentation, but charisma. It is solid and trustworthy, humble and collaborative, attentive, and based on values. We like fair play and rules: peace, order and good government. We are an honest broker. As the world becomes smaller and more global, the Canadian style is more prized." (Dr. David Walker, Dean, Faculty of Health Sciences, Queen's University)

Our style is eminently suited for the global realities of the 21st century, but, to leverage it, we must assert our leadership identity. A better understanding of ourselves will enable us to commit to leadership and select appropriate avenues suited to our skills, temperament and values.

It is impossible to strengthen Canadian leadership without improving public leadership. The first step is to elaborate a strategic framework for the country, including vision, mission, values and priorities to guide and align politicians' decisions regardless of their political allegiance. The second step is to put in place extensive development and talent management infrastructures for elected officials at all levels of government. Reviewing stakeholder roles (citizens, public servants, elected officials and media) and clarifying their accountabilities will also increase participation and performance.

CONCLUSION

We are fortunate to live in one of the best countries in the world. It is our collective responsibility to maintain and enhance this state of affairs. And to do so, requires abundant and competent leadership.

We hope that this book will contribute to the leadership development field and make us more aware of the value of leadership and the contribution it makes to every enterprise. As authors, this book is our way to give back to the country we love so much.

All Canadians will benefit from expanding the leadership talent pool. Leadership is like a chain, a flexible series of joined links used to pull or to transmit power. As leaders continue to grow and develop, they add links to their chain and expand their leadership capacity.

Happy trails on your leadership journey.

PART I

DEVELOPING COMPETENT LEADERS

Section A

What Is the Process?

To begin, we will take a look at leadership … from the inside. In other words, how does leadership feel to the leader? How is it defined, viewed and experienced from within? How does the leadership journey begin? What sparks the flame? How does the path evolve towards maturity? Are there predictable stages and obstacles along the way? Let's find out in the next four chapters.

CHAPTER 1

LEADERSHIP ESSENTIALS

Great leaders just step up when others are stuck; they develop people and help them realize their full potential. So take charge, rise above confusion; be accountable and responsible; understand relationships between people and events to get to the desired outcome. Not being sure about everything helps you stay grounded, forces you to listen and avoids arrogance. You need to be uncomfortable at times—it's part of humility.

Dr. Colin MacDonald
President and CEO, Clearwater Seafood

In the world, there are two polarities: negative and positive. Some people have an innate ability to stimulate the positive, revealing the treasure contained within each person. For instance, they can walk into a room without uttering a single word, and the energy changes. They possess the gift of establishing an intrinsic connection. This is a leadership quality that has nothing to do with status or position.

Clément Guimond
General Coordinator, Caisse d'économie solidaire Desjardins
(Credit Union)

THE VALUE OF LEADERSHIP

Leadership matters. More than any other factor, it affects the success of an enterprise. The Canadian military clearly understands this reality. "In life and death situations, good leadership makes the difference. Therefore, in the military, leadership is at the core of everything: process, goals and outcomes. Leadership is what we do," said our interviewees from the Canadian Forces, Captain (N) Alan Okros and Commander Gregg Hannah.

But what is leadership? How does it work? Since the world began, people have been fascinated by its magic and sought to unravel its mystery. Over the course of history, numerous explanations have been put forward, some emphasizing attributes, others circumstances, others yet, actions. In the past, many theories focused on leaders' identity: personality traits such as charisma, or characteristics such as physical ability, skin colour, gender, etc. However, personal attributes do not shed much light on how leadership works.

In the 20th century, Harvard professor John Kotter revolutionized the field with his landmark research and books about leaders. Studying leaders in action, Kotter concluded that they exhibited common practices while creating a change culture. Leaders:

- Scan the environment.
- Set a direction.
- Align constituencies to the direction.
- Inspire and motivate constituencies to reach the direction.

His studies shifted the focus from *who* leaders are to *what they do* and proved that considerations such as personality traits and characteristics are, in fact, secondary. His research also highlighted why powerful leaders who altered the course of history, including Gandhi, Mother Teresa, Martin Luther King and our very own Nellie McClung, often did so with no formal authority or status. Demonstrating Kotter's set of practices makes you a leader, regardless of background, appearance or schooling. In other words, effective leadership action topples the elitist approach.

James M. Kouzes and Barry Z. Posner reinforced Kotter's findings in their landmark book, *The Leadership Challenge* (Jossey Bass, San Francisco, 1987). For this research, they surveyed 550 leaders and conducted 42 in-depth interviews to identify 'personal best' leadership experiences. The aggregated data produced five best practices. Leaders:

- Challenge the process.
- Inspire a shared vision.

- Enable others to act.
- Model the way.
- Encourage the heart.

These studies revealed that anyone can become a leader if able to demonstrate the required behaviours and take appropriate action. In the 20th century, we finally turned the page of prejudice and entered the realm of possibility. "Leadership is about behaviour more than position. It has to do with the person, and doesn't necessarily come with the status or authority granted by a title … Everyone is called to and can provide leadership regardless of position or any other characteristic. There is now a greater recognition of this state of affairs." (Eleanor Rivoire, Senior Vice-President, Patient Care Program & Chief Nursing Executive, Kingston General Hospital; Vice-President, Patient Care & Chief Nursing Executive, Quinte Health Care)

In our professional practice and in society in general, we have observed the benefits of this new paradigm and have seen, to our great satisfaction, leaders of all kinds emerge and soar, unrestricted by artificial limitations. Picture Sam Sullivan, Mayor of Vancouver, accepting the Olympic flag from his wheelchair during the 2006 Torino Winter Games closing ceremony—a proud moment for him, his city and Canada, and a glorious victory for leadership spirit. During a CBC Television interview, Mr. Sullivan reported frequently hearing comments like these in Torino: "In my country, a person like you could never become the mayor of a large city. You must come from a great country if people can see the ability beyond the disability." A moving tribute to the progress accomplished and a strong testimonial to the leadership skills we Canadians could not overlook.

Greater access to leadership has also prompted another paradigm shift. In the past, much has been made of the hero rising during a crisis and saving the day. As appealing as this concept might be, superheroes are few and far between. The Romeo Dallaires of this world will show up, but in numbers too small to meet the world's growing leadership needs. A critical mass of effective leaders is required in all sectors.

Therefore, armed with a fierce belief that leadership can and has changed the world, the conviction that leaders come in multiple packages, and the realization that society needs an abundant supply of capable leaders in order to thrive, we set out to discover critical leadership development success factors in our big, beautiful country and made some amazing discoveries.

THE NATURE OF LEADERSHIP

What is leadership? It's certainly not one clear thing, but rather many. "Leadership is a complex grouping of various abilities. It is not a single ability but a cluster of abilities." (Luc Nadeau, Executive Vice-President, Corporate Communications and External Relations, and President of the Luxury Products Division, L'Oréal Canada)

For the sake of clarity, we organized respondents' feedback into four categories, the 'four Ps':

- **Purpose**—What is leadership's reason for being? In other words, why lead?
- **Person**—In order to play a leadership role, what does a person need to do?
- **Partnership**—Since leadership always involves others, how can we manage the leadership relationship in a productive way?
- **Process**—How does leadership work?

Purpose

To our delight, leaders overwhelmingly identified the purpose of leadership as service, espousing the 'servant leader' philosophy of Robert K. Greenleaf, illustrated by this beautiful quote: "The first responsibility of a leader is to define reality. The last is to say thank you. In between, the leader is a servant." (Max DePree, *Leadership Is an Art* [Doubleday: New York, 1989])

Here's an example of service: Newfoundland interviewee Gladys Osmond, after retiring from a multifaceted career in her sixties, started The Granny Brigade, dedicated to writing letters to Canadian peacekeepers and militaries around the world to provide support and encouragement as well as a connection to home. In 2006, the Brigade sent ten thousand letters and she received from Canada's top soldier, General Rick Hillier, a medal for distinguished service recognizing her 20-year letter writing campaign. Gladys' life and leadership are a testament to the power of service.

People in Atlantic Canada were acutely aware of the crucial importance of service and spoke about it in moving and eloquent terms. We linked it to the legendary community orientation this region is famous for. Service acts as the dominant colour of the leadership landscape in Atlantic Canada. We found this very inspiring.

Even in business, service is the paradigm of leadership. Interviewee Cora Tsouflidou, founder of the successful restaurant chain Chez Cora/Cora's, shared a real turning point from her early days: realizing she was in the counselling, as well as the food business. Regulars came for the sympathetic ear and the caring as well as the comfort food. Providing sustenance for the body and the soul made her business a tremendous success. Today, close to one hundred Cora restaurants can be found all over Canada and the expansion process is not over!

"There is a spiritual dimension to leadership. It has to be centred around service." (David Todd, General Manager, Shell Canada, Drilling) Without service, there is no leadership, or not for long. "Leadership is about serving others, creating an environment conducive to their professional and personal development." (Stéphane Gonthier, Senior Vice-President, Eastern North America, Alimentation Couche-Tard Inc.)

Consequently, upon taking the mantle of leadership, leaders need clarity about service. Antoni Cimolino, General Director, The Stratford Festival of Canada, expresses it eloquently: "It's a three-step process. Identify:

- the real nature of the entity you serve, and stay true to its character;
- who (stakeholders) and what (cause, goals, meaning) you are serving;
- how (strategy) to best serve the needs of this entity."

If leaders serve their ego, interest or greed, they soon lose the ability and credibility to lead. Leadership's soul dissipates and eventually evaporates, leaving nothing but an empty shell. History abounds with leaders who committed atrocities in the name of an ill-conceived cause, to expand their own power or feed their greed. Remember Enron? Regardless of their abilities, they become monsters abusing their leadership gifts.

Self-serving leaders are remembered negatively, while those who served well retain their ability to lead beyond the grave, becoming inspirational role models for all times. "It is not about me, it is about 'we.' Set the vision, and give the group the grounding and ongoing coaching. It is about competence, not ego." (Sarah Raiss, Executive Vice-President, Corporate Services, TransCanada Corporation)

Therefore, effective leadership is anchored in a clear service philosophy. "I think we must re-invest in society and develop a social conscience. Consequently, I get involved in everything; it's hard to say no. My leadership vision is a community vision: create infrastructures that allow society to affirm its voice and become aware of its identity." (Honourable Herménégilde Chiasson, Lieutenant Governor, New Brunswick)

Gifted leaders can lead people into trouble or into greatness. The outcome will depend, first and foremost, on deciding on which basis to lead.

Person

To become servant leaders, people have to rise above their own concerns and focus their energies on the leadership purpose at hand. "Leadership is an act of courage and generosity that requires going beyond self and ego to inspire people to believe in something that does not yet exist. It takes a great connection to self and strong conviction to stand firm and persist when you are paddling upstream or making unpopular decisions." (Yvon Bastien, Former President and General Manager, Sanofi Synthelabo Canada)

Leadership is demanding. It's all or nothing. It requires that leaders marshal their resources to serve the role. This begins with taking responsibility: you are in charge, accountable for a situation and its outcomes. "Accept responsibilities and share success." (Rob McEwen, Chairman and CEO, U.S. Gold and Lexam Explorations)

Leadership is not just about being on top, having a bigger office or more money; it's about taking care of your people, helping a cause, fulfilling a purpose. "Leadership is a big responsibility. You have to ensure you are operating for the greater good of the group. It's not about you, it's about them." (Peter Eriksson, Olympic and Paralympic National Coach, Track and Field) That is why most interviewees saw leadership as both a tremendous privilege and a responsibility. "Leave the world better than you found it." (Barry Lindemann, Manager Community Affairs, Canadian Paraplegic Association, Alberta)

Leadership can be lonely and risky, so you must commit to the role: lock, stock and barrel, with the glory and the pain, victory and defeat, and above all, responsibility. You will be rewarded with tremendous opportunities for maturity.

Second, identify what you need to do in order to play this demanding role. Interviewees recommended building bench strength, much like raising fitness levels for a marathon. The process encompasses:

- Determining the foundations of your leadership practice: values, mission, vision, ethics, guiding principles, etc. The key word is 'platform.'
- Developing the skills to succeed such as influencing, team building, negotiating, etc. The key word is 'competence.'
- Fortifying character: resilience, determination, ability to bounce back, etc. The key word is 'strength.'
- Acquiring useful outlooks, such as a sense of humour. The key word is 'attitude.'

All steps in the process of building bench strength are important, and we will discuss them in detail in later chapters, but for now, let's look at outlooks in more detail. Outlooks are like guides attitudes that help you stay on the leadership path and prevent derailing.

- **Optimism**—Leaders soon realize they are merchants of hope, and, as such, they need a positive outlook. They must display and instill confidence, recognize and control negative energy, and be able to frame issues in a balanced way. Doomsayers and victims quickly lose their ability to lead because no one wants to follow somebody into a future that's poorer than the present.

- **Humour**—Humour is a good companion when facing difficulties: it makes light of adversity and builds character. It also breaks down barriers and creates a comfortable atmosphere. Humour exposes the 'human' in the leader. "Humour is important to break stress and tension. Ability and willingness to have fun are key components." (John Knebel, Co-founder, KWA Canada)
- **Energy**—Leadership gives and takes energy. "It is the capacity to set things in motion, generate action, stand at the epicentre of movement, like an agent provocateur." (Chantal Petitclerc, Paralympic Athlete and Champion). To sustain the strength you're trying to build, you need to identify and tap into sources of energy. What recharges your batteries? What promotes renewal? Finding the answers can make the difference between longevity and burnout.
- **Creativity**—Since leadership is about transformation, it requires thinking outside of the box. "There is a pioneer, creative aspect in leadership that takes leaders where no one has gone before or inspires them to find new ways of doing things." (Francine Brousseau, Vice-President Development, Canadian Museum of Civilization Corporation) Innovative thinking will pave the way to vision.
- **Uncertainty**—Overall, respondents saw benefits in uncertainty. Certitude can lead to staleness and stagnation. Although uncertainty creates stress, leaders learn to find comfort in discomfort. "Embrace uncertainty without letting it destroy you." (James [Sa'ke'j] Youngblood Henderson, I.P.C., Research Director, Native Law Centre of Canada; Professor, Aboriginal Law, College of Law, University of Saskatchewan) So, learn to trust your ability to improvise!

Together, these outlooks maintain leaders' focus on the vision ahead, instead of on the obstacles in their path. They help leaders stay the course towards the destination, instead of focusing on the treacherous rocks.

Finally, align words and actions. 'Walking your talk' and 'talking your walk' are the hardest and most beneficial leadership pursuits, said interviewees. Alignment leads to optimal effectiveness and maximum follower loyalty. It is also the work of a lifetime and the object of constant striving. When words and actions are inconsistent, people believe the actions and start suspecting leaders of ulterior motives. Likewise, if leaders cannot or do not explain vision, goals and strategies, followers are left guessing and immobilized. Proficiency and alignment of both dimensions provide the 'all access pass' to leadership greatness.

Donald Dion, Elite Sports Consultant, City of Montréal; Diving Olympic Coach, summarizes the process as follows: "First, you must have a clear and precise vision. Second, commit to the vision and its objectives. This assumes mobilizing the passion and motivation required for achievement. Third, put in place the necessary environment: systems, human and financial resources, project management process, etc. It is crucial to transmit your vision and objectives to the people who will contribute to their realization, whether they are volunteers or employees."

The road to leadership is a life-altering experience during which a 'person' becomes a 'leader,' transcending their own limitations and those of current reality. The person has to be ready and willing, to say the least…

Partnership

Leadership is an act of collaboration. It happens through people and for people. "I appreciate that leadership has a collaborative component. I am a big proponent of leading from the front, the middle and the back. I feel that ineffective leaders lead themselves into the sunset and find out they are alone. You need to generate collaboration in order to lead." (Dr. David Walker, Dean, Faculty of Health Sciences, Queen's University)

It's is a unique type of relationship. "Since leadership is first and foremost an influence process, it's important to create a warm environment where people feel comfortable without denying or abdicating the boss-employee relationship. Relationship quality is important, as it represents the fertile ground where vision takes root." (Lorraine Pintal, C.M., General and Artistic Director, Théâtre du Nouveau Monde)

Establishing authentic relationships that don't excessively emphasize hierarchical differences is paramount.

A fine balance has to be struck between the authoritarian style where the leader is cold, distant and inaccessible and the buddy-buddy style where the leader is just another team member, overly familiar with associates. To a degree, it is cruel and dishonest to pretend being your employees' friend. For instance, when leaders must address a difficult performance issue, it is wise to reflect on the tone to take. One doesn't want to come across as a heartless and dictatorial brute, but as both firm and compassionate. Not the parent punishing the small child, but the strategic thinker with an overall and integrated view of the big picture. Humour can work well in such situations; a lighter tone allows the message to be conveyed without offence since someone who made a mistake already knows it. There is no need to lay it on thick. Employees should feel that the leader doesn't hold a grudge and is willing to give them another chance, but within boundaries. (Marc Mayer, Director, Montréal Museum of Contemporary Art)

The relationship needs to be appropriately framed because it contains polarities that require balancing: the leader is caring but not blind, involved but not familiar, firm yet compassionate, empathetic yet demanding—not an easy feat to accomplish while maintaining authenticity and yielding trust. "Leadership takes on many forms: action leaders who achieve, determination leaders who defeat adversity, visionary leaders who see differently, inspiration leaders who stimulate others, peaceful leaders who defuse tense situations, etc. Many never make it into the media, but are nevertheless great leaders, essential to our successes! Leadership is not owned by a particular group, a specific style or personality, but available to everyone: we are all potential leaders." (Bruno-Marie Béchard, Rector, Université de Sherbrooke, excerpt from a speech given at the Fête du Nouvel An [New Year Celebration] on February 2, 2006)

It starts with establishing rapport. "This type of connection is not based on superficial small talk or sterile courtesy, nor motivated by a mercenary instinct or power hunger. When it happens, it is a privileged moment when two people 'see' each other and know they will be able to work together. A form of communication is established, on an intuitive level, and both parties become aware of the other's presence and essence. The relationship aspect is as important as the task aspect in the practice of leadership." (Marc Mayer, Director, Montréal Museum of Contemporary Art) When this happens, "You will lead people to a place they did not think they would be able to go to." (Marge Watters, Co-founder, KWA Canada)

Next, get acquainted with the constituencies you serve. This means getting to know individual team members: What are their strengths? What gives them satisfaction? What stimulates their passion? "Leadership is about getting the best out of people." (Monique Lefebvre, Executive Director, Défi Sportif and AlterGo, People with Disabilities in Action)

Understanding psychology is a great asset. What drives motivation? What increases or destroys loyalty? What urges achievement? Great leaders know their people. "I have a passion for studying people and understanding how they work." (Chris Rudge, CEO and Secretary General, Canadian Olympic Committee)

Surround yourself with people who have complementary skills, talents and strengths. The cookie-cutter approach limits perspectives and weakens the team. "You are only as strong as the organization you build." (Dr. Joseph Segal, C.M., O.B.C., O.St.J., President, Kingswood Capital Corp.) "Smart leaders find smarter people to work with them." (Paul Zarnke, Executive Director, Children's Aid Society, Region of Peel)

Provide opportunities for development and growth. "Allow people to have a good experience." (May Brown, C.M., O.B.C., Former Councillor, City of Vancouver, B.C.) It's your duty to perpetuate the leadership legacy. "Good leaders develop good leaders." (Kevin Cameron, Consultant; Former President, The Halifax Mooseheads Hockey Club)

Most importantly, create a web of inclusion. "It is important to bring people to the table, plant seeds and let them appropriate the vision. The greatest successes are through persuasion, not confrontation." (Honourable William G. Davis, P.C., C.C., Q.C., Former Premier, Ontario) "Others need to own the problem and the solution to make change happen. Telling people what to do is not effective if you want change to be sustainable." (Dr. Carol Herbert, Dean, Schulich School of Medicine & Dentistry, University of Western Ontario) Be open to changing your mind. "If not supported, compromise." (Dr. Gloria Gutman, Professor Emerita, Gerontology Department; Director of the Dr. Tong Louie Living Laboratory, Simon Fraser University)

Process

The process is the methodology, the 'how to.' It divides into three components:

1. **Seeing**—the eyes.
2. **Believing**—the heart.
3. **Acting**—the hands.

The first two seem fairly interchangeable. For some leaders, seeing comes first; for others, believing comes first. Richard Blackburn, General and Artistic Director, Théâtre de la Dame de Cœur, describes the whole process:

Eyes: Seeing
"Leadership is being inhabited with a shifting and mobilizing vision. Shifting, for it changes and evolves; mobilizing, for it spurs us into action."

Heart: Believing
"The how is not always clear but the vision stirs our emotions and awakens passion."

Hands: Acting
"The next step is to harmonize the project with the team's energies. People should wrestle with interesting challenges and get something out of it for themselves, ending up with a big slice of the pie."

Eyes: Seeing

Seeing refers to two different types of 'eyesight.' Seeing current reality (external landscape) uses the cognitive power of the left brain. Visioning (internal landscape) calls upon the imaginative powers of the right brain. These two very different skills are both necessary for effective leadership.

- **External landscape**: "As one learns on the Prairies, vision requires a 360 degree view of one's surroundings and a climate that will allow ideas to grow into actions." (Lyn Wray, Division Manager, Financial Planning and Corporate Risk Management, Manitoba Hydro) People in the Prairies had a wonderful sense of the possible and exhibited the resilience and determination to turn possibility into reality. We were very impressed with their courage and pioneering disposition.

  Grasping the complexity of a situation and sizing up the big picture is essential for effective leadership. 'There are tree and forest people,' goes the saying. Some embrace the big picture, while others focus on specific details. Leadership requires an aerial view and, at times, diving to intervene; remaining close to the ground means losing sight of the landscape. "Leadership is about asking: Are we in the right forest? Not: Which trees to chop?" (Judy Murphy, COO, Royal Winnipeg Ballet)
- **Internal landscape**: Imagining the best possible future and seeing the vision shimmering in the distance is equally seminal. The importance of visioning has been abundantly stated in leadership literature; in fact, without visioning, there is no leadership. "In order to reach their goals, leaders must be passionate visionaries, who see far ahead and know how to use their intuition." (Alban D'Amours, President and CEO, Desjardins Group) This requires seeing possibilities and opportunities yet invisible to others.

Heart: Believing

Believing speaks to the power of faith and emotions. It stirs passion, which can then compel people to lead. "At eighteen, I became disabled. I had to re-evaluate my life and became more understanding with a compassionate approach. Positive Mental Attitude (PMA) made a huge difference." (Marni Abbot-Peter, Provincial Coach and Player, BC Wheelchair Basketball Society) Passion sustains the flame during the long and difficult haul towards the vision. Leaders need a strong 'passion connection' because it provides fuel and energy.

Passion is required to inspire. By believing in the possible, leaders attract followers like magnets. The might of faith mobilizes. "Don't be afraid to take a

position, even if it requires fierce combat. You will find people to stand by you."
(Honourable John C. Crosbie, P.C., O.C., Q.C., Former Minister, Government
of Canada) Communicating the vision and its rationale in a compelling manner
transmits passion. "Leadership is the ability to envision possibilities and find the
best path to reach the goal. Feel the passion to inspire others and lead them."
(Kathleen Bartels, Director, Vancouver Art Gallery)

Inspiring followers is a fundamental link in the leadership process. If
the leader is unsuccessful in that juncture, the leadership process aborts. "The
fundamental axis of leadership is inspiration. There's no escaping it. To inspire,
leaders must shift their focus away from the self towards a vision to achieve, a
project to realize. The project injects energy and hope in the hearts of those who
then turn to making the vision a reality." (Denise Verreault, C.M., C.Q., President
and CEO, Groupe Maritime Verreault Inc.)

Hands: Acting

When you take action, each step brings you closer to the vision. Denise Amyot,
Vice-President, Leadership Network, Public Service Human Resources Agency,
Government of Canada, uses a sailing analogy to illustrate the process:

- "Know where you are going, have a clear sense of your direction;
- Adjust your sails to the wind, using it to your advantage. It is okay to take a
  different route;
- Take care of crew, be good to people, help them grow as leaders;
- Be prepared to play different roles. Others will have to take the lead at times,
  and will require your support;
- Ensure you have the energy you need; make sure your personal tank is full. Be
  able to bounce back as things will not always go the way you want to."

Therefore, leadership requires skilful navigation between polarities.

Table 1.1

YIN	YANG
Set direction	Adjust sails
Set roles	Adjust roles
Show determination	Show flexibility

It also requires adapting to the wind. "Roadblocks on the journey to
transformation form an integral part of process steps by shaping the final outcome

and indicating the path to transformation. Obstacles and accidents along the way often reveal growth opportunities. Deciphering their meaning is more productive than resisting them. Which way is the current flowing?" (Richard Blackburn, General and Artistic Director, Théâtre de la Dame de Cœur)

The process demands strength and also constructs it. Adversity builds character and requires balancing strength so it doesn't become brutal force, and appreciating that "there is a great deal of gentleness in strength and a great deal of strength in gentleness." (Mavis Staines, Artistic Director, Canada's National Ballet School)

Moreover, the process breeds new leaders. Successful leadership includes preparing the next generation to take the helm. Developing talent is one of the most gratifying and meaningful leadership acts. It's about leaving a legacy and building the future: a significant 'rite of passage.' In this capacity, leaders play a similar role to people who manage artists. They need to have an eye for talent, believe in potential and nurture the person through the inevitable setbacks. "Developing people is like developing artists; the most active ingredient is support provided by individuals respected by the artist. I am convinced that encouragement acts on cells at a biological level. The greatest gift to bestow is confidence, for it provides the person with the strength to build on their assets." (Marc Mayer, Director, Montréal Museum of Contemporary Art)

Developing talent is about fostering maturity and judgement, not possessing infallible expertise. "You need to create an environment where people are heard, allowed to explore and ask questions. Real leaders facilitate, encourage and listen. They get people to participate. When things are not going well, I will step in and lead. However, it is important to allow others to experience leadership." (Mel Benson, Board Member, Suncor Energy Inc.)

CONCLUSION

Leadership is like a chain whose ultimate purpose is service. The person who accepts the role must ascribe their whole being to serve it. Through the process of seeing a desired future, believing in it passionately and taking action, leaders and followers create a new reality and reinvent themselves.

Therefore, the leadership *partnership* is about giving life to a new world and accepting the wisdom of natural laws. "When the hearts of women are on the ground, the nation dies," said Joseph Paquette, Mixed Blood Elder. This means that life givers must be treated with respect and reverence if the community is to survive and thrive. In the leadership relationship, followers give birth to the leader's vision. Without them, leadership cannot fulfill its destiny.

Leadership is a catalyst for greatness or disaster. Used wisely, it can propel individuals to impossible heights. Abused, it can drive them to unspeakable atrocities. Embedded in its DNA is the power of transformation, but beware: "When the focus of leadership becomes privilege instead of service, leadership self-destructs. It will not survive such a violation of its essence." (Antoni Cimolino, General Director, The Stratford Festival of Canada)

Before embarking on the leadership adventure, clarify your purpose and intentions. Go within to survey the assets you possess to serve the role. Build a solid foundation to your leadership practice—it will help chart your course and guide your decisions. Set up a solid partnership with your followers, a relationship of mutual respect and caring, for together, you are about to make magic.

CHAPTER 2

THE LEADERSHIP RIDE

There's a huge satisfaction in accomplishing something that is there for others to enjoy.
Donna Scott, O.C.
Former Vice-President, Canadian Publishing, Maclean Hunter Ltd.

It is a reward, helping people achieve great things. Success breeds success. It is fun!
Serge Rancourt
President, Publicis Canada

Development is never without costs. It requires a lot of work but must be viewed as an investment. You should also constantly question yourself and not rest on your laurels. Comfort is risky. Don't become too cozy. It's important to face new challenges and move on. Success can be dangerous if it creates too much comfort.
Luc Nadeau
Executive Vice-President, Corporate Communications and External Relations, and President of the Luxury Products Division, L'Oréal Canada

VIEWS FROM WITHIN

The leadership experience is a journey with many twists and turns, unique to each leader.

For instance:

"I moved up in different organizations. You start leading a department, move on to leading a company, then participating in leading the industry. You become more and more influential. The next stage is to develop in societal leadership." (Jane Peverett, President and CEO, British Columbia Transmission Corporation)

"At first, I led by expertise—a model based on having the answers and being right. Then I became a facilitator helping the organization change. I learned how to ask questions rather than give answers. The next phase was to work with larger groups and processes: this was more akin to re-engineering. I learned a lot about the business and strategy." (Bill Hamilton, Executive Coach, W.J.A. Hamilton & Associates; Former Senior Vice-President, BMO and CIBC)

As we can see from these examples, the journey is unique to each person, but how is it experienced from the inside? How does leadership feel to the leader? Much headway has been made in the field of developmental psychology by studying, for instance, how adolescence feels to teenagers: the quest for identity, the need for assertion and differentiation from parents, the requirement to choose a career, etc. Developmental psychology provides guidance on how to optimize internal dynamics for performance and development.

In the leadership field, much has been written about the impact of leadership from the *outside*, but less research has been conducted on the view from the *inside*. This chapter opens a window onto the leadership experience from the leaders'—not the followers'—point of view.

Not surprisingly, respondents perceive leadership as a very deep, intense, almost extreme experience. There is nothing casual about it. We identified four main themes from respondents' descriptions:

- **Vocation:** focus on dedication to service.
- **Transformation:** focus on the change process.
- **Roller coaster:** focus on the highs and lows.
- **Energy field:** focus on energy flow and transfer.

These focal points act as anchors for the internal experience of leadership and shape leaders' perception.

Vocation

Some respondents see leadership as a sacred endeavour not to be undertaken lightly. "It enriches your mind and troubles your conscience." (James [Sa'ke'j] Youngblood Henderson, I.P.C., Research Director, Native Law Centre of Canada; Professor, Aboriginal Law, College of Law, University of Saskatchewan) For them, leadership is a mission, a pilgrimage towards a worthy higher purpose.

People in this category view leadership as an all-consuming pursuit, requiring devotion to the cause and purity of intent. "I sought to change perceptions about disabled people: from victim to hero. I wanted to enable them to lead more active lives and experience competitiveness to outdo themselves. When people look at Chantal Petitclerc, it's with pride, not pity." (Monique Lefebvre, Executive Director, Défi Sportif and AlterGo, People with Disabilities in Action)

These people speak of leadership with reverence. They reported being engaged in something meaningful at a spiritual level. Words like honour, privilege and destiny kept recurring. "I feel a great satisfaction knowing that a certain part of my destiny is being fulfilled. Leadership provides an opportunity to make a difference in a positive way and to pass on values to the next generation." (Joseph Paquette, Mixed Blood Elder)

For those, leadership is a noble calling. "As a leader, you are constantly watched and you have to display selflessness and caring. Otherwise, followers won't give you their trust. You have to show greatness, not just speak of it. Leadership is not a popularity contest or an exercise in self-aggrandisement; it's about the service of a greater cause." (Antoni Cimolino, General Director, The Stratford Festival of Canada)

Like everything worthwhile, it takes discipline, courage and "an insane level of commitment and stubbornness to achieve things." (Albert Schultz, Founding Artistic Director, Soulpepper Theatre Company) But it's a blessing. "I have a wonderful job, travel and get to meet fantastic people from all walks of life, and all over the world. Leadership gives me freedom to bring about change. Several years ago, we decided we needed a Cancer Research Institute, and now it's here! It's very satisfying." (Dr. David Walker, Dean, Faculty of Health Sciences, Queen's University)

Transformation

Other respondents focus on metamorphosis and view the purpose and process of leadership as transformation: vision calls for action, action creates outcomes and outcomes result in transformation.

For those, leadership follows the path of 'The Quest,' mapped out by Joseph Campbell in *The Hero's Journey* (Harper & Row, San Francisco, 1990). Leaders hear a call to action and in responding, embark on a journey full of obstacles in order to fulfill their mission. Throughout the process, they become stronger and wiser, bringing back the ultimate treasure: transformation. As a result, reality expands, development occurs and leaders mature. The ripple effects are far reaching and unpredictable.

It is hard work and not every battle is won, but in the process, leaders transcend their limitations and reshape their world. "Leadership sets the bar high; it gives you purpose and allows you to excel. As you grow, you understand more and continue to assess yourself. Through leadership, we have built a business from the ground up and we have the satisfaction of seeing it grow through many battles, both won and lost." (Dr. Colin MacDonald, President and CEO, Clearwater Seafood)

Transformation takes place on the inside *and* the outside: dreams come true, goals are accomplished, the value of the enterprise grows, fears dissipate, life is lived according to values. Always, leaders make a difference and touch others. "I believe that people want to be successful. As a leader, you need to provide them with opportunities to do so." (Janet Knox, President and CEO, Annapolis Valley District Health Authority) Leadership is like the philosopher's stone, transforming whatever it touches into gold.

Roller Coaster

Still others focus on the ride. Leadership is like a roller coaster: thrilling and devastating, exhilarating and exhausting, exciting and crushing. "Leadership is not for the timid." (Doreen McKenzie-Sanders, C.M., Executive Director, Women in the Lead Inc.)

The path propels you out of the mundane into a realm of possibilities, pushing all of your buttons. "Leadership is about changing things or our attitude towards things. How do we react to the earthquakes of our lives? Are we victims or partners? We must grab the reins of our destiny. To help others, you have to help yourself first." (Natalie Choquette, Diva)

Through the roller coaster ride, leaders experience 'the rapture of life,' to paraphrase Joseph Campbell. They are fully engaged, not sitting on the sidelines. "Leadership is about living to the max, dangerously, on a tightrope. Hovering over the precipice, facing failure and confronting your mistakes. It's like mountain climbing: between life and death. Adrenalin rushes in. When you reach the summit, you see the next path to take as well as the next mountains to climb." (Yvon Bastien, Former President and General Manager, Sanofi Synthelabo Canada)

Risk is a constant factor that cannot always be mitigated. You have to find ways to live with it.

> Leadership can bring about great things, such as satisfaction from accomplishments and knowing you can transform things; however, one must be aware that there are risks. Even with the best plan powered by the best intentions, failure can happen, like an accident. It's the theory of probabilities. As a leader, you can't live in constant fear of failure—it comes with the territory. Leadership is not a world of certitudes. Just roll with the punches. You must believe in yourself and your goal, pull up your sleeves and carry on. When bad things happen, if you are sincere, people will rally to overcome obstacles instead of falling apart. (Marc Poulin, President Operations, Québec Region, Sobeys Inc.)

Energy Field

Another group concentrates on energy flow and transfer. Leadership requires and gives vast amounts of energy. Sustaining it as you climb the hill towards the vision is an issue all leaders face. How will you avoid crashing? How will you be renewed and reinvigorated? Just like in the environmental realm, the key word is sustainability.

There are four key sources of energy leaders can tap into to sustain their practice:

1. Passion.
2. Vision.
3. Support.
4. Success.

Passion

Leaders need to be plugged into their passion through a 'high-speed connection.' Otherwise, the burden becomes too heavy. Passion creates commitment, which sustains the leader during hard times and fosters resilience. When people are passionate, learning is less of a burden, and skill-building seems fun rather than taxing. Passion is the adrenalin charging the leader's batteries and supporting performance. "It is personally satisfying to see a better organization. Changing culture and gaining traction can feel like berthing the Queen Mary with a canoe." (Kevin Marshman, Vice-President and General Manager, Worldwide Customer Services, NCR Canada Ltd.)

Vision

The more clearly leaders see their vision, the more deeply they feel it and the more motivated they are to reach it. "Leaders must not suppress their vision but surrender to it. Without it, it is impossible to inspire people. Vision awakens passion in others, joining their lives to the collective enterprise." (Richard Blackburn, General and Artistic Director, Théâtre de la Dame de Cœur)

Support

Another key energy source is support, vital for leaders to ease growing pains, maintain momentum and remain focused on goals.

In general, leaders seem satisfied by the level of challenge provided by leadership; however, they overwhelmingly say they lack support. The vast majority reported experiencing these kinds of emotions:

- Stressed.
- Unable to share.
- Isolated and lonely.
- Burdened by responsibility: people's employment is in their hands.
- Targeted by criticism.
- Scrutinized.
- Disliked and misunderstood.
- Pressured to sacrifice their personal life.
- Pulled in too many directions.
- Unable to control their schedules.
- Guilty: they have to make unpopular decisions and take drastic actions, such as firing people and closing plants. At times, they also make errors and experience failure.

Moreover, they believe isolation comes with the territory and has to be stoically endured. This mindset is reinforced by popular wisdom like 'it's lonely at the top.' Since leadership is so crucial to organizational success, why is there such widespread lack of support for this key resource? Why should they have to tolerate this sad state of affairs? Are these attitudes a result of the lone ranger hero myth that keeps leaders isolated and lonely? The time has come to let go of the legend and face reality.

Our leaders need support, just like top athletes and performers do. The tremendous growth and success of individual coaching demonstrates the size of the gap to fill. Executive networking groups also help. "I really enjoy meeting with my eight colleagues of the Young Presidents' Association. Each month, we convene for four hours and exchange on a wide range of topics. It is a great source of support and learning." (Pierre Dion, President and CEO, TVA Group Inc)

Much more support is needed. Contrast, for instance, the amount of support artists like Céline Dion, Shania Twain or Michael Bublé get from their record labels and management. At this level, stars get advisors of all kinds, from nutritionists to tax lawyers. They also receive TLC from a plethora of caregivers, like massage therapists, counsellors and fitness trainers. The entertainment industry understands that 'someone has to care for the caregiver.' If artists feel depleted, they can't perform. The same logic applies to leaders: to sustain leadership momentum, they need and deserve ongoing acknowledgement, gratitude, advice, praise, etc.

We must face this problem and become creative about filling the support void. Moreover, since the majority of leaders jump into the fray propelled by external circumstances instead of internal drivers, they might not withstand the rigours of leadership without adequate support. How many leaders quit because of chronic support scarcity? How much leadership potential is lost? How many casualties litter the leadership road? Let's get out of our lone ranger paradigm and create vibrant, abundant and adequate support mechanisms to enable our leaders to thrive and soar.

Success

Of course, success motivates, providing energy. Without at least some success, leaders may get discouraged and paralyzed; with success, they get recharged and motivated to go further. Pierre Morin, Former Director, Parks and Recreation, City of Montréal, recounts the following tale: "When I was 20 years old, I became director of a family camp for disadvantaged families. I told them that, by pooling their resources, they could save and enjoy a two-week camping trip in beautiful surroundings. I obtained subsidies from the government, hired a cook, organized transportation, borrowed tents, etc. ... It was an incredible high to see the joy on these people's faces and I discovered my calling: community development through recreational activities."

Success is intoxicating—the best incentive to persist on the leadership road and face new challenges. Success affirms and validates leaders and leadership, proving that transformation is possible and that things can improve. Success is the active ingredient of growth and meaning. "Reward comes from working with people as they grow, expanding the business, creating something new. It is exhilarating!" (Paul Hayman, Executive Vice-President, The Franchise Company)

IS THE RIDE WORTH IT?

The leadership journey is an extraordinary adventure that demands great effort and sacrifice. But is it worth it? In general, interviewees said yes, rewards outweigh costs. "Leadership has given me a sense of pride and accomplishment, self-esteem, the feeling that I have touched people's lives." (Louis O'Reilly, President, O'Reilly International Entertainment Management)

There is, however, a cost, and it is not negligible. "To reach excellence, the price to pay goes with the territory. You can't have one without the other." (Charles Cardinal, Consultant in Planning, Periodization and Long-Term Athlete Development [LTAD])

Once leaders embark on the journey, it's hard to abdicate or abandon it.

Leadership can become all-consuming. Like a treadmill, where the speed and the incline continually increase, you have to keep pace or you will fly off. It continues to drive you. The path is littered with the bodies of those who have fallen off. Unfortunately, many never realize that their lives are being controlled by the ever-challenging treadmill. More and more of one's life can become consumed by it. The price of leadership is what you don't see. (Bruno Biscaro, COO, Accucaps Industries Limited)

The key is finding ways to make it work. "It is not really a cost, but a choice. I arrive at work every day at 5 a.m. and I love it. It gives me time to go over files and understand issues at stake." (Michèle Thibodeau-DeGuire, C.M., C.Q., President and Executive Director, Centraide [United Way] of Greater Montréal)

Pain and Gain

You can plot the dimensions of gain (what you get out of it) and pain (the cost to you) on two axes, producing four quadrants.

- **Q1: Low Gain/Low Pain**—Q1 is often an entry point where people decide if leadership is for them. As such, it is characterized by low involvement and trial and error. Q1 can also be a waiting room before exiting the field: a place of disillusionment. Alternatively, it can offer a rest area while recharging batteries. None of our leaders were in Q1, since they are all established and committed to leadership.

- **Q2: Low Gain/High Pain**—Q2 is a crucible of intense pain. All leaders travel through it during crises and ponder questions like *Can I survive? Should I quit?* If it lasts too long, discouragement sets in and people leave or crash. We

Illustration 2.1

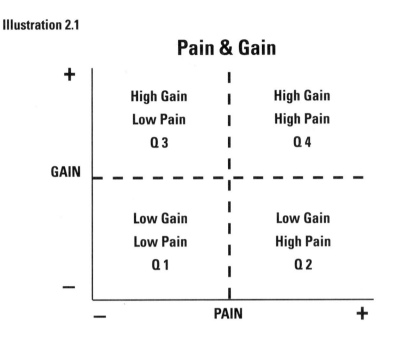

Pain & Gain

could not assess with certainty if any interviewees were at this place in their journey. However, many recounted having at times experienced this black hole.

Q3: High Gain/Low Pain—Q3 is a place of flow and energy. People know they are in the right 'zone' and trust their abilities. They have the confidence to improvise and find creative solutions. Foundations are solid. Q3 is where 40% of interviewees stated residing: low or no pain with high gains.

- **Q4: High Gain/High Pain**—Q4 is a place of adrenalin and of living on the edge. It's like flying a 747 and wondering if you can land it. You feel alert and alive, bursting with energy. It can also be the zone of catastrophe where your gamble didn't pay off, you made a major mistake or you are fighting a desperate battle. It is where the majority (60%) of our interviewees thought they resided.

To summarize, respondents primarily clustered into three groups:

- The first (20%) thinks the ride is eminently worthwhile: no or little pain, big gains.
- The second (20%) views it as an investment: short-term pain for long-term gains.
- The third (60%) thinks it is a high-stakes game: high risk, big gains/losses.

Illustration 2.2

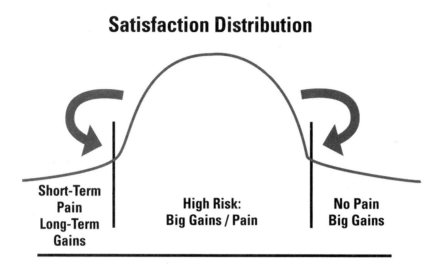

Satisfaction Distribution

| Short-Term
Pain
Long-Term
Gains | High Risk:
Big Gains / Pain | No Pain
Big Gains |

Group 1: Nirvana

About 20% of interviewees think there is no price at all. For these, leadership requires less effort, maybe because it's in their flow. "Leadership gives me energy. I enjoy seeing others grow and develop. To me, growth is more important than other measurements of success." (Judy Murphy, COO, Royal Winnipeg Ballet)

They really value the benefits of leadership. "I like having control of my own destiny and do not like being dependent on someone else. In the beginning, there was an element of social status. Later on, I became more interested in the mission/purpose of contributing as much as possible. I want to leave a legacy." (Dr. Sean Riley, President and Vice-Chancellor, St. Francis Xavier University)

Leadership has become a key part of their identity. "Leadership is my life!" (Guy Babineau, Director of Wellness, CBC/ Radio-Canada)

This group is the happiest with their leadership experience. "Leadership has enabled me to blossom. I feel like a butterfly spreading its wings. I have confidence in myself; therefore, I take risks. The worst is not to act. I am both pleased and surprised with my success and the friendships I have built along the way." (Louise Pelletier, Regional Director, Mauricie Region, Production of the Cascades, Hydro-Québec)

Group 2: Short-term Pain for Long-term Gain

Another 20% feel that, eventually, leadership pays off: it is a long-term investment. Over time, reward will exceed effort, and the price is reasonable. Overall, the trade-off is more than adequate. "Return is greater than investment: efforts expanded produce results and enable the team to achieve the vision. Another benefit is to be liked and appreciated." (Pierre-Marc Tremblay, President and CEO, Restaurants Pacini Inc.)

This group is quite happy with the leadership experience. "It's not heavy, it just takes time." (Honourable John C. Crosbie, P.C., O.C., Q.C., Former Minister, Government of Canada)

Group 3: High-stakes Game

The majority (about 60%) associates leadership with a high-stakes card game: expensive to play and risky, with the potential for big rewards and losses. You can lose your reputation, health and family, but success is the thrill of a lifetime. "Just like in sports, everything aches but when you win, it's fantastic!" (Jean Houde, Deputy Minister, Ministère des Finances du Québec [Québec Department of Finance])

Cora Tsouflidou, founder of the restaurant chain Chez Cora/Cora's, believed her formula would work in the rest of Canada and held fast against some advice to the contrary when she decided to expand outside Québec. Through this process, she had to face adversity and take action, which tested her commitment. In the end, she was proven right.

EXPLORING DYNAMICS

Leadership is an ecosystem that needs to be sustained in order to survive. Therefore, leaders must stabilize the pain/gain dynamics, ensure sources of renewable energy and monitor their flow to avoid stagnation. Even though leaders accept the responsibilities and challenges of the role, they must receive something in return to carry on. But what do they get out of it and how much does it mean to them?

Dynamics break down into three categories: people (self and others), why and how (purpose and process) and outcomes (results and impact). Each category can be a source of satisfaction or a cause of pain, accruing high costs for the leader. Like in a balance sheet, sources of satisfaction nurture leaders and costs deplete them.

Table 2.1

Gain	Pain
PEOPLE	**PEOPLE**
Self Intrinsic sources of satisfaction	**Self** Intrinsic costs
Others Extrinsic sources of satisfaction derived from interacting with others	**Others** Extrinsic costs derived from interacting with others
WHY and HOW	**WHY and HOW**
Purpose Satisfaction derived from connection to purpose and meaning	**Purpose** Costs derived from lack of connection with purpose and lack of meaning
Process Satisfaction derived from leadership activities	**Process** Costs derived from leadership activities
OUTCOMES	**OUTCOMES**
Results Satisfaction derived from results	**Results** Costs derived from lack of results, or negative results
Impact Satisfaction derived from the consequences of results	**Impact** Costs caused by the consequences of results

On the satisfaction side, internal factors, such as self-actualization or being connected to a higher purpose, seem more meaningful and lasting than external ones, such as status and awards. Vicarious components, such as seeing others succeed and grow, are deeply fulfilling and heartwarming. Sources related to growth and development are viewed as invigorating and affect motivation and energy levels.

In general, interviewees felt that the rewards outweigh the costs but that doesn't mean that the price is negligible. In general, costs accrued in the people category are very high, such as having to terminate someone or close a plant. Likewise, toll on family life hurts more than missing an important target.

Costs derived from a lack of connection with purpose will end up in leadership abandonment. Moreover, the need to keep an eye on the long term versus the short term, the bigger picture versus details, can cause intellectual fatigue. Finally, costs incurred from conducting leadership activities can be minor or major irritants. For instance, many leaders reported that they hate making speeches or doing public relations, but feel they have to. Others stated that they feel 'on' all the time and cannot, for example, go to the grocery store in a grubby T-shirt. Another heavy burden is the cost of failure and its impact.

People

The people continuum is personal and intensely felt. Therefore, it brings the most joy and pain. Joy speaks to the leader's value as perceived by self and others. The main source of satisfaction is a sense of self-worth. Pain is caused by the heavy burden of isolation and responsibility. When things go wrong, the drain on the leader's energy is enormous. Respondents spoke of the physical, emotional and intellectual endurance required for the role. Here are some sample comments:

- "Sense of fulfillment and joy about my ability to contribute."
- "Extraordinary privilege to draw people into your beliefs."
- "Seeing results through people. Their success becomes yours."
- "The price has been loneliness. It's a scary responsibility and I have to exercise it with empathy and fairness."
- "Impact on health; burnout factors at times."
- "When you succeed, some people are jealous."

Table 2.2

PEOPLE			
Self: Gain	**Self: Pain**	**Others: Gain**	**Others: Pain**
EMOTIONS	**EMOTIONS**	**PEOPLE**	**EMOTIONS**
Inner peace	Sacrifices	**DEVELOPMENT**	Jealousy
Pride	Worry	Seeing the best	Resentment
Joy	Vulnerability	in people	Criticism
Fun		Watching others	Envy
Passion	**TIME**	succeed, grow,	
	Your time is not	become leaders	**RELATIONSHIPS**
WORTH	your own		Toll on family life
Being the best	Toll on personal	**RELATIONSHIPS**	Family break-ups
you can be	life	Developing a	Loss of friends
Skill deployment		large network	Fans more than
Confidence			friends

Continued

PEOPLE			
Self: Gain	**Self: Pain**	**Others: Gain**	**Others: Pain**
DISCOVERY Self-knowledge Personal growth **QUALITIES ACQUIRED** Positive attitude Resilience Self-sufficiency Detachment Sensitivity Compassion	**RESPONSIBILITY** Pressure Expectations and demands Hard to set boundaries **PERSONAL** Intensely personal Self-doubt, criticism Attacked ego Loss of personal identity to leadership role **ISOLATION** Loneliness Alienation Distance **HEALTH RISKS** Stress Lack of sleep Fatigue, exhaustion	Working with high-performing teams Quality relationships and partnerships **GREATER GOOD** Having people's trust Touching their lives Sharing your dream Bearing people's hope Being a safety net Making others happy	Distant relationships Not everyone will like you **VISIBILITY** Everyone has an opinion of you Scrutiny Exposure Loss of anonymity Media target

Purpose and Process

The second continuum speaks to the why and the what. The stronger the alignment to purpose is, the greater meaning and satisfaction. From a process perspective, leaders need the competence and will to run the 'business' of leadership, which provides stimulating adventures and opportunities. Pain is primarily caused by challenges requiring courage and discipline. Here are some sample comments:

- "Independence to plan strategy, analyze problems and come up with solutions."
- "Joy to see vision and ideas unfold and become real."
- "Enjoy challenge and making progress, making a difference."
- "You can't show when you're down."
- "Need to take a position and it's not always easy. You can't waffle."
- "Risk of failure is always there."

Table 2.3

WHY and WHAT			
Purpose: Positive	**Purpose: Negative**	**Process: Positive**	**Process: Negative**
MEANING	**FOCUS**	**STIMULATION**	**DISCIPLINE**
Finding meaning in what you do	Keeping your eye on the long term, which sometimes means short-term losses	Charting one's own voyage	Long hours
Doing something you love		Continuous improvement	Hard work
Doing the best possible job		Variety and challenge	Setting an example, no matter what
Being a catalyst		Amazing experiences	Showing confidence in very tenuous situations
Doing what's right	Focus on the big picture, which means specific components can be sacrificed for the greater good of the whole	Learning about complexity	
Living according to values		Opportunities	**CHALLENGES**
Having a sense of the possible		Travel	Difficult performance conversations
			Terminations
SERVICE		**ACTIVITIES**	Corporate politics
Contributing to a worthwhile cause		Visioning	Trusting people sometimes means you will be taken in
Striving for a common goal	Loss of connection to purpose and meaning amplifies irritants and almost makes them unbearable	Strategizing	
		Planning	
Giving back		Driving change	**DECISION-MAKING**
Greater good more important than self-interest		Aligning	Having to make decisions
		Motivating	Element of risk not shared by everyone
		Shaping things and events	Making trade-offs and compromises
Doing something for the country		Innovating	Being as good as your last decision

Results and Impact

The third continuum speaks to results and their consequences; intangible rewards, such as influence and appreciation, are more valued than tangible ones. Here are some sample comments:

- "Satisfaction to know I moved things up a notch."
- "Leaving a legacy."
- "Accomplishing something that will be appreciated by others to come."
- "Need to confront difficult issues and people for the greater good of the organization."
- "When someone is not doing well, you wonder what you failed to do."
- "You lose some of the battles."

Table 2.4

RESULTS AND IMPACT			
Results: Positive	**Results: Negative**	**Impact: Positive**	**Impact: Negative**
SPECIFIC	**LOSSES**	**GENERIC**	**EMOTIONS**
New products and services	Failures	Rewards	Internalized failures
Breakthroughs	Errors	Recognition	Disappointments
Everyday miracles	Lost battles	Money	Helplessness
Finding solutions	Unpopular decisions	Appreciation	when you can't
Small victories	Opposition and disagreements	Quality of life	help
Measurable improvements		Leaving a legacy	Frustration when
Accomplishments		Leaving the world a better place	you can't find a solution
			Guilt
GENERIC		**SELF-**	Blame
Success		**ACTUALIZATION**	
Long-term transformation		Control	**OTHER**
Dreams come true		Freedom	Premature ageing
Realizing your vision		Driving the bus	Lack of financial rewards
Seeing your team win		Being a player instead of a spectator	Danger of taking yourself too seriously
Solving major problems		Influence: a voice that matters	

CONCLUSION

Leadership is a peak experience: intense, risky and involving the leader's whole being; there are no half measures. As such, it requires and provides considerable energy, affects people deeply and exposes vulnerabilities.

It is a vehicle for growth, leading to maturity and meaning. Through it, people expand their capacity to serve and become better human beings. When all is said and done, individuals appreciate the contribution they make through leadership and the contribution it makes to their life. "Fifty families or so depend on our firm for their livelihood. It's a burden and an honour. I deeply believe in people development and am happy when people leave to go on to something bigger and better. I want people to reach their potential." (Mark Surrette, President, Robertson Surrette)

They also value the experience and wisdom leadership provides. "In the twilight of your life, to be able to say that you added your grain of sand, and leave the world in better shape than you found it." (Gilles Harvey, Executive Director, Land Register, Ministère de la Justice du Québec [Québec Department of Justice])

So buckle up for the leadership ride. You will need a map and a compass, food for the road and tools for maintenance and repair. To get to the maturity destination, you must have a good sense of direction and keep your eye on the vision while enjoying the landscape you are traveling through. Make sure to manage fuel consumption, recharge your batteries at times, and rely on your travel companions for support and input.

In the next chapter, we will look at how the process unfolds. Ready to start your engines?

CHAPTER 3

THE LEADERSHIP GARDEN

Leadership is about becoming comfortable in your own skin. It is a gradual process like losing weight. You don't always see the changes but others notice them. You learn to focus on others instead of yourself; it's all about them. Mary Kay said, "Behave as if every person you meet has a sign on their forehead saying, 'make me feel important.' " I believe that. It is also about developing confidence in your own vision and opinions, finding your voice and speaking up.

Vickie van Dyke
Midday Host, Smooth Jazz Wave 94.7; Singer and Writer

Leadership allows leaders to realize their dreams and enables others to share them. It's important to make room for others; they must believe in the leader's dream and be happy to associate with it, in fact, make it their own.

Honourable Céline Hervieux-Payette, Q.C.,
Senator; Lawyer, Fasken Martineau DuMoulin

THE PATH TO MATURITY

The field of developmental psychology has been useful to millions insofar as it has identified predictable stages of human growth and mapped the path to maturity. For instance, the terrible twos, adolescence, the mid-life crisis, etc., are now familiar milestones, preparing people for what lies ahead and normalizing foreseeable crises. As a result, there is less blindsiding and better planning. Is there a similar map outlining predictable steps to leadership maturity? Our research clearly indicates that there is.

To describe the predictable steps to leadership maturity, we use a gardening analogy because the process is organic in nature, starting with a seed, which turns into a plant, blossoms and finally pollinates. Growth happens in fits and spurts: periods of acceleration alternate with plateaus and periods of regression. The onset of a new stage can be activated by external events, such as a promotion, or internal motivations, such as the desire to take on a greater challenge. "Difficult experiences triggered the onset of new phases and I took another step in my development as a leader." (Dominique Anglade, Consultant, McKinsey & Company)

Each stage produces a different result—leaves, flowers, pollen—and presents different challenges, stimulating the acquisition of new perspectives. "You are always on a learning curve. You get better at it. Next stage, I would like to provide leadership in the community to help people resolve complex issues." (Janet Milne, Former Assistant Deputy Minister, Finance and Administration, Government of Canada)

Each stage expands your comfort zone and requires the completion of specific developmental tasks. "It's both a liberating and humbling process to go through the stages." (Mavis Staines, Artistic Director, Canada's National Ballet School) By completing them, leaders emerge with an expanded capacity to contribute, greater self-insight and better understanding of the meaning of leadership and of life. "Through the development process, I was aware of setting targets to assess my progress, much like milestones. For instance, at some point, I realized that I was behaving like an entrepreneur." (Donald Dion, Elite Sports Consultant, City of Montréal; Diving Olympic Coach)

Perceptions

Respondents reported various levels of awareness. Most were not conscious of the stages as they unfolded, but perceived them in hindsight. "Like in a novel, a narrative emerges." (Peter Herrndorf, O.C., President and CEO, National Arts Centre) Many believed that awareness increases with maturity.

Others did not perceive separate stages, but instead a seamless flow. "Leadership development is fluid. There are no clear-cut building blocks." (Laura Collings Parsonson, Head of Library, Assistant Curriculum Leader, Program Support, Martingrove Collegiate Institute)

Some described an expansion in size, scope, complexity and responsibility. Geographical examples, such as moving from a local, to a regional, or national focus abound, as well as organizational ones. "It's not necessarily a hierarchical progression but a widening of the scope of responsibility." (John Bales, CEO, Coaching Association of Canada)

A few stressed adaptability as various challenges and opportunities are presented. "You learn at each stage. Different environments require different types of leadership. Even if the foundation is the same, dynamics vary." (David Levine, President and CEO, Montréal Regional Health Authority)

Many observed an emphasis shift, for instance, from results to process, then to people. "First, my focus was on anticipated outcomes. Then it moved to the process, the path that leads to results. Finally, to the people who make it happen." (Charles Cardinal, Consultant in Planning, Periodization and Long-Term Athlete Development [LTAD])

Others describe a change in direction, moving from a vertical focus in their early career (as followers and superiors command most of their attention) to a horizontal dimension (such as peers, clients and stakeholders, entities over which they have no authority, but must influence) at a later stage. "As my career progressed, I had the opportunity to broaden my sphere of influence, both vertically and horizontally. Now, I want to focus on the global scene." (Marie-France D'Auray-Boult, General Director, Performance & Knowledge Management Branch, Canadian International Development Agency [CIDA])

Many reported experiencing several types of shifts, depending on circumstances or desire. All movements can lead to leadership mastery; one is not necessarily superior to the other. However, movement *must occur* for growth. Otherwise, the leader becomes a signpost along the path, instead of traveling on it. "You sharpen your skills. You can't rest on your laurels. You have to find a way to lead. It's an incredible challenge, the most exciting time of my life." (Sunni Boot, President and CEO, ZenithOptimedia)

THE MAKING OF A LEADER

The overall outcome of the leadership journey is expanded capacity. Along the way, leaders gain a wider, more integrated outlook, learn to play different roles and acquire new skills ranging from facilitation to strategic planning.

Early in my career, I was in a hurry, provoking and sometimes rushing things. My style was more directive, and at times, I stepped on other people's toes. Now, I am more careful and seek consensus. My style has become well-rounded, integrated, not just based on logical and intellectual arguments. I suggest alternatives but let people draw their own conclusions. My current goal is to develop other leaders. Credit for achievement is a lesser concern. I try to simplify things, act as a facilitator and see my role as the architect, instead of the expert. I behave with more subtlety and less precipitation. My focus is on the broader picture and the long term. (Marc Poulin, President Operations, Québec Region, Sobeys Inc.)

The process is about giving life to the leader within. "As a leader, you must be aware that you are constantly in the spotlight and cast a shadow. This shadow dictates the leader's impact; all you say or do is a lightning rod for action—both positive and aligned, or destructive and misaligned. Your communication and actions must be in synch in order to sharpen the focus of the organization." (Bruno Biscaro, COO, Accucaps Industries Limited) Challenges rise, the bar is set high, victories are sweet and failures are crushing, but the outcome is priceless: expanded capacity coupled with sound and reliable leadership judgement.

Phases

The process unfolds in three phases:

- **Phase 1, Immanence:** In each of us, rests the presence of leadership. The first task is about making the connection.
- **Phase 2, Emergence:** Once awakened, leadership potential seeks expression. The second task is about manifesting leadership.
- **Phase 3, Transcendence:** Through leadership, leaders alter reality and transform themselves and others. The third step is about transformation.

Immanence

In every one of us, lies the presence of leadership. The question is how to awaken and activate its potential. The leader within is like a pilot light in a gas stove; always on, ensuring that the appliance is ready for operation: immanent because it is internal, pilot because it acts as a guidance system, light because it indicates active presence.

Illustration 3.1

The Making of a Leader

Here are some examples of how respondents access their 'immanent pilot':

"I first listen and observe in the back. Then a switch goes off, the light comes on and leadership emerges. I see something that can be changed or improved and I step up to the plate. I speak up and that seems to rally others." (Patrick Cuenco, Co-founder, Junior Hong Kong-Canada Business Association)

"I studied the great Indian Masters and follow their example. I access the leader within by adopting a loving attitude, which automatically predisposes me to lead. This leadership of the heart suits my emotional nature." (Pierre-Marc Tremblay, President and CEO, Restaurants Pacini Inc.)

Immanence confirms that the inside is more important than the package. Contrast "I cannot lead because I am disabled, too young, a visible minority, etc." with "If I concentrate on the potential inside, it will show me how to actualize it." As such, it flies in the face of the 'private club' approach to leadership, and in these times of leadership high demand, immanence is indeed a reassuring concept.

Emergence

Emergence is the moment when leaders step up to the plate and take a stand. It is the passage between latency and manifestation, potential and action. And it's up to every leader to find their life-giving process.

Here are some examples of how the leader within emerges:

"The leader emerges at peak moments; for instance, during an organizational crisis when you must be present and speak with the troops. You have to prepare your message with great care. In my case, I rehearse, visualize and ponder what will impact the audience. I also consult key people who will 'tell it like it is' to verify my assumptions." (Alain Cousineau, Chairman of the Board and CEO, Loto-Québec)

"Preparation is the key. You need to understand the situation from the stakeholders' perspective and strategize accordingly. Then, you have to communicate, listen to their points of view and foster collaboration. Without followers, you are not a leader. A critical mass must feel that they are part of the effort. Then comes implementation; that is the challenge." (Dr. David Walker, Dean, Faculty of Health Sciences, Queen's University)

Transcendence

Transcendence is the result: the transformation of reality, self and others. Leadership enables people to reach a vision and to exceed what they thought was possible. Leadership is essentially a transformation compound; in many ways, it is a form of alchemy.

Here are some examples of how leaders can transcend reality and reach a higher level of performance:

"Leadership enabled me to reach my objectives, to realize my dreams. In fact, I have now surpassed them." (Kazimir Olechnowicz, President and General Manager, CIMA+)

"Through leadership, I have had the satisfaction to make things better, to see progress. It has also given me the privilege of influence. In the health care field, you deal with people when they are at their most vulnerable. They entrust themselves to you, body and soul. It's an awesome responsibility and privilege. You have to take it seriously. It's also very rewarding." (Eleanor Rivoire, Senior Vice-President, Patient Care Program & Chief Nursing Executive, Kingston General Hospital; Vice-President, Patient Care & Chief Nursing Executive, Quinte Health Care)

THE LEADERSHIP GARDEN

Here's an overall illustration of the process, provided by Marg McGregor, CEO, Canadian Interuniversity Sport:

The first stage was planting: I was bright eyed and bushy tailed and thought I knew it all in high school. I moved to the growing stage in university when I became interested in social issues. The blooming stage was characterized by opportunities to lead national and international sporting events. I then detoured through a clipping stage, taking time away to raise kids and focus on the local environment. Now, I am re-blooming, preparing to lead the team at the Commonwealth Games. Next stage, I will pollinate in another sector.

Stages

The three phases—immanence, emergence and transcendence—can be broken down into four stages, each with a distinct focus:

Stage 1—**seeding**—is about gaining access to the leader within, getting the job done and acquiring basic skills. This stage involves expertise-based leadership and is focused on the individual asserting his/her leadership.

Stage 2—**growing**—is about serving others, becoming a facilitator and acquiring process skills. This stage is focused on mastering the intricacies of team leadership.

Stage 3—**blooming**—is about strategy, transformation, and serving the organization. This stage is focused on the organization and involves flagship leadership.

Stage 4—**pollinating**—is about skill and leadership transfer, giving back, and grooming the next generation. This stage is focused on the community and involves legacy leadership.

Here are some comments illustrating the process:

"The first phase of my leadership career was tied to expertise; the next, linked to team success and goal achievement. Currently, my focus is on vision, strategy, action plans etc. …" (Isabelle Courville, President, Hydro-Québec TransÉnergie)

"The first stage of leadership is often based on technical skills and academic knowledge: guiding others through that knowledge. The second stage is more focused on team responsibilities. I believe the next stage will harness public recognition for expertise and making an ever greater contribution to the community." (Doreen Malone, General Manager, Neptune Theatre)

Here's a summary of the big picture:

Table 3.1

PHASE	STAGE	FOCUS
1. IMMANENCE	1. Individual: Seeding Accessing the leader within	Task
2. EMERGENCE	2. Team: Growing Demonstrating leadership in a visible way	Service
3.TRANSCENDENCE	3. Organization: Blooming Transforming current reality, self and others	Transformation
	4. Community: Pollinating Nurturing future leadership	Legacy

Stage 1: Seeding

You cannot lead others without leading yourself. This requires character and skill building and takes time and effort. A lot of soul-searching is involved in finding your leadership identity: you have to take the *role* seriously, without taking *yourself* too seriously, a paradox.

Here's an illustration from 25-year-old Patrick Cuenco, Co-founder, Junior Hong Kong-Canada Business Association:

> I was born in Canada of Filipino parents. My mother was a Human Rights activist and had to flee the Philippines during the dictatorship of Ferdinand Marcos. She ingrained in her children respect for individual rights, justice, diversity, and taught us how fortunate we were to live in Canada. She brought us to love our country and contribute to it to the best of our abilities.
>
> Unfortunately, she passed away when I was 14 and the family spiralled into a crisis. I had to move to student housing and learn to cope with my grief, family chaos and living in difficult circumstances. I decided I had to lead myself out of this and applied for a scholarship to France. I was thrown into an immersion situation and had to learn the language to survive. This was a real confidence builder. It taught me I could survive

on my own, that I was tougher than I thought. I said to myself, "Life doesn't have to be depressing. I have to lead myself if I want to lead others, be positive and strong." When I returned to Canada, I embarked on a conscious leadership path and never looked back.

As we can see from this story, leaders need to lead themselves first, because leadership requires a strong self (assertive, not passive or aggressive), which does not mean an arrogant ego. "You must learn to check your ego at the door." (Janet Austin, CEO, YWCA of Vancouver)

Leadership also requires the ability to involve and engage others. Therefore, finding the right balance is tricky. Often, leaders start out being too democratic or laissez-faire and have to learn to assert themselves. Likewise, others start out being too autocratic or controlling, and have to learn to collaborate and trust. "Leadership evolved through more listening and being less bossy. I realized that asking people for opinions and ideas is important. It makes the employees feel that they can be part of the business and I learn from their ideas. We come up with the big picture as a team and help formulate a number of solutions to make it better." (Jane Cooney, President, Books for Business) Others remember this stage as a curious blend of confidence and doubt—being alternatively elated and terrified, adrenalin running high.

All agree this stage is focused on contents: issue at hand, problem to solve, cause to advance. Leaders enjoy 'fixing' things and being 'hands-on.' Getting the job done provides deep satisfaction. In fact, new leaders often access leadership through expertise. "The first step involves taking a process and sharpening it, pushing for results." (Dr. Teresa MacNeil, C.M., Director, Extension Department, St. Francis Xavier University)

Most recall being amateur at the seeding stage. "In the early stages, you sense the emergence of leadership and its potential. You are rough around the edges and impatient to get things done, which at times can be perceived as pushy." (Jack Graham, Partner, McInnes Cooper) However, leaders are propelled by enthusiasm. "There were lots of things I did not know, but I compensated for the lack of knowledge with energy, belief in the cause, and passion." (Nalini Stewart, O.Ont., Chair and Director of numerous community organizations and charities)

Invariably, the first stage involves self-doubt and not always knowing what to do. "At first, I wanted to get things done and became frustrated when I couldn't." (Jeannie House, Director, Advocacy & Information, Newfoundland and Labrador Health Boards Association) It is a formative time characterized by improvisation and following your instincts. It is the realm of trial and error, or, possibly, trial and terror.

Stage 2: Growing

A huge paradigm shift occurs when leaders comprehend that to succeed, they must serve their team. "Leadership has been a progressive learning. In the early days as a leader, you think you have to know it all yourself. Then, you tend to know what you have to know, and where you should rely on others." (Rose Patten, Senior Executive Vice-President, Human Resources and Strategic Management, BMO Financial Group)

That is when focus moves from self to team.

In the theatre, it's all about the group. A play is an act of collaboration, a form of progressive synergy. Everyone needs to be heard (literally and figuratively) or they won't play their part effectively. Negotiation must happen to get to the best possible results. The role of the leader/director is to understand the underlying theme of the play and excite people about the text, making the story and the issues it wrestles with as compelling as possible. Then, it is enabling people to make a contribution. Even bad ideas help the process because as people discuss them, they get clarity about how to proceed. It looks good on everyone.

It's important not to shut people down, not to exclude them. If they withdraw, everyone loses the benefit of their ideas. The leader has to model this; he has to be the conduit, the role model so people will develop pride in the show. If it's about you, it dies; if it's about them, you can't stop it. (Antoni Cimolino, General Director, The Stratford Festival of Canada)

At this point, leaders recognize that people are the primary conduit of leadership and become students of human nature. What follows is an intense interest in psychology. What motivates people? How can they understand and leverage personality differences? How can they actualize potential?

This realization promotes the onset of a facilitative, instead of a directive, approach. "Understand that leadership is composed of a million decisions. Bring everyone along with you. Engage and empower others. Fit their input into the final goal." (Dr. Colin MacDonald, President and CEO, Clearwater Seafood) Leaders grasp that results come from good facilitation, not expertise. In fact, they are often surrounded by experts whose technical knowledge is far greater than their own. Their job becomes asking the right questions, not knowing all the answers. This means learning the tools of the facilitation trade: soliciting input, listening, summarizing, etc. At this stage, leaders become less forceful and more insightful. "I listen and ask questions and push for clarity so everyone understands the direction. People feel more secure when they know the direction.

I want everyone to contribute, have fun, get involved, participate, and take control of their decisions." (Marc-André Dépin, President and CEO, Norampac)

Accordingly, they see the benefits of improving their communication skills: speaking up, painting the big picture, and motivating. Their role becomes "the one who can see the opportunities and excite people about them." (Fred Mattocks, Executive Director, Regional Programming, Production and Resources, CBC English Television) The mastery of human dynamics, facilitation, and communication skills dominates the landscape at stage 2.

Stage 3: Blooming

The leader's focus is to serve the organization, help it reach its goals and ensure its viability. "Now I have a broader role in the leadership of the company, fitting in the bigger picture, understanding how to help peers and how to bring about the overall success." (Sarah Raiss, Executive Vice-President, Corporate Services, TransCanada Corporation)

When they reach the third stage, leaders awaken to an environment that is more complex, volatile and public and their focus moves to the long term and the big picture. "Now I am able to deal with bigger issues due to breadth and depth of experience. I am currently involved in a huge transformational project that has the potential to leave a significant cultural legacy for Canada. At this stage, you know that what you do is worthwhile and significant. You believe deeply in it and you become a champion for the cause." (Mary Hofstetter, President and CEO, The Banff Centre)

To be effective, leaders need a system's view, as they must ensure that their organization's culture and infrastructure are conducive to high performance. Ultimately, "leaders must create respectful, supportive environments where results can be achieved." (Paul Zarnke, Executive Director, Children's Aid Society, Region of Peel) This means becoming more strategic and learning to balance a variety of interests. Their decisions affect more people and their horizon goes beyond the short term.

At this stage, leaders are more mature, practiced and comfortable. As figureheads, their leadership operates from symbolism as well as from direct intervention.

Stage 4: Pollinating

During this phase, leaders live and breathe the credo of service. They want to give back and develop other leaders. It's often a once-removed position where influencing is more indirect. It's time to let go of the reins and set upcoming leaders on the right course. Some take on mentor roles. "Leaders work for change because it is right. Their legacy is a better world, not fame. As Geronimo said, 'Once we were like the wind.' " (C.T. [Manny] Jules, Chairman, Indian Taxation Advisory Board)

They are so accomplished that they can apply their skills to a multitude of environments. It is time for altruism and succession planning. Many leaders engage in volunteer work or join a community organization to influence social change and improve quality of life. Passionate about a cause, they want to give it their all. They reach out to alleviate the suffering of others. "Leadership is a form of moral authority and it's the only one I seek." (Françoise David, Co-Spokesperson, Québec Solidaire)

Others guide corporations' destinies by serving on boards of directors or chairing them. Some endeavour to create a culture of talent in their organizations. They become the keepers of values and ensure that the organizational culture is value based and sustainable.

Watching leaders grow gives them great satisfaction. They use skills like coaching, mentoring, counselling, teaching, advising and guiding. The mindset is *I will teach you facilitation skills so you can help others find their own solutions.* "Now, I consciously try to mentor, guide and be a spiritual leader. Potential leaders need to be encouraged to develop and grow. Spend time with them to help them." (Mel Benson, Board Member, Suncor Energy Inc.)

As they mature, leaders realize their responsibility in the leadership development process. "Empowering people to become leaders adds to your credibility as a leader." (Byron Pascoe, Business Manager, Let It Out Entertainment Inc.)

Producing leaders is a significant outcome of effective leadership. "Teach everyone that they have something to offer and should not shy from opportunities. Leaders develop a following; they expand the qualities of others." (Graydon Oldfield, Canadian Downhill and Combined Champion, Canadian Alpine Ski Team Association; Branch Manager and Associate Director, Financial Services Scotia-McLeod)

Each and every leader has a part to play to develop the next leadership generation. "When I was younger and a follower, it was often hard to get help. Now when people ask for my assistance, I give it willingly. I take the time because I remember what it was like to want help, or advice, or mentoring. It's like a chain; you need to give back but more importantly, pay it forward. After helping someone I ask, 'What have you learned from me? How can you pass it on to another person? Who could you mentor?' " (Vickie van Dyke, Midday Host, Smooth Jazz Wave 94.7; Singer and Writer)

This phase also marks a renewal where people reflect, retreat, make new choices and revitalize. "I am driven by happiness, passion and curiosity. Right now I am at a turning point. I will consider taking a step in the political world, in science, or singing." (Joan C. Gibb, President, Canadian Cancer Society, Oakville Unit)

They seek to leave the world a better place. Don Yamkowy, Owner, Nishi-Khon/Key West Travel Ltd., hopes to "leave a legacy for my children. Grow the business and continue community involvement." Not only are leaders considered role models, but almost legends.

Here's an overall summary:

	PHASE 1	PHASE 2	PHASE 3	PHASE 3
	Immanence	Emergence	Transcendence	
	Stage 1	Stage 2	Stage 3	Stage 4
Who	Individual (Me)	Team (We)	Organization (Us)	Legacy (All)
Metaphor	Seeding	Growing	Blooming	Pollinating
Focus	Task	Help others to grow— service	Lead change and renewal— transformation	Pass on knowledge— succession planning
Recipient	Self	Team members	Other leaders	Leadership development process
Authority comes from	Expertise— having knowledge	Facilitation— sharing knowledge	Decision-making—using knowledge	Mentoring— transferring knowledge
Learning	Skills acquisition	Skill fluency	Skill mastery	Skill transfer
Ability	Rough around the edges	Polishing	Polished	Smooth edges
Vision	Reach my dream	Help others reach their dream	Help the organization reach its dream	Leave the world a better place
Position	Lead from the front	Lead from the centre	Lead from the top	Lead from the back

Continued

| | PHASE 1 | PHASE 2 | PHASE 3 | PHASE 3 |
	Stage 1	Stage 2	Stage 3	Stage 4
Power	Finding your own power	Empowering others	Enhancing organizational power	Transferring power
Problem solving	Finding solutions	Helping others find solutions	Solving organizational problems	Transferring problem-solving skills
Coaching	Doing it	Coaching others to do it	Coaching coaches	Teaching, coaching
Growth	Novice	Practitioner	Master	Elder
Learning states	1st—unconscious incompetence	2nd—conscious incompetence	3rd—conscious competence	4th—unconscious competence

The process is about finding your leadership voice. First, you do so by honing your natural instrument to expand its capability. The goal is to never turn a tenor into a baritone, but to widen range and power.

Then, you have to serve the role, using your gifts for a higher purpose and transcending limitations. It's not about hiding your identity under the role, but letting it shine through it, maintaining your authenticity. "You must remain authentic through good and bad times. People admire perfect leaders from a distance but seek to walk near the authentic ones, for they identify with them. In the case of hero leaders, identification fades, dissociation sets in and little by little, they morph into legend, myth." (Clément Guimond, General Coordinator, Caisse d'économie solidaire Desjardins [Credit Union])

Interviewees agreed that leadership maturity broadened understanding of their responsibilities. "Like a captain, I am in charge of steering the ship, which is the external, visible part of the role. The equally important part is to instil confidence, to reduce fear and to give hope. I must show that I believe that what we are doing will work." (Antoni Cimolino, General Director, The Stratford Festival of Canada)

Not surprisingly, the process awakens spirituality. The majority of leaders evoked an enhanced connection with Spirit as they progress towards maturity. "First you become aware of your own power, second you learn to empower others, and then you become aware of a higher Power." (Dr. Gary McPherson, C.M., Executive Director, Canadian Centre for Social Entrepreneurship, University of Alberta)

This spiritual awareness is not necessarily connected to organized religion. Leaders feel guided by Spirit and report that there is something like Divine Order at play. Therefore, their antennas are attuned to the guidance of Spirit.

Aboriginal leaders, in particular, are extremely aware of this dimension. "I have gone through many stages at various times in my life. For me, true leadership does not come from power and control. This would be denying others their gift of choice, for in so doing, we enslave them into our own beliefs and agenda." (Joseph Paquette, Mixed Blood Elder)

CONCLUSION

On their way to maturity, leaders go through predictable steps, each focusing on specific aspects and challenges. As leaders grow, they expand their capacity to lead and fine-tune their judgement, increasing its accuracy and reliability. Just like any human dynamic, the process has an inner logic that cannot be bypassed; the only way *out* is *through*. Leaders cannot move to the next step without meeting the objectives of the current one. Nature is indeed wise in organizing all growth processes according to the same steps.

CHAPTER 4

THE 'FORCE' AND THE 'BLUEPRINT'

It's natural; I don't have to think about it. I sense that something needs to be done and I volunteer. There is no calculation; I throw myself into the battle, body and soul. I don't weigh the odds. If I decide it's worth getting involved in an adventure, I do so with no regrets: noblesse oblige. Crises often provoke leadership emergence. I feel like a firefighter that others must hold back as he plunges into the flames! Leadership is a vocation.

Stéphane Gonthier
Senior Vice-President, Eastern North America, Alimentation
Couche-Tard Inc.

It happened by accident. I started as an individual contributor. When I became a people manager, my boss did not provide much direction. After I outlined my plans/actions, he would typically say, "Well, let me know how things work out." I was left to my own devices. Later, I was offered a much larger leadership role spanning across the whole of a manufacturing operation that was struggling to survive. It was there that I truly began to realize that I could lead an organization/business successfully. The expectations were "Make sure the wheels don't fall off." Upon arrival, I realized that the team had been decimated but the ingredients for success were there. All the team needed was focus, encouragement and determination. We did much more than just keep the wheels on!

Bruno Biscaro
COO, Accucaps Industries Limited

THE CALL TO LEADERSHIP

In each of us rests the potential for leadership but the response and measure depend on us. Whether we lead ourselves or others, we are all called to lead. How do people hear and respond to the call? Are there different ways to connect with the leader within?

This chapter will take you on a fascinating exploration of the 'Force' and the 'Blueprint', the two main access routes to the immanent leader. They are as different as night and day and were a surprise discovery of this research.

But first, let's look at early influences, as they provide the first exposure to leadership models and the first glimpse of the value of leadership. As such, they can create conditions for the immanent leader to emerge.

Early Influences

Are some environments particularly conducive to stimulate leadership? The answer is yes. People are the product of their environments. Influences encountered at a young age are extremely significant.

Family

There seems to be a strong link between parental influence and leadership identity. Parents who value and demonstrate leadership provide a head start: leadership is discussed, encouraged and part of the family culture. "I was very influenced by my parents. My father was a principled man who never went to beer parlours. My mother was a strong believer in people development: a music teacher, active in the community, interested in people, positive. I applied what I learned as a child in my career. Just like my parents, I love to see people grow." (Bill Hamilton, Executive Coach, W.J.A. Hamilton & Associates; Former Senior Vice-President, BMO and CIBC)

Many spoke of the compelling role played by other relatives. "My vision came from my grandfather and it is based on principles. You never steal a carpenter's hammer or a fisherman's net. You never look down on people and you don't allow them to look down on you. You own up to what you do." (Mel Benson, Board Member, Suncor Energy Inc.)

Place in the family is also significant. "I am the eldest of eight kids, so I had to assume leadership responsibilities early within the family context." (Simon Brault, O.C., Director General, National Theatre School of Canada)

Large families seem to promote leadership. "I come from a farming family where we worked together as a team, the oldest helping the youngest. At 16, I became the leader of a work group in a peat bog operation, partly located on our family's farm. I realized then that I enjoyed leading." (Yves Filion, President, CIGRÉ [Conseil international des grands réseaux électriques] [International Council on Large Electric Systems]; Former President, Hydro-Québec TransÉnergie)

Family crises can provoke leadership emergence. "I was a natural leader. As my dad passed away when I was six, I kind of took on his role. I first tried out my hand at leadership within the family environment." (Sylvie Paquette, Executive Vice-President, Corporate Development, Desjardins General Insurance Group)

Parents' expectations condition the child to espouse the family tradition. Monique Lefebvre, Executive Director, Défi Sportif and AlterGo, People with Disabilities in Action, remembers her parents' credo: "You can succeed at anything you put your mind to. A Lefebvre is a leader, not a follower.' In our family, we learned to behave as leaders, to be leaders."

Therefore, as a parent, don't underestimate your impact as a leadership role model. The family is the first milieu where children get leadership exposure. Parents who act irresponsibly, selfishly or weakly, hamper their offsprings' leadership potential. By contrast, parents who take on an active role in the community or in politics will teach that taking a stand and giving back are important. Likewise, if the family atmosphere promotes discipline, teamwork and accountability, kids will pick up leadership skills early on.

The bottom line is to make leadership visible. "It started with my family. I came from a military background. My father was a soldier and my mother's father served in the RAF as a very senior officer. I became aware of the whole idea of leadership as it related to war. It fascinated me. I was sent to an English boarding school at 15 and was given leadership responsibility over younger boys. I began to understand the broad range of skills that were required. As Head of House I had to set an example." (Piers Handling, Director and CEO, Toronto International Film Festival Group)

First Filters

First filters also colour leadership outlook. For instance, those who encounter leadership through sports share a similar mindset: teamwork, discipline and fair play. "I learned leadership through sports and use those principles to succeed: clear vision of a high-performing team, honest feedback about performance, game plan to move forward, acknowledgement that I may have to make tough choices at times." (Robert Kolida, Senior Vice-President, Human Resources, HBC Group)

Mr. Kolida's comments echo a mindset we often encountered in Ontario, where respondents spoke eloquently of fair play, discipline and responsibility. Ontarians seemed very realistic about the 'facts of life' of leadership, embracing it with their eyes wide open and a calm demeanour. This fortitude was very comforting.

Those who first meet leadership through community work also share a similar mindset: values, service and compassion. "From a young age, I was involved in the community in advocacy roles: a strike to save covered bridges, and the establishment of a Recreation Centre for youth, where I wrote the constitution, distributed membership cards and was elected to the executive." (Guy Babineau, Director of Wellness, CBC/ Radio-Canada)

Those who first hone leadership skills within the family learn the value of harmony and consensus. Family influences and first filters are enduring, their imprint permanent. Therefore, parents have a responsibility to act as role models and expose their children to a variety of healthy settings where they can witness quality leadership in action and start learning the skills. Isolation, TV, the Internet and video games are counterproductive to leadership emergence and development.

Leadership is essentially a *relationship* that cannot exist in a vacuum. To become leaders, kids need to acquire interpersonal, team and influence competencies. There is no shortage of opportunities to contribute in sports, community groups and in schools. So parents, provide exposure to leadership by getting involved yourself and involving your children.

ACCIDENTAL AND INNATE

When asked how the leadership journey began, participants gave responses that fell into two distinct categories: accidental and innate.

Accidental

Much to our astonishment, two-thirds of interviewees said things like *I never set out to be a leader*; *I had to lead because no one else would do it*; and *I did it because I deeply believed in a cause or really wanted to help*.

This majority group claims that leadership was 'thrust upon them.' "I backed into it. I had no leadership aspirations. I come from a field of individual contributors but as an emergency physician, I enjoyed the challenge of organizing 30 people in a chaotic environment. I found it satisfying as well as engineering change. As time went by, I discovered more things I wanted to change." (Dr. David Walker, Dean, Faculty of Health Sciences, Queen's University)

Innate

By contrast, one-third of interviewees detected a strong interest in leadership at a young age. We often heard things like: *Leadership is my life*; *I like to start something new and go into uncharted territory*; and *I see possibilities that others don't*. These leaders feel an inclination for the role and it quickly becomes part of their identity. "At 10, I was president of a bowling league. I thought it was natural ... Meanwhile at school, I became a cultural counsellor, going to the theatre and buying tickets for classmates. When I was 13, I produced a Molière play. I had a natural ability to facilitate, to act as a catalyst. The energy of others sustained me." (Pierre Morin, Former Director, Parks and Recreation, City of Montréal)

We called the first group 'accidental,' because these individuals often stumble upon leadership by accident, and the second group 'innate,' as they have a passion and disposition for leadership early on.

Getting Started

These groups begin their leadership careers differently.

At first, 'accidentals' experience reluctance and tend to resist leading; however, due to a service agenda, they move to acceptance. Over time, they feel more comfortable and their willingness to lead increases. Therefore, their path moves from surprise to acceptance. "I did not see myself as a leader. However, I was driven by passion for ideas and a cause. A void had to be filled. It is a learning process." (Marjorie Bencz, C.M., Executive Director, Edmonton Gleaners Association [Edmonton's Food Bank])

'Innates,' spurred by instinct, jump into the fray; leadership feels good to them. Over time, they become more rational. Their path moves from instinct to integration. "In Grade 3, I steered a class project. It gave me internal satisfaction and external praise. I acquired confidence and self-esteem." (Louis O'Reilly, President, O'Reilly International Entertainment Management)

Characteristics

Let us examine how different characteristics play out for both types.

Illustration 4.1

Different Paths

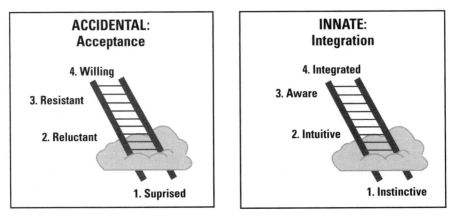

Effectiveness

Both innates and accidentals can be extremely effective. The issue is not which is better, but how to create the conditions so the two-thirds majority (accidentals) will accept leadership opportunities. "As a young person, I did not see myself as a leader but experience has helped shape me: I keep on learning and growing." (Becky McKinnon, Executive Chairman, Timothys' World Coffee) Innates will certainly show up, but their number is insufficient to meet our vast leadership needs.

The accidental/innate pattern is a new dynamic uncovered by our research. As such, we have no ways of knowing whether this holds true in other countries or if the two-to-one accidental-to-innate ratio applies. However, we presume that our sample mirrors the distribution in the overall Canadian population.

Development

Both types stress the importance of development—the gateway to skill, confidence and adaptability enhancement. All emphasized having a lot to learn before achieving maturity. Since accidentals enter the field somewhat reluctantly, nurture can certainly help nature.

Role-Modelling

Both types are acutely aware of the responsibility to act as role models and feel bound by it. Accidentals have a strong sense of duty and innates feel compelled to provide good leadership when they see a vacuum. "People looked to me for leadership." (Donna Scott, O.C., Former Vice-President, Canadian Publishing, Maclean Hunter Ltd.) "I have a desire to leave a legacy and make a difference. I aspire to develop a strong character to help through good and tough times. In the difficult times, character will see you through." (Doug Walker, CEO, Noise Solutions Inc.)

Gender Issues

There are more similarities than differences across genders; views are remarkably aligned and type distribution is similar. Only two females did not initially see themselves as leaders because of gender; however, many still feel external limitations to reaching their leadership potential. Therefore, differences are about aspiration, not understanding or practice. In other words, women feel they don't have as many leadership opportunities as men do (although the situation is improving), but the accidental/innate dynamics and corollary views are the same for both men and women.

Both genders are aware of the importance of blending and balancing male and female energies for effective leadership. "In this day and age, we need to inject feminine sensibility into the political system. Debate is a masculine format. We should replace it by a model based on dialogue, a feminine framework. The container is masculine; we require a feminine content." (Yvon Bastien, Former President and General Manager, Sanofi Synthelabo Canada)

Personality Traits

Innate leaders share common personality traits: they are often driven, restless and achievement oriented. For them, the clock is ticking and they are impatient to dive into leadership. To paraphrase Mae West, so many opportunities, so little time! An overtone of urgency colours their discourse and the need for speed imprints their actions.

Accidental leaders, whose identity is not necessarily tied to leadership, exhibit a wide diversity of personality traits and unlike innates, are not found under a common umbrella. They are as diverse as the overall population, their discourse and actions as varied.

INTERNAL WIRING

Accidental and innate leaders are 'wired' differently.

Starting Point

Where does the impetus for leadership come from? For accidentals, it is external (cause, environment, situation, etc.), while for innates, it comes from within (a burning desire to do something). Accidentals tune their antennas first to the external environment and secondly, to the internal one. For innates it's the opposite. Therefore, the accidental path is from the *outside in*, while the innate path is from the *inside out*.

Accidentals

The leader within an accidental is not initially visible. They see themselves as leaders through others' eyes first. "I did not have the motivation to be a leader; others saw that I had the ability." (Robbie Shaw, President, IWK Foundation) For them, the proof is in the pudding. "I do believe that if you look over your shoulder and nobody is there, then you clearly are not a leader." (Brian Semkiw, Chairman, Rand Worldwide) Opportunities occur and they step into the vacuum to seize them. "I had a strong reaction against discrimination towards those living on the border of the city. I rallied others, including businesses, to deal with the issue." (Alexa McDonough, MP; Former Federal NDP Leader, Canada)

Accidentals' relationship with leadership evolves like a friendship slowly morphing into love. "You step into a situation and gradually people see you as a leader; you have to earn people's respect." (Dr. Alan Bernstein, O.C., President, Canadian Institutes of Health Research) Leadership acts like a magnet pulling them in. "There's a point when you are called upon to lead." (Victor Lachance, Consultant; Former President and CEO, Canadian Centre for Ethics in Sport)

For accidentals, it is the power of attraction, the energy of the yang. They become gradually aware of their impact as a leader and end up wanting more. "I was shy and quiet growing up. One summer, I went to camp and was given a leadership role for a group of kids. Much to my surprise, I was awarded the best staff member award. I became hungry to lead and do more. At university, in the beginning my motivation to get involved was to meet people, but ultimately leadership opportunities came and gave me the confidence to lead further." (Byron Pascoe, Business Manager, Let It Out Entertainment Inc.)

Their approach tends to be intellectual, rational; they plan and reflect. Their style is characterized by quiet determination. Tone is measured, calm. "I just wanted to do the right things. In Grade 8, I was asked to help coach broomball at school. My father was a coach and I knew the importance of motivating and encouraging others to build a team. The team won despite not being the best, as they played for the team rather than for themselves." (Paul Bowes, Head Coach, Men's National Team, Canadian Wheelchair Basketball Association)

Innates

Innate leaders are very aware of the power within. The presence of leadership is palpable and tangible. "As a young person, there was a desire to lead. I wanted to show the way, to be the best. I felt an enormous competitiveness to be the best I could. I also had a desire to see others succeed. I had innate abilities and allowed them to play out." (Rose Patten, Senior Executive Vice-President, Human Resources and Strategic Management, BMO Financial Group)

They choose leadership, feeling entrusted with a mission and sensing they can carry it out. "I felt that I could make things happen and bring about change." (Janet Milne, Former Assistant Deputy Minister, Finance and Administration, Government of Canada)

They are consumed by possibilities. "I come from a family of leaders, which influenced me. I felt comfortable leading at a very young age. As people follow action rather than words, I tried to be a good role model." (Christiane Germain, Co-President, Groupe Germain Inc.) Or they look for vacuums to step into. "When teachers asked for volunteers, I always raised my hand. It is not an effort to take initiative. I strive to learn and challenge myself." (Joan C. Gibb, President, Canadian Cancer Society, Oakville Unit)

Their relationship with leadership is passionate and immediate, like a whirlwind romance. "I was impatient when things were not happening on a project. I would step in and fill the gap." (Dr. Colin MacDonald, President and CEO, Clearwater Seafood)

Innates push out the leadership force seeking to manifest. In other words, they are trying to express the leadership from within them. "You have to start listening to yourself and not worry so much about other people's opinions. My dreams were screaming." (Natalie Choquette, Diva) For innates, it is the power of creation, the energy of the yin.

Rapidly, they become aware of their impact. Leadership ignites and they burn. It's a "fire in the gut." (Veronica Lacey, President, The Learning Partnership) Their approach tends to be intuitive; they focus on their intuition and quickly come to conclusions. Their style is characterized by instinct and action. Their tone is breathless, urgent. "I have limited patience and want to learn quickly. I also want to get to the goal and have fun. I realized I had to lead others to get activities moving quickly and reach the point of having fun." (Laura Collings Parsonson, Head of Library, Assistant Curriculum Leader, Program Support, Martingrove Collegiate Institute)

Motives

Motivation can be described as fuel. Accidentals are initially fuelled by factors outside of leadership dynamics. For them, leadership is a means to an end, for example, achieving a goal, solving a problem, advocating for a cause. For innates, motivations are intrinsic to leadership dynamics. They feel compelled to lead, have a burning desire to do something and have to step into the fray or they will burst. Therefore, leadership is an end as well as a means; it moves passion to action and provokes transformation.

Accidentals

Accidentals are very aware that service is leadership's ultimate purpose and are less likely to misuse leadership for other reasons. "I wanted to serve the community in any form." (Doug McCallum, Former Mayor, Surrey, British Columbia)

They are motivated by outcomes and results. Leadership is a means to an end. "You reach as far as your arm span and if you want to reach higher, you have to hold hands with more people. Then, your reach expands. In the process, you learn to delegate." (Dr. Joseph Segal, C.M., O.B.C., O.St.J., President, Kingswood Capital Corp.) Consequently, they are less aware of vision and integrate it later. "The vision keeps on growing." (Bernadette McDonald, Author; Former Vice-President, Mountain Culture, The Banff Centre)

They drive change through a linear process, like conductors at the front or back of a train. "You can sit and talk about it, but unless words are moved to action you are not a leader." (Ben Nind, Artist; Executive and Artistic Director, Northern Arts & Cultural Centre)

Innates

Initially, innates are less aware of service. Later, they realize its importance. "I could lead people into trouble or into greatness. That made me realize that, if I wanted to be a leader *in* life, I had to learn to be the leader *of* my life, which meant I had to take charge and determine on which basis to lead." (Yvon Bastien, Former President and General Manager, Sanofi Synthelabo Canada)

Innates are often motivated to create something new. Innovation is, in itself, a pursuit. "It started in school. I was impatient, wanted to move on, to create something new, bringing people together in the process." (Antoni Cimolino, General Director, The Stratford Festival of Canada) As a result, they are more aware of vision, which acts as a powerful driver. "Very young, I was clear on what I wanted and how I saw the world. I was able to establish a vision." (Bonnie Dianne DuPont, Group Vice-President, Corporate Resources, Enbridge Inc.)

Leadership is an end as well as a means to getting things done. Intrinsic leadership dynamics, such as making a difference, being challenged, and able to influence, also act as motivators. "I had a burning need to do something, to make change happen." (Joanne Therrien, President, Vidacom Inc.)

They feel at the epicentre of change and fuse with it in a form of alchemy. "A leader is a catalyst of people's wills: His role is to inspire, bring together, stimulate and support their progress toward achieving a vision. Collective will then becomes a tremendous strength." (Bruno-Marie Béchard, Rector, Université de Sherbrooke)

Identity

For accidentals, the challenge is to turn leadership on. For innates, it's turning it off.

Accidentals

Initially, accidentals are something else: experts, problem solvers, advocates. ... Leadership is not, at first, directly tied to their identity. "I never wanted to be a leader. I saw challenges and did something about them." (Dr. Fraser Mustard, O.C., O.Ont., Founding President, The Canadian Institute for Advanced Research) "It took a long time for me to acknowledge that I had leadership skills. I thought it was just common sense." (Anne McGuire, President and CEO, IWK Health Centre) "When you see a vacuum, determine whether or not you are the right person to fill it. Then either step up or allow someone else to do so." (Janet Milne, Former Assistant Deputy Minister, Finance and Administration, Government of Canada)

They are happy following, but end up leading to get things done. They see leadership as an activity to perform some of the time. "I can't think of a time when I consciously set out to be a leader. I was more interested in working within successful teams and trying new things. When it was the right fit, I ended up in leadership roles." (Dave Mowat, CEO, Vancity Credit Union)

Innates

For innates, leadership is deeply tied to their identity. "From grade school on, whenever I joined different organizations, I eventually became the leader of most of them." (Dr. Carol Herbert, Dean, Schulich School of Medicine & Dentistry, University of Western Ontario)

They are less flexible about following. Although they intellectually know they can't always lead, they are emotionally attached to leadership and the urge to lead is strong. "I have little insight on what it's like to be a follower because I haven't played the role that often. There are so many styles of people and therefore, different ways to lead them. When I was young, I assumed everyone was like me. I now know that is not the case." (Louis O'Reilly, President, O'Reilly International Entertainment Management)

As a result, they view leadership as a relatively permanent condition; leadership is a way of life. "I am more comfortable leading than following." (Judy Murphy, COO, Royal Winnipeg Ballet)

Advantages and Disadvantages

Each type starts out with advantages and disadvantages. What leaders make of them tells the rest of the tale.

Table 4.1

ACCIDENTAL	INNATE
Advantages	**Advantages**
Service focus	Early start
Tend to use a consultative approach	Tend to use an inspirational approach
Take careful risks	Take bold risks
Dedication	Courage
Disadvantages	**Disadvantages**
May step up to the plate too infrequently	May step up to the plate too often
Have to work to acquire an inspirational voice	Have to work to acquire a consultative approach
Have to forge an identity as a leader	Have to develop a conscious service focus
Can under-utilize their leadership gifts	Can over-utilize their leadership gifts

Blind Spots

For the most part, each side assumes theirs to be the only reality. For instance, accidentals do not believe that people set out to be leaders. "People don't grow up wanting to be leaders." (Don Yamkowy, Owner, Nishi-Khon/Key West Travel Ltd.) They presume the way to mastery is learning, hard work and development.

Innates wonder why everyone isn't consumed by leadership and are baffled by those who appear indifferent to its wonders. "Leadership is the desire to change things, to make a contribution. It is a responsibility." (Honourable Carole Taylor, O.C., Minister of Finance; M.L.A., Vancouver-Langara, British Columbia Government; Former Chair, CBC/Radio-Canada) They doubt that leadership mastery can be achieved without a natural inclination.

THE 'FORCE' AND THE 'BLUEPRINT'

In our research, we discovered two primary and fundamentally different access routes to the leader within, which we called the 'Force,' used by innates, and the 'Blueprint,' used by accidentals. This is a very important discovery because connection is the first step in the making of a leader. Both routes are effective and both appear strange, if not downright bizarre, to the other type.

Accidental leaders focus on situational analysis, and subsequently, draw conclusions whether to lead or not. When sufficient evidence accumulates, they step up to the plate. Over time, they develop a 'blueprint' that guides their leadership decisions.

Innates focus on their internal landscape, and when a critical mass of energy mobilizes, they move to lead. They have a deep and intimate connection with a 'force' that urges them to act.

Accidentals are akin to anointed knights on a mission, while innates follow a visionary quest, much like Joan of Arc.

Innate Leaders: The 'Force'

Innate leaders' conversations gravitate towards the 'Force,' an inner presence that provides impetus for leadership and guides their actions. They have a deep and intimate connection with it, and, with time, become increasingly aware of its shifts and their meaning.

The Force is experienced as an electrical current in perpetual motion. There is a surge of power when activated, and as the Force reaches a certain threshold, it becomes irresistible and innates step into its vortex. As a result, they view leadership as a *transfer of energy.*

The Force is a shortcut to knowledge. It is strong and never lets innates down, providing courage, resilience and determination. It enables leaders to jump into the precipice with total confidence.

Here are some statements about the Force:

- "Something stirs; passion wells up inside and it calls. I need to act on it or I will burst. I can act on it by verbalizing or taking action. The leader within accesses you, not the other way around." (Louis O'Reilly, President, O'Reilly International Entertainment Management)
- "Intuition takes charge. A quiet, calm sense of being in control fills the space." (Piers Handling, Director and CEO, Toronto International Film Festival Group)
- "I'm not conscious of a deliberate series of steps. Leadership just surges up in me as the right thing to do." (Lyn Wray, Division Manager, Financial Planning and Corporate Risk Management, Manitoba Hydro)
- "I listen to the internal voice that guides me." (Natalie Choquette, Diva)

Here's how the Force works:

- The leader is plugged in through a 'high-speed connection.'
- The 'Force' pulsates and flows and the leader is attuned to its movements.
- It surges and reaches a critical mass.
- The leader succumbs to it and leaps into the fire, pushing leadership out. (Passion fills the reservoir: "Let's get it done!")
- Spirituality fills the leader with reverence for the 'presence' within.
- Followers say, "Lead on, we are with you!"
- As the leader acts, the process reveals itself, and energy transfers from leader to follower.

We were absolutely fascinated by the universality and comprehensiveness of the descriptions of the Force. The understanding is the same regardless of age, ethnic background, region or sector. For instance, there are no gender differences. One might think men could be uncomfortable describing what is essentially an intuitive process, but they are not.

For innates, the Force is a tangible entity that nurtures vision and passion and provides sustenance, but also demands action. One could almost say that the Force is the creative energy and the leader, the vessel that enables it to manifest.

Accidental Leaders: The 'Blueprint'

The 'Blueprint' is the approach used by accidentals to determine whether and how to lead. It is primarily a rational method, since they must find compelling reasons for leading.

Accidental leaders get pulled into leadership by external triggers, as well as their own desire to make a contribution. "Make sure your antenna is up. Where are the opportunities to facilitate change?" (Paul Zarnke, Executive Director, Children's Aid Society, Region of Peel) The Blueprint gives them the framework and safety required to gather data, analyze situations, make decisions, determine action plans, guide group processes, etc.

It develops over time and evolves into a familiar pathway. It doesn't operate by critical mass like the Force, but by accumulation of evidence. If the reasons to lead add up to a reasonable total, leaders take on the role. If not, they are happy to contribute in other ways.

Here are some statements about the Blueprint:

- "I don't always have to lead. The main thing is to make a contribution. I am happy to be part of a team and will take leadership roles to fill gaps when required. The climate has to be right, as well as the goal." (Susan Mitton, Regional Director, CBC Radio, Maritimes)
- "Know yourself and what types of environments get the best and the worst out of you." (Carmela Porco, Former Vice-President and COO, Doubleday Canada)
- "With anticipation, fear and trembling, I took on this position." (Paul Henderson, Founder and President, The Leadership Group; Maple Leafs Hockey Alumni)
- "Care enough to do the right thing." (Sue Lee, Senior Vice-President, Human Resources and Communications, Suncor Energy Inc.)
- "Get an idea, brainstorm with the team and reach an agreeable course of action." (Ann MacKenzie, President and CEO, Nova Scotia Film Development Corporation)

Here's how the Blueprint operates:

- External triggers surface.
- Followers ask, "Will you be our leader?"
- Assessment takes place: to lead or not to lead?
- When enough evidence accumulates, the leader is pulled into leadership. ("Understand what you are being called to do. Rise to the role; it will give you the strength to carry through.")

- Spirituality fills the leader with reverence for the mission.
- Conscious choice: "I do."
- The leader creates a solid process for leading, fulfilling a duty.

We were excited to discover such distinct and reliable approaches to leadership emergence and are in awe of their governing intelligence and powerful designs.

The Force and the Blueprint: a Summary

Here's a summary of the two access routes to the leader within.

Table 4.2

Accidental: The Blueprint	Innate: The Force
Trust your head	*Trust your gut*
FOCUS	**FOCUS**
External landscape	Internal landscape
Attuned to opportunities	Attuned to inner flow
Doing	Being
Action	Movement
Ponder leadership	Inhabited by leadership
Reflection	Energy
PROCESS	**PROCESS**
Analysis	Instinct
Decision	Intention
Back into leadership	Seek leadership
Accept mission	Volunteer for mission
Judgement call: depends on situation	Impulse: depends on vision and passion
Slow	Fast
Penny drops	Adrenalin rushes
Pulled into leadership	Push leadership out
Step out of comfort zone	Step into chaos
Temporary role	Permanent vocation

Accidental: The Blueprint	Innate: The Force
Trust your head	*Trust your gut*
CHARACTERISTICS	**CHARACTERISTICS**
Analyze situations	Read situations
Trust good planning and sound process	Trust intuition and ability to improvise
Displaying confidence is often an acquired skill	Find it easy to display confidence
Find it easy to seek input	Seeking input is often an acquired skill
Seek consensus	Seek alignment
Inspiring and motivating are often acquired skills	Find it easy to inspire and motivate
Find it easy to listen and support	Listening and supporting are often acquired skills
ROLES	**ROLES**
Facilitator	Driver
Convener	Catalyst
Enabler	Context provider
Mission keeper	Vision keeper
Role model	Role model
CHALLENGES	**CHALLENGES**
Analysis paralysis	Too much gut and not enough thought
Overcoming reluctance to lead	Assuming they should lead
Not stepping up to the plate	Stepping up too often
Leaving too early	Leaving too late
Concerned by what they lack to succeed	Less concerned by what they lack to succeed

THE PATH TO MATURITY

As leaders mature, the desire to become whole propels them to connect with the 'other side.' Maturity means acquiring the *opposite flow*. For instance, accidental leaders learn to trust their gut and, with time, use instinct, intuition and passion. Innate leaders, for their part, learn to analyze, consult and make more conscious choices about whether to lead or not to lead. It is as though each side needs to get in touch with the wisdom of the opposite side and experience its validity.

Maturity teaches accidental leaders to learn to trust their gut. This means finding quick access routes to instinct and intuition, key building blocks to a sound and accurate leadership judgement. They learn to balance analysis with intuition and eventually see wisdom in the path of the innates. "You get called and it happens at the gut level. If you wait for the intellect to kick in, you can't react in time because it's too slow!" (Antoni Cimolino, General Director, The Stratford Festival of Canada)

Maturity teaches innate leaders to trust their head and become more reflective, analytical and thoughtful. They learn to seek input, consult, listen, facilitate and eventually see the wisdom in the thoughtful path of the accidentals. "When I was young, I acted on instinct. In university, I received formal leadership training and I started to read authors like Covey and Maxwell. Studying leadership helped me hone and improve my leadership skills." (Louis O'Reilly, President, O'Reilly International Entertainment Management)

With the comfort of experience and maturity, both types can venture in each other's territory to find their shadow.

Similarities

The two types share many similarities:

The Role of Spirituality

Although their paths differ greatly, both accidentals and innates agree that connecting with the presence of leadership, and the subsequent emergence of the leader, are profound experiences. All leaders feel a sense of reverence and awe for the calling. 'Tapping the spirit within' is a spiritual encounter.

- "Go inside and listen. Let the answer come." (Dr. Gary McPherson, C.M., Executive Director, Canadian Centre for Social Entrepreneurship, University of Alberta)
- "Contact is made in silence where ideas take form and substance." (Richard Blackburn, General and Artistic Director, Théâtre de la Dame de Cœur)
- "I respectfully ask the Great Mystery for guidance so that I don't hurt anyone." (Joseph Paquette, Mixed Blood Elder)

The Role of Duty

Noble duty features into the equation. "I was trained as an actor and understand the importance of putting yourself aside to play a part. It's the same for leadership.

You must forget your own fears, frustrations, sorrows, and rise above your personal concerns in order to lead. The self can always feel sorry for itself in private, later." (Marc Mayer, Director, Montréal Museum of Contemporary Art) This sentiment is echoed by both types. They talk eloquently about responsibility, accountability and standing on principle.

Leading by Example

All are aware of the necessity of leading by example and taking the high road. "Don't cave in to what is easy." (Chris Rudge, CEO and Secretary General, Canadian Olympic Committee) The result is mutual respect between leaders and followers. "With my leadership roles from summer camp to university, I aimed to lead by example. I put in a lot of time and effort and I want people to also work hard at what they do. This creates respect on both sides; respect is all important. I try my best to earn it." (Byron Pascoe, Business Manager, Let It Out Entertainment Inc.)

CONCLUSION

The discovery of the accidental/innate dynamics has profound implications for leadership emergence and development. It raises important questions. For instance:

- How can we create the conditions for the accidental majority to step into the leadership role?
- How can we increase and vary support so that more accidentals stay on the leadership path?
- How can we help innates acquire consultative and analytical skills?
- How can we help accidentals get in touch with their intuition?
- How can we encourage both innates and accidentals to focus early on service, the purpose of leadership?

Understanding and validating these different access dynamics will promote the design of programs tailored to their styles. Individual leaders can also use these patterns to self-explore. Are you an innate or an accidental? How can you leverage your type to become a better leader? How can you reach out to the wisdom of the other type and learn from it?

Section B

How Can We Optimize the Process?

In the previous section, we saw how leaders grow. They begin by connecting with the leadership presence within (immanence) through two primary access routes: the 'Force' and the 'Blueprint.' Once leadership potential is activated, it seeks to manifest itself (emergence). From the first leadership act, leaders are on their way towards maturity through predictable stages of development, which deploy in an organic form: from seeding to growing, blooming, and, finally, pollinating. Each stage has specific goals and developmental tasks to be accomplished before the leader can 'graduate' to the next stage.

From within, the leadership experience is intense and emotional, engaging the leader's whole being. It is a powerful crucible for promoting growth and strengthening character. Staying on course means managing the pain/gain equation and energy flow.

To succeed, leaders must focus on how to best serve their constituencies, devise a vision for a desirable future, infuse it with passion, and partner up with followers to make it happen. It starts with taking responsibility for leadership and owning the role: subscribing all their assets, skills, qualities, etc., to serve it. This doesn't mean obliterating their identity, but letting it shine through the role.

As they lead, leaders surpass the limitations of current reality to create a new one, transforming themselves and others in the process (transcendence). Leadership's DNA is a transformation compound.

In this next section, we will examine how best to optimize these dynamics and leverage their nature. Let's begin with what individuals can do to facilitate their own development.

CHAPTER 5

INDIVIDUAL LEADERSHIP STRATEGY

The difference between leadership and manipulation is small and measured by intent. The difference is what goes to my heart.
David Todd
General Manager, Shell Canada, Drilling

I believe true leadership begins with being clear about values and beliefs. Knowing who you are is the key to believing in your dreams and having the courage to see them through, particularly when things get challenging. If you can stay true to this inner compass, then success will follow.
Rick Hansen, C.C., O.B.C.
President and CEO, Rick Hansen Foundation

Leadership is hard work. Face reality and be willing to take steps, to change and move with the times. Be ready for challenges and be tough on yourself. Look in the mirror and behave the way you are expected to.
John Furlong
CEO, Vancouver 2010 Olympic and Paralympic Winter Games

YOU ARE IN CHARGE

Development is necessary to become an accomplished leader. "The natural desire to lead does not equate success. You have to improve your skills and abilities." (Fred Mattocks, Executive Director, Regional Programming, Production and Resources, CBC English Television)

Development is a constant evolution: growth follows stagnation, sharp awareness alternates with denial, and clear direction interchanges with reactive coping. "Every stage is a stepping stone to the next." (John Sleeman, Chairman and CEO, Sleeman Breweries Ltd.)

It does not follow a set route, but a path unique to each person. Its destination is leadership *identity*. It works through discovery and revelation. At times, leaders set out to explore, and, at others, things are revealed to them. "You realize you are a leader when you start saying things you didn't know you knew." (Bruce Harber, President and CEO, York Central Hospital)

The journey provokes shifts of consciousness, triggered by external events, such as challenges, and internal realizations, such as insights. The process is as valid as the conclusions reached. "The way to get to a goal is as important as achieving the goal." (Sue Lee, Senior Vice-President, Human Resources and Communications, Suncor Energy Inc.)

The greater the awareness, the faster the ride; oblivion slows it down. Consciousness also brings higher levels of articulation and a sense of control. "At first, I worked a lot on myself. I wanted to know myself better and understand my impact as a leader. I did a lot of self-analysis, which made me aware of my strengths and areas for development, and built my confidence." (Sylvie Paquette, Executive Vice-President, Corporate Development, Desjardins General Insurance Group)

Striking a healthy balance between phases of soul-searching and reflection, and phases of intense activity will assist the process. For instance, relentless action without introspection results in endless repetition of the same mistakes. Likewise, too much contemplation without action stifles skill development. "Learn through observation and experience. Take on responsibility for a project and see it through." (Honourable Joseph Handley, Premier, Northwest Territories)

Intuition plays a major role, partnering with cognition to integrate development. Of the two, intuition acts faster. When making an important decision, leaders always heavily lean on it. A lot of information is stored in the unconscious, just below the surface, and is activated through intuition. Therefore, a strong intuition expands leadership capacity. Accessing intuition means tuning in to your gut, your right brain, your unconscious; paying attention to your dreams and learning to notice impressions. A wonderful book on the topic is Julia Cameron's *The Artist's Way* (Tarcher, New York, 2002).

Learning takes time and requires dedication. The good news is you can learn from anything—good or bad. Your ability to leverage learning will make a difference in how quickly and effectively you develop as a leader. "Keep track of the results you are achieving and your impact on staff. Seek out assistance for areas of weakness." (Lyn Wray, Division Manager, Financial Planning and Corporate Risk Management, Manitoba Hydro)

Development is not a passive process. Learners should be much more than simple recipients, compliant and placid. They should be in the driver's seat! "You must take charge of your own leadership development process. Don't wallow in comfort and ease. Become the architect of your path. Ask, 'What did I learn today? And if I haven't learned much, what do I set out to learn tomorrow?' " (Luc Nadeau, Executive Vice-President, Corporate Communications and External Relations, and President of the Luxury Products Division, L'Oréal Canada)

Even the best programs will fail if learners are not engaged. Moreover, learners are most in tune with their own needs and best placed to make strategic decisions about next development steps, like choosing assignment A over assignment B.

Therefore, to increase your chances of success you need to plan your approach. All respondents recognized the need for a well-articulated, conscious learning strategy to maximize learning and fast-track development. "I feel that I still have a lot to learn and look for a continuous learning environment." (Valerie Payn, President, Halifax Chamber of Commerce) You can improve your strategy by:

- Adapting it to your learning style.
- Adjusting it as situations evolve. "Keep on learning, adjusting your approach." (Donna Scott, O.C., Former Vice-President, Canadian Publishing, Maclean Hunter Ltd.)
- Increasing awareness. The more conscious the strategy, the faster the learning.
- Finding ways to overcome obstacles. "Think like a spider and spin the web wider. If you think like a spider, you discover that there are always ways to go around hurdles." (Denise Amyot, Vice-President, Leadership Network, Public Service Human Resources Agency, Government of Canada)

MAXIMIZING YOUR DEVELOPMENT

Getting results means following three key steps:

- '*Going in*' focuses on exploring your motivations for leading, discovering your leadership identity and, most importantly, designing your platform, the foundation of your leadership practice. On a smaller scale, it also means setting learning objectives and crafting a development plan.

- *'Reaching out'* deals with experimenting with leadership and expanding your capacity.
- *'Stepping back'* concentrates on learning from experiences and understanding your impact.

  Here's an illustration:

- *Before:* Say you are a young team leader in a large organization and want broader exposure. You decide to get involved in the United Way Campaign at work. What do you expect to learn from this experience? How will you prepare for it?
- *During:* As the campaign unfolds, you take on the task of delivering presentations to all departments to stimulate participation and practise public speaking. How can you derive maximum learning from this opportunity?
- *After:* At the end of the campaign, it's time to reflect on the experience and analyze it. What did you get out of it? Process both positive and negative feedback—it will help you become a better leader. If your presentations lacked pizzazz, how can you inject it the next time? You might join your local Toastmasters Club to get more practice and coaching. The cycle will then begin anew.

The *going in/reaching out/stepping back* dance is a perpetual cycle. "It's a continuing process: education, experience, reflection, listening to people and reviewing results of my actions." (Dr. Colin MacDonald, President and CEO, Clearwater Seafood) It will make you more conscious and more strategic, and you will get better, faster results. Let's now explore each step in detail.

Going In

Going in is about preparing for leadership. Here are some tips:

Clarify Your Purpose

Leadership requires courage, a deep connection to purpose, passion and engagement. "If you make a commitment, be prepared to invest the energy needed to succeed. Take on extra responsibility to make a difference. Don't be complacent but engage, commit and deliver." (Larry Berg, President and CEO, Vancouver International Airport Authority)

Identify your motivation, interests and passion. What excites you? What gets your juices flowing? Where can you make a difference? Who and what will your leadership serve? "Lead for the right reasons, not photo ops. Look into your own heart. Why do you want to be a leader?" (Johanna Maria Bates-Van der Zeijst, President, Johanna M. Bates Literary Consultants Inc.) The bottom line is: "Take your place. Make your mark." (Isabelle Hudon, President and CEO, Board of Trade of Metropolitan Montréal)

Connect with the Leader Within

To lead, you need to awaken the leader within and facilitate its emergence. It starts with tuning in. What guidance is it giving you? "Listen to your inner voice and be alert to opportunities life throws your way to seize them. You should combine both: listening to yourself and getting involved. What do I value? What are my interests? In what should I get involved? To find your way, you have to listen to your own voice." (Denise Verreault, C.M., C.Q., President and CEO, Groupe Maritime Verreault Inc.)

Build Your Foundation

A firm foundation acts as a compass, guiding decisions, informing behaviour and providing consistency. Interviewees view foundation building as the first step in becoming an effective leader and a *fundamental* leadership act. "It's like building a house. You start with the foundations and add on progressively. The basis of my leadership not only rests on my own choices, but stands on the shoulders of people who came before me. My parents passed down values and ideals to me, forming a leadership chain that I will continue with my children and others." (Patrick Cuenco, Co-founder, Junior Hong Kong-Canada Business Association)

Erecting a strong foundation will solidify your leadership edifice. "Through the years, I realized that people want to follow leaders equipped with a solid foundation: values, goals and vision. I believe that they will forgive errors if they believe leaders are sincere and honest. Therefore, I worked hard on this basis." (Marc Poulin, President Operations, Québec Region, Sobeys Inc.)

So, budding leaders should ponder questions like *What are my values? What principles will guide my decisions? What is my vision of effective leadership? What kind of leader do I want to be? What is my mission? Who am I serving through leadership and what is the best way to serve them? What legacy do I want to leave behind?* "I built my foundation by asking questions such as 'Why not?' and by refusing the status quo. Also, by embracing change and being open, improving my skills and knowledge and pushing myself everyday. It is important to imagine possibilities and bring people on board in order to achieve the goal." (Kathleen Bartels, Director, Vancouver Art Gallery)

A platform is like a home: The work is never done. Just when you think you've got it right, the roof needs repairs, the basement floods or you decide to redo the landscaping. It's a labour of love and requires time and constant tinkering. "Mistakes are great teachers. I made my own and grew as a result. I observed other leaders and learned from them. I also studied leadership at Harvard during an MBA. It took me a long time to develop a behavioural code and an instinct for leadership but it was worth it as it guides my practice, informs my decisions and provides consistency." (Peter Herrndorf, O.C., President and CEO, National Arts Centre)

Construction Process

In order to structure their platform, leaders engage in deep reflection, especially about intention, vision and values. Reflection is based on introspection. "In the silence, leaders perceive their intention. They must find their centre, like tennis players who quickly return to centre court." (Richard Blackburn, General and Artistic Director, Théâtre de la Dame de Cœur)

Various techniques can be used, such as contemplating issues, journaling, yoga, walking, etc. "Keep a journal—be reflective on your growth as a leader. Create opportunities to get feedback. It is an individual learning process." (Dr. Jacquelyn Thayer Scott, O.C., Past President and Professor, Cape Breton University; Deputy Chair, Prime Minister's Advisory Council on Science and Technology) Here are some 'construction materials' to help you build your platform:

Intention

Intention infuses action, and followers 'buy in' to leaders depending on how they perceive their intention. "What I did was based on strong belief in a cause and passion for it. Coming from a small town in Cape Breton with no sense of hierarchy, my outlook is to help others. I am motivated and prepared to sacrifice for others." (Dr. Ruth M. Goldbloom, O.C., Chair, Pier 21 Foundation)

It is important to set the bar high. Here are a few examples of elevated intentions:

- "Being the best I could be was behind what I did to make my organization the best it could be." (Allan Taylor, O.C., Former Chairman and CEO, Royal Bank of Canada)
- "When my belief of equity and accessibility was challenged, I stepped into a leadership role to address the issues properly." (Patrick Jarvis, Owner and

President, Amarok Training Services Ltd.; Former President, Canadian Paralympic Committee)

- "Putting more humanity in the workplace is the legacy I want to leave behind." (Denise Amyot, Vice-President, Leadership Network, Public Service Human Resources Agency, Government of Canada)

Vision

Leadership is tied to vision. "In order to lead, you need a compelling vision; without it you are incapacitated. Make sure the vision is compelling enough to give inspiration." (John Furlong, CEO, Vancouver 2010 Olympic and Paralympic Winter Games) Therefore, leaders must articulate a vision. Without it, there is no leadership. Here are some pointers:

- Select a vision distant enough from current reality to be inspiring. "Think of the most important and worthwhile thing to do. Imagine how to get there. Focus on the first right step and the next will follow. Others will supply the push to go on, as it will become their plan." (Honourable Ken Dryden, MP; Former Minister, Social Development, Government of Canada)
- Make it tangible enough to guide action. "It is not necessary to have all the answers but to know where you are going." (Guy Babineau, Director of Wellness, CBC/Radio-Canada)
- Evolve the vision as you progress. "It's important to find the means, time and energy to realize your dreams. You must give it a try and see if it's possible. Ninety percent of obstacles are in our heads." (Honourable Céline Hervieux-Payette, Q. C., Senator; Lawyer, Fasken Martineau DuMoulin)
- Take a risk. No risk, no vision. "My father taught me: if you are taking a risk, take a big one—the dividends will be worth it. He helped me reflect afterwards on the impact of my actions." (Susan LaRosa, Director of Education, York Catholic District School Board)

Eleanor Rivoire, Senior Vice-President, Patient Care Program & Chief Nursing Executive, Kingston General Hospital; Vice-President, Patient Care & Chief Nursing Executive, Quinte Health Care, summed it up well: "I am idealistic and optimistic by nature. I dream, which makes it easier for me to create leadership visions. Then I test them through trial and error. I take risks and watch the results, as well as listen to feedback and suggestions. It's an organic, interactive process."

A clear vision acts like the North Star through the transformation voyage. Without it, leadership is aimless and cannot rise above the mundane. Its absence is crippling.

Values

The majority of interviewees chose values as the most important component of their platform. "I created the foundation of my leadership practice by defining and actualizing my values and beliefs. I realized early on that in order to generate and maintain follower loyalty, leaders must have a value system and put it in practice. When leaders are congruent and consistent with their values, it is a source of motivation for employees and of credibility for leaders. The value system guides decision-making, especially in difficult situations like budget or staff cuts: Who to protect? What to slash?" (Michèle Fortin, President and CEO, Télé-Québec)

Obviously, upbringing plays a role in value selection. "I learned watching my mother treat everyone with respect regardless of title or position." (Nancy Lee, COO, Olympic Broadcast Services; Former Executive Director, CBC-TV Sports; Chef de Mission, CBC Olympics) "My mother was the quiet backbone of the family and would offer support, whatever the outcome. My father set high aspirations and offered strategies to reach them." (Cary Mullen, Olympian and World Cup Champion; Serial Entrepreneur; Professional Speaker)

However, no matter how potent these influences are, leaders have to define their own set of values. "Values are the context within which you win or lose." (Steven Parker, Chairman, CCL Group) Respondents were positively adamant about values' vital importance to a successful and sustainable leadership practice. "When you leave a position, you leave with your reputation. Therefore, stand on your principles." (Sandra Stevenson, President and CEO, Sport BC)

Leaders also appreciate the guidance of values when faced with difficult choices. "Defining values is important. For instance, how do you react when faced with a bribe doing business in a foreign country?" (Peter Robinson, CEO, Mountain Equipment Co-op)

Top-Ranking Values

Here are the most important values to the practice of leadership, according to respondents:

Integrity—Integrity cements trust and, without trust, there is no leadership. It acts like a compass pointing to the 'true north.' "Integrity is critical. If you don't demonstrate the values you expect from others, you sabotage your ability to lead." (Jim Mills, President and CEO, Office Interiors)

Respect—Respect defines the playing field. By giving respect, the leader receives it. A disrespectful leader breeds resentment, contempt and over time, rejection.

Honesty—Honesty serves leaders well in good and bad times. 'Telling it like it is' is by far the best approach in the long run. Transparency is important, because either followers will see the truth or it will come out in time.

Fairness—Fairness enables followers to accept difficult choices. They may not like a decision, but they will rally if they feel they have been fairly treated. Fairness implies equitable treatment regardless of differences. In today's diverse workplace, it's an essential leadership condition.

Ethics—When all is said and done, ethics are more important than results. Many interviewees mentioned having their own code of conduct. No matter how good results are, if they are achieved through shady means, constituencies will eventually withdraw their trust and respect. Simply put, success without an ethical foundation erodes ability to lead. That is why corporations nowadays balance the 'what' with the 'how.' For instance, a manager who gets great numbers by bullying his team is no longer considered a good performer. And to find out what followers really think, corporations increasingly rely on mechanisms like employee engagement surveys, 360-degree feedback instruments, exit interviews, etc. They know that if the 'how' is not taken care of, the 'what' is not sustainable.

More than anything else, values influence *every choice* leaders make. "I observed role models and emulated what worked, copying their approach. My style is probably a combination of my personality and a composite of my role models. The underpinning though was defining my values: integrity, truthfulness, honesty. They permeate everything I do." (Mark Surrette, President, Robertson Surrette)

Reaching Out

You have to take action. "Leadership is not a spectator sport." (Honourable William G. Davis, P.C., C.C., Q.C., Former Premier, Ontario) "Take the bull by the horns and point it in the direction you want to go." (Joseph Paquette, Mixed Blood Elder)

Without action, the best vision remains a fantasy. Start with sharing your vision and ask for input. People will get excited and give you feedback and ideas. Once it has taken shape, begin crafting a plan that together, you can make happen. You don't need a document detailing every move, but a blueprint for moving forward. Diving into action makes the vision real and gives people a sense of control over their destiny.

Action promotes skill building. For knowledge to transfer into know-how, nothing replaces practice. The accumulation and variety of experiences has a high impact on leadership development. Whether positive or negative, reactive or deliberate, experience allows leaders to find out where they excel and how to adapt to diverse circumstances. It is an opportunity for exploration, testing and learning through trial and error. "The longer I am a leader, the better I get at it." (David Carey, President, Volleyball Canada)

Experience moulds leaders into greatness; however, waiting for what life throws at you is not sufficient—you have to engage it. Respondents repeatedly stated the importance of seeking experiences to spur development. Carefully and strategically select opportunities, take a risk and do it! For instance, the CEO of a large organization showed one of the authors a picture of a cow herd and asked, "Do you think I know anything about raising cows?" "No," replied the puzzled author. "That is precisely why I am doing it. You have to push yourself out of your comfort zone. That is how you grow." The same leader later went on a solo quest in the wilderness and traveled alone through Europe.

The theory of immunization states that by injecting a little virus into an organism, it learns to combat it. What chaos do you need to inject in your life so you can grow? How can you temporarily destabilize yourself to achieve a new, more solid balance? Since people don't usually change unless the pain of change is less than the pain of status quo, what patterns in your life are you sick of? How can you break the routine to go further and spread your wings? How can you activate all parts of yourself to become more whole?

Therefore, as mentioned earlier, build your bench strength through experience. "If people want to become leaders, they have to do more. Practice and discipline produce strong leaders, just like in sports. Pull up your sleeves, work hard and put in the effort." (Suzanne Blanchet, President and CEO, Cascades Tissue Group)

Of all types of experiences, adversity is the strongest developer. "Leadership is like tea; it reveals its essence in hot water." (Gilles Harvey, Executive Director, Land Register, Ministère de la Justice du Québec [Québec Department of Justice])

Respondents often indicated that they learned more from adversity than from success. Therefore, leaders must develop a resilient and almost welcoming attitude towards adversity. What is the silver lining, the blessing, the learning behind the crisis? What is it trying to teach you? What does it want you to pay attention to? How can you face it squarely? "Leadership requires the courage to take ownership of a crisis and to put a plan together to deal with it." (Susan LaRosa, Director of Education, York Catholic District School Board)

Leadership requires a considerable amount of power, especially during hardships, and power, much like endurance, builds over time. Power is about capacity, like megabytes in a computer. Leaders need great reserves of power to enact their vision and promote transformation, and capacity expands through action.

Stepping Back

After action comes reflection: How did it go? What did I learn? What would I do differently the next time? Reflection is as important as action. Without it, you will endlessly repeat the same mistakes and get into a rut. Action builds muscle and reflection injects meaning.

Maximize Learning

The more learning you extract from an experience, the better. "Throughout my career, I was exposed to a lot of people and learned from them. I soaked in all the information and consciously reflected on my learning." (Mel Benson, Board Member, Suncor Energy Inc.) It's important to process developmental experiences. "Take the time to reflect—you need to look at what happened, what worked or did not work, and evaluate situations." (Richard Cameron, Senior Vice-President, Canadian International Development Agency [CIDA]) In other words, analyze and assess both the experience and your performance. Look at your behaviour with detachment, said the interviewees; it can be changed if it doesn't work. Adopt the mindset of an actor analyzing his performance. How can you better convey the essence of the leadership role using your gifts? How can you serve the role with *your* voice? Be willing to experiment. If something doesn't work, ask what would. People will tell you because they have your success at stake. Listen to their advice and try again. You might be surprised.

Mistakes are great teachers; admit when you make one, learn from it and move on. Nothing is more disarming than a person who admits their errors—anger dissipates almost instantly. Likewise, nothing is more irritating than not admitting you are wrong when it's blatantly obvious. Credibility is an important currency for leaders. Saying you erred will increase your credibility and make you more human. "Know your capabilities and shortcomings. Seek evaluation. Be insightful. If you are open to receive feedback, you continue to learn and grow." (Scott Logan, CEO, Halifax 2014 Commonwealth Games, Candidate City)

Great learning can be derived from analysis. "Go back to the drawing board when you fail. I debrief in the car on my way home every day to learn from my experiences." (Judy Murphy, COO, Royal Winnipeg Ballet)

Understand Your Impact

What you say and do has an impact. Understanding how you come across is necessary to leverage influence and avoid being blindsided. Impact, of course, means results and progress towards the vision. It also means inspiring dedication, awakening imagination and galvanizing a team through a collective effort. "I develop insight on my impact in two ways: First, assessing progress towards the vision. Second, paying attention to feedback, particularly from those who question the status quo or disagree. I like listening to people on an improvement quest. I think one can learn a lot from them." (Yvon Bastien, Former President and General Manager, Sanofi Synthelabo Canada)

Leadership, like beauty, is in the eye of the beholder. For better or worse, effectiveness is a matter of perception, far more subjective than objective. "Leaders are like sculptors of human potential. I feel responsible to develop potential, using all the means at my disposal. I see my impact through the gratitude of those I have helped to grow." (Glenn Hoag, Head Coach, Team Canada Men's Volleyball; Head Coach, Men's Volleyball Team Vert & Or [Green and Gold], Université de Sherbrooke)

Leaders live in the eyes and hearts of followers and must behave accordingly. "Look at yourself from the outside. Question your actions and goals." (Elaine Taranu-Teofilovici, Former CEO, YWCA Canada) Impact is less visible to leaders than to followers. In general, leaders have a clearer grasp of their intentions than of their actions, and blind spots can also block the view. For followers, the reverse is true. They 'feel' the leader's impact on their motivation and are either mobilized, indifferent or turned off. Each side has a lot to gain from sharing perspectives with the other: followers get clarity about the leader's intention and meaning, and leaders get a better appreciation of their impact.

Respondents indicated that over time, they learned to observe their own behaviour with detachment. If a given behaviour doesn't work, replace it with another: adjust until you find what works. "I want to be aware of my impact without succumbing under its weight. I want to be conscious, yet detached." (Chantal Petitclerc, Paralympic Athlete and Champion)

Sooner or later, leaders realize that understanding impact is the only way to get consistent outcomes. It starts with assessing results, such as targets, which are quantitative and external in nature. This 'hard' side of impact is relatively easy to measure with good metrics. The 'soft' side is more challenging to evaluate, because it is qualitative and internal, hence more difficult to apprehend. For instance: how do you affect people's motivations, productivity, loyalty?

To assess your impact, you need to look at yourself from the outside and get abundant feedback. This way, you will see yourself through *their* eyes and come to understand how you are perceived by those you seek to influence. "Seeking to understand my impact is a recent pursuit. I think it comes with maturity. I now want to deepen my understanding of how I impact others, which is not the same as impacting situations or results. I assess more now; before, I did not question as much." (Stéphane Gonthier, Senior Vice-President, Eastern North America, Alimentation Couche-Tard Inc.)

Leaders generally underestimate their impact out of modesty or lack of appreciation. Because their intent is clear to them, they assume others perceive it as well. Moreover, impact sometimes takes followers years to grasp. How often do we hear things like: *Now that I have children, I appreciate the value of guidance, and have become full of gratitude for the advice my Grade 10 teacher gave me when I was struggling.*

When they realize the extent of their impact, leaders are surprised, even astounded. "The power of impact has been an amazing revelation. When you operate on good intentions and truly want to help, people recognize it. Students I taught in the 1940s come back and tell me what a difference I made in their lives. It's magical." (Gladys Osmond, Leader, The Granny Brigade) Therefore, presume that you have considerable impact and act accordingly.

Seeking Input

Leaders need to take the issue of impact seriously. Comedies use, to great effect, characters who don't know how they come across. Think of social climber Hyacinth Bucket (pronounced 'bouquet') in the British sitcom *Keeping Up Appearances*. She sees herself as the hostess with the mostest, when, in reality, everyone wants to avoid her social functions. Because they are so oblivious, such characters are laughable. In leadership, however, this must be avoided at all costs. For example, think of a dictatorial leader who thinks that bringing donuts to the office will fix the tension between him and his followers … how sublimely naïve!

To be effective, you have to align intent and impact. Does what you *do* actually mirror what you *want to do*? If so, blind spots shrink and consciousness expands. Remember, it is important to *talk the walk* and *walk the talk*, aligning action and communication.

To understand impact means actively seeking feedback. But what exactly is it? Feedback is information that indicates whether the mark has been hit. Psychology borrowed the term 'feedback' from the field of aeronautics, where feedback devices enable rockets to stay on target. Likewise, feedback enables us to modify our behaviour in order to be more effective.

Feedback can be objective, quantitative and hard. In this case, it can be tracked and measured; for instance, results, achievements, ideas turned into actions, progress towards goals, changes implemented. "I use results to measure my leadership impact. Often, I go back to my inauguration speech as President in 2000 and ask myself, 'Where are we now in relationship to this original vision?' It's reassuring to see how much progress we have made." (Alban D'Amours, President and CEO, Desjardins Group)

It can also be subjective, qualitative and soft. In this case, it is perceived through the senses and intuition; for instance, thriving employees, leader's passion mirrored by others, buy-in, commitment to decisions, quality of work life and lasting relationships.

Both types of feedback are equally important and help leaders acquire an accurate perspective on how they perform. Interviewees strongly emphasized the vital importance of feedback for effective leadership. Diva Natalie Choquette shared her thoughts: "I don't seek to understand my impact on others as much as to have one. Each smile is a victory and I enjoy creating a sense of wonder. Over the years, I have received many moving testimonials. For instance, after touring Japan, I got thank-you letters from an association whose goal is to teach people how to work joyfully and relax. A doctor also told me I transformed his way of working. I dare to be all kinds of things on stage and hope to give people the courage to do the same in their own lives. It is a transfer of energy, like making people laugh, a liberating therapeutic folly!"

Let's now explore the best ways to seek and obtain feedback.

What to Expect

Leadership is not a popularity contest, nor is its purpose self-aggrandisement. Therefore, don't expect everyone to like you all the time. According to the laws of probability, reactions will follow the 'bell curve': the majority (60%) will think you are average to very good. A minority (20%) will support you unconditionally and another 20% will oppose you no matter what.

Illustration 5.1

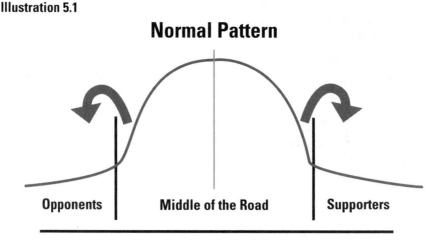

Normal Pattern

Opponents   **Middle of the Road**   **Supporters**

Leadership Performance

Here's an example from someone who knows: "In politics, we get a lot of feedback. People assess our performance and share their thoughts and suggestions. It's like a bell curve: there are the unconditional fans who always support you, the people who are unhappy, and the majority who have more specific and nuanced opinions. You must find a balance between listening to yourself and to others. It is a privilege to serve and represent citizens." (Yolande James, MNA for Nelligan, Québec)

Typical mistakes include taking supporters for granted, paying too much attention to opponents, and overlooking the 60% majority. This is an error, for the majority's top 30% can easily convert into supporters if handled well, and the bottom 30% can just as easily turn into opponents if poorly handled. Typically, leaders spend too much time and energy on opponents and not enough on the majority. This group should get the most attention.

How to Get Feedback

There are two ways to get feedback: *formal* and *informal*. The informal route includes asking questions, seeking input, listening to comments, welcoming unsolicited feedback, and seeking those who don't agree and finding out what their concerns are. Body language can also be very telling, as can be anecdotes, testimonials and input from superiors. "I pay attention to feedback, applause, individual comments. I remember receiving a letter from a listener who said I brightened his mornings. He said he felt compelled to let me know how important I was to his day. It made my day. So now, I make a point of letting people know when they have somehow touched my life. I feel that we should talk about the positive more often. I hope to give joy to people through radio and when someone gives me joy, in any aspect of life, I tell them!" (Vickie van Dyke, Midday Host, Smooth Jazz Wave 94.7; Singer and Writer)

The formal route is more structured and includes 360-degree assessments, psychometric instruments, performance appraisals, and employee and customer survey results. Using systemic devices allows 'soft' data to become 'hard,' enhancing its credibility. The benefits of formal feedback protocols have now been recognized and many organizations are well-equipped with regular feedback mechanisms.

Interviewees spoke especially highly of 360-degree processes, because the variety of respondents offers an array of perspectives. Moreover, since anonymity is protected, raters can be straightforward. Processes are generally conducted by a professional, objective third party and results are discussed with qualified experts. Respondents indicated that 70% to 80% of the results confirm what they already knew. This far outweighs the surprises, which represent only 20% to 30%. Furthermore, surprises are not always negative. "360-degree feedback has generally validated what I already believed, but it has also provided new insights that have caused me to modify my behaviour with others. I have also learned that I have to create a safe environment in order to receive candid feedback." (Kevin Marshman, Vice-President and General Manager, Worldwide Customer Services, NCR Canada Ltd.)

Mr. Marshman makes a very good point: if you want to receive genuine and helpful feedback, provide the security required. Otherwise, people will only tell you what they think you want to hear, and your decisions will become stabs in the dark.

Moreover, you don't have to react immediately to feedback. Sit on it for a while; give your emotions time to settle and your brain an opportunity to formulate an adequate response. People will respect you even more. Feedback is the gift of learning. "I became president of a company when I was 30 years old and knew I had a lot to learn. People came to me with feedback, ideas, suggestions, and it helped me acquire a lot of knowledge. You either learn to be a leader from your people or you fail them." (Gregory Hines, President and CEO, Tm Bioscience Corporation)

Vacuum at the Top

It's difficult to get frank feedback at the top. "The higher you climb, the harder it is to get genuine feedback. People tend to say what they think you want to hear and avoid giving bad news. To counteract this, I engage in daily informal interaction with as many people as possible, and I find out what is really going on. Otherwise, if I confine myself to formal institutional structures, I lose touch. Orchestrated contacts yield less real data. I enjoy direct contact. It also allows me to explain how people's roles and responsibilities fit into the corporate strategy." (Marc Poulin, President Operations, Québec Region, Sobeys Inc.)

Here are some tips to break out of the *feedback-free zone* at the top:

FEEDBACK TIPS FOR DISCERNING EXECUTIVES
- Assemble a trusted group of associates who can tell it like it is.
- Seek out feedback, not just from supporters and like-minded associates, but from opponents, dissidents and radicals.
- Practise 'managing by walking around.' The more accessible you are, the higher the chances that you will receive candid feedback.
- Pay particular attention to bottom-up feedback.
- Conduct employee/customer surveys tied to leadership effectiveness and act on results.

- Routinely ask powerful questions. *I can't see my own actions. Please give me your input on how and where I can improve. What am I doing that is helping/harming you? How can I support you? What would you wish to see done differently? If you were in charge, what would you do?* These discussions are best conducted one on one and with ground rules, such as confidentiality, no reprisals and a focus on solution finding, not blaming.

Getting useful feedback depends on the safety of the environment and the quality of relationships. Therefore, the leader needs to set up the right conditions. Here is our interviewees' best advice:

CREATING THE RIGHT ENVIRONMENT
- Generate a happy, productive environment that minimizes tension and conflict.
- Be there for people, despite the line of authority. Talk to everyone the same way, regardless of their level. Then, they will be more comfortable giving you feedback.
- Show interest in others' growth and development and they will do the same for you.
- Credit people for what they do. Celebrate success and acknowledge failures—consider them learning experiences.
- Act on feedback received. If people don't see any changes, they will be less likely to give you feedback the next time you ask for it.

The bottom line is *ask, understand* and then … *act!* "I like to get feedback, to bounce ideas off of people and surround myself with smart people. I always find that the team's wisdom is superior to the individual. However, once you have consulted, you need to act. Take a risk and pray to God that you are right. Ready, aim, fire is better than ready, aim, aim … Leaders make decisions and live with the consequences." (Dr. David Walker, Dean, Faculty of Health Sciences, Queen's University)

To summarize, there are three primary reasons for discerning impact: aligning intent and impact, harmonizing perceptions of self and others, and elevating intention for the greater good of those under your care. The process fosters maturity and growth, building a healthy ego and cultivating the practice of authenticity.

CONCLUSION

Followers give you their trust, so make sure they are in capable and caring hands by thoroughly preparing for leadership, expanding your capacity through practice, learning from experience and actively seeking to understand your impact. "Get out of your comfort zone, step up and take a leadership role, even if you don't have all the competencies. You learn the most when you are fearful of the experience and you grow from it." (Diane Rabbani, Human Resources Consultant; Former Deputy Minister, British Columbia)

Just as sea captains have a plan to get to their destination, you need a strategy to guide your development process. Don't leave it to chance.

CHAPTER 6

THE MASTER AND THE APPRENTICE

To be able to trust instinct, accept the fact that you might feel lost at times. Instinct is a process, not an end result. It is like a compass needle in the hand of an explorer—it will always hold a true course despite the path that is taken to follow it.

Ben Nind
Artist; Executive and Artistic Director, Northern Arts & Cultural Centre

Role models have been a great inspiration. They help you see things from different perspectives. My former boss was the CEO of CEOs; he mentored people who developed and took on CEO roles.

Nancy Myers Johnson
Director and Vice-President, Huntley Communication Services Inc.

CAN LEADERSHIP BE TAUGHT?

"Leadership cannot be taught, but can be developed," said Ken Dobell, Former Deputy Minister and Cabinet Secretary, Office of the Premier, British Columbia. In other words, leadership is not a topic like geography, but a process like acting. Therefore, it has to be developed from the *inside out*, not acquired from the *outside in*. Reaching leadership mastery requires extensive practice through which leaders and actors alike find their voice and learn to use their gifts to serve the role. Education can provide frameworks, context, theories, etc., but alone, is insufficient to achieve mastery. "You can teach peripheral skills, such as listening and watching, picking up verbal and non-verbal signals, being sensitive to the environment. ..." (Bonnie Dianne DuPont, Group Vice-President, Corporate Resources, Enbridge Inc.)

Therefore, the optimal leadership development structure has to be practice-heavy, reinforced by extensive modelling, coaching, support and reflection. An appropriate model can be found in the arts in general and the theatre in particular. Let's venture backstage. ...

THE LEADERSHIP ROLE

Transforming from 'person' to 'leader' assumes accepting the mandate and being willing to perform the role.

Taking On the Role

Taking on a leadership role means experiencing the same dynamics as actors. You must first connect with the role and second convincingly carry it out. Just like in the theatre, the leadership essence incarnates through the leader's personality, which gives it voice, form and substance. It's the classic case of 'self as an instrument,' the entire person being mobilized to serve the role.

Leaders' and actors' behaviours are on stage, visible, public. When the curtain rises, actors are left to their own devices to create a credible performance. The character they portray is virtually born in front of the audience. Likewise in leadership, the leader is born in front of followers who determine if the performance is believable and worth buying into. "Sometimes, I ask technicians to behave like actors when bringing props and equipment on stage during a performance. Even the most timid manage to do something interesting. There is poetry in every one of us that yearns to be liberated. Our bad habits turn us into prisoners. When technicians transform into actors, I look them deep in the eye and support them completely. The best in us emerges through the magic of the stage; likewise for leadership." (Natalie Choquette, Diva)

Preparing for the Role

Not surprisingly, leadership and actor development also follow similar paths. Actors and leaders cannot improve their craft simply by listening to experts and taking notes; they must experiment with behaviours, get feedback, integrate it and try again. Practice makes perfect. "Words inform; practice transforms. It's impossible to learn how to swim without jumping into the pool. Experience broadens the cosmos. Viewed from this angle, we never make mistakes. If we go through a negative experience, we needed to do so in order to learn. Action is always superior to deliberation." (Denise Verreault, C.M., C.Q., President and CEO, Groupe Maritime Verreault Inc.)

Development is not primarily about knowledge acquisition, but moulding over time. "It is not teaching as in lecturing, but a constant guiding, sometimes pushing and pulling along the course." (Gregory Hines, President and CEO, Tm Bioscience Corporation) Like a coach, you can guide your protégés, but they have to run the race. You need to know when you should push and when to step back and give them space. If they fall, pick them up and point them back in the right direction.

THE APPRENTICESHIP MODEL

In the arts, development is structured according to the apprenticeship model, a formula proven throughout the ages. For example, during the Renaissance, famous painters such as Leonardo da Vinci took on talented recruits to train. The process not only involved teaching but also coaching and practice. As the apprentice became more competent, he went from preparing canvases to painting backgrounds, then foreground elements and finally, his own creations. This system improved performance over time, while providing a lot of guidance and support along the way. Masters didn't expect a 'quick fix' and realized that proficiency doesn't happen overnight. Therefore, the pace was slow and the investment long term.

Structure

The apprenticeship model is eminently relevant to leadership development, with its combination of observation and emulation, practice, reflection, analysis and fine tuning. It is pragmatic rather than scholarly, and relies heavily on experimentation. It is not an exact science but a combination of art and science, polishing hard edges to achieve smoothness and brilliance. Here are some of the steps involved:

- Observe role models in action.
- Analyze their actions and derive learning.
- Engage in experimentation.
- Reflect on experience.
- Get feedback.
- Come to conclusions.
- Apply learning to the next experience.
- Hone skill.
- Transfer skill to a new context.

Richard Monette, C.M, Artistic Director, The Stratford Festival of Canada, illustrates with this impressive tale:

When I chose my profession, I followed a predictable path of leadership development. First I became an actor; at this point, I was concerned with my individual contribution and performance. Then I became a lead actor and, as such, I had to lead both the public and other actors. When I became a director, I had to focus on the big picture and making everyone look good in order to serve the play and the issues portrayed by it. I learned that craft by observing good directors in action. I was like a sponge: a good listener and learner. The artistic director job was thrust upon me; I never wanted it. But in the end, service prevailed. They needed me and I wanted to give something back. It was important to bring the ship to a safe harbour. I am amazed at how successful I have been. I never fancied myself as a sort of CEO but I found, to my great surprise, that I am good at programming and strategy and that I can live with tough decisions that are for the greater good of the whole. It has been a good experience combining business and art.

Models and Mentors

The apprenticeship system is based on observation, coaching and emulation of 'masters.' Likewise, the overwhelming majority of respondents declared models and mentors the *most* significant contributors to their development. "Life lessons and words of wisdom from elders influenced me the most." (Bernd Christmas, Lawyer and Mi'kmaq Leader) For interviewees, nothing rivals the significance of mentors and models; they are the ultimate catalysts of leadership development. "Most of my development stemmed from many people who mentored me. I come from a strong, loving family with values and principles. I was privileged to be with mentors I admired and whose values were in keeping with mine. They put challenges in front of me that stretched me." (Judy Rogers, City Manager, Vancouver, British Columbia)

During our interviews, we heard many touching stories about mentors and felt the caring presence of masters, alive and well in their protégés' memories. The masters' lasting influence was a source of endless fascination; it's as though they never leave the protégé and provide guidance in difficult moments. "I had terrific mentors who gave me the opportunity to acquire and enhance skills, who allowed me to make mistakes and learn from experiences. They were people who had faith in me early on in my career and gave me space to sink or swim; people who made me believe in myself and that I could succeed." (Mary Hofstetter, President and CEO, The Banff Centre)

Models and mentors seemed to work equally well for innates and accidentals, young and old, women and men, business and sports people, etc. They perform a multitude of developmental tasks, providing:

- **Grounding**—"Never forget where you came from." (Nancy Karetak-Lindell, MP, Nunavut)
- **Support**—"Role models for change took me where I was dreading to go." (Dr. David Walker, Dean, Faculty of Health Sciences, Queen's University)
- **Inspiration**—"I am where I am today because of role models." (Dr. Alan Bernstein, O.C., President, Canadian Institutes of Health Research)
- **Motivation**—"On the way, I met people who prompted me to reflect, provided me with feedback and pushed me to go further. I am grateful to them all." (Marc Poulin, President Operations, Québec Region, Sobeys Inc.)

Respondents were acutely aware of the value of mentoring. You receive the gift and pass it on. "I observed good leaders and integrated their best practices into my own style. I am also aware that I am a model for others; therefore, I aim for congruence in my actions. I help people find their own place under the sun." (Suzanne Blanchet, President and CEO, Cascades Tissue Group)

Here's a table summarizing the landscape:

Table 6.1

MODELS	MENTORS
• Can be distant or close, alive or dead. • Are not necessarily mentors but can be. • Provide a search image of what to do or not to do. • Their influence far outlasts their physical presence. • Learning occurs with both good and bad models.	• Actively take protégés under their wing. • Believe in the protégés and have faith in their capabilities. • Provide support, coaching and advice. • Allow protégés to stretch their wings and make their own mistakes. • Act as a sponsor/ambassador for the protégé.

Mentoring is the cornerstone of the apprenticeship model. Therefore, it's ideal for leadership development.

In the arts, particularly in the theatre, the apprenticeship is highly structured. In leadership development, it is still a haphazard affair driven mostly by learners. However, our program research points to an encouraging trend to replicate the apprenticeship system in a deliberate and strategic manner. More on this in Chapters 7 and 8.

Mastery

The ultimate outcome of artist, actor and leadership development is twofold: superb execution (mastery), supported by a reliable judgement,which enables them to make sound decisions, quickly and effectively. To paraphrase W.C. Howell's model for learning, it's about attaining a zone of *unconscious competence,* which surpasses rational thought in speed and accuracy. For instance, in a difficult situation, a good leader will rapidly size it up, come to a conclusion and move to action. That is why the Canadian Forces see leadership as the ultimate outcome of their efforts. In the thick of battle, when danger and risk abound, leaders have to make life and death decisions and exhibit solid, spot-on judgement.

Developing such judgement requires a facilitative, not a prescriptive, approach. It can only be drawn out, leveraging the *immanence/emergence/transcendence* dynamics. This means cultivating independent, not copycat thinking; autonomy, not compliance; self-reliance, not dependency. Richard Monette, C.M, Artistic Director, The Stratford Festival of Canada, explains: "In the theatre, we don't have to answer all questions. It's more important to put an issue in front of an audience and let them wrestle with it themselves. They can make their own decisions. Maybe it's the same about leadership: the question or the issue is more important than the answer. Therefore, the key is in presenting the issue accurately, from a rich and complex perspective."

Effective leadership development is not about prescribing formulas and recipes to reproduce, but about fostering the discovery and expression of a unique and authentic leadership identity. Therefore, enticing mastery is a 'good to great' process. It's about growing strengths, increasing flow, turning on the power—not fixing gaps or compensating for insufficiencies. For example, someone with no musical talent will never become an outstanding concert pianist, despite considerable effort. Focusing on weaknesses and shortcomings engenders a consciousness of lack, which at best, results in mediocrity.

What is required is an *awareness of magic*. Budding artists, for instance, blossom under the guidance of mentors who see their potential and nurture it. Armed with an iron-clad conviction, love and care, legendary Canadian producer David Foster turned 17-year-old Josh Groban into an international singing sensation by finding and guiding his flow. As a result, young Josh surpassed what he thought possible, and Foster redefined the pop/classical music genre.

THE ROAD TO MASTERY

In order to reach mastery, leaders need to progress through three stages:

1. **Knowing**—acquiring a knowledge base; *competence* is the goal.
2. **Doing**—practising knowledge, putting it into action; *know how* is the goal.
3. **Being**—integrating knowledge and know-how; *mastery* is the goal.

Advancing through the levels requires progression beyond cognition, as mastery calls upon the whole person: body and soul.

Here's another powerful illustration from Richard Monette, C.M, Artistic Director, The Stratford Festival of Canada: "You also need to be a master of your craft and know the tools of your trade. In my case, it meant training the voice, so it could be as good an instrument as possible. For instance, because of my French-Canadian and Italian background, I had to get rid of my accent when speaking in English. So when I was about 15, I went to a voice coach in Montréal and told her I wanted to become a Shakespearean actor. She replied, 'Well, Mr. Monette, we better get started; we've got a lot of work to do.' I regard the mastery of technique as the measure of an artist or a leader's sincerity."

In order to reach mastery, leaders use learning methodologies consistent with the apprenticeship model: observation, experimentation, reflection and support.

Observation

Observation is the first step to emulation, readily available and cost effective. "I became a shameless copier of great people." (Dave Mowat, CEO, Vancity Credit Union) "I was confirmed and affirmed by observation." (Diane Gorman, Former Assistant Deputy Minister, Health Canada, Governement of Canada)

It works by osmosis, learners absorbing more than they realize. "Since I had ongoing exposure to executives, I absorbed a lot from their discussions on business issues and corporate strategies. The information they shared enabled me to develop my own vision of leadership and its foundations." (Louise Pelletier, Regional Director, Mauricie Region, Production of the Cascades, Hydro-Québec)

Observing bad examples is as effective as observing good ones. "Observation enabled me to compare and contrast leaders." (Sarah Raiss, Executive Vice-President, Corporate Services, TransCanada Corporation) In a positive case, the observer feels admiration for effective behaviours and attitudes. Then, follows an analysis to enhance comprehension. Subsequently, the apprentice seeks to emulate the model. "I have always been intrigued by individuals capable of drawing people together and learned by watching them." (Mavis Staines, Artistic Director, Canada's National Ballet School)

In a negative scenario, the observer is repulsed by the model's actions. Then follows an analysis of what not to do in the future. The result is rejection ... and indelible memories. "Through life, you learn from different people. The best models are bad leaders. We have all been badly managed and gained from those experiences." (Paul Greenhalgh, Director, Corcoran Gallery of Art; Former President, NSCAD [Nova Scotia College of Art and Design University])

Reading is another form of observation. "I read a lot of leaders' biographies. I feel that history repeats itself. What lessons from the past can we apply today? I think that youth has to be shown that despite technology advances, humans are the same and lots can be learned from the past." (Patrick Cuenco, Co-founder, Junior Hong Kong-Canada Business Association)

Respondents commented that over time, they sharpened their observation skills, increasing their subtlety by watching energy levels, body language and paying attention to the unsaid.

Experimentation

For many, experience is the most defining contributor to development, because it tests and tries leadership. Any experience can be used for learning. "The universe provides an abundance of practice opportunities." (Cora Tsouflidou, President, Chez Cora/Cora's)

Gaining valuable experience means venturing outside of your comfort zone into unknown territory. "In the beginning, you must prove yourself and it is uncomfortable to live with the stress of challenge. But it's the only way to learn. When I started out, I set objectives and felt I had to succeed and deliver the goods; in fact, forcing my own hand. You have to plunge into the battle. Afterwards, it's a matter of refining your abilities." (Denis Losier, President and CEO, Assumption Life)

Respondents unanimously agreed that difficult experiences develop us more than easy ones. Challenge means complexity, unfamiliarity and confusion, etc., anything that demands stretching capabilities and builds character and resilience. "When something blocks your path, use it as a stepping stone. See the possibility beyond the obstacle. Never wonder if it is possible." (Denise Amyot, Vice-President, Leadership Network, Public Service Human Resources Agency, Government of Canada)

Experience is the fire through which steel blades are tempered. It is scary and risky, but immensely rewarding. Sometimes a crushing blow is the gateway to greatness. Experimentation, through trial by fire, moulds and toughens leaders. A variety of experiences promotes openness to diversity, flexibility, adaptability and resourcefulness. International exposure tops the list. "I went through a variety of environments: from military leader in war time, to running a police force in Singapore, to being the Minister at Canada House in London, to Chairman for many organizations, mostly as a philanthropist." (Patrick Reid, O.C., M.C., C.D., Chairman, Rick Hansen Foundation) There is a symbiotic relationship between experience and confidence. New experiences breed confidence, and more confidence spurs the quest for new experiences.

Developmental experiences can be chosen, for instance, an international assignment, or come at you like a curveball, like the departure of an excellent employee. Therefore, to select appropriate experiences, leaders need to be clear on their developmental needs, and maintain a positive attitude to overcome challenges that arise along the way. "Experiences, even the frustrating ones, are part of learning." (Dr. Mary Brooks, William A. Black Chair of Commerce, School of Business Administration, Dalhousie University)

Waiting for the right opportunities to come along is not sufficient; leaders have to actively seek them out. Pro-activeness increases choice and fast-tracks development. Therefore, the quality, quantity and sequence are important, and the value of any experience increases when properly processed.

Reflection

Reflection is the ability to make sense of experience and is a condition for learning. What did you learn? What would you do differently if the same situation arose? What patterns do you discern in your actions? "Look inside and reflect on best experiences when you felt good and empowered. Recognize what works and what doesn't." (Sue Holloway, Double Olympic Medalist, Kayak)

Reflection is a habit to acquire. Without it, leaders risk experiencing without extracting the relevant learning. Here's another powerful illustration from Richard Monette, C.M, Artistic Director, The Stratford Festival of Canada: "Even though it can be scary to go within, it's absolutely necessary both for the actor and the leader. The mindset of a gypsy or a bohemian is required to explore your internal landscape. Your essence and sincerity must come through for people to trust you."

Respondents use two main reflection avenues: individual and interactive. Individual techniques include reviewing, analyzing, journaling, debriefing their day on the way home, applying a series of questions to each experience, etc. Interactive techniques include partner or group activities. For instance, a significant number of respondents belong to networking, learning or support groups and take advantage of these settings for sharing and learning. Many also use partner vehicles, such as coaching, mentoring, counselling and buddy systems in a similar way. Individual and interactive avenues enable leaders to process their experience, making sense of it and setting goals for the next ones.

Reflection also enables leaders to distance themselves from their own behaviour. Behaviour can be changed and doesn't equate identity. Over time, most leaders learn to view behaviours as experiments and become less defensive when confronted about ineffective ones.

Reflection sharpens perceptiveness and the ability to see patterns and the big picture. Reflection guarantees that you will 'live and learn,' instead of just living without learning.

Support

Sharing with others helps the learning process. First, it alleviates the isolation often felt by leaders. 'It's lonely at the top' goes the saying and leadership resonates with this unfortunate truth. Therefore, forums, associations and committees of all kinds create a sense of belonging and normalize the leadership experience.

Second, these groups act as a community where participants can learn from each other. "I learned a lot from Tommy Douglas when he shared stories." (Honourable Bob Rae, PC, O.C., O.Ont., Q.C., Former Premier, Ontario) For instance, "the mandate of the Centre Québécois de Leadership [Québec Centre for Leadership] is to foster leadership excellence in the Québec public sector. As such, it organizes many activities and programs, including regular half-day Leadership Circles where leaders congregate to discuss issues and solve problems. Leadership Breakfasts are also set up quarterly to expose leaders to new topics and stimulate discussion and networking. Both activities are extremely well-received and growing." (Gilles Harvey, Former Director, Centre Québécois de Leadership [Québec Centre for Leadership])

Third, they sharpen communication skills. Leaders learn to listen deeply and ask better questions as well as express their thoughts more clearly. Leaders need to be "able to tell stories to convey meaning and illuminate." (Marg McGregor, CEO, Canadian Interuniversity Sport)

Fourth, these groups provide a pool of advisors, role models, mentors, coaches and learning partners. Many respondents think there is an insufficient number of leadership-focused groups, distinct from management or business groups.

Leaders need support to keep on leading and learning. In his landmark fable *The Little Prince*, Antoine de Saint-Exupéry recounts the adventures of a little boy visiting different planets and the wisdom he acquires along the way. Pierre-Marc Tremblay, President and CEO, Restaurants Pacini Inc., uses a potent example from the book to talk about responsibility: "I am in continuous improvement mode so I question myself, reflect, and as a result, become aware of my strengths and weaknesses. *The Little Prince* says, 'If you want a friend, bring him close. If you succeed, he becomes your responsibility.' It's relatively easy to start a friendship; much more difficult to maintain it and to assume responsibility."

As a society, we need to become more aware of the support vacuum our leaders often experience. Let's shoulder responsibility for leadership support. This way, we will keep the leaders we've already managed to develop.

STRUCTURED LEARNING EXPERIENCES

It is important to continue learning. Learning keeps you a fresh leader instead of a stifled one. "Early in my career I completed graduate studies in nursing. Ten years ago, I did an MBA, which gave me a different perspective. Over the years, I have continued my education and I am now a certified health executive. It is important to constantly be open-minded, learn, grow and develop." (Janet Knox, President and CEO, Annapolis Valley District Health Authority)

However, structured learning experiences, such as workshops and educational programs, are not viewed as a significant component of the learning strategy for several reasons:

- There are not enough programs specifically focused on leadership.
- Leadership programs are not widely available across the country, limiting access to a wider audience.
- School curriculum doesn't include leadership development, nor is it viewed as a legitimate field of study. This means that most children and youth are not exposed to it.
- Too few adults are exposed to leadership training.

Leadership development requires extensive practice, coaching and introspection to succeed, so traditional teaching methodologies, assumptions and classroom environments are not always optimal.

Most respondents perceive existing programs as better suited to management than to leadership development. Going back to the 'talk/walk' formula, programs rank average to good on 'talk' and poor to very poor on 'walk.' Perceived value increases with applications such as case studies, simulations and role plays, and practice opportunities such as workplace or community projects. "After working for 12 years with a company, I went to the Harvard leadership program and found that useful. This learning experience came at a good stage in my career. It was helpful to learn through case studies with people from different sectors who provided different perspectives to solve problems." (Murray Todd, President, Canada Hibernia Holding Corporation)

Participants find educational programs useful to acquire frameworks and theories and confirm what experience has already taught them. "A former employer offered a lot of leadership training. This allowed me to confirm things I intuitively knew but couldn't always articulate. So I learned models, theories and concepts that enabled me to create a mental infrastructure of the leadership field." (Dominique Anglade, Consultant, McKinsey & Company)

Interacting with other participants is also viewed as beneficial for acquiring different perspectives and expanding one's network. "What is helpful with attending programs is to meet people from around the world, and the subsequent exchange of ideas." (Dave Mowat, CEO, Vancity Credit Union)

Here's a summary of prevalent opinions on structured learning experiences:

Table 6.2

STRUCTURED LEARNING EXPERIENCES	
Not Useful	**Useful**
• Not enough practice and too much theory. • Academics don't always have leadership credibility. • You revert back to old habits upon returning to your normal environment. • Programs don't push you out of your comfort zone.	• Assessment and feedback. • Models and frameworks. • Common language. • Networking with fellow leaders. • Different perspectives. • Stepping back, seeing the big picture. • Filling gaps in the background. • Insights—'intelligence' into a field.

Structured learning experiences alone cannot develop leaders. Practice, self-discovery, support and community are also required. Therefore, we need to view them as a *component* of the development infrastructure, not the whole package.

CONCLUSION

The apprenticeship model is effective because it is empirical in nature. Therefore, leadership development works best when structured according to the following apprenticeship principles:

- **From the 'inside out'**—to allow the formation of a sound leadership judgement.
- **Focused on self–discovery**—to enable leaders to find their authentic leadership identity and voice, and encourage independent thinking, autonomy and self-reliance.
- **Emphasizing flow**—to optimize the expansion of natural potential and talents instead of fixing gaps.
- **Holistic**—involving the whole person, in order to stimulate integration and depth.
- **Practice driven**—to develop skills through experimentation, coaching and feedback.
- **Mentor dependent**—to expose the learner to role-modelling, foster emulation and provide guidance and protection.

- **Mastery focused**—to promote the acquisition and integration of knowing, know-how and being.
- **Progressively paced**—to reflect the nature of the development process.
- **Integrated:** linking learning, practice, self-discovery and support to produce lasting results.

The apprenticeship model works because it is pragmatic instead of scholarly, and focused on *drawing out* and *shaping* the leader within. "You need to connect with your leadership essence and allow it to express itself." (Yvon Bastien, Former President and General Manager, Sanofi Synthelabo Canada)

In Chapters 7 and 8 we will see how the apprenticeship model is being used effectively in successful programs.

CHAPTER 7

PROGRAM ARCHITECTURE

Managers manage complexity, leaders lead change.
   Corey Jack
   Executive Head, BMO Financial Group Institute for Learning

Success is thinking differently and acting accordingly.
   Sandra Gage
   Executive Director, Partnership Development, ESTEEM Team
   Association and
   Shelly O'Brien
   Executive Director, Programs, ESTEEM Team Association

PROGRAM ESSENTIALS

In this chapter, we will examine the optimal architecture for building effective leadership development programs.

Definition

To structure and optimize leadership development, organizations put in place programs, which we define as concerted efforts to expand leadership capacity in order to meet current and future leadership needs.

Programs include a variety of components, such as education, practice, opportunities for self-discovery, support and community-building. Ideally, these components reinforce each other instead of operating in isolation. Strategically integrated programs enable organizations to maximize their investment and have more control over the quality and quantity of results.

Research Process

To find out best practices, we interviewed 66 experts involved with leadership development programs in community groups, consulting firms, co-operatives, corporations, institutes, public sector entities, sports federations and associations, universities and youth institutions. A complete list of participating organizations can be found in Appendix III. In Chapters 10 and 11, we will review the co-op program findings in greater detail.

Purpose

Programs aim to produce well-rounded, skilful, strategic leaders (mastery component) equipped with a sound and reliable judgement (guidance system component)—people who can walk into any situation, come to conclusions, determine what to do and galvanize others into action. Nowhere is this more evident than in the military, where the goal is to develop leaders who can "formulate reasoned answers to unpredictable events: judgement, wisdom and response instead of knee-jerk reaction. As a result, leadership is pervasive and starts at the beginning of the training program. Socialization plays a central role, since leadership is essentially a relationship where influence is key. The military culture constantly reinforces the fact that leadership is important." (Captain [N] Alan Okros, Professor; Former Director, Canadian Forces Leadership Institute, Royal Military College)

Producing such leaders is no small feat and interviewees were cognizant of the magnitude of the task and the corresponding responsibility. Experts discerned that a 'service cascade' flows from their efforts; by creating stronger leaders, they help organizations, communities, the country, etc., enhance their capability and well-being. We found an acute awareness of mission and purpose among experts. They feel compelled to take exceptional care of their charges in all sectors and regions. As a result, they are tremendously motivated and passionate about their work. It was a privilege to benefit from their wisdom and expertise.

Types of Programs

Programs can be divided into two main categories:

- *Public* programs are offered by universities, institutes and others to their clients. In this case, the audience is composed of participants from various organizations and sectors.
- *Internal* programs are offered to an organization's employees and stakeholders. These are specific to the organization's mandate, needs and culture and delivered internally. Sometimes, these are provided to a sector instead of a single organization; for instance, programs made available by professional associations to their members.

Sometimes these two merge to create a blended category; for example, a university adapting a program to suit an organizational client.

Program Contents

Since the field of leadership is in constant evolution, expectations of leaders change, prompting content modifications. Take, as an example, the imperative to lead by influence instead of authority as well as the ability to lead across functional levels. Today's leaders must effectively drive change and manage transformation, particularly during times of uncertainty. Likewise, globalization requires leaders to work with a variety of international stakeholders and elicit collaboration from an increasingly diverse audience. Therefore, programs evolve, and professionals seek to make them as comprehensive and relevant to their audience as possible.

Frame of Reference

Developing competent leaders is time and labour intensive. Most programs in our research last between one-and-a-half to three years. Therefore, designing, implementing and delivering programs represents a considerable investment of human and financial resources. As a result, drivers must be clear and support, constant. Leadership development cannot be the flavour of the month: it simply takes too much time and money to make it happen. Just like parenting, leadership development requires years of careful, respectful and loving guidance. Leaving it to chance is naïve, if not downright careless; and expecting good leaders to pop up on their own is no longer considered a viable option.

HOW DO PROGRAMS GET STARTED?

What prompts organizations to set up leadership development programs?

Motivations

Motivations for program start-up are similar across the board, with the exception of sector-specific situations. Generic motivations include improvement and innovation.

Improvement

The first motivation is to improve a state of affairs found wanting; to fill a void, a need or a gap; to correct an imbalance or to raise the bar. Here are some examples:

- "Increase the number of women in sports leadership." (Karin Lofstrom, Executive Director, CAAWS [Canadian Association for the Advancement of Women and Sport])
- "Plan for the future and fill the expanding leadership needs of a fast-growth organization." (France Dufresne, Director, Organizational Development and Training, Cirque du Soleil)
- "Create leaders who are more complete and better integrated, endowed with depth and vast perspectives, and have better grasp of good management and leadership principles." (Richard Bégin, Director, Management Development Programs, Canada Revenue Agency)

Innovation

The second motivation is to innovate, to create something that did not previously exist. Here are some examples:

- "Equip multi-disciplinary teams with the skills to work together in a more productive way, and enable team members to take on leadership roles through jazz." (Brian Hayman, President, Getting in the Groove)
- "Provide ongoing skill development so manager-leaders can adapt to the changing business environment and capitalize on opportunities." (Tim Clark, Vice-President, Human Resources Development; Beth Shearer, General Manager, The Franchise Company)

Sector Specific Motivations

Here are some examples:

- Educational institutions and institutes aiming for quality programming. "Enhance the quality of Canadian leadership in business, government and non-governmental organizations." (John Rankin, Executive Director, Niagara Institute)
- Consultants designing innovative programs to elevate standards of excellence. "Raise the leadership bar for individuals, corporations, businesses. Help organizations bring a degree of excellence to their leadership, only seen in great organizations. And through this, create bottom-line results." (Dr. Rosie Steeves, President; Barbara Ross-Denroche, Principal, The Refinery Leadership Partners Inc., [Formerly CEL, Centre for Exceptional Leadership Inc.])
- Corporations seeking to: "develop leaders who can execute the business strategy. Create a leadership pipeline for the organization." (Corey Jack, Executive Head, BMO Financial Group Institute for Learning)
- Public sector organizations striving to produce a continuing supply of capable leaders. "We have many priorities, and one of them focuses on succession planning due to the impending wave of baby boomer retirement." (Jean-François Pinsonnault, Consultant, Learning and Development, Human Resources, Canada Mortgage and Housing Corporation [CMHC])
- Sport entities wishing to raise the calibre of coaching and support infrastructures, which in turn improve athletes' performance. "To sustain coaching groups who support Elite and Excellence athletes in the Québec City region." (Jacques Loiselle, Former President, Conseil du sport de haut niveau de Québec [High Level Sports Council, Québec City Region])
- Arts organizations paying particular attention to leadership culture. "We sought the digital imprint of the Cirque for our programs while implementing

best practices. We wanted to consolidate the foundations of our success, fuel passion, unite to move forward, push the limits and deliver the goods." (France Dufresne, Director, Organizational Development and Training, Cirque du Soleil)

Destination Excellence

Regardless of program type or sector, all experts aim for excellence, the key to a good reputation. "We rely heavily upon word of mouth. The reputation of our organization is very good." (Denise Coutts, Executive Director; Nancy McKinstry and Julia Kim, Board members, Minerva Foundation for BC Women)

Linda Arnoldussen, Director of Learning and Operational Excellence, Leadership Development program, School of Business, Executive Education and Lifelong Learning, University of Alberta, said that the key is the "reputation of the university and program; relationships with partners in the community, program structure and calibre of instructors." This is obvious for public programs that must attract clients to thrive and survive, but it also applies to internal programs, which are increasingly evaluated and fine-tuned to measure their effectiveness.

A Good Fit

Program format is also a big draw because participants look for a good fit. For instance, approach, methodology and relevance are high on the list. Karin Lofstrom, Executive Director, CAAWS [Canadian Association for the Advancement of Women and Sport], explains, "Not many programs exist in this niche. Participants have an opportunity to network with other women leaders in sports."

Circumstantial features, such as international exposure, location and learning space, also factor into the equation. "We offer a highly experiential program in a beautiful and inspiring location; it provides a sense of place for reflection and serenity." (Lisa Jackson, Associate Director of Operations, The Banff Centre) "Experience sharing, exchanges, cultural diversity and an international component; we have a growing number of participants from outside the country." (Georges Bourelle, President, and CEO Centre international de recherche et d'études en management (CIREM) [International Center for Research and Studies in Management])

The decision to attend a program is also influenced by easy access to clear information through websites, brochures and other marketing materials. More and more, people seek a quality and comprehensive learning experience that fits their needs and circumstances.

Reputation

Experts know program reputation is crucial. Currently, many use enrolment, retention levels, completion rates and participants' referrals as success indicators. A few are considering proactive research to understand the playing field *before* program design efforts begin. "We are conducting surveys and focus groups to proactively gather some intelligence on, for example, demographics and benchmark processes." (Linda Arnoldussen, Director of Learning and Operational Excellence, Leadership Development program, School of Business, Executive Education and Lifelong Learning, University of Alberta)

Both public and internal programs are continually striving to improve and taking innovative means to do so. Programs are getting more sophisticated, integrating special features such as field trips and artistic activities. The 'vanilla or chocolate' mode has been replaced by an impressive array of flavours. Pistachio-mango anyone?

AUDIENCES

Who attends leadership development programs?

Target Audiences

Target audiences are existing leaders at different levels, emerging leaders (up-and-comers), high potentials and new managers.

- **Existing leaders.** "Our audience is established leaders in mid-career operating in the domestic or international markets." (Brian Earn, Director; Michael Cox, Associate Director, Centre for Studies in Leadership, University of Guelph)
- **Emerging leaders.** "Leadership is thrust upon younger people now. We need to accommodate their development, not just the enhancement of proven leaders." (Dr. Nancy Greer, Acting Director, Professor and Academic Lead, School of Leadership Studies, Royal Roads University)
- **High potentials.** "To be selected for any of the Canadian Forces College's programs, participants must have strong performance and potential as they

will become the future generals and admirals." (Commander Gregg Hannah, Senior Staff Officer, Canadian Forces College)

- **New managers.** "For the new managers' program, we invite people to reflect on their own style by using a variety of psychometric instruments and a 360. They start with an individual assessment and build on it by acquiring skills such as coaching, team building, change management, etc." (Mona Jasinski, Manager, Learning and Development, Shell Canada Limited)

Broadening Program Audiences

Most programs begin with a generic offering and customize it for specific audiences, for instance, executives, middle managers, front-line supervisors and individuals considering leadership/management positions. Here's an example from Josh Blair, Senior Vice-President, Human Resources Strategy and Business Support, Telus Corporation: "We built a framework that applies to all leadership levels:

- Leading self, assessing your capabilities to continuously improve.
- Leading others: individual, teams or extended teams; leading through influence and inspiration; leading constant change.
- Leading business results: financial acumen; sales; how to take the business to new levels."

Some adventuresome programs expand their audience to include stakeholders beyond employees. "We have broadened the scope of applicants to include external partners such as suppliers and customers. So far, external participants rave about the program as much as internal participants." (Barb Tchozewski, Organizational Effectiveness Coordinator, SaskEnergy)

As clienteles broaden, the awareness of diversity increases, not just in terms of visible differences but in terms of invisible ones, such as thinking and learning styles, perspectives, etc. "We recognize there is greater diversity. As a result, alternative models requiring situational leadership, listening and getting different inputs are embraced." (Dr. Alan C. Middleton, Executive Director, Schulich Executive Education Centre [SEEC], York University)

There is a strong understanding that one size doesn't fit all, as well as a will to accommodate differences by offering options such as elective courses, tailored applications, formats, and regional variations. "The approach used was very consultative and participative. The model gives guidelines but allows each region to adapt it to their needs and circumstances." (Sylvain B. Lalonde, Executive

Director, Fédération de hockey sur glace du Québec Inc. [Québec Ice Hockey Federation])

PROGRAM ARCHITECTURE

Program experts confirmed what individual leaders stated: the optimal leadership development configuration is the apprenticeship model, because it emphasizes moulding over time to achieve mastery, and operates from the inside out to develop leadership judgement. For instance, Barb Tchozewski, Organizational Effectiveness Coordinator, SaskEnergy, stated that their organization uses a whole systems approach where "learners are responsible for their learning plan and the program is but one element of a personal life-long competency developmental strategy." Jean-François Pinsonnault, Consultant, Learning and Development, Human Resources, Canada Mortgage and Housing Corporation, said that CMHC's program blends "knowledge acquisition through education; knowledge application through practice; knowledge transfer through teaching, coaching and mentoring."

Components

In order to produce well-rounded leaders, equipped with both the right skills and judgement, education must be complemented by extensive practice. This way, developing leaders can gain experience and hone their craft.

Because leadership can only be developed from the inside out, leaders have to focus inwardly to identify strengths and areas for development, and understand motivations and impact. One cannot build a solid leadership identity without extensive introspection.

In order to alleviate the state of isolation leaders often find themselves in, they also require support to stay on the development path and a community of practice to belong to. Therefore, successful programs comprise the following components: education, practice, self-discovery, support and community. Please refer to illustration 7.1.

Illustration 7.1

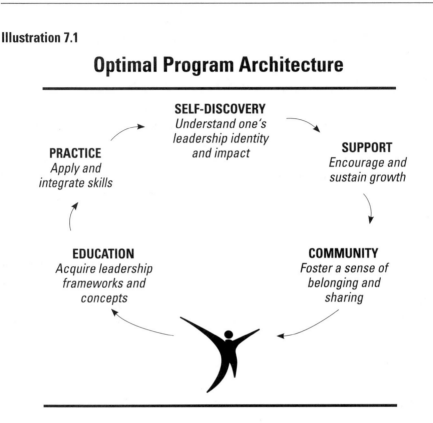

Optimal Program Architecture

Just like in the apprenticeship model, this blended approach is driven by a heavy experiential emphasis, both in and out of the classroom. Let's look at each aspect in detail.

Education

Education is often where leadership development design efforts begin. It provides a conceptual framework and an anchor for program architecture. However, professionals soon realize that it cannot, alone, bear the responsibility for effective development. Therefore, one must approach education with realistic expectations. Education can provide a common language, concepts, models, etc., but cannot, in and of itself, polish skills at a high level, nor develop a foolproof leadership judgement.

Contents

- *Public programs*, because they welcome participants from various organizations, are more generic in contents. They seek to impart leadership frameworks and concepts, develop skills and expand self-awareness. They appear somewhat firm in design and are based on academic research, market trends and a broad understanding of participants' needs. "It's a core program with only two elective courses. Students are required to complete a minor of their choice. The internship, however, is matched to their interest." (Dr. Pierre Zundel, Dean, Renaissance College, New Brunswick University)
- *Organizational programs* that welcome employees and other stakeholders offer contents tailored to the organization's objectives. They also make considerable efforts to understand and adapt to participants' needs. "The orientation of our program is to try to balance the needs of the individual with the needs of the organization." (Tim Clark, Vice President, Human Resources Development, and Beth Shearer, General Manager, The Franchise Company) Telus Corporation strives to achieve a "50/50 balance between company needs (framework is constant) and individual development (help with projects and mentoring)." (Josh Blair, Senior Vice-President, Human Resources Strategy and Business Support, Telus Corporation)

  Many organizations nowadays possess competency systems that define the landscape for effective leadership behaviours and provide a baseline to evaluate performance. Here's an example from Christine Brown, General Manager, Human Resources, HBC Stores and Specialty: "We have designed an internal leadership profile (competencies/criteria) to determine what the best looks like, by interviewing outstanding performers. It is based on four categories: people, results, service and strategy with accompanying behaviours. It is now integrated in our performance management system."
- *Field-specific programs,* such as community, sports and arts, offer contents relevant to their domain, as well as leadership topics. In other words, understanding field dynamics is required for effective leadership. "The Action Canada program includes leadership skills development and work on the major public policy issues facing Canada." (Cathy Beehan, CEO, Action Canada Foundation)
- *All programs* seek to provide a common leadership framework and language; for instance, purpose, role and responsibilities, expectations and principles. As such, popular models and tools relevant to the leadership field are found in most programs.

Therefore, many topics were similar across the board. They can be divided into the following categories:

- **Leadership skills**—visioning, motivating, strategy development, people and team development.
- **Process skills**—facilitation, problem solving, networking, negotiation, change management.
- **Communication skills**—listening, asking questions, speaking, writing, presenting, influence and persuasion.
- **Interpersonal skills**—establishing rapport, building relationships, getting along, building consensus, conflict resolution, emotional intelligence (EQ).
- **Business related**—finance, organizational systems, management, business strategy, customer service and marketing.

Most programs carefully articulate the relationship between management and leadership and provide models that represent their interdependencies and value both roles. "Leadership and management must not be seen as opposites. The two roles are linked and interdependent. It's important not to overshadow management; we need manager-leaders." (Gilles Harvey, Former Director, Centre Québécois de Leadership [Québec Centre for Leadership])

A lot of programs stress the importance of building a solid foundation and help participants design their leadership platform with activities such as value selection, visioning, code of ethics design and personal mission elaboration. This is a very good use of classroom time, because it provides a structured format to reflect and make decisions on these fundamental items. "We help participants articulate their vision and intentions; develop their authenticity, strength and adaptability." (Dr. Rosie Steeves, President; Barbara Ross-Denroche, Principal, The Refinery Leadership Partners Inc., [formerly CEL, Centre for Exceptional Leadership Inc.])

Obviously, curriculum evolves with emerging trends and needs. For instance, many leadership programs now include topics such as globalization, diversity, environmental issues and corporate social responsibility. These also develop cognitive abilities and conceptual thinking. "It's a blend of topics where critical thinking is woven through." (Dr. Patricia Bradshaw, Associate Professor, Organizational Behaviour, MBA Program, Skills for Leadership and Governance, Schulich School of Business, York University)

Outstanding programs are highly experiential, configured to accommodate individual needs and competently supervised. For instance, the Desjardins Cooperative Institute uses a variety of learning methodologies: "Lectures by instructors; opinions from specialists and interviews with national and international leaders on video; learning through games; individual work and group projects, etc." (Excerpts from www.desjardins.com, January 2007) They also require participants to create a Personal Development Plan, which serves as a map to their learning journey, fostering responsibility. As we discussed in

Chapter 5, individuals must be accountable for their own development, and a Personal Development Plan is a great tool for planning ahead and injecting strategic thinking into the process. Many organizations now require their leaders to craft one.

Education is important because it equips students with the basic models, theories and concepts that will frame their leadership practice. It also provides a common language, a network of fellow learners, and helpful resources. In other words, education anchors and supports the learning experience.

Practice

Developing leaders need practice to assimilate new learning and make it stick. It is also the crucible through which they find their voice, style and identity. Leadership, like sports, requires extensive practice to achieve proficiency. Therefore, programs have been gradually enhancing experiential components both within and outside the classroom. "Students have to function as a team. They are presented with activities and challenges and as a team, they decide how to master them. The ability to communicate and work together is important." (Theresa [Therri] Papp, Consultant, Rotary Youth Leadership Awards, Rotary International)

Inside the classroom, this results in many interactive activities, such as simulations, case studies, role plays, etc. "Our basic program comprises assessments, exercises, journaling, application, simulations during which participants are videotaped and can see themselves in action. This is very revealing and complemented by facilitated group feedback and a one-to-one executive coaching sessions. We also ask them to select a goal to enhance their leadership practice after the program." (Donna Porter, Lead Facilitator, Niagara Institute)

Outside the classroom, the practice component, often called practicum, must be strategically chosen, extensively supported and analyzed to derive maximum benefit. "The model for the integration and application of leadership learning is customized by each learner, based on the personal leadership challenge faced. For example, in pre-residency online orientation, students discuss a current challenge they are facing; they then work on creating an action plan." (Dr. Nancy Greer, Acting Director, Professor and Academic Lead, School of Leadership Studies, Royal Roads University) We found a growing trend to this effect, particularly in organizational programs; however, market reality does not currently reflect this as a consistent best practice.

Practicum activities can include intra-organizational activities, such as assignments, affectations, job shadowing and problem solving. Because organizations want optimal ROI, practicum assignments are increasingly tied to real issues. They can also include external activities, such as community projects, field trips and exchanges. For instance, the range of practicum assignments is becoming more adventurous and global. "We have co-operative internships, one in Canada and one overseas." (Dr. Pierre Zundel, Dean, Renaissance College, New Brunswick University)

While on assignment, learners always stretch outside of their comfort zone, venture into unfamiliar territory and meet challenges head on. In other words, they broaden their capacity. Therefore, it is important to strategically select assignments to fit each participant's current needs and goals. Richard Bégin, Director, Management Development Programs, said: "The Canada Revenue Agency ensures that candidates get a variety of assignments during their leadership and management development three-year program. For example, if a person has been working in a specialized area, a broad assignment is provided; if someone has only had head office experience, a regional posting will be arranged; if a person is not fluently bilingual, a move to a location where they can practise their second language will be offered."

Assignments need to be as carefully analyzed as they are planned. "We work closely with the workplace to see how clients are adapting their knowledge to specific situations and what they need to do to close the gap. Their assignment lasts between one to two years." (Mervin Hillier, President, The Corporate L.I.F.E. Centre Inc.)

A popular model features classroom education followed by a practical assignment, both supported by virtual methodologies.

Action Canada Fellows attend three 8-day working conferences in different Canadian cities, including Vancouver and Ottawa, to improve their understanding of the major policy issues facing our country. In the first three years, Fellows have traveled to Newfoundland and Labrador, Yukon and Nunavut. They also work in task force groups to determine how these policy issues might best be addressed. In addition to the three working conferences, each task force convenes two face-to-face meetings during the fellowship year and connects weekly by conference calls and emails. The task forces are supported by Action Canada Advisors who work with the Fellows throughout the year." (Cathy Beehan, CEO, Action Canada Foundation)

Practice makes perfect and enables apprentices to integrate leadership behaviours. Through practice, skills become ingrained and judgement is refined. Through practice, leaders connect with the role's essence and learn to express it through their unique gifts. "All the world's a stage," said Shakespeare, and leaders grow on the many stages created by practice opportunities.

Self-Discovery

As we saw in Chapter 5, it is fundamental for leaders to understand themselves (motivations, drivers, strengths and limitations) in order to avoid blind spots and increase their effectiveness. In other words, they must align intent with impact.

To this end, the vast majority of programs use formal and informal activities enabling self-discovery. On the formal side, extensive assessment instruments—both psychometric and 360-degree feedback devices—are used. These offer a professional, research-based, objective picture of how participants are wired from the inside and perceived from the outside.

Psychometric instruments are like X-ray charts providing a glimpse of internal wiring, exposing its inner logic and illuminating strengths to be leveraged and weaknesses to solidify. Most programs offer a wide range of psychometric instruments and expert coaches to assist with their interpretation. Interviewees find these very useful because instruments make sense of personality traits, normalize growth challenges and legitimate needs. As such, they offer a blueprint for planning development.

On the other hand, 360-degree feedback devices are like snapshots, taken at a point in time by the participant's stakeholders. They are extremely valuable, since leadership effectiveness, like beauty, is in the eyes of the beholder. In the influencing game, perception is reality.

The 360-degree process invites participants to select a cross-section of stakeholders, including direct reports, colleagues, clients, associates and superiors. These individuals rate the person on a number of competencies, behaviours, skills, etc., and provide qualitative feedback as well. To accurately portray reality, a representative and fair stakeholder list should contain friends and foes alike. It is recommended that there be 12 to 18 people in a stakeholder group.

Respondents find these devices very powerful, for 360s provide a glimpse of themselves through other people's eyes. Here's a sample of typical insights:

- Participants underestimate themselves.
- Areas important to stakeholders come into sharp focus.
- Impact is greater than expected.
- Clear direction is provided on how to align intent and impact.
- Stakeholders offer new and surprising sources of support.
- Participants get a better appreciation of the value of people skills.

As a result, 360-degree feedback devices are gaining in popularity and becoming commonplace. Many organizations have developed specific 360 feedback devices based on their internal competency systems to further align the process to organizational realities. "We use a 360 feedback device linked to a competency-based system for many of our programs. We provide pre-course learning information through a Web-based portal, and follow up with additional tools and materials 14 days after the program." (Lisa Jackson, Associate Director of Operations, The Banff Centre)

It's important that attributes and behaviours be measured within a specific context. "A good leader in a community of monks is not the same as a good leader in a biker gang. Therefore, respondents must know the candidate well to give adequate feedback. We ask respondents to provide nuanced opinions and we guarantee confidentiality." (Dr. Mario Roy, Chair, Organization of work studies, Department of Management, Faculty of Administration, representing the Centre d'Entreprises [Centre for Business], Université de Sherbrooke)

Psychometric and 360-degree feedback results are frequently integrated to present a complete picture of internal wiring and external perceptions. By understanding both, leaders can align intent and impact to become more effective. Often, the combined results serve as a starting point for Personal Development Plans. Many programs give participants coaching time to debrief results and begin the Personal Development Plan process.

Other formal strategies to promote self-discovery include videotaped simulations and role plays subsequently analyzed. Through these interactive activities, leaders see themselves in action and get a glimpse of their behaviour as it appears to others.

On the informal side, interpersonal activities, such as peer and instructor feedback and group discussions, are extensively used. Likewise, individual activities such as journaling, exercises, readings and action planning allow participants to look within and reflect in a structured manner.

Self-discovery is the work of a lifetime and, as such, never ends. But getting a head start during a program gives leaders an advantage as well as good learning habits.

Support

Let's face it: development is hard work. To sustain the effort, people need support and lots of it. Nothing is more ineffective and irresponsible than throwing people into the deep end of the pool without assistance.

And yet support is often the most misunderstood and underestimated component of leadership development programs. Maybe it is equated with an admission of weakness or a state of vulnerability. It should not. Support is the safety net that enables developing leaders to venture out of their comfort zone without falling apart, and to take risks without being paralyzed by fear. Jean-François Bouchard,

President, Sid Lee, put it well: "First you take them under your wing, then you push them off the branch so they can try their own wings, finally you mend their beaks when required."

In the apprenticeship model, extensive support is provided to facilitate emulation, lessen growing pains, normalize mistakes, provide advice and, in general, lend a helping hand. Given that the learning process is fraught with anxiety and extensive support is needed to alleviate it, its presence needs to be more visible and substantial in the course of programs.

The best programs use formal and informal means of support from a variety of sources. "Students enrolled in international exchanges get a lot of coaching, mentoring and help, both here and abroad, from faculty staff members and each other. We orient international students to different aspects of Canadian life and organize social activities during the first few days of their arrival to facilitate their integration. Many are not used to group work, so we find ways to help them through coaching, buddy systems, etc. We are also putting together a glossary of colloquial expressions and business terminology that puzzle international students." (Angela L. James, Director, Centre for International Management, School of Business, Queen's University)

Formal support generally includes coaching and mentoring. Mentoring is provided by internal leaders who take a participant under their wing to show them the ropes. Coaching is generally delivered by external professionals who perform specific expert functions, such as debriefing assessment results, conducting career discussions, helping participants start their Personal Development Plan, etc. Informal support is provided by everyone involved in the program, including faculty, peers and administrative staff.

Over time, organizations become more creative and polished in the variety and scope of support mechanisms provided. Corey Jack, Executive Head, BMO Financial Group Institute for Learning, said his company provides "coaching from line managers, and mentoring by program graduates. In the case of longer programs, involving cohort groups of students, additional support is provided by resources who act like guidance counsellors."

Often, participants are presented with options and invited to select the most suitable to their circumstances, temperament and objectives. Here are some examples:

- Learning assistance offered by facilitators who help students integrate learning—this can be provided on an individual basis, such as coaching sessions, or in small groups, such as labs. One-on-one activities allow faculty and participants to develop a more personal relationship and enable instructors to better understand their students. Group activities promote peer and faculty support and deepen the learning experience. Methodologies include live and distance.

- Coaching offered by professionals, instructors, peers or bosses—the explosion of the coaching profession in the last 10 years attests to the vast needs to fill. Today, many organizations hire professional coaches for their executives and equip managers and employees with coaching skills. "Peer coaching (giving and receiving feedback) is fundamental to all components of our Leadership Program, as a significant expectation of all participants is that they will not only take care of their own learning, but will also meaningfully contribute to the learning of others—something that we believe is an essential role of all leaders today." (Dr. Nancy Greer, Acting Director, Professor and Academic Lead, School of Leadership Studies, Royal Roads University) An innovative approach is being used in the MA in Leadership at University of Guelph. Students in the coaching program provide leadership participants with coaching: a win-win formula that helps coaching students hone their skills and provides leadership participants with support.
- Mentoring supplied by executives, former graduates and bosses—mentoring, like marriage, succeeds when the match is right and when both parties are committed to the relationship and dedicated to making it work. As we have seen earlier, flourishing mentoring relationships have the most profound and lasting impact on leadership development. Therefore, an increasing number of organizations are implementing formal mentoring infrastructures to expose more people to its benefits. Several create 'mentor databases' that enable participants to select a mentor suited to their needs, and ensure there are no mentor shortages. Mentoring by former graduates is a growing trend because it gives students the support of someone 'who's been there.'
- Sponsorship provided by executives who offer project support and act as career advisors and promoters—executive attention is a powerful gift, greatly appreciated by developing leaders. For instance, SaskEnergy involves its Executive Committee in presentations made by program participants on ROI projects completed during their practicum.

Support acts as a growth enabler; it is the ingredient that turns raw potential into competence, the pat on the back that makes a difference, the advice that reframes a failure. Support allows more people to stay on the leadership track. It is food for the learner's soul.

Leaders give a lot but who cares for the caregivers? The vast majority of interviewees reported living in a 'support vacuum'. This needs to be addressed and redressed. Montréal's Martin Neufeld, a.k.a., the Hugger Busker, came up with an original solution: He started offering 'free hugs' on street corners as a "practical approach to living kindness through human interaction and shared intimacy." (www.huggerbusker.com, January 2007) It has now become a worldwide movement, a testimonial to the widespread need for support and human contact in our society. Why are we denying our leaders the support they need?

Community

Not only do leaders need support to grow, they need community to feel a sense of belonging. A frequent complaint during the interviews was *I have nobody to talk to.* To counteract the state of isolation leaders often find themselves in, an increasing number of programs feature communities of practice where leaders can congregate to share, learn and help each other. These allow leaders to problem solve, facilitate access to resources and foster career development.

Sharing with like-minded others is very important. Leaders spend a lot of time in vertical relationships with direct reports and superiors. Horizontal relationships are required to offer camaraderie, but in the hustle of everyday life, little time is available for those.

Communities of practice represent a legitimate approach to fill that void. Moreover, these groups foster innovation instead of the constant reinventing of the wheel which takes place when people operate in isolation. Once leaders share the same knowledge base, they can use it to jump together to a new level of creative solutions.

Communities allow leaders to discuss issues of concern, innovate and network in a safe and confidential environment. "We create a community of practice, a safe space where participants can share openly about their management challenges, and where they can pursue their quest for meaning. We are concerned with the whole person, not just the manager-leader." (Dr. Mario Cayer and Dr. Marie-Éve Marchand, Professors, Programme Complexité, Conscience et Gestion [Complexity, Conscience and Management Program], Département de Management, Université Laval)

Through these circles, leaders are renewed and invigorated. They benefit from each other's expertise and know-how, sharing on a wide variety of issues such as performance management, career progression and business strategy. They use each other as sounding boards for solutions and advice. The level of satisfaction derived from communities of practice far outweighs the effort to set them up.

We found a variety of formats, such as councils, conferences, exchanges and forums, offered to various audiences, such as current and former program participants; executives; middle managers; supervisors; high potentials; unit, branch and regional leaders; and women leaders.

Many are initiated by leaders themselves, seeking to belong to a community. Often, organizations or programs will provide an infrastructure and the leaders do the rest. For instance, an organization might announce that it is launching 'leadership networks' and provide a blueprint for start-up and governance, leaving the initiative in the hands of the leaders. Consequently, many networks will spring up for technical leaders, new leaders, plant leaders, etc. These practically run on their own and provide incredible value to their members.

Participants meet on a regular basis to dialogue on specific topics. "There are meetings four times a year and regional tours. Group work is focused on leadership in action." (Sylvain B. Lalonde, Executive Director, Fédération de hockey sur glace du Québec Inc. [Québec Ice Hockey Federation])

These discussions enrich participants' thinking and their repertoire of concepts and solutions. If support is the misunderstood program component, community is the new kid on the block. But it's growing fast. Program experts interviewed reported a tendency to enhance this best practice. Not only that, but the leaders themselves are demanding it.

CONCLUSION

Leadership development programming is becoming a competitive, sophisticated and international field of research and practice, as well as a booming business worldwide. This is highly encouraging because it means that, increasingly, people realize that producing the required quality and quantity of leaders demands solid and stable infrastructures.

People and organizations are also becoming more realistic about what it really takes to produce outstanding leaders. The naïveté that assumes a short leadership workshop will do the trick, is slowly being replaced by a more down-to-earth attitude which involves pulling up your sleeves and working for the desired outcome … over the long term.

CHAPTER 8

PROGRAM ENHANCEMENT

The program framework is holistic: e-learning, classroom, experiential through special projects, mentoring and coaching, as well as involvement in the local community. There are also assessment devices such as the Myers-Briggs, 360 feedback instruments, and a values core assessment to measure behaviours. Participants present to a panel on how they lead, and get feedback. The focus is on actual performance, versus style.

Josh Blair,
Senior Vice-President, Human Resources Strategy and Business
Support, Telus Corporation

They become well-rounded people with a wide range of interests. They exhibit leadership skills. They can sustain commitment to a program.

Jill Hermant,
Executive Director, The Duke of Edinburgh's Award, Ontario Division

THE MAKING OF A PROGRAM

How are programs born and how do they evolve?

Design

Most respondents indicated that, at the onset, they were chiefly preoccupied with *curriculum* design. Over time, they start integrating self-discovery, practice, support and community components; consequently, the focus shifts to *infrastructure* design.

Once programs evolve into an infrastructure composed of several components, orientation is required to help participants see the big picture, understand each module and how they fit together. Orientation provides a map to the program, facilitating navigation and enabling participants to adapt it to their own needs.

As a result of adding more components, program duration expands and people realize leadership development is a long-term investment. "The program lasts for 18 months. It starts with an orientation and a pre-program 360. Then, they study for four weeks over six months—very intense and lots of content. The next step is a project that needs to bring back 25% ROI. The executives give feedback on projects and sponsor them. In a lot of cases, recommendations are implemented. The last step is a post-program 360." (Barb Tchozewski, Organizational Effectiveness Coordinator, SaskEnergy)

In order to accommodate practicum needs and encourage participants to venture out of their comfort zone, locations become more varied and strategic. "Future executives participating in our programs undergo six weeks of training including two one-week-long field trips where they are exposed to dynamics profoundly different from their day-to-day reality. For instance, a trip to Goose Bay to study the complexity of local issues and relations between stakeholders as well as leadership dynamics of Aboriginal people." (Richard Bégin, Director, Management Development Programs, Canada Revenue Agency)

To get the desired results requires a significant investment of time, money and resources. "One hundred percent of costs are covered by the company at the corporate level. We did not cut funds for training during difficult financial years and spend about 3% of payroll on training and development. Investing in people is asset building." (Dr. Robert W. Hedley, Vice-President, Leadership, Maple Leaf Foods Inc.)

We were encouraged to find that, increasingly, organizations are willing to make the investment required to get a reliable supply of competent leaders.

Evolution

Programs evolve as professionals seek to improve them, align them to a changing environment, or endeavour to meet participants' needs. Most interviewees reported that goals and vision haven't changed, but means have.

Improvements

Over time, programs are fine-tuned and get better structured. "We have modified the program to include formalized mentoring by Action Canada Advisors who are assigned to each Fellow's task force group. After the initial years, we also added a program component focusing on developing Fellows' commentary writing skills, where they work with prominent Canadian editors and journalists to produce and submit for publication, articles on public policy issues." (Cathy Beehan, CEO, Action Canada Foundation)

Here are examples of typical improvements:

- Design becomes more elaborate. Extensive needs analyses are conducted, pilots run and delivery streamlined. Keeping programs current and interesting is a major concern. "Our guiding principle is: you're never done; once you stop learning, you stop leading. Therefore, our program is based on models, concepts and principles that are constantly reinforced in practice and in the culture." (Captain [N] Alan Okros, Professor; Former Director, Canadian Forces Leadership Institute, Royal Military College)
- Metrics increase in sophistication. "We ask participants to reflect on the program ROI. For example, how will a behaviour change translate to the bottom line? When you add up the numbers, it becomes amazing: last session totalled $2 million for 15 people! Participants experience a huge 'aha' when they realize the cost of lost productivity and people replacement due to ineffective leadership." (Dr. Rosie Steeves, President; Barbara Ross-Denroche, Principal, The Refinery Leadership Partners Inc., [Formerly CEL, Centre for Exceptional Leadership Inc.])
- Creativity is injected through techniques from the world of arts, sports, spirituality, etc. For example, Brian Hayman, President, Getting in the Groove, shares that his program exposes learners to a live jazz band so they can learn the intricacies of team membership and leadership. Lisa Jackson, Associate Director of Operations, The Banff Centre, recounts that the centre's program blends arts, ecology and culture dynamics in an integrated approach to leadership. Susan Szpakowski, Executive Director, The Shambhala Institute for Authentic Leadership, tells us that the institute's development programs

include the study of organizational disciplines, meditation practice, artistic processes and dialogue.

- Designs become more open and fluid. Instead of cramming every minute with contents, program designers learn to leave breathing space to allow reflection, integration, networking and relaxation. "We modified the program's format to provide more space instead of jam-packing it with activities." (Denise Coutts, Executive Director; Nancy McKinstry and Julia Kim, Board members, Minerva Foundation for BC Women)
- Practical toolkits are provided, containing elements such as decision-making paths, problem-solving models, checklists, reminders, etc. These result in "business models tailor-made for clients." (Mervin Hillier, President, The Corporate L.I.F.E. Centre Inc.)
- Faculty diversifies. "We have a blend of faculty, augmented by practitioners and scholars (250 associates) who bring a variety and richness of experience. This enables us to configure the optimal faculty team for a given offering." (Dr. Nancy Greer, Acting Director, Professor and Academic Lead, School of Leadership Studies, Royal Roads University) There seems to be an increasing trend to rely on executives who move from sponsors to facilitators, presenters and coaches. Many organizations train them so they can competently play those roles, which they seem to really enjoy. "We use senior executives and take steps to maximize their skills as facilitators." (Tim Clark, Vice-President, Human Resources Development, and Beth Shearer, General Manager, The Franchise Company) Graduates become mentors. This has several benefits: participants get coaching from someone who 'has been there,' programs get additional resources, and graduates expand their skills.
- Partnerships multiply. For instance, universities now partner with others to offer double degrees and international exchange programs. In the community sector, innovative partnerships are formed between individuals, corporations and government agencies. "Enbridge and the Ontario Trillium Foundation provide the funding for our community program." (Michael Rosenberg, Founder, Peel Leadership Program) If possible, the goal is to offer community programs free of charge. "Program participants don't have to pay. Everything is donated as a result of our corporate sponsors and partners." (Denise Coutts, Executive Director; Nancy McKinstry and Julia Kim, Board members, Minerva Foundation for BC Women) These community partnerships make everyone look good in win-win scenarios. "Participants do not pay to attend programs. They are sponsored by the Rotary Clubs." Theresa [Therri] Papp, Consultant, Rotary Youth Leadership Awards, Rotary International)
- Programs expand. Regional programs grow nationally and national ones, internationally. "International students outside of NATO want to gain a

better appreciation of Western ethics and values as well as *savoir faire*. Ethics has become a major attraction for Canada. People want to learn our ethical system. Over time, as a result of participation in the Canadian Forces College's programs, relationships develop between the Canadian Forces College, The Canadian Forces, and Canada and other nations and their institutions, such as Singapore." (Commander Gregg Hannah, Senior Staff Officer, Canadian Forces College)

Programs become more professional and strategic. "Custom programs are totally tailored to needs analysis results, culture and style of the organization." (Dr. Alan C. Middleton, Executive Director, Schulich Executive Education Centre [SEEC], York University) They closely align to contexts like business strategy and culture. "We need leaders who can provide coaching on artistic and management issues. We seek to define the required attributes for effective leaders, for instance, generous, transparent. …" (France Dufresne, Director, Organizational Development and Training, Cirque du Soleil)

As a result, programs intimately mesh with the community they serve. "The military is a profession and professionals have an identity, responsibilities, expertise and a code of ethics based on values. In the military, our values are discipline, sacrifice, duty and honour. It is important that the Canadian military represents the values and aspirations of the nation. The value system is like a magna carta; militaries act like ambassadors of the aspirations of the Canadian population." (Captain [N] Alan Okros, Professor; Former Director, Canadian Forces Leadership Institute, Royal Military College)

The field of leadership development is in constant evolution. As we explored the various initiatives taking place across the country, we came to the conclusion that practitioners would benefit from learning from each other instead of operating in isolation and reinventing the wheel. We will examine this issue in greater detail in Chapter 12: National Leadership Strategy.

PARTICIPANT SELECTION

How are participants selected?

Basic Approaches

Programs select participants based on different underlying philosophies:

- Opportunities for everyone. Some programs cast a broad net to attract as many leaders as possible. Those tend to keep admissions criteria at a minimum and allow participants to self-select. This philosophy is inclusive. "Programs are open to individuals interested in pursuing a leadership path. They can self-select with their immediate manager's approval and the programs are available at different levels." (Mona Jasinski, Manager, Learning and Development, Shell Canada Limited)

- Opportunities for the majority. These programs want to catch a lot of fish in their net while levelling the playing field with entry criteria, such as academic credentials, GMAT scores, and years of experience. "Admission requirements are a four-year Honours undergraduate degree from a recognized university with a minimum average of B and a minimum of five years of relevant work experience." (Brian Earn, Director; Michael Cox, Associate Director, Centre for Studies in Leadership, University of Guelph) This philosophy is based on the belief that certain knowledge and skills are required to succeed. For instance, Dr. Patricia Bradshaw, Associate Professor, Organizational Behaviour, shared that 70% of York University's MBA program students are international. Therefore, an English-language fluency criterion has been added.

- Opportunities for specific candidates. This group wants to catch only certain fish in their net. This is the case of programs aimed at specific groups, such as elite sports coaches, girls in Grade 11, and hockey players. They have strict criteria, such as professional qualifications, gender, age, and level of accomplishment. "Action Canada seeks Canadians in early career years, who have a record of leadership or extraordinary achievements apart from academic studies, and who have a passion for Canada, the potential to become a Canadian leader, and the commitment to make a positive contribution to our country." (Cathy Beehan, CEO, Action Canada Foundation)

This is also the case for high-potentials that organizations want to fast-track and invest heavily in. It also applies to succession planning programs designed to groom the next generation of executives. For instance, HBC Group focuses on talent management to ensure that the right people are in the right positions, for now and the future. This is not a training program, but a strategic talent management initiative.

Programs targeting candidates most likely to succeed also use this approach. "Students selected to go on international exchanges must have good academic standing, 70%+, no failed courses, be accepted by the partner university and behave as a good ambassador of Canada. They must complete an application process where they are assessed on a point system. For instance, extracurricular activities and language fluency are important. They must also answer essay questions as to why they want to do the exchange and how it will be beneficial to their commerce degree." (Angela L. James, Director, Centre for International Management, School of Business, Queen's University)

Contrasting Approaches

These three approaches are now better defined and understood. In fact, they complement each other. For instance, many organizations clearly differentiate between leadership development initiatives (wide net) and succession planning initiatives (small net). Broad leadership development initiatives create opportunities for the employees at large, while succession planning ensures the next generation of executives is prepared and ready.

As a result, succession planning selection criteria are more rigorous and the process is generally driven by talent review. Here's an example shared by Christine Brown, General Manager, Human Resources, HBC Stores and Specialty: "We start with a talent review. As a group, executives assess their direct reports according to a nine-box grid based on two dimensions: performance and potential; and three levels: low, medium, high. The results are a collective view on how an employee is perceived by executives. People end up in three categories: high potential, stability talent, cautioned risk."

When organizations confuse generic and specific initiatives, employees get the impression that leadership development is elitist. As a result, organizations have learned to spell out the rules of the game. Here are a few examples:

- "Selection criteria combine education, experience and competencies. Participants must fill out a form, add their resumés and take part in a number of selection activities, such as tests and simulations of all kinds. The process takes approximately six months. For instance, this year 740 people applied and 50 were chosen. The selection is based on the best individual performances." (Richard Bégin, Director, Management Development Programs, Canada Revenue Agency)
- "The first step is to look at transcripts; the second is to view applicants' résumés and/or videos outlining the unique talents and experience they bring to the program, and specifying their career interests. The selection committee reviews applications and all the material provided." (Dr. Pierre Zundel, Dean, Renaissance College, New Brunswick University)

The guiding principle seems to be to let everyone into reception, but only allow suitable and interested candidates farther into the building.

IMPACT

Leadership impact is palpable. "There is curiosity about leadership and a desire to learn. When people see others changing, it becomes even more interesting."

(Dr. Rosie Steeves, President; Barbara Ross-Denroche, Principal, The Refinery Leadership Partners Inc., [Formerly CEL, Centre for Exceptional Leadership Inc.])

Therefore, it is important to evaluate the effectiveness of leadership development programs, as they most certainly affect leadership impact itself. Most programs link evaluation with objectives. In other words, the expected ROI should be as clear as possible. 'Beginning with the end in mind,' to paraphrase Stephen Covey, makes it easier to structure programs that fit a specific context and can succeed in a given environment. "Approach, methodology and processes are linked from a holistic perspective." (Mervin Hillier, President, The Corporate L.I.F.E. Centre Inc.)

Ties between organizational goals, leadership requirements and program contents should be crystal clear. This way, professionals can easily see the big picture, articulate linkages and select appropriate evaluation methods. Here are comments that illustrate clear goals and objectives:

- "Fulfill the organization's succession planning needs in a strategic way." (Dr. Patricia Hedley, Director of Professional Development, Humber Institute of Technology and Advanced Learning)
- "Give students the ability and confidence to make a sustained difference." (Dr. Nancy Greer, Acting Director, Professor and Academic Lead, School of Leadership Studies, Royal Roads University)

How to Measure Impact

Professionals interviewed referred to Donald Kirkpatrick's four levels of evaluation—Reactions, Learning, Transfer and Results—to frame their comments (*Evaluating Training Programs: The Four Levels*, Berrett-Koehler, San Francisco, CA, 1994).

Reactions are most consistently evaluated, followed by *Learning*. There is a growing awareness that *Transfer* and *Results* must be more comprehensively assessed to prove program impact and improve credibility, particularly with executives. Many have started to use a balanced scorecard. Others correlate evaluation results with measures like employee satisfaction, engagement surveys, promotions, etc. "The program is proven, as several executives are former attendees." (Josh Blair, Senior Vice-President, Human Resources Strategy and Business Support, Telus Corporation)

Reactions

Programs evaluate participant satisfaction either at the end of the program or afterwards, in a recurrent fashion. For instance, participants might get an evaluation form six months after the end of the program and again, a year later. Professionals were keenly aware of the value of formal and informal feedback and the need to take into account participants' suggestions for program improvements. "Participants recommended creating management circles to enable interaction with leaders from inside and outside their immediate working environment. Discussion groups facilitated by management consultants, are held every four to six weeks. Each group is composed of about eight participants, which allows them to explore issues relevant to their daily lives. It's a formula in expansion." (Gilles Harvey, Former Director, Centre Québécois de Leadership [Québec Centre for Leadership])

To evaluate reactions, most use a combination of quantitative and qualitative methods, such as questionnaires, surveys, interviews, testimonials and anecdotal evidence. "Participants report that learning is more than the accumulation of technique. Often they suggest the experience was transformative and enabled them to function more effectively in their organizations. We have a growing catalogue of stories of organizational change, alliance building and cultural shifts, arising out of these kinds of personal transformations." (Susan Szpakowski, Executive Director, The Shambhala Institute for Authentic Leadership)

Learning

Evaluating learning often starts with evaluating understanding. Did students 'get' the contents and the context? For instance, Michael Rosenberg, Founder, Peel Leadership Program, said the goal is to "understand community needs."

Learning always involves an awareness of transformation: paradigm shifts, insights, broader perspectives. "It's about expanding consciousness, not skill building. It affects more deeply organizations who need to improvise, or people who have an inkling for it, those who can tolerate risk and ambiguity." (Brian Hayman, President, Getting in the Groove)

The result of combining greater understanding and skills with expanded awareness is personal growth. "Participants become bolder, no longer victims— they deal with issues." (Dr. Rosie Steeves, President; Barbara Ross-Denroche, Principal, The Refinery Leadership Partners Inc., [Formerly CEL, Centre for Exceptional Leadership Inc.]) They develop a sense of empowerment and confidence. "They acquire the knowledge that they can do more than they thought possible." (Jill Hermant, Executive Director, The Duke of Edinburgh's Award, Ontario Division)

Through it all, participants develop a clearer view of themselves as leaders and build their bench strength. "Participants report they sharpen their awareness of their strengths and weaknesses. They create developmental action plans." (Linda Arnoldussen, Director of Learning and Operational Excellence, Leadership Development program, School of Business, Executive Education and Lifelong Learning, University of Alberta)

To assess learning, many use pre- and post-program 360s, which are very useful to measure awareness and behaviour shifts. Some use tests and control groups and many favour integrated approaches. "Higher-level evaluation is rigorous. It includes observation, log books, assignments, exams, assessment. There is a practicum at the higher level, under a master coach set-up." (John Bales, CEO, Coaching Association of Canada)

Transfer

All programs are aware of the need to better measure transfer of knowledge. Can participants apply newly acquired skills in their own environment? Just like in chef training, the proof is in the pudding: can the student actually execute a recipe? Some programs have begun implementing smart and effective evaluation systems.

Transfer starts with empowerment, the desire to act. "They return from the program charged up and wanting to apply new skills." (Karin Lofstrom, Executive Director, CAAWS [Canadian Association for the Advancement of Women and Sport]) "The leadership program is a gift. We motivate and inspire our participants to envision what they will do in return for their community—it is that wonderful pay-it-forward phenomenon." (Denise Coutts, Executive Director; Nancy McKinstry and Julia Kim, Board members, Minerva Foundation for BC Women)

As a next step in the transfer process, participants need to apply their skills by getting involved. "They shine in community projects." (Michael Rosenberg, Founder, Peel Leadership Program) Then, they accomplish. "They become well-rounded people with a wide range of interests. They exhibit leadership skills. They can sustain a commitment to a program." (Jill Hermant, Executive Director, The Duke of Edinburgh's Award, Ontario Division)

Over time and through extensive practice, they master a complex array of skills. "They acquire capabilities and tools, and become proactive in their environment. Their ability to self-assess expands, as well as their skill at analyzing and putting forward hypotheses and scenarios. Finally, they act in accordance with their values." (Dr. Jean-Pierre Brunelle, Professor, Faculty of Physical and Sports

Education, Université de Sherbrooke; Francophone Program Lead, Leadership and Ethics Module, Montréal National Coaching Institute, Coaching Association of Canada)

Transfer of knowledge is most visible through practicum activities, so these are increasingly tracked. "In custom programs, we do tracking in three months and six months with participants and their supervisor." (Dr. Alan C. Middleton, Executive Director, Schulich Executive Education Centre [SEEC], York University)

The ultimate test, of course, is in actions. "We ask ourselves: are participants living by the values and principles they learned in the program?" (Barb Tchozewski, Organizational Effectiveness Coordinator, SaskEnergy)

Results

Results can be broken down into two categories: organizational and individual.

Organizational

In terms of organizational results, participants described cascades of benefits, such as performance improvements, increased customer satisfaction, culture change and higher profile. Some see a "major impact on athlete performance through better qualified coaches and improved retention of coaches." (John Bales, CEO, Coaching Association of Canada) "Team members have more engaging leadership with better results. Customers benefit from crisper and stronger relationships. Company and shareholders see improved business and financial results. The community witnesses more involvement." (Josh Blair, Senior Vice-President, Human Resources Strategy and Business Support, Telus Corporation)

Success invariably means quantitative and qualitative results are achieved. "All objectives have been reached: competency acquisition, positive experience for leaders, multiplication of leaders, implementation of relevant regional infrastructures, team proliferation, better coaching for players, access to the major leagues for more players." (Sylvain B. Lalonde, Executive Director, Fédération de hockey sur glace du Québec Inc. [Québec Ice Hockey Federation])

Results are measured in many ways. Some link program evaluation to organizational results. Others ensure practicum assignments are tightly linked to organizational context. "We look at performance indicators and their progress. Maximizing shareholders' values is an objective. We use a balanced scorecard to determine improvements." (Mervin Hillier, President, The Corporate L.I.F.E. Centre Inc.)

Tailor-made questionnaires following action plan steps are also popular. "We have designed a questionnaire that follows action plan steps and allows regions to reflect on mandate, activities, roles and responsibilities, etc. This enables every leader and region to track progress and has proven very motivating. The process allows the Federation to measure best leadership practices and to take the pulse of regional leadership." (Sylvain B. Lalonde, Executive Director, Fédération de hockey sur glace du Québec Inc. [Québec Ice Hockey Federation])

Many organizations also conduct internal and external benchmarking, and grant awards. "Recognition of achievement is community based at the bronze level, provincially at the silver level, and federally at the gold level." (Jill Hermant, Executive Director, The Duke of Edinburgh's Award, Ontario Division)

Individual

For individuals, results range from promotions to role expansion and career development. "A number of participants move on to expanded leadership roles, such as board members, politicians, etc." (Michael Rosenberg, Founder, Peel Leadership Program) It also means higher profile, better credentials and greater connection to community through the expansion of networks.

The bottom line is long-term progress. "We measure athletes' progress over the long term. We focus on their overall journey, not incidents along the way, such as winning or losing a race. We watch rising stars like those who placed fourth or fifth at the Torino Winter Olympics. A large segment of those came from the Québec City region. Therefore, we know our system is working." (Jacques Loiselle, Former President, Conseil du sport de haut niveau de Québec [High Level Sports Council, Québec City Region])

CONCLUSION

Leadership development programs are critical to meet current and future leadership needs, both organizationally and nationally. Here are a few recommendations that will help structuring effective programs:

- Define the leadership value proposition. All interviewees identified leadership as a critical factor to the success of any organization; therefore, the value of leadership in a given context must be spelled out and development strategies defined to ensure a sustainable supply of effective leaders to meet current and future needs.
- View leadership development as a long-term ROI. It takes considerable time (most programs last from six months to three years) and is anything but a quick fix, so the investment and expected returns must be clearly communicated to

stakeholders. Considerable resources are required to produce quantity and quality returns.

- Connect leadership development to organizational context, culture and desired outcomes. Linkages between goals, leadership contribution and development efforts must be explicit. Leadership is a natural resource like oil: many steps are involved to ensure a regular supply.

- Use the apprenticeship model including the following components: education, applications through experience, opportunities for self-discovery, support mechanisms and access to a community of practice. Integrating these five components into a tightly knit, seamless infrastructure requires extensive monitoring and coordination.

- Foster diversity and inclusion. To achieve the critical mass of required leaders means providing development opportunities at large. Not everyone will step up to the plate, but no one will feel excluded. Moreover, programs should present and allow numerous perspectives and styles, and vary instructional approaches and settings. It's important to create a space large enough for leaders to find their own place and identity. This sometimes means redressing imbalances of the past, and letting go of simplistic cookie-cutter formulas.

- Clarify program offerings. Many organizations now offer a suite of leadership programs intended for various audiences and purposes; therefore, it's crucial to define the rules of the road. Selection processes should be spelled out.

- Expand evaluation span. To clearly demonstrate the ROI of leadership development, transfer of knowledge and its results need to be better measured.

Setting up effective leadership development programs is no small feat, but it is possible to do so by emulating the apprenticeship model, including the five key components and linking them to organizational strategy, culture and context.

PART II

ENSURING A RELIABLE LEADERSHIP SUPPLY

In the previous section, we looked at how the leadership development process works and how to optimize its inherent dynamics. Now we are ready to examine how to ensure a reliable leadership supply for the country. To do so, we will look at various strategies that can be implemented by organizations and by the nation. We will also learn from best practices from co-operatives that can transfer to other sectors.

CHAPTER 9

ORGANIZATIONAL LEADERSHIP STRATEGIES

In my organization, 1% of work hours and revenues are dedicated to education. We are committed to grow, allow our employees to grow and help the community. The CEO needs to know all employees. An encouraging indicator is our low 2% absenteeism and turnover rate.

Frederick MacGillivray
President and CEO, Trade Centre Limited, Halifax

We have done very little to advance the development of leadership. It needs to be more structured. Not enough attention is being paid to leadership development, just like parenting. Leading has become more complex and the process of development hasn't kept up. Forty years ago, being a CEO was easy; all you had to do was tinker with the previous incumbent's positions and you were okay. ... Now there is a need to spend more time developing and actualizing core values and defining a leadership platform. Organizations need sound models to evaluate and support good leadership behaviours. The stars should not be the types who deliver results but have no values. Most organizations do not have what it takes to identify and develop stars.

Bill Hamilton
Executive Coach, W.J.A. Hamilton & Associates
Former Senior Vice-President, BMO and CIBC

ENVIRONMENT FOR SUCCESS

If programs are the *architecture* of success, organizations provide the *environment for success*. In other words, they can create conditions that facilitate leadership emergence, foster its development and encourage the practice of excellence. The right conditions will nurture leadership and allow it to blossom. The wrong ones will stifle and suppress it. This is a serious responsibility and we were delighted to discover that many organizations are taking action to make their environments 'leadership friendly.'

What steps are involved in designing such an approach?

Leading by Example

First and foremost, organizations must behave like leaders themselves. Over and over, interviewees stated that organizations who act like victims, losers or gangsters don't exactly foster the practice of exemplary leadership among employees. In other words, organizations must practise what they preach—demonstrate leadership if they want their employees to do the same.

It starts at the top: Executives should exemplify quality leadership and leaders all around should model the right behaviours. "Leadership exists at all levels. Be diligent when you choose leaders and pay attention to the ones who become role models. They need to be inspirational, not negative examples of poor leadership. Leading is a sacred trust." (Lorene Reist, Business Director, Western Canada, NYCOMED Pharma Inc.)

This supposes that individuals assume responsibility for leadership. In order to do so, they must know what they are getting into. "People need to understand the expectations placed on leaders; then they can determine if they want to play a leadership role." (David Carey, President, Volleyball Canada)

Good leadership should be acknowledged and rewarded, because 'what gets reinforced, gets repeated.' Likewise, poor leadership must be dealt with. "Walk the talk. Have a business vision and create a culture of success for your staff. Measure results against the vision and hold people accountable. Solicit feedback from employees regarding your own accountability as a leader." (Gregory Hines, President and CEO, Tm Bioscience Corporation)

THE FOUR PILLARS

To be successful at leadership practice and development, organizations need to build a leadership 'house,' or container, supported by these four pillars:

Conscience: defining a leadership foundation and making leadership a top priority

Configuration: putting in place strategies, infrastructures and systems to sustain and promote effective leadership and to provide opportunities for systemic development

Caring: adopting a nurturing attitude towards employees and their development

Climate: creating an environment conducive to leadership.

Illustration 9.1

The 4 "Cs" for Creating an Organizational Environment Conducive to Leadership

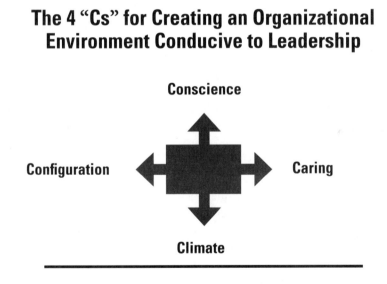

Conscience

Organizations must be cognizant of the importance and value of leadership. Sustaining a viable leadership practice requires making it a priority, devising a leadership stance and applying it in a consistent manner.

Awareness

It starts with affirming the value of leadership. Leadership has to count, be visible. "Position leadership as a desirable role by explicitly stating how it contributes to the success of the organization. Articulate that leadership matters. Celebrate leadership success and value those who make a contribution to the community. Foster a culture of leadership." (Fred Mattocks, Executive Director, Regional Programming, Production and Resources, CBC English Television) Leadership must be in the forefront of organizational consciousness. This means putting in place infrastructures, programs and events that will keep it a priority. For instance, many organizations now boast a leadership council, steering and coordinating leadership efforts. Others have leadership awards, networks, conferences, etc. The keys to success are integration and visibility.

Platform

Just like individuals, organizations need to erect a solid foundation. This platform will align leadership practice and spell out expectations of leaders, making it easier to assess and manage their performance. Platforms also minimize dissonance between what is being said and done, and send a clear message about the organization as a leader.

A platform is like the framework of a strategic plan. It contains stable elements, such as mission, vision, values and code of ethics. It also contains variable elements, such as specific priorities, targets and action steps that can change every year. In other words, the framework acts as the stable core, and the plan, the flexible surrounding. It's important to review and renew the core, but it evolves more slowly and gradually, due to its nature.

Platform definition clarifies leadership issues for organizations and gives them 'a leg to stand on.' It provides an umbrella under which to regroup and integrate everything that pertains to leadership, avoiding departmental silos and turf wars.

In order to construct their platform, organizations have to search their collective soul to define their essential beliefs about leadership. It can be hard to step back from the bustle of day-to-day operations and reflect on leadership issues, but it is fundamental. Here are some BIG questions to start the process:

PLATFORM-BUILDING QUESTIONS

Value

- Why is leadership important in our organization?
- How critical is leadership effectiveness to our success?
- What is the organization willing to do to ensure an abundant supply of competent leaders to meet its current and future needs?
- What investment will the organization commit to in order to develop effective leadership from a long-term and global perspective?

Definition

- What does leadership mean? How has it evolved over time? How will it need to change to meet future needs?
- What is our leadership brand: competencies, key leadership processes like decision-making, problem solving and conflict resolution?
- As a leader, how does our organization define its vision and mission?
- What is the ideological framework (values, principles, guidelines, ethics, etc.) guiding the day-to-day practice of leadership?

Expectations

- What do we expect of our leaders: competencies, results, behaviours, norms, role-modelling, etc.?
- How do we recognize and reward good leaders?
- How do we deal with ineffective leaders?

Alignment

- How linked is leadership to the strategic framework, business strategy and departmental action plans?
- How linked is leadership practice to internal and external image and communication?
- How linked is leadership to the needs of various stakeholders: employees, shareholders, customers, community, etc.?

The platform provides both an anchor and a compass. "Codes of ethics are important; you need to live by them. Leaders personify them." (Allan Taylor, O.C. Former Chairman and CEO, Royal Bank of Canada) Chronologically, it should be the first step to take, because everything else rests on it. Again, our program research is encouraging: Many organizations now possess complete platforms or some components.

Community Service

It's not enough for organizations to win in the marketplace, delight their customers or garner awards; they have to demonstrate community leadership through service. "Organizations can get involved in the community, for instance, in United Way Campaigns, and encourage employees to play a role in their immediate environment. Leaders must provide their organization with philanthropic projects." (Raymond Côté, President, Sports Québec)

Not only is community involvement a great opportunity for organizations to give back to the groups that support them and to fulfill their corporate social responsibilities, but for employees, volunteer work is fertile soil for leadership development. "Provide opportunities and allow aspiring leaders to get involved in the community—it is a great training ground." (Dennis Skulsky, President, CanWest MediaWorks Publications Inc.)

Many opportunities exist and it is up to organizations and employees to show their creative involvement. "Our organization supports community leadership programs and we also have a project for families in transition where employees volunteer to help families in need." (Bonnie Dianne DuPont, Group Vice-President, Corporate Resources, Enbridge Inc.)

So, to erect the conscience pillar, organizations must make leadership a top priority, define their platform and serve their community.

Configuration

Structures contain power; they can help or hinder achievement, stifle or enable success. At their best, structures invite and empower contribution. "Put in place structures that foster meaningful participation." (Alexa McDonough, MP; Former Federal NDP Leader, Canada) What structures are best suited to leadership practice and development? Here's what our interviewees had to say:

Conducive to Leadership Practice

Structures should facilitate, not obstruct, the practice of leadership. They have to be solid but not rigid, overpowering, nor too complex. People and ideas must travel freely to stimulate productivity and development. Here are the main attributes of structures conducive to effective leadership practice:

Flat

Cumbersome, heavy structures block the flow of initiative, information and energy. They simply are not suitable to the level of entrepreneurship required for leadership practice. "Break with formal, hierarchical approaches; flatten work organization; do not reduce people to doers." (Gérald Larose, Professor-Researcher, School of Social Work, Université du Québec à Montréal [UQAM])

Structures should be enablers, not obstacles, provide support and require low maintenance. When they demand too much care or become the focus of attention instead of substance, something is wrong. Just like in design, elegance and clean lines are best.

Decentralized

Overly centralized structures are powerful deterrents to leadership, because they create huge bureaucracies where pressures to comply and conform are relentless.

> Centralization is the enemy of leadership, as it destroys it. In order to create a critical mass of leaders, leadership must be awakened and developed in a lot of people. For leadership to thrive, a fluid environment and numerous practice opportunities are required. That is why mergers don't work: They remove leadership opportunities, and institutionalize. Leaders at the helm of these super-sized organizations must be so good that they are few and far between. It's the Alexander the Great syndrome: how many can appear in a generation? (Marc Poulin, President Operations, Québec Region, Sobeys Inc.)

In overly centralized organizations, ownership is reduced and visibility is low, leading to apathy, not to leadership. "Large organizations possess vices inherent to their nature as well as centralizing systems. To create success conditions, it's important to provide responsibilities and stimulate entrepreneurship from within instead of crushing it." (Jocelyn Deschênes, Producer, President, Sphère Média Plus)

Over the course of our careers, we have witnessed constant swings of the pendulum as organizations alternatively centralize and then decentralize in futile attempts to achieve balance. The issue is not *whether* to centralize or decentralize, but rather *what* to centralize and decentralize. Which processes should be common to all parts of the organization? What should flex according to market and regional realities? These are much better questions.

Participative

When people can provide input, and feel that their points of views have been considered, engagement and alignment naturally follow. Therefore, participative structures produce more innovative outcomes and encounter less resistance. "Involve more people in decision making. Allow young bright people to express themselves. Reward them." (Honourable Carole Taylor, O.C., Minister of Finance; M.L.A., Vancouver-Langara, British Columbia Government; Former Chair, CBC/Radio-Canada)

Such structures also promote drive, dynamism, novel solutions. "It's important to put in place a culture and create infrastructures to encourage people to formulate projects. We implemented this here with great results. People propose initiatives and action plans that partly shape our business plans and budgets. It stimulates creativity, risk, and an appetite for calculated risk. Leadership is everything but being passive. It's about encouraging action, engagement." (Simon Brault, O.C., Director General, National Theatre School of Canada)

Empowering

What constitutes an empowering environment? A place where people know what's going on and feel they can make a difference. "Do not stifle people. Reward achievement properly. For example, we have a number of employees who started as crew and moved up to the most senior positions in the organization. Jobs should not be dead ends." (George Cohon, O.C., O.Ont., Founder, McDonald's Restaurants of Canada and McDonald's in Russia)

In order to feel motivated, people want control and to feel that their decisions matter. "Push authority down as far as possible to motivate people. It is risky but worth it." (Bernadette McDonald, Author; Former Vice-President, Mountain Culture, The Banff Centre)

Ultimately, people need to know that their contribution *has* value and *is* valued. "Let's empower people to become actors and fully participate in their own life, leading their work life instead of being led by it. Organizations must have confidence in their employees' intelligence and build their confidence." (Clément Guimond, General Coordinator, Caisse d'économie solidaire Desjardins [Credit Union])

Conducive to Leadership Development

Structures should also facilitate leadership development, not hinder it. "Move people out of their comfort zone across and around the organization. Stretch them and allow for the kind of discomfort required for growth. Breadth of experience and exposure are the best way to expand knowledge." (Diane Rabbani, Human Resources Consultant; Former Deputy Minister, British Columbia)

It starts by making leadership development a priority, rather than an afterthought. "Organizations must be mindful of people development in general and leadership development in particular." (Alban D'Amours, President and CEO, Desjardins Group)

An emphasis on development does not only mean training but also a multitude of methods that expand individual and organizational capability. "Develop an environment of lifelong learning (training allowance, mentoring, volunteering). Make sure you recognize the best out of people, not just what they do wrong." (Sandra Stevenson, President and CEO, Sport BC)

In this perspective, organizations should focus primarily on mastery, not gaps. It's not about compensating for people's weaknesses, but increasing their flow. This is a mindset first, and an infrastructure second. In such a climate, "Everyone is a student and a teacher. People learn from each other and everyone feels important." (Joseph Paquette, Mixed Blood Elder) There is much power and flexibility in this approach: people coaching people in an expanding circle. And through it, individuals gain respect and appreciation for each other's skills, experience and perspective. As the wheel turns, sometimes you receive and sometimes you give, but you always learn.

Here are some of the essential building blocks *besides* programs to construct and reinforce a good leadership development infrastructure.

Framework and Resources

How can you ensure all the pieces of the 'people puzzle' are in place and fit together? "Leaders create a strategic alignment model that aligns culture, structure and processes to achieve strategy. This promotes system thinking and leveraged actions. Balanced Scorecards align initiatives, resources and accountabilities. Balanced Scorecards are about execution of strategy and driving change management." (Bruce Harber, President and CEO, York Central Hospital)

People Strategy

How can you manage your most valuable resource effectively? "Have a well-defined HR strategy in all aspects. Companies should not take employees for granted." (Jim Mills, President and CEO, Office Interiors)

Talent Management

How can you attract, select, orient, develop and manage the 'lifeblood' of your organization? "Identify the leadership competencies that are required. Hire based on these competencies. Assess employees' competencies and recognize the gaps, then have a plan to help them achieve the goals. Provide them on-the-job training, mentoring, coaching, etc." (David Szwarc, Chief Administrative Officer, Region of Peel)

Orientation and Induction

How can you ensure new employees quickly become more productive? Employees need to be embraced by the organization they join. In-depth orientation to the company's values and business are the first steps to solidify a successful and smooth integration. "I believe that support is the essential component in new leader development, as it builds confidence. Therefore, I never refuse to meet young people seeking employment. To develop leadership, we must put our energy in the right places: invest in youth." (François Rebello, President and CEO, Groupe Investissement Responsable [Responsible Investment Group])

Resources

How can you ensure developing leaders are supported as they grow? "Make leadership development one of the company values and make more resources available to support it, from education to experience. All existing leaders should be required to become mentors. We need to teach them to be effective mentors." (Anne McGuire, President and CEO, IWK Health Centre)

Performance Management

How can you reinforce good leadership performance and deal with poor performers? "Commit to performance management with feedback on leadership aspects. When there are gaps, identify and address them." (Joseph Randell, President and CEO, Air Canada Jazz)

Incentives

How can you put in place incentives that truly motivate? "Incentives are often too homogeneous. You need to think outside the box to come up with a variety of incentives. For instance, opportunities to accomplish goals, extra time off, money, responsibility, etc. Overall, you need to understand people." (Graydon Oldfield, Canadian Downhill and Combined Champion, Canadian Alpine Ski Team Association; Branch Manager and Associate Director, Financial Services ScotiaMcLeod)

Succession Planning

How can you make sure your organization is prepared for the future? "Have a succession plan. Take experienced people who have retired and retain them as mentors for fast-track individuals to rejuvenate the organization and improve the next crop of leaders." (Patrick Reid, O.C., M.C., C.D., Chairman, Rick Hansen Foundation)

To summarize, configuration affects outcomes. Your organization's infrastructure will either hinder or facilitate effective leadership practice and development. The choice is yours.

Caring

Just like parenting, leadership development requires a caring atmosphere to promote growth. A punitive, stifling or overly competitive climate will constrict leadership emergence, practice and development. Ample evidence of this phenomenon is visible in dictatorial regimes where people become compliant and subservient, losing the initiative and creativity required to lead.

Johanna Maria Bates-Van der Zeijst, President, Johanna M. Bates Literary Consultants Inc., puts a good principle forward: "Watch out for your employees and they will watch out for the organization." If employees feel important and appreciated, they will give their best. Employees should sense that they are more than a means to an end, a number or a machine. "Learn how to give credit to employees and praise them in a meaningful way." (Peter Istvanffy, President and CEO, Calgary Academy)

Competent but cold leaders have trouble reaching the hearts of their followers; however, competence and caring together constitute an unbeatable combination. "An organization is but an empty shell to be brought to life by the spirit and intent of leaders who should be interested in people, not only in money. People are at the heart of success." (Louise Pelletier, Regional Director, Mauricie Region, Production of the Cascades, Hydro-Québec)

So, show your employees that you care and they will repay a thousandfold. Yvon Bastien, Former President and General Manager, Sanofi Synthelabo Canada, believes the following statement has the power to completely transform the culture of an organization: "The heart, the mind, *and then* the bottom line."

If, like children, employees feel cared for, they blossom, and this includes achieving their leadership potential. This is not just a psychological reality, but a business imperative. In our consulting practices, we are exposed to many organizations and notice the enormous impact corporate cultures have on employees. Caring cultures produce innovative, free, confident employees, while cold, impersonal cultures produce employees who only use a fraction of their abilities and end up being shadows of themselves. Caring matters; it's not a fluffy issue but a condition for success.

Caring for employees means developing the following characteristics:

Holistic

Increasingly, workers can bring more than their head and hands to the workplace—they can also bring their hearts and spirits. Not only is it saner, but more productive, because healthy, integrated individuals tend to be more creative and resilient. Fostering a culture of creativity enhances productivity.

Worldwide, there is now considerable experimentation with the 'whole person at work' concept. Organizations are looking for ways to ensure employees' health and wholeness. "In Japan, they exercise at work and everyone participates, including bosses—very good for team building and physical well-being. For emotional well-being, some organizations provide daycare centres in the workplace, which allow parents to see their children at lunch and to intervene if required. Another idea is to offer horse whispering workshops, which completely transform leadership outlooks, helping leaders focus on their employees." (Natalie Choquette, Diva)

Resilient

Organizations must care enough about their employees' development to allow them to fail without too many negative consequences. Occasional mishaps are unavoidable in order to learn and grow. Organizations must "allow risk, which inevitably means error. We have to demystify risk phobia and build resilience." (Francine Brousseau, Vice-President Development, Canadian Museum of Civilization Corporation)

It is important to put in place systems that allow experimentation while mitigating risks. "Give people opportunities and provide feedback and advice. Assign them in areas of the organization where the risk is not too high to start with; if they are successful, move them to more strategic areas of the business. Set a system to test people and see if they can achieve results." (Gerry Duffy, Strategic Management Consultant; Former Senior Vice-President, Methanex)

Mistakes are great teachers and should be celebrated as character builders. "We need to change our attitude towards failure. Most successful entrepreneurs have had failures; we should not be so intolerant. Being truly negligent is one thing, but if not, let us give people a second chance." (Dr. Jacquelyn Thayer Scott, O.C., Past President and Professor, Cape Breton University; Deputy Chair, Prime Minister's Advisory Council on Science and Technology)

After a setback, it's important to rebuild self-confidence. At this time, employees need more, not less support. "Be willing to give people a chance—coach them. Take extra time to help them learn from their mistakes and … failures." (Michael Pfeiffer, President and CEO, QC Data International Inc.) It's important to enable them to move on, otherwise they get stuck. "Don't constantly look back; recognize your failures and move on. Having the courage and confidence to move on is important." (Frederick MacGillivray, President and CEO, Trade Centre Limited, Halifax)

Most interviewees indicated learning more from adversity than success. Therefore, processes to learn from mistakes are essential—debriefing discussions, tools for reflecting and planning, etc. "Give people opportunities to learn new things and develop. Celebrate accomplishments. View failure as an opportunity to learn, get over the failure and move on." (Mary Hofstetter, President and CEO, The Banff Centre)

Once again, Personal Development Plans can help by providing a structure to make sense of learning experiences. Likewise, coaching and mentoring conversations can be useful to normalize mistakes, putting them in a larger context.

Some organizations promote learning partners, a peer system for providing support and accelerating learning. Other organizations pair up newcomers with established employees as part of a 'buddy system.' This facilitates new employee integration through coaching and learning assistance.

Appreciative

Human nature tends to focus on the negative. As a result, people are starved for appreciation and acknowledgment and low on self-esteem. This can have a devastating impact when times get hard, because self-esteem is the foundation of resilience.

Somehow, people worry that praise will create conceit or that providing it will diminish one's own value; it's quite the opposite. 'A candle loses nothing by lighting another candle.' A wise statement. Here is advice from an expert: "It's important to publicly recognize a job well done. Since I became Lieutenant Governor, I have become more aware of the value of symbols such as medals and other awards, which enable people to walk with their heads held up high." (Honourable Herménégilde Chiasson, Lieutenant Governor, New Brunswick)

The key to successful rewards and recognition programs is variety. Not everyone will consider hockey tickets a reward; therefore, organizations need to have a wide range of rewards and ways to recognize people, publicly and privately. Some high-performing employees feel uncomfortable being recognized during a big event, but will enjoy lunch with the boss in a fine dining establishment.

Determine what is meaningful for the individual. For many, peer recognition is very important. Therefore, several organizations have put in place peer-nominated awards and incentives, a good way to add value and to bring teams together.

In our opinion, organizations are a long way from overdoing rewards and recognition. We need to build workplaces where support and gratitude abound. "Celebrate and recognize leaders on an ongoing basis. Catch people doing something right. Create opportunities to lead." (Marg McGregor, CEO, Canadian Interuniversity Sport)

Climate

One of the most powerful tools to breed quality leaders is a nurturing ecosystem providing possibilities, learning, support and recognition. "Stretch people's potential; conspire for their success by creating an environment within which they are motivated to stretch." (Bruno Biscaro, COO, Accucaps Industries Limited)

There should be an abundance of moments to seize, risks to take, heights to reach. The operative word is 'variety.' "When I worked at the Mississauga Hospital, I was president of the social club. This experience exposed me to many people and I learned a lot. Small things are as important as big things. Encourage people to get involved. How you lead is as important as what you do." (Suzanne Christie, Project Manager, Peel Mentoring Network; Instructor) The climate should literally 'buzz' with possibility. "Give people opportunities to practise leadership. Push for expanding the envelope of opportunities offered. Let them lead and fail—we can be so intolerant of failures." (Mark Surrette, President, Robertson Surrette)

This means freedom to act. "Provide challenges for people to prove their measure in action. Offer opportunities to take on responsibilities and risks. Give them autonomy and a free hand to act." (Pierre David, Executive Director, CMHC International [Canada Mortgage and Housing Corporation])

It is important to encourage everyone to step up to the plate and provide support so they can take the leadership risk. "Create situations where people are stretched. Create programs to give people leadership roles with mentorship to help them. Don't take the easy road of having the same people take on leadership roles all the time; discover others." (Albert Schultz, Founding Artistic Director, Soulpepper Theatre Company)

Tight leashes and plush cocoons are not conducive to responsibility. "Make people accountable; give them, not only the impression they are making a contribution, but provide them with the real means to do so." (François Saillant, Coordinator, Front d'action populaire en réaménagement urbain, FRAPRU [The Popular Face of Action in Urban Refitting])

In order for people to take responsibility, they need the authority and the means to accomplish the job. "Take people out of their comfort zone. Put them in deep water, but if they can't swim, you have to help them. Accept that everyone's level of capability is different." (Paul Henderson, Founder and President, The Leadership Group; Maple Leafs Hockey Alumni) You have to give people room to manoeuvre and relinquish control. "Be open to letting go. You can't be in control all the time. Give support and resources to allow people to succeed. Organizations sometimes set people up to fail. Environments should recognize that failure is not the end of the world, only a setback. It is a stepping stone." (Sue Holloway, Double Olympic Medalist, Kayak)

Climates are by-products of cultures, which, in turn, are anchored by values and behaviours. To create an environment conducive to leadership emergence, practice and development, organizations need to consciously work at shaping their corporate culture.

The best organizations spend a lot of time, not only defining their values and accompanying behaviours, but integrating them into all of their people systems, from recruitment to performance management and promotions. This way, the culture is kept alive and reinforced by systems.

Moreover, they take great pains to articulate their culture and communicate about it through various means, including symbols and slogans that grab people's attention. For instance, one organization has a 'value garden' in its lobby, representing its value structure and interdependencies. In another organization, the finance department rebranded its image by redefining the value its members bring to their internal customers and capturing it in this catchy slogan: 'Not just dollars, but sense!'

As practitioners, it has been our experience that cultures are like gardens. Neglect means that weeds eventually take over. To achieve the desired garden or culture requires a plan, nurturing and ongoing maintenance.

CONCLUSION

Organizations, like individuals, must shoulder some responsibility for leadership emergence, practice and development. Organizations can do a lot to create an environment where leadership will flourish. Moreover, it is to their advantage to do so: The more quality leaders they produce, the better off the organization will be. It requires an investment, but eventually produces a good return. "The organization will be as strong as its staff. Investing in their development is the same as investing in R&D." (Ben Nind, Artist; Executive and Artistic Director, Northern Arts & Cultural Centre)

Organizations need to view these efforts as 'hard,' not 'soft.' "There is reluctance to invest in employee learning. Progressive employers should invest a percentage of their budget towards education." (Robbie Shaw, President, IWK Foundation)

Bottom line: You get what you pay for and work for.

CHAPTER 10

CO-OP FUNDAMENTALS

We started with a premise: With great leaders, great things happen. There is a strong correlation between good leadership and high performance.
Grace Pulver
Vice-President, Human Resources, Vancity Credit Union

Leadership has many faces. Too often, it is seen as the 'I have the microphone' skill set, but it is much deeper and more influential. The most important leadership role is people development; not just lip service, but leaving behind a legacy of leaders. Often I hear, 'He is not a leader.' I disagree. A better phrase is 'our environment does not promote leadership.' Are leaders born? I don't believe so. Are leaders developed? Always! If leadership does not involve people, we are lost.
Michael Barrett
Vice-President, Human Resources and Corporate Secretary
Gay Lea Foods Co-operative Limited

AN INTERESTING ALTERNATIVE

Throughout our research, people said that the leadership style bound to succeed in today's global and interdependent world is democratic and based on common interests. It is anchored in influence rather than authority, empowerment not control, collaboration instead of dominance. It's looking for the win-win solutions that have a chance to last.

Likewise, interviewees expressed doubts about the pyramid still being the optimal structure. Instead, they talked about networks, circles, teams, etc., which seem more conducive to today's realities and mindsets.

Why Co-ops?

We researched co-operatives, organizations that, by nature, are configured accordingly: Co-ops seek to balance their social and economic mandates and are acutely aware of the need to provide leadership to the community.

We interviewed a representative sample of co-ops in all sectors of the economy and regions of the country, in order to understand how leadership is practised and developed in this environment. We spoke to a variety of co-ops in retail, financial, farming, health care, forestry, energy, food and funeral services.

We were extremely impressed by the level of resourcefulness and community spirit encountered, and learned a lot about sustainable economic development and the power of people pulling together to achieve goals.

This research yielded a high number of best practices applicable to other sectors; we've listed them at the end of Chapter 11: Best Practices from the Co-op Sector. In this chapter, we will provide some context and define the co-op framework.

What Is a Co-operative?

In 1995, as part of the Manchester Conference, the International Co-operative Alliance approved the following definition of a co-operative: "A co-operative is an autonomous association of persons united voluntarily to meet their common economic, social, and cultural needs and aspirations, through a jointly-owned and democratically-controlled enterprise."

The Canadian Co-operative Association (CCA) expands on this definition: "A co-operative is an organization owned by the members who use its services.

Co-operatives can provide virtually any product or service, and can be either a non-profit or for-profit enterprise. Co-ops and credit unions provide consumers with a distinct values-based, community-owned and controlled alternative. Unlike the private, public, or voluntary sectors, all co-operatives around the world are guided by the same seven principles:

1. Voluntary and open membership.
2. Democratic member control.
3. Member economic participation.
4. Autonomy and independence.
5. Education, training and information.
6. Co-operation among co-operatives.
7. Concern for community."

(Excerpt from www.coopscanada.coop, Canadian Co-operative Association [CCA], January 2007.)

This blueprint is used worldwide. It emphasizes inclusiveness, heavy member participation and control, autonomy, continuing education and interdependence. As you can see, only one of these principles is concerned with finances. Therefore, the 'bottom line' is by no means the only driver for co-operatives—social and economic mandates both matter. "Contrary to the scandals, skepticism and concerns that the sole pursuit of profit generates, the co-op movement brings a breath of fresh air, an ethical flavour." (Bruno-Marie Béchard, Rector, Université de Sherbrooke, excerpt from a speech given at the Gala du mérite coopératif de l'Estrie [Gala celebrating Co-operative Merit in the Eastern Townships] on October 29, 2005)

Here are some interesting facts about the vibrancy of the co-op sector. "Co-operatives exist in every sector of the economy and can touch every aspect of our lives. You can be born in a health care co-op and buried by a funeral co-op. In between, you can work in a workers' co-op, live in a housing co-op, buy your groceries, clothing and other items from retail co-ops, send your children to a child care co-op, do all your banking at a credit union, and purchase your insurance from an insurance co-op.

In the World

- Co-operatives around the world employ 20% more people than do large multinational corporations.
- Worldwide, 800 million people are members of a co-operative or credit union.

- In the UK, the London Symphony Orchestra, Philharmonic and London Philharmonic are all run as co-operatives.

In Canada

- There are 9,500 co-operatives and credit unions in Canada. The earliest Canadian co-operative began with the formation of a farmers' mutual fire insurance company in the mid-1800s. Co-operatives and credit unions employ over 155,000 Canadians.
- Four out of every ten Canadians are members of a co-operative or credit union. Over 70,000 Canadians volunteer their time to serve on co-op and credit union boards. Three-quarters of co-ops consult with members and board members to determine community needs.
- Canadian co-operatives and credit unions give approximately $60 million annually to their communities through donations and sponsorships.
- Canadian co-operatives and credit unions have combined assets of approximately $300 billion. In 900 communities across Canada, a credit union is the only financial institution." (Excerpt from www.coopscanada.coop, Canadian Co-operative Association [CCA], January 2007.)

As we can see from these examples, co-ops represent a vibrant and viable formula for economic and social development.

How Do Co-ops Get Started?

Often, the motivation to start a co-op is a need that cannot be met through traditional means. For example, "In Vancouver, the Tech Co-op was founded by computer users and technology professionals frustrated with conventional approaches to computer servicing." (Excerpt from 'Co-ops in British Columbia' leaflet, www.coopscanada.coop, Canadian Co-operative Association [CCA], January 2007.)

At other times, the impetus is solving a persistent problem, improving community well-being or responding to emerging needs, thereby innovating. "The Harrop-Procter Community Co-operative used the co-op model to advance a new approach to forestry in B.C. For the first time, local loggers and environmentalists are working together to harvest trees." (Excerpt from 'Co-ops in British Columbia' leaflet, www.coopscanada.coop, Canadian Co-operative Association [CCA], January 2007.)

In the same vein, Desjardins, the largest financial co-op in Canada, with $118,068 billion dollars in assets and counting (December 2005) as well as more than 5 million members across Canada, was founded by Alphonse Desjardins in 1900 to "facilitate access to savings and loans for the average person. Through research, he came up with a project for a new kind of savings and loan co-operative that would enable the working class to become its own banker and provide communities with an instrument for economic organization and development." (Adapted from www.desjardins.com, Desjardins Group, January 2007.)

Similarly, the United Farmers of Alberta Co-operative was formed "over 90 years ago to give Alberta farmers a voice in shaping the future of their province and enable members to co-operatively purchase farm supplies and other goods or services, combining maximum economic benefit and service." (Adapted from www.ufa.net, United Farmers of Alberta Co-operative Limited, January 2007.)

Because co-ops fulfill unmet needs or solve problems in a new way, they often pioneer trends that may seem marginal at first, but soon become commonplace.

For example, co-ops started the health food revolution in the '70s. A similar phenomenon happened in agriculture, where they led the push for organic foods, and in retail, where they showed the way to less and more healthy packaging. Currently, some co-ops are innovating with the introduction of bio-fuels. Co-ops are now at the forefront of innovation in the field of alternative energy and in such areas as fair trade. (John Restakis, Executive Director, British Columbia Co-operative Association)

Not only do co-ops come up with innovative trends, but they also develop new mindsets that eventually transfer to other sectors of the economy. For example, 'Corporate Social Responsibility' (CSR) and 'ethical investments' were brainchildren of the co-op movement. They now permeate the private sector, where they have become a *fait accompli*. Co-ops are indeed hotbeds for innovation.

Bottom line, the birth of a co-op is always about a group of people who pull together to improve a state of affairs and create a new reality. As such, empowerment, not passivity, is fostered. "Co-ops represent an important means for people to take control of their destiny and develop their leadership skills. As such, they counteract the tendency to let the state take charge and create dependency." (Alban D'Amours, President and CEO, Desjardins Group)

How Do Co-ops Function?

"The primary purpose of co-operatives and credit unions is to meet the common needs of their members, whereas the primary purpose of most investor-owned businesses is to maximize profit for shareholders. Co-operatives and credit unions use the one-member/one-vote system, not the one-vote-per-share system used by most businesses. Co-operatives and credit unions share profits among their member-owners on the basis of how much they use the co-op, not on how many shares they hold. Co-operatives and credit unions also tend to invest their profits in improving service to members and promoting the well-being of their communities." (Excerpt from www.coopscanada.coop, Canadian Co-operative Association [CCA], January 2007.)

Therefore, co-ops are like organic ecosystems that must manage several dynamics to achieve a healthy and sustainable balance. For instance, financial health is a legitimate goal, but not at the cost of social responsibility and ethics. Community growth is desirable, but not without considering its long-term implications. Success is sought after, but not if it means losing one's identity. Balancing and reconciling polarities, which are at times opposites, is a constant concern. "SaskCentral and the credit unions of Saskatchewan share a common vision of growing communities through innovation, social responsibility and financial strength." (Excerpt from www.saskcentral.com, SaskCentral, January 2007.)

Accordingly, the notion of balance often came up in interviewees' discourse. For example, respondents were acutely aware of the imperative to keep the past, present and future in their sightlines—staying connected to their roots, while strategically envisioning the future and effectively managing the present. For instance, succession planning strategies for the Ontario Co-op Association include "an internship program offered to young interns annually and the appointment of one board member under 25." (Denyse Guy, Executive Director, Ontario Co-operative Association)

As mentioned earlier, while co-ops operate like businesses, profit is not the sole decision-making criterion. Stakeholder relationships between customers, members, employees and the community also require attention. Task and process are two other critical components to balance—it's not just what you do, but how you do it. Interviewees reported a tendency to focus on common interests and resolve tensions instead of letting them escalate. For instance, Co-op Atlantic "recently went through an extensive strategic planning process. Not only did we reflect on issues such as niche markets and competitive advantages, but also on openness to members and building trusting relationships." (Léo LeBlanc, Vice-President Human Resources and Corporate Affairs; Corporate Secretary, Co-op Atlantic)

Therefore, concepts like *win-win solutions, sustainable development* and *balanced scorecard* peppered respondents' comments, as did words like *consultation, input* and *transparency*. Co-ops seem to function according to this popular adage: 'If you plan the battle, you don't battle the plan.' Inclusive decision-making may take more time, but once decisions are made, people move forward in an aligned and determined fashion, speeding up implementation. Therefore, the only issue is where you want to spend your time: combatting resistance, or consulting people to achieve better decisions and less resistance.

As a result, co-ops' interests span over a long-term horizon, reflect the multiplicity of stakeholders' perspectives, and balance drivers such as financial health, community growth and social responsibility. By driving balance and responsibility, the co-op culture is eminently conducive to leadership emergence, practice and development.

How Are Co-ops Organized?

We soon realized that the co-op world is made of networks of networks, forming and reforming to foster greater collaboration, efficiency and economies of scale. Firstly, co-ops group individuals or entities who can benefit from working together. For example, Agropur coopérative, a dairy co-op, enables "4,060 Canadian dairy farmers located in four provinces to benefit from a system integrating collection, production, packaging and distribution for their products. Generating sales of over two billion dollars, the resulting products grace the tables of thousands of Canadians from coast to coast." (Adapted from www.agropur.com, Agropur coopérative, January 2007.)

Secondly, wholesaler co-op organizations provide services to member co-ops. Co-op Atlantic is a dynamic wholesaler providing "goods and services to 129 member co-operatives across Atlantic Canada. Our member co-operatives, in turn, are community businesses owned and operated by the people they serve. Collectively, these co-ops serve over 200,000 families and employ over 5,000 people, generating annual sales of $500 million." (Adapted from www.coopatlantic. ca, Co-op Atlantic, January 2007.)

Thirdly, sector co-ops congregate to better serve and represent common needs and interests. Usually, these groupings are called federations and act like professional associations, advocating with governments on policy issues that matter to the sector. For instance, the Canadian Worker Co-operative Federation (CWCF) provides "a voice for worker co-ops on the national stage and encourages the development of more worker co-ops. Worker co-ops aim to improve the lives of working people and increase democracy in the workplace through worker ownership and control." (Excerpt from www.coopscanada.coop, Canadian Co-operative Association [CCA], January 2007.)

Fourthly, co-ops regroup geographically to represent their members in a given territory, such as a province. For instance, the Nova Scotia Co-operative Council "brings all types and sectors of co-operatives together to form a strong co-operative movement in Nova Scotia. It acts as an advocate for co-operatives with the municipal, provincial, and federal governments and encourages the development of a 'co-operative identity' among the public of Nova Scotia." (Dianne Kelderman, Chief Executive Officer, Nova Scotia Co-operative Council)

How Do Co-ops Evolve?

Co-ops are like 'the little engine that could,' started by groups of determined people. Some grow very big. "Mountain Equipment Co-op was conceived in 1971 within the cozy confines of a storm-battered tent. While enduring a savage mountain storm, a small group of students agreed they needed a place to buy gear not carried by conventional retailers. Today, MEC is Canada's largest supplier of quality outdoor equipment. With more than two million members in 192 countries, we're a vibrant retail co-operative." (Adapted from www.mec.ca, Mountain Equipment Co-op, January 2007.) Peter Robinson, the CEO, added, "Co-ops give people opportunities to learn and contribute. People go through rich experiences and come back enthused and with more knowledge. The co-op model becomes an experience-based opportunity."

In his landmark book, *The 7 Habits of Highly Effective People* (Simon & Schuster, New York, 1989), Stephen Covey suggests that as they grow individuals and organizations move from dependence to independence and finally to interdependence. First, become autonomous, next, collaborate and synergize. Interdependence is a partnership between independent entities, not an alliance between co-dependent beings. Interdependence should not be confused with co-dependency.

Like other organizations, co-ops evolve according to L.E. Greiner's 'Growth Curve' model presented below:

Illustration 10.1

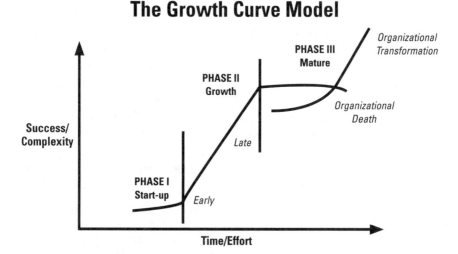

The Growth Curve Model

Adapted from L.E. Greiner, Evolution and Revolution as Organizations Grow, *HBR*, July-August 1972, no. 4. P. 37-46

Co-ops undergo the same challenges as other, more traditional organizations: survival during start-up, infrastructure development during growth, and renewal during maturity. For instance, Gay Lea Foods Co-operative, a mature organization, "has recently undergone a process of renewal and revitalization through a redefinition of business focus and an injection of fresh leadership," said Michael Barrett, Vice-President Human Resources and Corporate Secretary. Therefore, leadership requirements change according to growth stages.

For community-based entities, the growth phase presents special difficulties because of the extensive capitalization required to fund infrastructure investments in technology, human resources and physical assets. Moreover, expansion can trigger an identity crisis: How can a co-op grow while preserving the co-operative identity? How can it broaden the definition of community to include people in other provinces or sectors of the economy? A lot of soul-searching takes place at this critical juncture. "I came at a difficult time. The co-op had, to a degree, lost touch with its identity, was not paying enough attention to clients, and had little sense of shared vision. So I spent time connecting with our people and soon realized the flame was still flickering, but strong winds were blowing all around. I really listened and found ways to allow people to be part of something inspiring." (Kathy Bardswick, President and CEO, The Co-Operators)

As a result, a variety of solutions emerge, ranging from adopting 'niche market' or 'regional' strategies, which dictate slower growth, to rolling out 'identity preservation' strategies while pursuing aggressive development. "Even though this is a large enterprise, the co-op fibre is nurtured through various roles: a VP of institutional affairs, eight co-op advisors who provide a helping hand to co-op members, and facilitators who manage groups of producers where co-op business is discussed." (Robert Lavallée, Director, Organizational Development, Agropur coopérative)

Growth requires adopting a valid business model, said Quintin Fox, Manager of Member Services, Canadian Co-operative Association. "The history of co-operative development shows that the replication and development of a limited number of proven models normally tends to be the main driver of growth of the co-operative system, rather than across-the-board surges of interest in co-operation in all its forms."

Dianne Kelderman, Chief Executive Officer, Nova Scotia Co-operative Council, added, "We are doomed to fail if the image we project is 'poor us, we need help, charity and special treatment.' We don't play that game. The image we project is one of action and delivering. We do what we say and we can demonstrate that we are making a significant difference."

This means becoming more businesslike, which can present capability challenges. Do people have the required skills? If not, how quickly can imported external resources acquire the co-operative mindset? Raising the skill level of current stakeholders or inducting new resources into the co-op mentality invariably involves a considerable investment in development. Co-ops demonstrate a realistic outlook about these issues. They know that culture fit is important to succeed in a given environment.

Like all entrepreneurial organizations, co-ops are hotbeds of innovation and resourcefulness, but when growth comes, they need to become efficient and effective. Implementing operational excellence can prove demanding. "I think the co-op sector generates many innovative best practices. The challenge is to execute well." (Kathy Bardswick, President and CEO, The Co-Operators)

Once these growth issues are resolved, however, they can move forward with confidence. For instance, "Desjardins wants to become the best integrated co-operative financial group in the world. This means getting international recognition for the ability to combine co-operative and financial performance. In this regard, it can count on the assistance of Développement International Desjardins, active for 35 years in 50 countries, all over the world. The co-op formula offers new alternatives because its outlook goes beyond quarterly results to embrace the long term, and enables values sharing. Développement International Desjardins attests to Desjardins' commitment to fight against poverty on a global scale." (Alban D'Amours, President and CEO, Desjardins Group)

LEADERSHIP STYLE

"The co-op model is not based on a win-lose approach: bringing value to both sides is important. This doesn't mean we don't negotiate, but we are careful to bring value to the other side. We aim for win-win solutions." (Sid Bildfell, CEO, SaskCentral) This statement sums up the overall style, focused on common, rather than opposing, interests. Because collaboration is important, co-ops value relationships and are willing to invest time to build them. "We don't have a standard approach; others are different and it takes time to adapt and work together. We learn to respect differences," continued Mr. Bildfell.

A Blended Approach

Therefore, co-ops combine business, community and democratic styles, inspired by their social and economic mandates. Both mandates must be balanced to maintain equilibrium in the ecosystem. As a result, leadership style tends to be inclusive and consulting processes are extensively used. "Democratic processes are a key operational component of co-op enterprises. Co-op leaders are elected by the membership to serve on the co-op's board of directors. The board develops a strong working relationship with management and employees. The board is also required by legislation to consult with the members, particularly on policy issues that affect the overall operations of the co-op." (Glen Fitzpatrick, Managing Director, Newfoundland and Labrador Federation of Co-operatives)

In many ways, co-ops are typical of the blended model currently sought after by both the public and the private sectors. The last 10 to 15 years have witnessed a spectacular evolution as both sectors endeavour to acquire their counterpart's best attributes. The public sector has deployed tremendous efforts to become more efficient, transparent and service oriented—upgrading technology, streamlining processes and consulting citizens. Meanwhile, the private sector has become more socially responsible and community invested, while striving for a longer-term perspective and implementing balanced metrics that go beyond the bottom line.

Nowhere is this blended approach better illustrated than in Crown and Government Corporations, which, when successful, manifest the best of both worlds, combining bottom-line concerns and efficiency with lofty ideals and sound public policies. Blended approaches constitute a growing trend in organizational infrastructure and strategy design.

They also mirror the organic reality of family life, where people have to make it work over the long term and reconcile different agendas and viewpoints. Pierre Dion, President and CEO, TVA Group Inc, said, "You can't run a family like a business. At home, you can't delegate like at the office. Transitioning between both is not always an easy task. To demonstrate good leadership, you must balance family, work, personal life, mental, physical and financial health, and giving back to the community. It's quite a challenge."

Solid Foundations

Co-operatives have a firm grasp on leadership's purpose: service. "The ultimate goal of co-operation is to improve quality of life. Therefore, all co-operative activity is inspired by service to people and their community. Service is perceived as both the source and purpose of the economy." (Alain Leclerc, Executive Director, Fédération des coopératives funéraires du Québec [Québec Federation of Funeral Co-operatives]) Cheryl Byrne, Vice-President, Knowledge Services, Credit Union Central of Canada, summed it up well: "We have come to realize that we are servant leaders." Because of the need to balance social and economic mandates, co-ops tend to be very aware of the service dimension.

What and who is the co-op serving and how? Once these questions are resolved, the next step is to put the foundations—values and ethics—in place. Although also used in other sectors, these seem pervasive in the co-op world, anchored in the fabric of everyday life, not an add-on. Most interviewees prefaced their comments by stating their organization's values and explaining how they act as a foundation for everything else:

- "Our values and code of ethics are present all over our documentation. The code is discussed during performance discussions. It is used through our value proposition. We do not shy away from talking about values." (Sid Bildfell, CEO, SaskCentral)
- "Our values constitute the basis of our organization's business ethics and form the underpinning of our entire set of relationships. Applying our values represents a distinctive competitive advantage. Passing on values is more than just communicating them. To integrate co-op values, you have to live by them." (Ernest Desrosiers, Former Chef de l'exploitation [COO], La Coop fédérée)

Over and over, respondents stressed that, for the organization and its stakeholders to succeed, the first and foremost condition is abiding by the co-operative's principles, values and code of ethics. As a result, co-ops expend huge efforts to make sure foundations are alive and continue to provide a framework for decision-making, which in turn impact actions and behaviours. In other words, an effective leadership style combines appropriate behaviours based on strong principles.

Concern for People

"Among the co-op movement's assets is a preoccupation above all for people. In order for co-operation to blossom, concepts like teams, empowerment, equitable sharing, participation and democratic management are absolutely necessary." (Bruno-Marie Béchard, Rector, Université de Sherbrooke, excerpt from a speech given at the Gala du mérite coopératif de l'Estrie [Gala celebrating Co-operative Merit in the Eastern Townships] on October 29, 2005)

For co-ops, people are both the reason for being, and the means to success. "You need to see people as the root of success instead of concentrating first on strategy, otherwise you will not succeed. First, spend time with people and see what they think, and then, together, come up with the best strategy to achieve desired results. Buy-in is important." (Dave Mowat, CEO, Vancity Credit Union) Therefore, co-ops seek to create environments where people can make a contribution, express their individuality and collaborate.

Mutual Assistance

Co-ops help each other in all kinds of ways. For instance, large financial co-ops provide funding and sponsorship to start-up co-ops. Sometimes, co-ops band together to form a united front. For instance, in response to an 'American invasion' of their marketplace, Funeral Co-ops in Québec joined together to offer competitive prices and compassionate services, hence the inception of the Fédération des coopératives funéraires du Québec [Québec Federation of Funeral Co-operatives], the largest service-delivery network in the province, with over 100 locations.

Co-ops also create alliances to achieve efficiencies and economies of scale for the benefit of their members. "In today's financial services marketplace, credit unions have better reasons than ever to work together across local and provincial boundaries to achieve efficiencies and economies of scale, and to make possible service offerings to members." (Cheryl Byrne, Vice-President, Knowledge Services, Credit Union Central of Canada)

Resourcefulness and Creativity

Resourcefulness and creativity constitute another trademark. Because of their inception patterns, co-ops travel in uncharted territory. This requires a firm belief in possibility and a 'can-do attitude' coupled with fierce determination. "Boisaco Inc. was born of the will of the community to take charge of its future, following three successive entrepreneurial bankruptcies. Our goal was to make profitable a large sawmill and provide employment for the local workforce. Today, Boisaco Inc. is one of the largest independent producers of softwood lumber in Québec." (Alain Dufour, Executive Director, Co-op Cofor)

Innovative thinking is required to generate new ideas and alternatives. Here are some examples:

- The **Multi-Cultural Health Brokers Co-operative** is a unique worker co-op of "mostly foreign-trained health professionals who provide culturally appropriate health services to immigrants and refugee families living in Edmonton." (Excerpts from 'Co-ops in Alberta' leaflet, www.coopscanada. coop, Canadian Co-operative Association [CCA], January 2007.)
- The **People's Car Co-operative** of Kitchener-Waterloo became the first "legally incorporated car-sharing co-operative in Ontario in 1998. Since then, it has provided a growing fleet of co-owned vehicles to its members." (Excerpts from 'Co-ops in Ontario' leaflet, www.coopscanada.coop, Canadian Co-operative Association [CCA], January 2007.)

- **Evangeline Community Health Services Co-op** in Wellington, PEI, was founded when "local residents organized to fill the gap created by the retirement of their local doctor. It was chosen by the province as a pilot site for a community health centre in the region, focusing on prevention and health maintenance." (Excerpts from 'Co-ops in PEI' leaflet, www.coopscanada. coop, Canadian Co-operative Association [CCA], January 2007.)
- Québec boasts **42 co-operatives** providing "at-home services such as cleaning and meal preparation for seniors and others who need them. In 2003-2004, these co-ops generated revenues of $42.6 million." (Adapted from 'Saviez-vous que?' [Did you know that?] leaflet www.coopQuebec.coop, Conseil québécois de la coopération et de la mutualité, January 2007)

The possibilities are endless and only limited by imagination.

CONCLUSION

Balance is the word in the co-op sector: between social and economic mandates, business and community needs, short and long term. In many ways, co-ops have more experience with the fine art of balance than the private and the business sector. Let's see how this applies in the next chapter.

CHAPTER 11

BEST PRACTICES FROM THE CO-OP SECTOR

Whether for the CEO or a clerk, job performance includes values like honesty and respect. These must be expressed in a concrete way, such as community involvement: to learn and share.
   Barry Delaney
   Senior Vice-President, Governance and Strategy, Envision Financial

Our objective is to attract and keep highly skilled, well-educated and experienced people. By creating excitement around the work they do, we shape an environment where they choose to stay. We want success and innovation. Co-ops are doing a good job and people attracted to them are looking for collective action.
   Dianne Kelderman
   Chief Executive Officer, Nova Scotia Co-operative Council

LEADERSHIP PRACTICE

In co-ops, leadership practice is as interesting as their blended leadership style. For starters, co-ops operate according to the critical mass paradigm—everyone is expected to lead in some capacity. Therefore, co-ops provide numerous opportunities to lead and to grow as a leader. They also set up smart structures to facilitate leading. Let's examine this issue in more detail.

Infrastructure

If structure drives outcomes, than the co-op container has a better chance of producing the critical mass of leaders required today. "Everyone has to play a part. The organization supports leadership from all quadrants because of who we are and whom we serve." (Sid Bildfell, CEO, SaskCentral)

Co-ops can draw from a vast pool of potential leaders, including members, elected officials, employees and managers. They also attract leaders from their customer and community bases. For instance, a person from the community might become a member and, eventually, an elected official.

Illustration 11.1

Co-op's Leadership Pool

Moreover, the infrastructure fosters empowerment instead of dependence and passivity. For instance, "Arctic Co-operatives Limited is a significant economic force in the Artic. It is owned and controlled by 35 community-based co-operative business enterprises. In 2004, co-ops reported a total revenue increase of $127 million." (Excerpts from www.arcticco-op.com, Arctic Co-operatives Limited, January 2007.)

Expectations

Because of the community orientation, everyone is expected to demonstrate some leadership, regardless of position. In other words, show up, pull up your sleeves, and lead. This expectation is grounded in necessity as well as in co-operative philosophy: Leadership potential exists everywhere. It's almost like growing up on a farm and having to pitch in. Level of interest or capability doesn't matter; somehow, you must find a way to contribute.

To illustrate this concept, here's an anecdote shared by Jean-Guy Vienneau, Professeur, École de Kinésiologie et de Récréologie [Professor, Kinesiology and Recreology Department], Université de Moncton: "In the beginning, we wanted to equip community leaders with the tools to lead. We defined competencies and designed training programs, for instance in facilitation skills and conflict resolution. We sought to develop principles to guide community leaders in the decision-making process. We also helped them craft a vision for their community." In creating these programs, the university demonstrated leadership and gave community leaders the tools to get on with the business of leadership.

Not surprisingly, this expectation is more conducive to leadership emergence than stifling hierarchical systems. It almost mirrors the V flying formation pattern of Canadian geese, in which different birds take the lead in succession. You have to 'sail your ship' and that is all there is to it.

On top of applying to all stakeholders a generic leadership expectation, co-ops are increasingly defining expectations for specific leadership groups, such as members, officers, employees and managers. "We expect employees to be proactive, make decisions and demonstrate innovation. As for elected officials (Board of Directors), we expect them to make sound decisions to support the growth of Agropur coopérative in the long term." (Robert Lavallée, Director, Organizational Development, Agropur coopérative)

Therefore, co-ops, in expanding numbers, boast competency systems that clearly identify expectations and put in place systems to support the acquisition and application of those competencies. "For management, the practice of leadership is supported and reinforced through eight competencies and a leadership enhancement program." (Nancy Rooney, Director, Organizational Development, Co-operators General Insurance Company)

Not only are expectations spelled out, they are integrated into the business strategy and reinforced at the individual level. "The skills required to drive forward are communicated in the strategic plan and present in personal performance plans." (Michael Barrett, Vice-President Human Resources and Corporate Secretary, Gay Lea Foods Co-operative Limited)

Moreover, they continually rise. "Expectations for elected officials used to be: provide good direction, oversight and financial prudence. Now the Board has to take a more active leadership role." (John Restakis, Executive Director, British Columbia Co-operative Association)

Officers are required to take a proactive role. "We assign each Board Member to branches and they visit them three times a year to talk with staff, meet members and learn more about our business. We also want them to participate in community events four times a year." (Barry Delaney, Senior Vice-President, Governance and Strategy, Envision Financial)

Walking the Talk

In such a context, co-ops better behave like leaders or they will be taken to task by their many stakeholders. This mindset is illustrated by the new direction forged by Bruno-Marie Béchard, Rector, Université de Sherbrooke, for his institution, "Sherbrooke: a Leading University and a University of Leaders."

This kind of organizational leadership is eminently visible in Saskatchewan, where "co-ops were a force before the birth of the province. Today, the province boasts 1,300 co-ops in virtually every sector, providing employment for 15,000 people, controlling $10 billion in assets. Three of Canada's top 100 employers, as ranked by *Maclean's* magazine in 2004, are Saskatchewan-based co-operatives." (Excerpts from 'Co-ops in Saskatchewan' leaflet, www.coopscanada.coop, Canadian Co-operative Association [CCA], January 2007.)

It starts with field leadership. "The Newfoundland Filmmakers Co-operative was born in 1975 from the desire to tell Newfoundland stories on the big screen and work in the field without having to leave the province. To date, over 200 films have been produced ranging from short animations to feature-length dramas, television series and documentaries." (Excerpt from 'Co-ops in Newfoundland and Labrador' leaflet, www.coopscanada.coop, Canadian Co-operative Association [CCA], January 2007.)

Behaving like a leader organization requires heightened awareness of community responsibility and understanding of the change agent role. "Our people will change roles, be volunteers and take on projects. Executives will spend time sharing community work with staff. A big focus is corporate responsibility." (Nancy Rooney, Director, Organizational Development, Co-operators General Insurance Company)

Stakeholder Alignment

How is this kind of organizational leadership possible? Through alignment. Because co-ops are democratic organizations with many stakeholders, alignment around a common vision is critical. "No clans, one vision: buy-in, commitment and boldness!" (Guy Benoît, President, Coop Santé Aylmer Health Co-op)

A strong and clear vision literally holds these stakeholders together. "We have a vision and involve staff about how we can work together. Today, healthy employees want to have a say, and for us to succeed, they have to support the vision." (Barry Delaney, Senior Vice-President, Governance and Strategy, Envision Financial)

Alignment is no small feat. Extensive rounds of consultation and approval are required. "We use the **W** technique, which consists of the following steps: First, a mandate is obtained from the Board; second, input is solicited from people and their ideas synthesized; third, the Board is asked for feedback. The Board will then fine-tune the proposition, and stakeholders will be consulted about it. Finally, the input-loaded proposition is brought back to the Board for final approval." (Ernest Desrosiers, Former Chef de l'exploitation [COO], La Coop fédérée)

Here's another powerful technique shared by Barry Delaney, Senior Vice-President, Governance and Strategy, Envision Financial: "The vision is communicated by the management team. One technique that we use is to go to a branch before they open the doors, and have what we call a coffee session. We always talk about vision and strategy and how they relate to the issues of the day. As each Executive Team Member has high-level speaking notes, the result is that staff gets a consistent message delivered face to face. The *Globe & Mail* highlighted this as a best practice."

Once everyone is aligned, the four primary stakeholder groups—members, elected officials (sometimes called Officers or Board Members), employees and managers—need to:

- Understand and commit to executing their organization's strategic plan: directions, priorities, objectives, etc.
- Know their respective roles and responsibilities.
- Possess the knowledge, competencies, *savoir faire* and professional dedication to play their part.
- Work collaboratively.

These inclusive practices are increasingly adopted by other sectors. Inclusion and alignment currently constitute a powerful trend. In co-ops, it's a way of life.

Continuous Improvement Strategies

How do co-ops improve the practice of leadership? We discovered many creative practices that are eminently transferable to other sectors.

Board Members

"Leadership on governance is the prime role of the Board, as they need to carry the vision of the co-op. Managing and doing the work of the co-op is usually carried out at the staff level. That said, leadership and management should also be shared responsibilities, and the Board and staff need to find a comfort level in dividing up responsibilities and leadership roles." (Carol Murray, Co-op Resource Specialist, Alberta Community and Co-operative Association)

Board Officers play a crucial role in governance, especially because members own their co-operative and elect their leaders according to the one member/one vote system. Therefore, like in any democracy, it's in everyone's best interest to elect competent and trustworthy individuals. On this front, co-ops face the same issues as the public sector: How can they attract quality candidates? How can they set up optimal infrastructures and provide support?

On the attraction/selection front, many co-ops have defined criteria for effective officers and are taking proactive steps to solicit quality candidates. "In the past, directors were not well-prepared to play their role. Therefore, we developed pamphlets to provide information for Board Members and now engage in more promotion to recruit strong officers." (Léo LeBlanc, Vice-President, Human Resources and Corporate Affairs; Corporate Secretary, Co-op Atlantic)

Co-ops have also clarified the profile of a good candidate for their context. Understandably, this picture varies across the land. Here are a few things said:

- "We look for candidates with high morals and ethics and who can commit to the principles governing co-op life. Modesty and sobriety are also high concerns; we don't want to mix with alcohol." (William Lyall, President, Arctic Co-operatives Limited)
- "We are starting to look for directors who are business minded, engaged in the community, and within the 28 to 35 age bracket." (Barry Delaney, Senior Vice-President, Governance and Strategy, Envision Financial)
- "We want committed people, who can easily get involved in their environment. Community spirit can be developed over time. Moreover, the Maritimes culture really helps foster this kind of community spirit." (René Legacy, Vice-President, Communications and Strategy, Fédération des caisses populaires acadiennes [Federation of Acadian Credit Unions])

Recruiting candidates with strong leadership skills makes it easier to develop their governance skills, which can be nurtured through a number of strategies. "Groups, such as the Association of Credit Union Presidents, were set up to help board members make enlightened decisions. (René Legacy, Vice-President, Communications and Strategy, Fédération des caisses populaires acadiennes [Federation of Acadian Credit Unions])

Extensive development is required. "It's important to invest time developing officers and help them transition from an operational focus to a more involved, strategic stage." (Jocelyn Lessard, Executive Director, Fédération québécoise des coopératives forestières [Québec Federation of Forestry Co-operatives]) Many have come to the conclusion that a formal *certification* process is required. This is a fantastic idea to even out the playing field. "The certification process is emphasized for elected officials and gaining in importance. It is increasingly taken seriously." (Claude Gauthier, Director of Operations, Growmark Inc.)

A certification process ensures elected leaders acquire a common knowledge base, language, values and skills. For instance, La Coop fédérée offers a "certification program for elected officials, comprised of 15 credit courses and three levels. The program also credits participation in co-op activities." (Adapted from www. coopfed.qc.ca, La Coop fédérée, January 2007.)

Currently in Ontario, there is even a movement to standardize certification. "There is no national unified system to certify officers of the non-financial co-operatives. We would like to collaborate with the co-operative sector to develop a common governance approach for Boards." (Denyse Guy, Executive Director, Ontario Co-operative Association)

Certification is exactly what should happen in the public sector to familiarize elected officials with their new career, for which they have not specifically been trained. These programs could comprise components like codes of ethics, education, exams, coaching, mentoring, support and community activities. Certification is definitely a best practice other sectors could emulate.

The container is also important: What is the optimal structure to keep boards fresh and membership renewed? How to minimize conflicts of interests? How to define roles and responsibilities so staff and officers have clear and distinct mandates? How to ensure that boards are truly representative of member diversity? Many have introduced fixed terms for officers. "We have 12 directors on the Board and each year, four seats come up for election. Each director serves a three-year term." (Barry Delaney, Senior Vice-President, Governance and Strategy, Envision Financial) Others, like Desjardins, are starting to compensate officers. In summary, the trend is to *professionalize* elected leadership. The prevailing opinion among our respondents was: "In the past, people were well-intentioned but did not necessarily have the right skills." (Dianne Kelderman, Chief Executive Officer, Nova Scotia Co-operative Council)

Staff

Co-ops are seeking to optimize the talent management pipeline. In general, their efforts are similar to those in other sectors. Therefore, we will only highlight the differences. The first is attraction. "What attracts people is an environment where *they* can make decisions at a local level as opposed to other organizations that have centralized their decision-making process." (René Legacy, Vice-President, Communications and Strategy, Fédération des caisses populaires acadiennes [Federation of Acadian Credit Unions]) This idea of local empowerment is indeed seductive—nothing like controlling your destiny and innovating.

This 'empowerment/innovation' mindset is in keeping with basic human aspirations: to have a voice, matter, belong, contribute and be acknowledged. "From modest beginnings in the agricultural and fishing industry, Envision Financial has provided people in B.C. with locally responsive decision-making, exceptional service and innovative products for nearly 60 years." (Barry Delaney, Senior Vice-President, Governance and Strategy, Envision Financial)

Co-ops' empowerment of their staff is a breath of fresh air, compared to the depersonalized, centralizing models in vogue today. For instance, many organizations have located their call centres in other countries with disastrous levels in customer service and productivity. Others have centralized accounts payable so that no one 'owns' an account, with the result that customers have to start all over again every time they call the department. Because co-ops are community based, impersonality is simply *not* an option.

Attracting young people has become a concern; therefore, outreach programs abound. "We try to recruit young people through trade shows and fairs. However, they are hard to find because retail is not the preferred option for young people." (William Lyall, President, Arctic Co-operatives Limited)

Internships often constitute a good way to bring young people in. "We have an internship program intended for university students, such as from Guelph and Laurier Universities. Our program provides a work experience in a co-op setting. In our record year, we welcomed almost 20 young people. Normally, about 12 positions are actively occupied by interns. The objective is to groom the next wave of leaders." (Claude Gauthier, Director of Operations, Growmark Inc.)

The second difference is the emphasis on the practice of leadership in the community. "Community involvement helps to make the community be a better place to live. It's also a great leadership development opportunity." (Nancy Rooney, Director, Organizational Development, Co-operators General Insurance Company) Employees are strongly encouraged to take part in community projects, which are viewed as both opportunities to give back and to polish skills. "Board members realize they have received a lot from their community and want to give back to their community." (Guy Benoît, President, Coop Santé Aylmer Health Co-op)

To summarize, leadership in the co-op environment is driven by the 'critical mass' paradigm. All stakeholders are expected to provide leadership and this fosters leadership emergence. Opportunities for leadership practice and development abound, both inside the organization and in the community—a good model to emulate.

LEADERSHIP DEVELOPMENT

In co-ops, leadership development comprises the same five components as everywhere else: education, practice, self-discovery, support and community. Let's see how these components are carried out.

Education

In co-ops, leadership education is part of a larger educational context, which comprises many levels, starting with:

Co-op Education

Co-ops are aware that their members and employees have to be in sync with the co-op mindset to succeed. "To support new individuals in our organization, we have devoted a portion of our orientation program to informing staff about co-operatives and our co-operative heritage; this is a key piece of information that will assist them with understanding who we are and adapting to our organization." (Nancy Rooney, Director, Organizational Development, Co-operators General Insurance Company)

As a result, co-ops expend considerable effort inducting new stakeholders to the co-operative mindset. "The priorities of every co-operative organization must be based on the education, training and information of its administrators, employees and members. Every year, the network invests an average of 1.5 million dollars in the training of its employees and volunteer administrators." (Excerpt from www.acadie.com, Fédération des caisses populaires acadiennes, January 2007.)

It starts with citizen education: democratic principles, civil responsibilities, relationships and accountabilities between individuals, communities, society and various levels of government. In other words, to be a good co-op member or employee, you first have to be a good citizen.

The next component, co-operative education, introduces newcomers to co-operative principles, values, governance models, and economic and social mandates. This means acquiring a long-term and holistic view, learning to balance multiple interests, and working collaboratively. For instance, Arctic Co-op wants "to improve the understanding and effectiveness of the co-op movement, by providing co-operative training and education programs to inform members, elected officials and employees of their roles and responsibilities." (Excerpt from www.arcticco-op.com, Arctic Co-operatives Limited, January 2007.)

Co-ops realize that, individually and collectively, stakeholders act as change agents, and provide them with tools to act accordingly. Considerable financial and human resources are invested to align everyone to the foundations. It is viewed as a fundamental condition to success.

Finally, newcomers are oriented to their organization. "It is important that co-op members develop a good understanding of co-op principles and the fundamental requirements for the effective functioning of a co-operative enterprise. Both members and staff should be part of this process, in order to facilitate common understandings of the role and function of all stakeholders involved." (Glen Fitzpatrick, Managing Director, Newfoundland and Labrador Federation of Co-operatives) Like an iceberg, what is underneath the water is more significant than what floats above, because it supports the whole edifice. It allows everyone to share the same frameworks, values and guidelines. In difficult situations, people are likely to make similar judgement calls based on a common understanding. Once again, the co-op sector provides a viable model.

Professional Education

Next, people are ready to develop specific competencies related to their position. Co-ops nurture entrepreneurial development. "A fisherman, for example, who is a member of a fisheries co-op, will have an opportunity to learn new skills. As a member, the fisherman would learn how to read the co-op's annual financial reports and participate in democratic decision-making processes. As an elected board leader, skills would include how to run a business meeting, board/management relations, group consensus building, etc. We support this personal development process so that co-op leaders become increasingly effective in running their co-op. It also improves their entrepreneurial skills and their ability to run their own fishing enterprises." (Glen Fitzpatrick, Managing Director, Newfoundland and Labrador Federation of Co-operatives)

Co-ops use a blend of internal resources and external providers for educational delivery. On the internal front, some create separate entities to handle training and development. For instance, the Desjardins Co-operative Institute "provides a time and place where elected directors and managers exchange ideas, enrich their knowledge, adapt behaviour and integrate Desjardins governance and management practices. The Institute plays a mobilization role by conveying and sharing the values, vision, orientations and strategies." (Adapted from www. desjardins.com, Desjardins Group, January 2007.)

Likewise, "Envision University is a way for us to value our people and help them grow educationally. Some of our staff have wanted to get a university degree but were not afforded that opportunity when they were younger. These staff members, over the years, have taken many industry-related courses that are challenging and relevant. Our credit union has obtained accreditation for these internal courses. As a result, some staff have earned two years' worth of credits recognized towards a four-year university degree. This is good for our employees and for our business. It also helps us attract and retain talent." (Barry Delaney, Senior Vice-President, Governance and Strategy, Envision Financial)

External providers include consulting firms, colleges and universities. "There is now a Master's Program in Co-operative Management at St. Mary's University. We also have an agreement with the Nova Scotia Community College to include a co-op section in their program, which comprises internship and staff exchanges." (Dianne Kelderman, Chief Executive Officer, Nova Scotia Co-operative Council)

External resources also include co-op wholesalers, federations and provincial associations. "Training and education is based on competencies of the job. We have a series of internal and external programs. We use CUSOURCE as well as university MBA programs, online education, etc." (Sid Bildfell, CEO, SaskCentral) CUSOURCE is a division of Credit Union Central that provides educational services to the credit union network. By taking advantage of entities like CUSOURCE, co-ops reinforce their culture.

Leadership Education

Finally, we get to leadership education, which comes in all shapes and forms. For example, "there is a three-week program at the University of Bologna, Italy, that allows co-op leaders from all over the world to meet and to exchange outside their normal environment. Bologna boasts some of the most successful co-ops in the world. The program has been in existence for five years and can be seen as a way to explore the operations of a co-operative economy, a source of best practice, and a good way to energize people and provide a source of new ideas and inspiration." (John Restakis, Executive Director, British Columbia Co-operative Association)

Some partner up with renowned institutions. "We offer leadership education through the Niagara Institute. Programs include comprehensive assessments,

including 360-degree instruments, and encourage personal development plans."
(Robert Lavallée, Director, Organizational Development, Agropur coopérative)

Large co-operatives offer comprehensive leadership development programs.
For instance, Vancity Credit Union has developed a "suite of leadership programs
aimed at different audiences, from executives to new managers." (Grace Pulver, Vice-
President, Human Resources, Vancity Credit Union) The Desjardins Co-operative
Institute provides extensive leadership education for both elected directors and
managers. "The program Destination Excellence incorporates Desjardins' frame
of reference of sustainable overall performance in a co-operative organization
and presents the challenges of organizational and personal leadership in achieving
balanced performance management." (Adapted from www.desjardins.com,
Desjardins Group, January 2007.)

Succession Planning

Succession planning is a big concern. Baby boomers are retiring, urbanization
is increasing, and diversity must be taken into account. "The demographics and
diversity of Boards are a concern. Currently there are few youths, women and immigrants engaged at this level. Youths want to get involved to match their values.
The interest is there. We got 2347 e-mail applications for 23 positions." (Denyse
Guy, Executive Director, Ontario Co-operative Association)

Co-ops work hard to attract and develop the next generation of leaders. "Co-
operatives have a great appeal for the young leaders that we will need to sustain our
future. We need to promote the co-operative brand and attract this much-needed
talent." (Cheryl Byrne, Vice-President, Knowledge Services, Credit Union Central
of Canada) There is a definite trend towards sophisticated approaches combining
the power of attraction with creative outreach and talent identification. Here are
a few examples:

- **Reputation.** "We are a values-driven organization and we look at the social,
  environmental and financial impact of our actions. As a result, we attract
  people in line with our company values." (Grace Pulver, Vice-President,
  Human Resources, Vancity Credit Union)
- **Internships.** "We hire more than 75 students a year. If they are interested, they
  join us and we pair them with employees recognized for their success. This
  enables them to journey through the co-op movement." (Ernest Desrosiers,
  Former Chef de l'exploitation [COO], La Coop fédérée)
- **Talent pools.** "We offer training and development to our new employees
  because they build the future. Not having the required experience, they
  operate within a framework which enables them to achieve and grow in their

development. There is no fast-tracking; all potential candidates are part of a process, which gives us the assurance that future leaders are available." (René Legacy, Vice-President, Communications and Strategy, Fédération des caisses populaires acadiennes [Federation of Acadian Credit Unions])

To summarize, leadership education in co-ops is viewed as part of a continuum that begins with citizen and co-op education, proceeds to professional and organizational education, and, finally, on to leadership education. Although different respondents emphasized some aspects over others, they viewed them as linked. Layers upon layers of knowledge, know-how and consciousness combine to produce practised and integrated leaders who can make sound judgement calls on a consistent basis.

Practice

There are ample opportunities for supervised leadership practice in co-ops, both within the co-op and in the community. To select assignments wisely and strategically, co-ops use a number of guiding tools:

- **Curriculum.** An intact intern cohort will go through the same steps, and assignations are chosen according to contents.
- **Position.** If you are, for instance, an executive, you have to sit on ABC Committee or lead the United Way Campaign.
- **Personal development plans (PDPs).** Well-crafted, individualized PDPs are useful tools where goals pursued drive assignation selection. PDPs also assume careful monitoring of progress and debriefing of assignments.
- **Interest.** Demonstrating interest for a particular assignment also plays a part. Likewise, a repeated lack of interest to various offerings can be detrimental to a person's career.

Here are a few interesting examples of practicum assignments:

- **Exchanges.** "We have had success trading resources with credit unions. They acquire the wholesale side, while we acquire the credit side." (Sid Bildfell, CEO, SaskCentral)
- **Secondments.** "Secondments are used for grocery managers, who are sent 400 miles away to acquire the skills." (William Lyall, President, Arctic Co-operatives Limited)
- **Projects.** "Practical applications occur through projects. Yearly, we have between 150 to 200 projects in progress with over 60 project managers taking part." (René Legacy, Vice-President, Communications and Strategy,

Fédération des caisses populaires acadiennes [Federation of Acadian Credit Unions])

- **Community involvement**. "Our employees act as Youth Counsellors in the community. Also, we recently sent 12 employees on a work team to El Salvador at the company's expense as part of our outreach. What a movement!" (Michael Barrett, Vice-President, Human Resources and Corporate Secretary, Gay Lea Foods Co-operative Limited)
- **Problem-solving**. "We set up groups of eight to ten people and provide them with a problematic situation to resolve." (Robert Lavallée, Director, Organizational Development, Agropur coopérative)

Selecting an appropriate assignment is crucial to ensure a good fit. However, it's equally important to analyze the assignment. What did the person learn about himself as a leader? What was his impact? What would help him get to the next stage? In light of these discussions and progress made, selection parameters for the next assignment may be adjusted.

Self-Discovery

Self-discovery methods are similar to those used in other sectors: psychometric instruments, formal and informal feedback mechanisms, analysis and debriefing tools, etc.

Support

As developing leaders go through assignments, they need formal and informal support. On the formal side, it is often part of a set program. "In the Management Development program, participants benefit from six individual coaching sessions. A lot of informal mentoring also takes place." (Grace Pulver, Vice-President, Human Resources, Vancity Credit Union)

Informally, support is often offered through mentoring, and co-ops, much like other organizations, are increasingly structuring their mentoring programs. Mentor-protégé matching is key to the success of mentoring programs. Personal chemistry matters as much as relevance of experience. That is why mentoring programs are becoming more flexible—to allow both parties some choice. "We pair up people who want to set up similar organizations to ours with mentors from our organization. We bring them on site for a first-hand experience." (Guy Benoît, President, Coop Santé Aylmer Health Co-op)

Mentoring also works best when mentors are trained and have an interest in 'taking younger ones' under their wing. Therefore, a growing number of organizations are providing mentor education and assessment to enable people to determine whether this role is for them.

Although coaching and mentoring constitute the primary forms of support, it can also take many other forms. "The Federation gets involved in support and development. This includes building renovations, consulting, business plan review and funding." (Alain Leclerc, Executive Director, Fédération des coopératives funéraires du Québec [Québec Federation of Funeral Co-operatives])

Co-op representatives had a sharp awareness of the value of support and a great willingness to provide it. They also firmly believed that, by supporting each other, they could go through anything and 'figure their way out.'

Community

It is important for leaders to belong to a community of practice for sharing, problem-solving and networking. The multiplicity of co-op networks, wholesalers, sector federations and provincial associations provide numerous opportunities. "Networking with other co-ops is also considered to be critical to long-term success. When we assist with the development of a new co-op, we try to link it with the existing sector to facilitate access to their knowledge and expertise, and provide positive reinforcement during the first years of operation" (Glen Fitzpatrick, Managing Director, Newfoundland and Labrador Federation of Co-operatives) This way, people have numerous opportunities to belong to a community, inside their workplace or through a work-related group.

Internal opportunities also abound. "Task forces are a major focus and tool in our organization. For example, when selecting a new head office, a cross-functional team came together to organize the move, select furnishings, colours, etc." (Michael Barrett, Vice-President Human Resources and Corporate Secretary, Gay Lea Foods Co-operative Limited)

Of course, networking with the executives doesn't hurt. Both Agropur coopérative and La Coop fédérée organize functions where young leaders can meet with executives, including the co-op's President, as part of the orientation process. This is a good opportunity to observe executives in action and project themselves into the future. Executive exposure provides visible, tangible role-modelling and develops interpersonal skills communication.

BEST PRACTICES

Balance

As the world gets more global, complex and interdependent, organizations must learn to balance numerous dynamics to ensure sustainable development and stakeholder satisfaction. Co-ops, because of their nature and structure, already do so; therefore, they have extensive experience, for instance, in balancing social and economic mandates, long- and short-term perspectives, stakeholder interests, etc. In many ways, co-ops are masters of the balanced scorecard.

Co-ops are acutely aware of the need to balance giving and receiving. For instance, giving back to the community is a priority. They view such projects as an opportunity to help and practise leadership. Likewise, community activities give co-ops opportunities to demonstrate organizational leadership, modelling the right behaviours for stakeholders.

Solid Foundations

Today, public and private sector organizations are seeking to better define and implement their leadership platform and strategic framework. Because co-ops are member-owned and democratic in nature, they have a lot of experience in getting input and commitment from a variety of stakeholders to shape and implement both platform and framework.

The integration of foundations into everyday life and organizational systems seems very advanced in co-operatives. Interviewees frequently referred to them with feeling, if not passion. Foundations seemed more alive and tangible than in the other sectors. Respondents were extremely aware of the link between organizational and individual success and foundations.

People First

Concern for people is a definite priority. Because co-ops are more attuned to a variety of dynamics, they are more realistic about human nature and expectations. As a result, they see people as multi-dimensional, not just workers, and are more willing to accommodate realities outside the workplace.

Co-ops are also very in tune with human needs, such as the need to be appreciated, to matter, to make a contribution and a difference, to receive and provide assistance, and to belong. Moreover, they understand that work systems and structures must be configured to meet those needs, not the other way around. Therefore, corporate infrastructures and cultures seem more human.

Resourcefulness and Creativity

Because co-ops are community based and often begin in small towns and rural areas, members have to demonstrate resourcefulness. Therefore, they learn to think creatively, innovate, and keep trying until it works. Creative resilience is definitely a culture feature. Since they are less under the influence of big business, they think outside the box and come up with original ways of solving problems. And, due to their community orientation and holistic perspective, they are more open to pioneering alternative trends such as Corporate Social Responsibility (CSR), organic foods and biofuels than other sectors. As a result, they are often at the forefront of the next big wave.

Everyone Leads

Co-ops have adopted the 'critical mass' leadership model and embrace its imperatives. Because co-ops are community based and democratic, everyone is expected to provide leadership to some degree, and the pressure on the organization to behave as a leader is strong. Therefore, both individual stakeholders and co-ops understand they have to deliver the goods in the leadership department and put in place enabling systems and infrastructures to do so.

They also have a large leadership talent pool to draw from—members, employees, community stakeholders and customers. As a result, the conceptual model is the circle more than the pyramid. In co-ops, members elect their leaders, including Board members and CEOs. This democratic bent means that leaders have to earn the support of their followers, keep tabs on their needs and make balanced decisions. As a result, much time is spent consulting and communicating to determine strategies and align stakeholders to them.

Educating the Whole Person

The holistic educational view, starting with civic and democratic education, moving to co-op education, and then on to orientation to the organization,

Continued

the role and leadership, is bound to produce people with a broad perspective and awareness of their responsibilities as well as their rights.

Inducting newcomers to the co-op mindset by matching them with a 'buddy' facilitates and accelerates orientation. Likewise, upgrading existing employees' skills so they can be on par with the marketplace enables them to stay current. Once culture and skills are in place, employees can be effective in the co-op context.

Professionalizing the Officer Role

Co-ops are aware they need to provide elected officials with the tools to do their job competently. As a result, they define the required profile, actively recruit star candidates, clarify roles and responsibilities and limit terms of office. Certification programs, though, are a capital idea. They ensure a common language and knowledge base, which evens out the playing field.

This practice is transferable to board members in the private sector, but most importantly, to elected officials in the public sector at all levels: municipal, regional, provincial and federal. Imagine a certification program for MPs!

RECOMMENDATIONS

We asked co-op respondents to share their best advice about leadership practice and development. Here it is:

Ongoing leadership development. Numerous leaders are needed and organizations must seize every occasion for their development. Anything can be turned into a leadership development opportunity. Extensive practice, feedback and coaching are required to make training stick. "People need feedback to get perspectives on who, where they are as leaders. Is what you are doing really developing you? What could you do outside your comfort zone? What can you learn from that? People find they grow most during hardships." (Nancy Rooney, Director, Organizational Development, Co-operators General Insurance Company) "We focus on people who want to learn from those in the know. Matching a developing leader with a successful one who can coach is effective." (Ernest Desrosiers, Former Chef de l'exploitation [COO], La Coop fédérée)

Foundations and know-how. Respondents stressed the importance of both foundations and know-how to succeed. People must be connected to the leadership platform, as well as have the right competencies to do their jobs. One without the other simply doesn't work. "What co-ops need are good skills and people committed to a particular agenda and vision." (Dianne Kelderman, Chief Executive Officer, Nova Scotia Co-operative Council) "A committed and competent co-op leadership, supported by a network of technical assistance providers is a critical factor in ensuring a co-op is successful in its early stages and is able to oversee implementation of a long-term business strategy." (Glen Fitzpatrick, Managing Director, Newfoundland and Labrador Federation of Co-operatives)

Leadership talent. Leaders come in all shapes and sizes and sometimes through non-traditional channels. Having objective criteria to identify leadership potential is key. "We have to open up to new horizons. In order to get employment in the Credit Union, a financial background is not a guarantee. We need to leverage other areas. One of my most performing employees in marketing used to sell dog food." (René Legacy, Vice-President, Communications and Strategy, Fédération des caisses populaires acadiennes [Federation of Acadian Credit Unions])

Leadership skill differentiation. Skill requirements vary for different leaders: Officers and executives need to be able to think and act strategically; frontline supervisors must be able to organize workload and build teams, etc. And, as organizations grow, skill diversification intensifies. Therefore, it is imperative to have a clear picture of competencies and devise development plans specific to each group—employees, managers, members and officers

Certification program for elected officials. Respondents overwhelmingly agreed that, to be effective, officers need extensive orientation and development, and that these efforts must be structured to provide purpose, measure progress and integrate learning. "Board members are committed to their own development and development of the structure. They bring experts in governance and are not afraid of challenging themselves." (Sid Bildfell, CEO, SaskCentral)

CONCLUSION

Our incursion into the co-op world proved fruitful, surprising and refreshing. Everyday, co-ops prove that leadership is about service and empowerment. "You realize true results when you facilitate others to be successful. Finding success is making people successful around you." (Dave Mowat, CEO, Vancity Credit Union)

It's also about nurturing a *pioneer* spirit in order to grow and innovate. "Put yourself in a position to do more. Make an intentional effort to experience something new. Do things outside of your boundaries that expose you to new learnings." (Peter Robinson, CEO, Mountain Equipment Co-op)

Nowhere is it more obvious that leadership is from the inside out. "Speak with personal passion. Listen to your heart. Put less reliance on structures and more on people. The starting point is to find where your values lie." (Kathy Bardswick, President and CEO, The Co-Operators)

Co-ops are about people who improve their community and create successful organizations by the sheer strength of their conviction and the power of their dreams. "I became a leader by being good at farming and doing things right on the farm; by listening and being accountable; by having a passion that I put my whole life into. Leaders don't stop, they just keep going." (Clarence Olthuis, Chairman, United Farmers of Alberta Co-operative Limited [UFA])

Through this journey, we discovered many innovative practices that can be transferred to other sectors. In the end, we agree with this statement: "The co-op movement is a leadership school. It's important to recognize its contribution to leadership development in Canada." (Alban D'Amours, President and CEO, Desjardins Group)

CHAPTER 12

NATIONAL LEADERSHIP STRATEGY

Foster leadership development with children. Significantly change the curriculum to make it more balanced in order to build confidence and self-awareness. Help kids understand what they are good at and how to leverage it, not spend their energy on their weaknesses and the negatives.
  Diane Rabbani
  Human Resources Consultant;
  Former Deputy Minister, British Columbia.

Give expression to Canadian leadership: a sense of valuing leadership through sharing of achievements and innovations. It then becomes part of our language domestically and internationally to talk about leadership, and allows Canadians to reflect on how they can contribute. It will also help to harness untapped potential to tackle vexing problems and build new realities.
  Victor Lachance
  Consultant;
  Former President and CEO, Canadian Centre for Ethics in Sport

THE CALL TO ACTION

To secure an abundant supply of capable leaders in all sectors of the economy, Canada must generate a critical leadership mass. "We can't expect leaders to 'pop up'; they have to be nurtured through a culture that values leadership, promotes good leaders and gives them opportunities to burnish their skills. For instance, what are universities doing to encourage the average student to step up to the plate and take on a leadership role?" (Dr. David Walker, Dean, Faculty of Health Sciences, Queen's University)

This means putting in place effective and abundant leadership development infrastructures. As Ken Dobell, Former Deputy Minister and Cabinet Secretary, Office of the Premier, British Columbia, said in Chapter 6, "Leadership cannot be taught, but can be developed." However, with the right programs, environments and structures, it is possible to develop leaders.

Wanted: A National Leadership Strategy

At this point in time, little is in place in the way of concerted and aligned efforts across the country. Let's act like leaders, and create a powerful vision. What would the ideal end state look like?

According to interviewees, the best way to meet our growing leadership needs and fill the leadership deficit is to design and implement a *National Leadership Strategy*, which would:

- Make leadership development a priority.
- Stress the importance and value of capable leaders.
- Reinforce the imperative to invest in this crucial resource.
- Emphasize the requirement for a strategic and long-term approach.

Putting this strategy in place amounts to a revolution like the implementation of Tommy Douglas' government-funded health care. It will take years to achieve and demand significant financial and human resources, but the alternative is not an option. As the saying goes, if you think education is expensive, try ignorance!

The strategy would comprise:

- A framework and plan to guide our efforts.
- Specific goals to set a direction.
- Infrastructures to support implementation.
- Financial resources to fund the project.
- Competent human resources to make it happen.
- Alignment and coordination of all stakeholders involved.

Just like government-funded health care, a National Leadership Strategy represents a vision for the betterment of our society. History repeats itself, for once again, such a blueprint is being developed in Saskatchewan, where the booming economy and the ensuing skilled workers shortage is prompting employers to heavily invest in training and development, and to reach out to less tapped employee markets, such as the Aboriginal community. Professional and trade associations are also jumping on the bandwagon, offering more training, including intensive apprenticeship programs. Meanwhile, the provincial government is providing training subsidies and has developed incentive-based policies to encourage immigration from other provinces to Saskatchewan.

Faced with a serious labour shortage, all stakeholders are pulling together: integration and alignment are starting to take place. In such a scenario, everyone wins. Workers become more skilled and face brighter career and economic prospects. Employers benefit from highly skilled employees and build multiple bridges to the community they serve. Professional and trade associations recruit new members and enhance their reputation. The government upgrades social and economic conditions and obtains more and better educated citizens. When faced with a crisis, people team up and make it work: pain drives change

A similar initiative needs to happen on the leadership front. For the last decade, we have identified, denounced and complained about the leadership deficit. It's time to pull up our sleeves and do something about it. Let's take our cue from Saskatchewan and move to action. And the development of a National Strategy is the right place to start.

To craft such a strategy would require assembling a group of representative and interested stakeholders. Then, using the **W** method described in Chapter 11, extensive consultation with relevant parties would be required to get input and buy in. Eventually, a finished product would emerge that would likely satisfy stakeholders and move them to action.

We don't pretend to have a full-blown strategy to offer, and, anyway, such things are better *created* than *prescribed*; however, we can share the components suggested by respondents, as well as our own thoughts. We will, therefore, focus on three cornerstones:

Leadership education. Currently, leadership is barely visible as a field of study. "How come I didn't learn anything about leadership until I was in the workplace? We need to focus on leadership development in early childhood and youth education." (Elizabeth Watson, Principal, Governance Advisory Services)

Sadly, this quote reflects most of our interviewees' experience. The invisibility of leadership as a field of study is pervasive at all educational levels. When asked if they had studied leadership, the majority of respondents replied in the negative. Even business schools have been slow to introduce it in their curriculum. Graduates may be well-versed in the intricacies of finance, but are often baffled by the leadership requirements of their jobs. "Academic studies must stress leadership and soft skills. Many graduates are not fully prepared to function without effective interpersonal and communication skills." (Joseph Randell, President and CEO, Air Canada Jazz)

To equip people with useful frameworks and skills, we propose including leadership education at all levels in all provinces, adapting it to age groups, and structuring it according to the apprenticeship model. "It would be nice if school curriculum included leadership education early on. I am not aware that the school system does much to foster the development of entrepreneurial or leadership mindsets. It is important to help students develop lifelong skills at an early age: focus more on curiosity and less on traditional content; kids don't always see the relevance of what they learn. It is too late to start thinking about leadership when leaving university." (Becky McKinnon, Executive Chairman, Timothy's World Coffee).

To be effective, leadership development needs to be practice-heavy. Therefore, students should be enticed to get involved in school or community projects. "Leadership education should be mandatory in primary and secondary schools, and project driven. For instance, my daughter has to organize a blood drive in her school." (Isabelle Courville, President, Hydro-Québec TransÉnergie)

These types of projects would not only develop initiative and entrepreneurship, but they also would build skills and benefit the community—a win-win all around. Through these, students would learn that as citizens, they have both rights and responsibilities.

So, just like in the co-op sector, leadership education should start with civic education, because the goal is to produce well-rounded, Canada-savvy leaders connected to the international context; people who are aware of their responsibilities and willing to contribute to the country. If we start now, we might see significant results in 10 to 12 years. "Leadership should be taught in public school. Later, the curriculum should include courses in philosophy so young people can learn to think, reflect and analyze. We must help students develop skills and take ownership. They should be given projects where they have to convince others to join. Boosting awareness of the importance of leadership is prime." (Ève-Lynne Biron, President and General Manager, Laboratoire Médical Biron)

Access to mentoring. Respondents selected mentoring as the most powerful leadership development method. Therefore, if more individuals have access to mentoring, more leaders will emerge. We propose expanding the scope and reach of mentoring programs to young people and adults, and linking them to various communities.

This assumes large quantities of well-trained mentors, 'matching systems' to connect mentors and protégés, follow-up and evaluation processes, integration of mentoring relationships in infrastructures such as schools, workplaces, communities, sports and arts, and more. With so many qualified baby boomers retiring, it shouldn't be hard. "Mobilize the wisdom of retirees who want to keep contributing" was a recommendation we frequently heard.

According to interviewees, mentoring is a priceless gift for both parties: Protégés benefit from guidance, caring and advice, and mentors feel good about sharing their expertise and being looked up to—a winning formula.

National Leadership Institute. We need a governance body to devise strategies, coordinate and align leadership development efforts in the country, and act as a catalyst for information sharing, education and resource development.

WIDESPREAD LEADERSHIP EDUCATION

Interviewees proposed introducing leadership as part of the curriculum at all levels and in all provinces. "Leadership education should be mandatory." (Patrick Cuenco, Co-founder, Junior Hong Kong-Canada Business Association) Cary Mullen, Olympian and World Cup Champion; Serial Entrepreneur; Professional Speaker, adds: "The education system should help young adults develop a vision of how they want to contribute instead of fumbling through life."

Leadership education should be conducted according to the apprenticeship model: practical, targeted to age group, project driven, and linked to the community. "There should be more service learning for young people. Parents are stretched, the community needs to help. Let's look at society and how to make it a better place to live. We need to build a caring infrastructure." (Dr. Jacquelyn Thayer Scott, O.C., Past President and Professor, Cape Breton University; Deputy Chair, Prime Minister's Advisory Council on Science and Technology)

Like anything worthwhile, leadership mastery happens progressively. As said earlier, if we start investing now, it might take a generation to make a significant difference in the quantity and quality of results. "We would have more leaders if, as a society, we invested more in leadership development, starting with young people." (Denis Losier, President and CEO, Assumption Life)

So, the sooner we start, the sooner we will see results. Leadership has to become a *visible* and *legitimate* field of study. The younger kids start, the more accomplished they can become.

Goal: Well-Rounded Leaders

"Begin with the end in mind," says Stephen Covey in his landmark book, *The Seven Habits of Highly Effective People* (Simon & Schuster, New York, 1989). But, just what *is* the desirable outcome?

Given the increased complexity and interdependence of our global world, the answer is well-rounded leaders—people who can interpret events, detect patterns, decipher trends and most importantly "formulate reasoned answers to unpredictable events: judgement, wisdom, response instead of knee-jerk reaction." (Captain [N] Alan Okros, Professor; Former Director, Canadian Forces Leadership Institute, Royal Military College) How can we produce such leaders?

Broad Knowledge

It starts by teaching them context to understand the world, how it works and where we fit in it. Context offers a framework to anchor ideas and link events. Skilled journalists excel at providing context by helping audiences make sense of happenings. This demands a broad knowledge on a variety of topics, such as philosophy, geography, arts, science, sports, etc. "Leaders need exposure to areas beyond their field of expertise to learn how to think outside the box; for instance, practise with team sports to integrate fair play, and speak in public to develop their own voice." (Richard Monette, C.M, Artistic Director, The Stratford Festival of Canada)

History sheds light on how events and ideologies are shaped and how we arrived at our current state. Canadian history, in particular, *affects* and *reflects* our national consciousness, identity and pride. "We need to study more history, particularly of great people, in a non-partisan way—what makes them great, their accomplishments. Role models are required in education. If they fit your style, they will inspire you." (Rob Dexter, Q.C., Chairman and CEO, Maritime Travel Inc.)

Big-Picture Thinking

Like helicopters, leaders need to hover over trees to view the forest. This requires training the mind to operate at a conceptual level, noticing linkages and patterns lurking below the surface. In other words, the mind must be able to synthesize, diagnose, deduce, strategize, etc. "Foster the development of perceptiveness and maturity. Offer philosophy courses to provide context and teach how to think. Add broad, global knowledge to technical competence. As a leader, you must have a connection with the universe." (Yvon Bastien, Former President and General Manager, Sanofi Synthelabo Canada)

These cognitive abilities can be sharpened. Some people are more gifted than others, but everyone can improve. Therefore, from a leadership development perspective, the ideal educational system should be geared to giving a good general education and to training the mind to think at an abstract, conceptual and contextual level.

Initiative

Leadership is about creating new realities and this means leaving the security of well-traveled roads. Becoming a leader requires initiative, and entrepreneurship provides an ideal vehicle to develop initiative. Entrepreneurship is not limited to business; as a mindset, it can be applied to anything: research, community, policy-making. The key is developing a culture where success is possible and everyone has a can-do attitude. "Entrepreneurship is an important vehicle for leadership development. As a young country, we have fewer traditions than others, so we must create them. Moreover, our culture is conducive to entrepreneurship because it is not elitist: anyone who works hard can succeed." (Yves Filion, President, CIGRÉ [Conseil international des grands réseaux électriques] [International Council on Large Electric Systems]; Former President, Hydro-Québec TransÉnergie)

In this regard, Québec is a leader we can all learn from. Since the quiet revolution, entrepreneurs have multiplied, forming 'Québec Inc.'—province-born corporate giants that are now taking the world by storm. Here is some information garnered from the websites of four examples:

- Hardware giant RONA (www.rona.ca, January 2007) has experienced phenomenal growth since its inception in 1939. It now boasts 620 stores and 25,000 employees across the country.
- Beauty and home products manufacturer Fruits & Passion (www.fruits-passion.com, January 2007) currently has 2,000 points of sale around the world. Outside of Canada, these are located in the U.S., Europe, the Middle East and Asia. Africa is next on their list.
- Drugstore chain Jean Coutu (www.jeancoutu.com, January 2007) operates 320 stores in Canada and 1,549 in the U.S. under the banners of Brooks and Eckerd drugstores. A tremendous success.
- With 5,000 stores, Alimentation Couche-Tard Inc. (www.couche-tard.com, January 2007) is the number one convenience retailer in Canada and the third in the U.S. It operates Couche-Tard, Mac's and Circle K brands. It has now started to expand internationally.

When speaking with Québec interviewees, we perceived a powerful sense of the possible, a true go-getter attitude and a relaxed confidence. We concluded that, as a minority, Québecers *had* to create in order to succeed, and along the way, forged a culture of entrepreneurship that supports innovation and risk taking. "Whether you think you can or cannot do something, you are right," says motivational speaker and writer Anthony Robbins in his landmark book *Unlimited Power* (Simon & Schuster, New York, 1986) He is right; more than a reality, entrepreneurship is an <u>attitude</u>.

So how can we instill in kids an entrepreneurial mindset early on? Many schools now feature projects where students have to start businesses and compete on the stock market; others get involved in sports or community projects. Some schools teach creative thinking and foster resilience through coaching and mentoring. All of these, and many other ideas, can work. Process matters more than contents. Cultivating inventiveness and confidence is the goal. "Leadership develops progressively: you can't expect overnight success. We should start leadership education in public school: Teach children to become responsible, to take initiative, to assert themselves in groups." (Françoise Bertrand, President and CEO, Fédération des Chambres de Commerce du Québec [Québec Federation of Chambers of Commerce])

Civic Responsibility

Regardless of how effective society's leaders are, they cannot move forward without committed, informed followers, so we must instill civic responsibility among citizens, particularly youth. "It is essential to invest massively in education in order to enable citizens to play an enlightened role in society. From an early age, people must be called to, not only exercise their rights, but fulfill their responsibilities." (Laure Waridel, Eco-sociologist; Author; Co-Founder Équiterre)

Citizens in general and leaders in particular must acknowledge the need to balance rights and responsibilities. "The education system should present both opportunities and responsibilities. Civic and civil education are not part of the formal education curriculum. Understanding responsibilities makes you understand leadership. We are missing fundamentals in the role that we all play in shaping our culture." (Fred Mattocks, Executive Director, Regional Programming, Production and Resources, CBC English Television)

To be assumed, responsibilities must be actualized. "Each high school student should get involved in a social project of some kind: illiteracy, disability, etc. It would provide opportunities to learn and awaken to social life and its attendant problems." (Gérald Larose, Professor-Researcher, School of Social Work, Université du Québec à Montréal [UQAM])

Civic education would go a long way to nurturing a service disposition in the future leaders. Leadership is first and foremost an act of service. It's about empowerment, not power.

Canada Savvy

Obviously, Canada needs leaders who intimately know and understand the country. Therefore, "In Canada, leadership must be taught emphasizing a context characterized, not by fierce competition or outlandish capitalism, but by cooperation, openness to common interests and win-win methods." (Alban D'Amours, President and CEO, Desjardins Group)

Canada-wide knowledge is a challenge because of our size, diversity and massive immigration. "Due to the size of our country and the difficulty to travel, there is ignorance about Canada and this creates a lack of understanding. Knowing our country will help build respect and leadership. People will know what they are talking about instead of making assumptions with no foundations. We should start exchanges at a young age. Though culture shock is a good thing, let's go beyond it, and find similarities. Let's awaken curiosity. ..." (Robert Lepage, President, Robert Lepage Inc.; Stage and Artistic Director, Ex-Machina)

We need wide-ranging programs to foster knowledge acquisition and appreciation of our geography, history and culture. "Encourage exchanges, a great platform to develop leadership as they broaden language and cultural understanding. Set up programs for inner city/disadvantaged groups. Reach out to new immigrants to help them get integrated. Benefits could be immense." (John Bales, CEO, Coaching Association of Canada)

It's important to start early.

Encourage young people to travel between provinces to discover the country. Send kids all over. Set up cheap fares on VIA Rail for them. Provide tax credits if they get a summer job in another province. Organize exchanges between provinces for high school students. For university students, set up a program for them to complete a semester in a university located in a different province. Make history more interesting by teaching linkages between events, currents, forces; we need a more common sense of history and Canadian values. We also must emphasize second-language acquisition. (Nalini Stewart, O.Ont., Chair and Director of numerous community organizations and charities)

This would reduce disparities in understanding the makeup of the country and align people from coast to coast. It would also infuse young people with a deep love for our country and motivate them to contribute. "Make a difference in the Canadian way: Engender a spirit of entrepreneurship, create opportunities, care about others, focus on what has meaning, and strengthen international activities." (James Gray, O.C., A.O.E., Chairman, Canada West Foundation; Founder and Former Chairman, Canadian Hunter Exploration Ltd.)

During our research, we had the opportunity to connect with people from all regions and walks of life. It left us hungry for more. We were deeply moved by respondents' willingness to participate and help. Many people opened their hearts and extended their hands to these two unknown women wanting to improve leadership. Our project was home grown and unofficial and the response was phenomenal, exceeding our wildest expectations. This taught us that Canadians have a real appetite to connect with each other across the land and get to know each other better. All we require are the vehicles to do so.

Language and Culture

Experts in linguistics claim that the hardest language is the second language you learn, because your brain resists integrating a new framework. That is why language acquisition is easier for children and for adults already acquainted with two or more.

Being a bilingual country gives us an advantage: we are used to second-language exposure and acquisition. Since the Official Languages Act of 1969, we have made tremendous progress through immersion schools and exchange programs. Not only are we increasingly bilingual, but we are not surprised by multicultural environments and are generally open to other perspectives. This has become a Canadian competency, useful in international trade and politics.

Can we take it even further? For instance, multiply exchange programs. Increasingly, universities offer their students the possibility of spending a semester abroad. How about applying this idea to exchanges between provinces, so a University of British Columbia student could spend a semester at Université de Moncton, for example? Travel and immersion work. How can we set up vehicles so that more Canadians become bilingual *and* bicultural?

On the culture front, we are fortunate to benefit from two prolific cultural traditions that expand our consciousness and enrich our heritage. And now, because of immigration, many more improve our quality of life. Think of the extraordinary contributions made by literature giants Michael Ondaatje and Rohinton Mistry.

Are we doing everything to ensure that all Canadians profit and derive pride from this precious resource? Internationally, we are known for our cultural products. Our writers, singers, painters, etc., carry the flag of Canadian creativity well beyond our frontiers, making us proud. But are they as well-known at home? How can we do a better job of sharing successes and expertise? We need to leverage the advantages of our rich cultural heritage. What is the core cultural knowledge we should all share? How can we disseminate it? "In contemporary art, Vancouver is looked at in great respect; not recognized enough nationally, but recognized internationally." (Kathleen Bartels, Director, Vancouver Art Gallery)

Design Principles

In order to design programs resulting in well-rounded leaders, interviewees recommended restoring balance in three areas:

1. **Personality components: intellectual, emotional, physical and spiritual.** Currently, there is too much emphasis on the intellectual.
2. **Content and process.** At this point, the balance is skewed in favour of content.
3. **Theory and practice.** Now, there is too much theory and not enough practice.

Personality Components

Leaders utilize their whole being to perform: physical, intellectual, emotional and spiritual components. However, education overly emphasizes the intellectual at the expense of others: the system is IQ obsessed.

As a society, we are doing ourselves a disservice by maintaining this imbalance. For example, many employees get terminated due to their lack of interpersonal skills. Others crack under pressure, and these breakdowns might be prevented by a good fitness regime. Others, still, cannot find hope and strength through hardships, due to a poor connection to their spirituality.

Leadership requires integrated, vibrant individuals who can access all aspects of themselves.

> The education system should provide young people with the opportunity to develop healthy bodies and minds. Our children don't have enough opportunities for physical development in school and it hinders their emotional development. We should have a curriculum addressing the whole person. Being well-rounded is very important. Interpersonal skills need to be developed; they just don't happen by accident. Learning personal accountability and goal achievement is also important when you are young. Our education does not prepare leaders. The earlier support is provided, the better the outcome will be. Leaders will then emerge. (Ken Shields, C.M., Former Head Coach, Canadian National Men's Basketball Team)

Content and Process

Attention given to content and process is uneven; there's too much emphasis on content and not enough on process. Obviously, learning content like geography, mathematics, biology and music is very important. But interviewees argue that learning process skills, such as problem-solving, decision-making, creative thinking and team-building, is just as important.

Indeed, regardless of career, problems will arise, decisions will have to be made, and creative solutions will need to be found. Moreover, the bar of quality is constantly raised in order to deliver mandates and remain competitive. In the global, complex, interdependent world of the 21st century, we are 'condemned' to perform and innovate. And performance and innovation require process skills; how to think outside the box, how to rally people to an idea, how to resolve conflict, how to negotiate a win-win solution, etc. They are the framework within which you win or lose. Shouldn't these skills be taught?

Process skills are the fabric holding teams, organizations and nations together. The ingenuity of solutions and decisions will often make the difference between success and failure. They are arrived at through solid processes that can be broken down, taught and practised.

People often find it hard to see the presence of process skills, but it is not impossible. For instance, when students take part in an exercise, debriefing it will make the process tangible and deepen learning. "Leadership development programs must involve real-life situations and projects, as well as simulations during which learners can observe what takes place. This way, leadership dynamics become visible." (Alain Cousineau, Chairman, President and CEO, Loto-Québec)

Theory and Practice

Theory alone is not sufficient to achieve proficiency; therefore, structured practice opportunities must be built in to ensure acquisition of in-depth *savoir faire*, not just superficial knowledge. Currently, our system is theory heavy. Introducing more practice opportunities will ensure the development of graduates who know what they are doing instead of *thinking* that they know.

This applies to many subjects, including presentation skills, computer science, mediation, etc., but it's particularly true about leadership. "Leadership development programs should include lots of practice opportunities. It is important to entice and stimulate interest for leadership and allow learners to experiment with it. This way they will find and express their leadership voice." (Lorraine Pintal, O.C., General and Artistic Director, Théâtre du Nouveau Monde)

Field trips, exchanges, community work, adventure, etc., broaden perspectives and foster openness and adaptability. "We can help motivate people at an early age. It is important to value and validate children. Some kids are abused and poor. What conditions can be put in place to address poverty? Camping programs and opportunities to volunteer could help kids develop and contribute positively. We have to develop a culture to celebrate and recognize leaders." (Honourable Bob Rae, PC, O.C., O.Ont., Q.C., Former Premier, Ontario)

Critical Success Factors

What will contribute to the success of leadership education? Our interviewees recommended these building blocks to design successful leadership development programs for all ages.

Experience

Programs must be highly experiential: There are no shortcuts to practice. "You have to get on a bicycle and ride it. Effective leaders will hone their skills by practising leadership and receiving feedback. There is no substitute for hands-on experience." (Jack Graham, Partner, McInnes Cooper) A series of well-planned learning experiences is required.

But which experiences are most enriching?

- They must **stretch** learners out of their comfort zone. "Set up programs that allow people to expand to different segments of the Canadian fabric, for example, indigenous society. Teach issues facing different communities from across Canada. Figure out solutions and take a leadership role. Foster leadership ability to act." (Bernd Christmas, Lawyer and Mi'kmaq Leader)
- They must be **varied.** "Start developing your view of Canada in the world. Everyone should travel the world and experience different environments, for example, the fast-paced Asia or unchanged parts of Africa—places with different priorities. People will then develop a greater appreciation for Canada." (Rob McEwen, Chairman and CEO, U.S. Gold and Lexam Explorations) Silos breed limited mindsets by confining people to a narrow specialty, function or region. "Go out of your environment and take part in activities that foster personal development, such as politics, community action, sports. It's important to seek opportunities to practise leadership." (Michèle Fortin, President and CEO, Télé-Québec)
- They must be linked to **community.** Volunteer work provides outstanding leadership development opportunities and puts learners in touch with service. "Engage in volunteer activity to see the world outside of your own interests. One person's actions contain the seeds of transformation and the capacity for revolution." (Ruth Kelly, President, Venture Publishing Inc.; Publisher and Editor-In-Chief, Alberta Venture) Due to the limited resources and funding available, learners have to become resourceful to succeed; in other words, entrepreneurial. Volunteer work is based on caring. "Find out what you can do to help. Get moving and stir people up. Do something about what you care about; it is so easy when you care. 'Who cares!' immobilizes, but 'I care' can

change the world—the power of caring is transformative." (Gladys Osmond, Leader, The Granny Brigade)

Space

The goal is not to produce cookie-cutter leaders but to enable people to find their own path. Therefore, it's important to design a learning space big enough to acknowledge the effectiveness of various styles—a creative place to experiment, risk, reflect, dream and express emotions. "Create an environment where people feel confident and fulfilled contributing to society—the type of environment where the power of positive reinforcement and caring will help people excel at what they do." (Dennis Skulsky, President, CanWest MediaWorks Publications Inc.)

It's about setting the context to embark on a leadership discovery adventure. "It's important to integrate sport, artistic, social and community activities, as well as to dream, innovate, and surpass perceived limitations." (Luc Nadeau, Executive Vice-President, Corporate Communications and External Relations and President of the Luxury Products Division, L'Oréal Canada)

Influence

Leadership is, first and foremost, a relationship, a bond between leader and followers. Here's a famous illustration: British Admiral Horatio Nelson, hero of the battle of Trafalgar, became a captain at age 21. When his ship docked in Portsmouth at the end of his first voyage at the helm, the crew stated they would stay on board for the next trip if he led. That's quite a testimonial from people often pressed into service and living in difficult and dangerous conditions. Throughout his illustrious career, Nelson was able to consistently elicit this kind of loyalty. When all is said and done, how strong is the bond between leader and followers?

Leaders need to be skilled at establishing, enhancing and repairing relationships. Interviewees validated the importance of interpersonal skills, particularly the complex ones, like conflict resolution. Moreover, our diverse world requires sophisticated capabilities to deal with people whose culture, values, customs and paradigms can be profoundly different. "Students need human relations training within a multicultural society to understand how to work effectively together." (Honourable Joseph L. Handley, Premier, Northwest Territories)

Leadership is a process of influence, and, as such, is based on good communication. Good communication requires openness, curiosity and interest. It's about the capacity to engage in meaningful dialogue to achieve agreement. Not as visible as debate or public speaking, dialogue is nevertheless an essential leadership competency. "Develop competencies like listening, adapting to change, being respectful, and presentation skills." (Lorene Reist, Business Director, Western Canada, NYCOMED Pharma Inc.)

Another key capability is persuasion, a complex amalgam involving psychology, perceptiveness and argumentation. It takes knowledge, practice and feedback to become an effective communicator—fundamental to success in every profession and at every organizational level. "Being an effective communicator will have ripple effects throughout the organization. Talk about it in practical terms, sell ideas and be focused. But also listen well; show flexibility and openness to advice." (Piers Handling, Director and CEO, Toronto International Film Festival Group)

MENTORING OUTREACH

Exposing developing leaders to successful mentors and models makes leadership tangible. "We need to encourage leaders from different walks of life to interact with younger people—talk to them and provide opportunities. It could be a structured program exposing potential leaders to established ones. If we focus on leadership development and allow people to realize their potential, it will provide young people with the opportunities they deserve to serve." (Dr. Alan Bernstein, O.C., President, Canadian Institutes of Health Research)

The power of mentoring is doubled when combined with leadership practice. "Start in the early days. Build a foundation of self-confidence. Give them opportunities to take on leadership roles at school while they grow. Support them through coaching and mentoring, so they can behave well in leadership roles. Above all, inspire them. People model themselves based on leaders they see." (Janet Milne, Former Assistant Deputy Minister, Finance and Administration, Government of Canada)

Since mentoring is perceived as the most effective leadership development technique, its power needs to be unleashed. "Every 13-year-old should be given a mentor to explore the height and depth of their potential and tap into their leadership capacity. Do it through the school system and beyond, for instance, outside geographic boundaries, or through volunteer activity, which is a key component in leadership development." (Ruth Kelly, President, Venture Publishing Inc.; Publisher and Editor-in-Chief, Alberta Venture)

In order to offer it to more people, mentoring capacity needs to be expanded. "Fund programs, provide staffing and opportunities to identify potential leaders and help them develop through positive fostering and mentoring. Currently, very little time is built into education for mentoring. Provide more time for those in leadership roles to help others." (Laura Collings Parsonson, Head of

Library, Assistant Curriculum Leader, Program Support, Martingrove Collegiate Institute)

Mentoring assumes having a pool of talented mentors. How can we identify leaders in the community? "Get prominent people to be in open dialogue with students; this will balance theory with experience." (Philip Owen, Former Mayor, Vancouver, British Columbia)

One solution, mentioned earlier in this chapter, is to tap into the mentoring potential of baby boomers looking for opportunities to give back. They still have the stamina and know-how to contribute. Enlist them to act as mentors to developing leaders and consultants to developing countries. When established leaders reach out to younger ones, they will energize each other. "There is a lot of baby boomer talent out there. How can we mobilize it? Should we set up programs where sponsors can mentor young cubs?" (Joanne Lalumière, Executive Director and Corporate Secretary, Société zoologique de Granby [Granby Zoological Society])

Mentoring is a gift we receive and need to learn to give. "Young people can mentor each other. For example, in summer camp, 11-year-olds can buddy up with eight-year-olds, etc. In grade school, Grade Five students can read stories to kindergarten kids. In high school, senior students can tutor freshmen. Share, learn to lead, mentor. It can be done within the existing structures, like a grassroots movement." (Vickie van Dyke, Midday Host, Smooth Jazz Wave 94.7; Singer and Writer)

The good news is that mentoring programs are fairly straightforward to set up and run. Basically, you need qualified and interested mentors, willing protégés and an effective system.

Participants

Mentors have to be oriented and trained to understand and competently play their role. Protégés require orientation: what to expect of the process, how to play their part and how to derive maximum benefits from the mentoring relationship.

Process

The process should describe selection, orientation, training, matching, duration, expectations, evaluation, etc. It works best when there is some flexibility in matching, so people can choose each other for maximum commitment and chemistry. The process should be an integral part of the organization's people management system. This means that mentor and protégé databases must be kept current, relationships documented and evaluated, operational systems fine-tuned, and that resources must be assigned to administer the process.

Many models are possible: projects, internships, community involvement and more. Be creative and create your own model. The ingredients are easy enough to combine. Start small and see how it goes. "Create the right environment. Invite people who have values similar to yours to join the organization. Create a development process. Allow people to take responsibility and accept their mistakes. Have mentors and coaches throughout the process. Invest in development of employees. Put people in 'stretch' jobs and measure their success." (Sue Lee, Senior Vice-President, Human Resources and Communications, Suncor Energy Inc.)

The possibilities are endless and beneficial for all parties. The power of mentoring and its lasting effects are easy to grasp. Mentoring acts like yeast, the active ingredient enabling leadership capacity to rise. Mentoring is like a seed, small and unobtrusive, but full of possibilities.

NATIONAL LEADERSHIP INSTITUTE

Many interviewees advocated the creation of a Canadian National Leadership Institute. "It is important to assemble people to talk about leadership, the experiences and aspects of the role. Let's set up an institute that will bring leaders together for this purpose." (Dr. Gail Dinter-Gottlieb, President and Vice-Chancellor, Acadia University)

This organization could be a partnership between federal and provincial governments and involve other parties, such as corporations, colleges and universities, and municipalities, whose roles and accountabilities would be defined. "Set up a leadership institute connected to many organizations, in order to showcase how to develop leaders. Stimulate and demonstrate leadership. Keep it simple and straightforward. Provide opportunities to exercise leadership in organizations and volunteer activities. Make learning and leadership development opportunities more accessible." (Glenna Carr, Corporate Board Director; Former Deputy Minister and Secretary, Management Board of Cabinet, Ontario)

This Institute would adopt the same philosophy as the Canadian military: "Leadership development is not part of what we do, *it is* what we do." (Captain [N] Alan Okros, Professor; Former Director, Canadian Forces Leadership Institute, Royal Military College) In other words, leadership is not an aside or a by-product; it is a relentless pursuit, a national obsession, much like hockey. "It would be useful to have a centre of excellence in leadership and set higher standards. It could be based on the military training principles." (Patrick Reid, O.C., M.C., C.D., Chairman, Rick Hansen Foundation)

The Institute's mandate would be to:

- Develop a National Leadership Strategy.
- Ensure that leadership stays at the forefront of our national consciousness.
- Make leadership development a priority in education, the workplace and the community.

The Institute would ensure that outstanding leaders in all walks of life are not taken for granted or forgotten, but revered and immortalized through awards; tributes; textbooks; TV series; and movies, such as the upcoming *Shake Hands with the Devil* about Roméo Dallaire. starring Roy Dupuis. "In Canada, there is a lack of leadership celebration. We need to recognize our extraordinary input and bring leaders together to cross-pollinate." (Marg McGregor, CEO, Canadian Interuniversity Sport)

The Institute would act as a catalyst for leaders to share information and best practices, solve problems and become the best they can be. "Identify and pull together people who could define ethics of leadership and develop a centre of excellence." (Rod Smith, Senior Partner, Focuspoint Strategic Management; Former President, Black Photo Corporation)

Here are sample activities the Institute could undertake:

Information Sharing

- Conduct and sponsor research.
- Disseminate research.
- Act as a clearing house for information sharing.
- Set up a variety of networks (sector, industry, occupational levels, gender, age, etc.) to help Canadians share best practices, resolve challenges and learn about leadership.
- Produce extensive databases of leadership resources, best practices, and other leadership-related information.
- Create a mentor resource pool.
- Publish and/or support the publication of leadership-related materials in various forms: Internet, books, pamphlets, etc.

Education

- Produce core educational materials.
- Provide funding to create dramatic series showcasing famous leaders.
- Support educational program delivery.
- Organize activities, such as forums, conferences and symposiums.
- Organize leadership exchange programs between sectors, provinces and countries, aligned with international trade or aid policies.

- Establish international placement or studies abroad as a core component of university programs.

Strategy

- Manage projects, such as a national dialogue on Canadian identity, vision for the future and code of ethics.
- Foster the development of Canadian Leadership in Canada and abroad.
- Mobilize the wisdom of retirees.
- Create a leadership Think-Tank across the country.
- Support the media in reporting leadership accomplishments, featuring successful problem-solving and profiling unsung heroes.
- Monitor progress and evaluate results.

Recognition

- Put in place various rewards and awards to acknowledge outstanding Canadian leaders.
- Create an Order of Canada category for emerging leaders.
- Each year, showcase the top 10 leadership development programs in the country and give them awards.

The possibilities are endless. "Do more of what we do, but do it better and massively expand on it. Provide opportunities for leaders to see the world and understand its needs." (Alexa McDonough, MP; Former Federal NDP Leader, Canada)

In order to fulfill its mandate, the Institute would need ample sources of reliable, consistent funding, clear roles and responsibilities for the various parties involved, a vision and a strategic plan. It would become to leadership development what the Canadian Olympic Committee is to elite athlete development.

CONCLUSION

As executives well know, nothing anchors and aligns efforts like a good business strategy. It's like a lightning rod pulling people and things together.

For example, the city of Barrie, Ontario, has created a fantastic strategic plan to guide its development. On its website, www.city.barrie.on.ca (January 2007), you can find the *Community-Based Strategic Plan*, a strategic framework arrived at through extensive consultation; the *2005-2006 Corporate Business Plan,* an elaborate document spelling out priorities, action steps, deadlines and accountabilities; and plan implementation, such as the *September 2006 Update.*

We were extremely impressed with the strategic capability, level of detail and diligence of these documents, which demonstrate Barrie's innovative and effective leadership as a municipal government.

Effective strategic planning and implementation is possible for governments as well as for businesses. Let's follow Barrie's example and craft our National Leadership Strategy. It is doable and it will be a giant step forward to structure our leadership development efforts and bring us closer to achieving a critical mass of competent leaders for our country.

PART III

STRENGTHENING CANADIAN LEADERSHIP

How can we build our leadership bench strength? How can we expand our leadership capacity and enhance our impact as leaders? In this next section, we will discover rich avenues to explore …

CHAPTER 13

OUR NATIONAL LEADERSHIP BRAND

We have a natural humility and are aware that promises made must be promises kept. Our moderate and inspired leadership is rooted in empathy with a sense of purpose. We are admired and judged based on the way we work.

John Furlong
CEO, Vancouver 2010 Olympic and Paralympic Winter Games

I think we have the best of all worlds in Canada. Our businesses are increasingly becoming world-class organizations, for we have North American know-how coupled with Europe's social conscience and good manners. Our belief in a balanced scorecard, not just the bottom line, is a success factor in the global economy. We are calm, rational and reasonable. We excel at creating win-win solutions. There is a way through most conflicts, and we can find it.

Mark Surrette
President, Robertson Surrette

OUR OWN WAY

To strengthen Canadian leadership, we first have to understand what it is. Canadian leadership can be understood from two points of view:

National Leadership Style. As a distinct cultural group, do we lead differently than other nationalities? For instance, how does our style compare to the Australian, the German or the Japanese leadership style? Style, like culture, happens whether people are aware of it or consciously try to mould it. We have our own leadership style like every other cultural group, shaped by our history, temperament, values, etc., and reflected in our consciousness.

National Leadership Impact. Nations, like other entities such as provinces, cities, regions and organizations, either act as leaders or they don't. For instance, England demonstrated exceptional leadership during World War II. Nations, just like individuals and organizations, have to define their leadership identity, find their leadership voice, and determine how they want to lead. The world is vast and leadership needs, enormous. What do we want to provide leadership on? Who and what do we want our leadership to serve? How do *we* want to lead?

In this chapter, we will examine the nature of our leadership style, and in the next chapter, we will discuss how the nation can expand its leadership impact: presence and capacity.

Perspectives

On leadership style, interviewees split into two clusters: a very small minority that doesn't think there is a specific Canadian style, doesn't know, or won't comment; and a large majority that can describe the style on its own merit, or by contrasting it to others.

Style descriptions were remarkably consistent across the country, with differences of emphasis. Most respondents described a 'core' Canadian leadership style, greatly influenced by the 'maverick' social thinking of the Prairies, which considerably shaped our society—hence the selection of Tommy Douglas as 'the Greatest Canadian of all time' in a 2004 poll conducted by the CBC. "The criteria were broad. To be eligible, a nominee had to be:

- Born in what is now Canada, or born elsewhere but lived here and made a significant contribution to this country.
- Real (no fictional characters or animals).
- An individual (no pairs or groups).

Beyond that, it was up to the public to define what 'greatness' meant. People sent in more than *140,000* nominations from all corners of the country!" (Adapted from www.cbc.ca/greatest, January 2007.) It seems that Tommy Douglas epitomizes greatness, 'the Canadian way.' But what does that mean exactly? Stay tuned. …

This core style manifests itself through regional and individual filters. For instance, when asked to share their definition of leadership:

- Respondents in Atlantic Canada emphasized service to the community, resilience and positive attitude.
- People from Québec focused on risk, innovation and entrepreneurship.
- Ontarians spoke of fair play, strategy and responsibility.
- Residents of the Prairies and the North zeroed in on courage, determination and resourcefulness.
- Those in British Columbia stressed balance, collaboration and resilience.

Immigrants and Canadians who have lived/worked internationally have an especially sharp view of the Canadian leadership style because they can see it from the inside and the outside. "When I was in Chile, people told me that I led in an inclusive way. I think it is true. Canadians are used to a lot of diversity, in contrast to countries that are more homogeneous in look and thought. Taking into account a variety of perspectives is a Canadian habit." (Patrick Cuenco, Co-founder, Junior Hong Kong-Canada Business Association)

Respondents from the arts/media were particularly articulate and enthusiastic about this topic. "As a nation, we are consensus builders due to two dominant cultures with much more diversity. We have embraced the mosaic, not the melting pot. Differences make us rich and unique, and we tend to use collaborative processes." (Albert Schultz, Founding Artistic Director, Soulpepper Theatre Company)

Since culture is the crux of the arts, people spend time reflecting on topics such as leadership style and are skilled at picking up patterns and linkages. "I am very proud of Canada's image. We are both speedy and thoughtful. We have a North American rhythm coupled with a social-democratic ideology. We are good in many sectors and are not pretentious, in fact, sometimes too modest. …" (Lorraine Pintal, C.M., General and Artistic Director, Théâtre du Nouveau Monde)

Respondents from Québec were adept at contrasting the Canadian leadership style with that of various others. Europe is their main reference point, while the rest of Canada generally uses the U.S. "The Canadian leadership approach is derived from the Anglo-Saxon tradition, which impacts other Commonwealth countries such as the U.K., Australia and New Zealand. It is a style that navigates between America and Europe. For instance, the Canadian style is more efficient, open, organized and less hierarchical than the European style, and more oriented towards balancing the interests of various parties. For Canadians, a deal has to be good for *all* parties involved." (Stéphane Gonthier, Senior Vice-President, Eastern North America, Alimentation Couche-Tard Inc.)

Blind Spot

Most respondents stressed that we must become more aware of our own style. "People love Canada and Canadians. However, we need to become more aware of our qualities. Here, we truly understand the value people bring to organizations and the difference they can make. We must capitalize on our human perspective." (Cora Tsouflidou, President, Chez Cora/Cora's)

The lack of a common understanding of our own leadership style can result in operating in the dark and underestimating ourselves. "As Canadians, we are reflective of our culture; polite, at times not quite aggressive enough, but respectful. However, we underestimate our own ability when we should not." (Joseph Randell, President and CEO, Air Canada Jazz) It can also prevent us from seizing opportunities. "We need to stand up and be counted." (Susan LaRosa, Director of Education, York Catholic District School Board)

TRADEMARKS

Our Canadian Leadership Brand is characterized by two trademarks or signatures: *inclusion* and *process expertise*. People often prefaced their comments by mentioning the above.

Inclusion

The first trademark is *inclusion*. "Canadian leaders are inclined to be tolerant and inclusive in decision-making. They think of the group as opposed to the individual. The style is consensus-minded instead of authoritarian or one-upmanship." (Alfred Smithers, O.C., President and CEO, Secunda Group of Companies)

Many respondents shared their delighted surprise at discovering the positive view of Canadian leadership due to its inclusive style. "During a big project in Singapore, local employees said they felt treated with respect by Canadian leaders, like equals and without prejudice." (Richard Blackburn, General and Artistic Director, Théâtre de la Dame de Cœur)

One of our interviewees, the Honourable Ken Dryden, MP; Former Minister, Social Development, Government of Canada, had a wonderful explanation for this phenomenon in an article published in *Maclean's* magazine on September 25, 2006:

> We started out as two communities side by side, with different languages, culture, religions and laws. We created a nation; more than a century later, Canada is an immensely successful country by almost any measure. And we are a true global country with an unimaginable mix of peoples, languages, religions. Because of our French and English history, we created institutions and developed understandings that have allowed differences to thrive. We have evolved a 'live and let live' attitude that allows a bilingual country to work. We didn't set out to do this. It happened because of our Canadian experience.

Our history and reputation reinforce the inclusion trademark. We do not have an imperialist past and never set out to rule the world; therefore, we are not viewed as conquerors. This enables us to get along with small and large powers, developed and developing countries, without being suspected of ulterior motives. "We seem to be able to build bridges and enable people to reach consensus." (Susan Mitton, Regional Director, CBC Radio, Maritimes)

Moreover, our political stability and balanced views project safety and moderation instead of fanaticism or extremism. The first reaction to Canadians is generally positive: People are open to our influence. "Canada is an affluent and non-aggressive country. We are seen as the good guys, The Blue Helmets, the pacifists who promulgate humanitarian values." (Honourable Herménégilde Chiasson, Lieutenant Governor, New Brunswick)

Our temperament leads us to suggest instead of dictate, build bridges instead of forcing issues. We are perceived as moderates, able to navigate between right and left and negotiate positions everyone can live with. The prevailing opinion about us is summarized by these two Ps: *Peaceful* and *Professional*. This ability to keep to the middle and rally people serves us well in an increasingly diverse and interdependent world.

In adversity, we are capable of great things and other countries recognize it. Under pressure, we remain level-headed, calm and reasonable, a reputation reinforced by the deportment of our militaries, aid workers and diplomats. Our inclusive style is a definite competitive advantage in the global marketplace, where we are sought-after partners. "Canada has a golden opportunity. We are well-respected because of our past, are a peaceful place and have a social conscience. Other countries are looking up to us and we need to step up to the plate. We should be a leader in helping people from around the world. In order to do this, we need to move more quickly and decisively, be proactive instead of reactive." (Doug McCallum, Former Mayor, Surrey, British Columbia)

Process Expertise

Our second trademark is *process expertise*, such as soliciting input, rallying diverse perspectives, building teams, resolving conflicts and leveraging complementary abilities. If content is the 'what,' the substance of a discussion, then process is the 'how,' the framework, including agenda, facilitation, climate, decision-making methods, etc. It is the procedure that allows people to interact effectively and democratically in order to reach sound and satisfying decisions.

Process skills are much like housework: invisible except for their result, and more noticeable in failure than success. But don't underestimate them—they can make or break relationships and profoundly influence outcomes. For instance, a good facilitator creates a warm atmosphere where everyone feels comfortable expressing ideas and people can respect other perspectives. Competent facilitators reframe issues and identify themes until a common platform emerges, ensuring discussions don't become polarized or personal. They also use solid and democratic methods for consulting, problem-solving and decision-making. Process skills *weave* various threads into a consensus and uncover win-win solutions that have a chance to last.

Because of our size, federative structure and diversity, we have learned to value and hone process skills. "We are thoughtful leaders who can bring consensus to difficult issues where there is a wide range of opinions. We can help solve problems, bridge gaps and implement change. We need to become more influential by stepping up behind the scenes to encourage a collaborative approach." (Shelley White, CEO, United Way of Peel)

Process expertise is useful in many areas, including project management, problem-solving, team-building, negotiating, mediating, coaching, mentoring and consulting. "Canadians are often very good consultants. We can listen with no pre-formed ideas." (Dr. Jack Mintz, Professor, Business Economics, Director, International Tax Program, Institute of International Business, Rotman School of Management; Former President, C.D. Howe Institute)

Process expertise makes us desirable partners in international business and politics. "Before something is presented, we make sure discussions have taken place so people are engaged and own the process and the results. People want Canada on their team because of our collaborative approach. Adaptable and flexible, we can play different roles." (Denise Amyot, Vice-President, Leadership Network, Public Service Human Resources Agency, Government of Canada)

In international aid, people notice we genuinely care and want to transfer our know-how. "Canada is considered a positive influence, well-received and well-perceived. People from other countries know we sincerely want to train their staff to help them become autonomous. In fact, there is more demand than we can supply. Canada Mortgage and Housing Corporation's international business has tripled in recent years. We could take on much more, but it would require redefining our mandate." (Pierre David, Executive Director, CMHC International [Canada Mortgage and Housing Corporation])

As the world reduces in size and increases in complexity, success will belong to the *integrators*, not the *bullies*. As a country with a good reputation, an inclusive style and solid process skills, we are well-positioned to influence. People are open to listen to us. But what will our message be? "We have to do something to help the world; we need to provide leadership based on ideas, ideals and values." (Pierre Morin, Former Director, Parks and Recreation, City of Montréal)

INFLUENCES

Our trademarks of inclusion and process expertise did not happen overnight. How did they emerge and evolve?

"Identity builds by layers: nation, language, culture. At different times, one layer or another becomes more or less important." (Honourable Herménégilde Chiasson, Lieutenant Governor, New Brunswick) Likewise, leadership style is constructed by layers and evolves over time. Respondents pointed to five major factors that have shaped our leadership style:

- Space
- History
- Immigration
- Legislation
- Political leadership.

Space

"We have a large country, thinly populated." (Gerry Duffy, Strategic Management Consultant; Former Senior Vice-President, Methanex) As a result, we generally believe opportunities abound or can be created, and that there is enough room for people to 'do their own thing' and express their individuality. The pressure to conform is not overly strong.

Our federative structure and size allow regional differences and strengths to flourish. We value the unique contribution each region brings. During our research, regional cultures became very visible to us and we were fascinated by their strength and uniqueness. For example:

- The community spirit of Atlantic Canada shone through loud and clear. Weeks after the interviews, people would call us back, asking if they could do anything else to help us.
- Likewise, the determination of the Prairies was evident throughout. People would say things like "We talked to each other and decided your book is a good idea. We are going to pull together and ensure that you have good representation from this region."
- The pioneer spirit of the North was admirable and heartwarming: Some interviewees from Yellowknife volunteered to travel to participate in leadership events in order to ensure that we had a Northern presence.
- People from Québec showed a lot of support by their willingness to 'take a chance' on us. Comments like "We want to be part of this adventure. This sounds exciting!" were frequently heard.
- Respondents from Ontario worked very hard to help us by activating and leveraging their networks.
- People from B.C. showed wisdom and caring by offering their help in clever ways and being steadfast through the whole process.

Throughout, even the busiest people found time to participate because they thought it was the right thing to do and wanted the project to show multiple opinions.

People bent over backwards to help us, some by suggesting other leaders or institutions to contact, others by providing resources, others yet by offering sponsorship and support. Some even invited us to stay at their homes when visiting their city!

After several months of talking to people, we realized how rich our differences are and how much we can benefit and grow through learning from each other. Canada is like a big salad where each ingredient retains its identity while combining with others to create an interesting and unique mix. The 'dressing' (core culture and values) binds us together, giving our salad a distinctive flavour.

"Canada has a lot to gain from understanding and appreciating regional differences; from working with what it is in a gentle way and valuing the contribution of diverse parties. Our country is first and foremost a network. We have to transcend infrastructures and congregate around common values." (Rémi Tremblay, President, Esse Leadership) Just like in mutual gains bargaining, we need to focus on common interests first, and let regional differences flourish.

Our size not only allows for physical space, but psychological space as well, which makes us tolerant and creative. It does, however, make it harder to reach across the land, so people link through smaller pockets, usually in a vertical way by sectors or regions. In order to join horizontally, leaders need a focus and enabling infrastructures such as national networks.

History

"Canada was forged out of conciliation. Politically, we are like this too. It makes us successful." (Chris Rudge, CEO and Secretary General, Canadian Olympic Committee) Canada is a young country; we are less hampered by established ways, open to finding new solutions, and confident in the future. Adversely, people can be too focused on the present and ignore the lessons of the past. Most respondents could articulate the 'Canadian consciousness,' but were not always clear on where it came from.

In order to create a strong Canadian identity, we need to define and disseminate a common baseline of historical knowledge that *all* Canadians can partake in. This would not only enable us to share a similar frame of reference, but help us position ourselves in trade, international aid and diplomacy. A clearer understanding of the forces that shaped our past and made us who we are will help us better grasp our uniqueness and make a convincing case to those we seek to influence.

Others seem to see us more clearly than we see ourselves, and this puts us at a disadvantage. We should be able to see ourselves clearly and with detachment. History is a powerful means to do so, because it *illuminates* the past and *enlightens* the present.

Immigration

Canada, Australia and the U.S. are the world's top three immigration countries. Because of our extensive immigration, we have now become a microcosm of the world and have devised leading-edge policies in the areas of human rights and multiculturalism to enable people from various ethnic backgrounds to cohabit peacefully. As well, church and state are separate, which permits multiple religions to coexist, most of the time peacefully.

In March 2006, the TV network France 2 aired a program entitled *Pourquoi le Canada fait-il rêver?* (*Why Canada makes us dream?*) which outlined how we welcome immigrants and allow them to flourish. The program proposed the Canadian model as a valid option for France to consider in their diversity efforts. "When people immigrate to Canada, we believe that they enrich our nation. We see diversity as a positive force and believe in its richness." (Nancy Karetak-Lindell, MP, Nunavut)

In today's global world, the ability to respect and productively manage differences is a strong asset. Because of our size, federative structure, bilingualism and extensive immigration, we are further ahead than other countries in this regard, and can leverage this competency in business, politics and international aid. But we need to become more aware of this asset and use it consciously and strategically. Expanding on our earlier salad analogy, we have done a good job of ensuring the various 'vegetables' retain their identity. What can be done so that the 'dressing' which binds us together sticks to all the ingredients? More on that in the next chapter...

Interviewees shared many stories about being selected for international projects or winning competitive bids, largely because of their nationality. They reported frequently hearing statements like these:

- "Canada has North American know-how and a social democratic conscience."
- "You have the best passport in the world. Make sure it stays that way!"
- "You are from Canada. Are you a mediator then?"
- "We want to work with you because you make us feel part of the team, not like second-class citizens."
- "We chose you because we can count on you. You won't let us down."

There are enormous possibilities for us to adopt a leadership stance suited to our temperament, size and values. The wind is favourable. How do we want to set our sails? Imagine, for instance, becoming champions and custodians of the environment, or fighting AIDS worldwide, or spearheading literacy, ethics or wellness? The sky is the limit; let's choose and move forward.

Legislation

Over the years, Canada has created a legislative framework that guarantees citizens a wide range of rights and freedoms and seeks to eliminate barriers preventing everyone from contributing to society. "We, as Canadians, must continue to work towards a balanced and compassionate approach to differences. Participation and involvement are the norm, instead of exclusion and ostracism. This is not the case in other countries." (Philip Owen, Former Mayor, Vancouver, British Columbia)

We owe gratitude to the wisdom and vision of previous legislators who crafted our legislative framework:

- **1867:** The Constitution Act defines the country.
- **1947:** The Citizenship Act defines what it means to be a Canadian citizen.
- **1960:** The Canadian Bill of Rights defines rights and freedoms of Canadian citizens, such as equality, liberty, security, property and justice.
- **1969:** The Official Languages Act asserts the status of French and English as the two official languages of Canada.

- **1976:** The Immigration Act defines categories of immigration and regulations governing them, establishes the respective roles of provincial and federal governments in the planning and administration of immigration, and abolishes discrimination in immigration.
- **1977:** The Canadian Human Rights Act establishes equal rights related to opportunity and accommodation and defines prohibited grounds of discrimination.
- **1982:** The Canadian Charter of Rights and Freedoms further defines fundamental freedoms, such as conscience, religion, thought, belief, press, peaceful assembly, and association.
- **1985:** The Canadian Multiculturalism Act acknowledges freedom of all members of Canadian society to preserve, enhance and share their cultural heritage.
- **1986:** The Employment Equity Act seeks to achieve equality in all aspects of employment and to eliminate systemic discrimination. It targets four groups: women, persons with disabilities, members of visible minorities and Aboriginal people.
- **1991:** The Canadian Race Relations Foundations Act creates a foundation aimed at eliminating all forms of racism in Canada.
- **2005:** The Civil Marriage Act extends the legal capacity for civil marriage to same-sex couples, while respecting religious freedom.

As a result, leadership in Canada is not tied to privilege, status or money, but to competence, performance and the ability to create opportunities. Today, anyone who has the know-how, desire and vision can aspire to leadership. Our leadership is *with* people, not distant *from* them. We have become "a capitalist system with a social conscience." (Gerry Duffy, Strategic Management Consultant; Former Senior Vice-President, Methanex)

The framework is laid out and it affects our attitudes, behaviours and leadership style. We can make it better by being strategic and thinking long term.

Political Leadership

A number of interviewees made reference to political leaders as symbols of our National Leadership Brand. Former prime ministers Lester B. Pearson and Pierre Elliott Trudeau were cited as most influential in shaping our leadership style: Pearson representing the humanitarian dimension, and Trudeau, the courageous one. Together, Pearson and Trudeau embody the qualities of diplomacy and assertiveness. "During Pearson's time, Canada was recognized for moderation and conciliation. We were respected as peacekeepers and provided stability at the UN.

Trudeau, for his part, added further dimensions to our international impression and reputation." (Honourable William G. Davis, P.C., C.C., Q.C., Former Premier, Ontario)

Pearson and his achievements exemplify cherished Canadian ideals that resonate with our sense of identity. "I am so proud of Pearson's accomplishments ... the voice of reason, harmony, collaboration and collective responsibility." (Paul Zarnke, Executive Director, Children's Aid Society, Region of Peel) Respondents felt very strongly that the role he created for Canada is appropriate for our *stature and nature* and needs to be carried forward. "Our role as a conciliator and peacekeeper is a good one; however, we need to act more quickly and decisively, take a stand and stick to it." (William Adair, Executive Director, Canadian Paraplegic Association of Ontario)

Pearson is remembered as someone who 'drew the best out of others.' "Lester B. Pearson was a leader with diplomacy and courage. This requires nerves and adherence to values." (Janet Austin, CEO, YWCA of Vancouver) Stephen Lewis is often mentioned as a spiritual heir to Pearson today. "The UN Secretary-General appointed him as his Special Envoy for HIV/AIDS in Africa. In March 2004, Mr. Lewis was honoured by the UN Association in Canada with the Pearson Peace Medal, which celebrates outstanding achievements in the field of international service. In April 2005, *Time Magazine* listed him as one of the '100 most influential people in the world.' " (Excerpts from The Stephen Lewis Foundation website, www.stephenlewisfoundation.org, January 2007.)

Trudeau represents the complementary pole: assertive and brave. "We need to recapture the voice we had when Trudeau was prime minister and stood up to the U.S." (Bill Hamilton, Executive Coach, W.J.A. Hamilton & Associates; Former Senior Vice-President, BMO and CIBC) He was admired for his boldness, his flamboyant style and his superb intellect. "Trudeau put us on the world map. Like him, we need to be fiercely independent, based on our values." (George Cohon, O.C., O.Ont., Founder, McDonald's Restaurants of Canada and McDonald's in Russia)

Trudeau was a transformational leader who worked tirelessly to achieve his vision of 'a just society.' He kept his eye on the mark and had the courage to say no to whatever strayed away from it. He made a lasting impression in our minds and in our hearts. People speak of him with longing and admiration. Interviewees often mentioned General Roméo Dallaire as his spiritual heir because of his courage and his efforts to strengthen United Nations peacekeeping.

The Trudeau and Pearson voices unite to form a complete whole: *courage* with *care*. It is easy to see that one without the other can lead to an incomplete outlook. To achieve maximum potency, they must be balanced. Interviewees recommended planning and acting strategically to affirm these voices. For instance, how can we express *care* effectively in international aid, humanitarian efforts and public policy? How can we express *courage* and take a stand on environmental issues, health care and culture? Respondents stated that we will be at our best when we consciously develop, affirm and express these voices in a concerted, deliberate and assertive manner.

This can even serve us in business, where being exploitative (lacking care) antagonizes stakeholders, resulting in a bad reputation and damaged relationships. Likewise, being weak (lacking courage) leaves you open to being taken for granted, swindled or used.

Still valid today, these legacies are deeply tied to the Canadian identity and need to be constantly affirmed. Many interviewees thought that some ground has been lost and needs to be regained. More on this in the next chapter.

NATIONAL LEADERSHIP BRAND

As the world gets smaller, more complex and interdependent, the importance of integrating various perspectives, achieving win-win solutions and collaborating with diverse people increases. Canadians are uniquely positioned to succeed. Here are a few of our assets:

- Experience and success in dealing with diversity.
- Federative structure, which requires managing regional differences.
- Size, which forces us to reach out across great distances.
- History, which has taught us that solutions that last have to work for all parties.
- Values that drive political stability and moderation: peace, order and good government.
- Bilingualism, which gives us an edge over unilingual countries.
- Reputation; with our lack of imperialistic baggage, no one suspects us of a domination agenda.
- Track record in defending democracy and in peacekeeping.

We stand at the crossroads of success if we play our cards right. As former prime minister Lester B. Pearson used to say, "The 21st century will belong to Canada."

Brand Structure

At the core stand values; next, cornerstone beliefs, which in turn produce attributes that go on to affect behaviours. It's like a cascade moving from the centre outwards. "The Canadian leadership style cannot be disassociated from

Canadian values, focused on consensus, honesty, conciliation and democracy." (Pierre David, Executive Director, CMHC International [Canada Mortgage and Housing Corporation])

Values

Values have an enormous influence on behaviours. Visualize a stained glass window, each piece of a different design and colour, held together with strong metal. The metal represents values.

Values guide actions. "We have a sense of fairness, consensus-building and getting everyone onside." (Dr. Franco Vaccarino, Chair, Department of Psychology, University of Toronto) "Recently, singer/songwriter and political activist Bono said, 'the world needs more Canada.' The image of integrity, trust … We are a values-based society. We use our values as a form of currency." (Victor Lachance, Consultant; Former President and CEO, Canadian Centre for Ethics in Sport)

Values are shaped by history, heritage and policy decisions. The Canadian military did extensive research on the topic. "As people, Canadians recognize a number of fundamental values that the nation aspires to reflect. We believe that such values can be woven into the fabric of our society and expect our leaders to preserve them throughout the governance system. Canadian values are expressed first and foremost in founding legislation such as the Constitution Act of 1982 and the Canadian Charter of Rights and Freedoms … as well as in a number of pieces of foundational legislation and … their preambles." (*Duty with Honour: The Profession of Arms in Canada*, published under the auspices of the Chief of Defence Staff by the Canadian Defence Academy, Canadian Forces Leadership Institute, 2003)

Canadian values can be organized in three groups: individual, community and country.

Table 13.1

INDIVIDUAL	COMMUNITY	COUNTRY
• Respect and dignity of all persons. • Rights and freedoms. **PEOPLE FIRST +**	• Democratic principles. • Abidance of lawful authority. **SOCIAL JUSTICE =**	• Order. • Good government. • Peace. **STABILITY**

(Adapted from *Duty with Honour: The Profession of Arms in Canada*, published under the auspices of the Chief of Defence Staff by the Canadian Defence Academy, Canadian Forces Leadership Institute, 2003.)

If individuals are respected and well-treated, communities can be built on democratic principles and citizens will abide by lawful authority. The result is a peaceful and orderly country, ruled by good government. Each of the three categories of Canadian values is governed by an organizing principle: People First + Social Justice = Stability, the basis of Canadian society. This infrastructure was mirrored in our discussions with respondents.

Individual

The foundation is respect, dignity and guaranteed rights and freedoms for all. Individual rights have to be balanced by collective responsibility for the care and well-being of community. "Our cultural heart is compassion, as evidenced by our safety nets." (Dr. Gary McPherson, C.M., Executive Director, Canadian Centre for Social Entrepreneurship, University of Alberta)

Community

Through democratic principles, we seek to build communities where everyone has a voice, is treated in an equitable manner and can contribute to the best of their abilities. If the legislative framework is fair and well-managed, citizens will abide by it, resulting in social justice. "Canada respects diversity. We understand multiple perspectives. Fairness and social justice are part of who we are." (Dr. Valerie Davidson, NSERC/HP Canada Chair for Women in Science and Engineering, School of Engineering, University of Guelph)

Country

"Our democracy and political stability rest on solid laws, a social fabric based on rules of right, and social-democratic and co-operative values influenced by Western Canada." (Jean Houde, Deputy Minister, Ministère des Finances du Québec [Québec Department of Finance])

Cornerstones

Flowing from the values are cornerstones or characteristics that define the brand. If values are the central core, cornerstones act as pillars to support the whole edifice. As our celebrated country star Paul Brandt says in his hit song *Canadian Man*, "Strong and free, that's the True North and, baby, that's me!" Values act like a compass setting the direction. And by being true to our values, we can point the way like the True North. Next, are attributes or qualities that exemplify or manifest the cornerstones. Finally, attributes condition behaviour selection.

Here's an illustration. Years ago, one of the authors ventured into a car dealership to have her car fixed. Although the only customer at the desk, she was ignored by service reps who were reading the paper, drinking coffee and chatting with each other. When one of them reluctantly approached the counter with much sighing and reluctance, she asked him to explain a banner prominently displayed in the waiting area, stating that *'customer care is our #1 priority.'* He replied that it was part of a 'head office campaign' and they 'had to use' the banner. Obviously, this organization did not hold customer service as a value. As a result, customer service was not a cornerstone of their culture. Staff appeared unresponsive, uncaring and negligent (attributes), and more interested in their own pursuits than customers' interests (behaviours). Needless to say, the author walked out of the dealership in search of a customer-responsive one—more proof that culture impacts the bottom line ... sometimes with a vengeance.

What individuals, organizations and nations hold dear can be clearly seen through their attitudes and actions, because values influence the whole chain: characteristics, attributes and behaviours.

The five cornerstones that shape our leadership brand are linked and synergize to create dynamics in constant evolution.

- **Principle**: an ethical and sound foundation for leadership practice; the key word is *integrity*.
- **Professionalism**: competence, know-how, accountability; the key word is *quality*.
- **Possibility**: can-do attitude and resilience to make it happen; the key word is *resourcefulness*.
- **Diversity**: ability to seek, respect and integrate various perspectives and work with different people; the key word is *inclusiveness*.
- **Peace:** collaboration, problem-solving and conflict resolution; the key word is *harmony*.

Principle

"Canadian leaders are visionaries, ambitious people able to demonstrate boldness and creativity. At a time when globalization makes constant innovation a prerequisite to remaining competitive, they are able to make their mark, never forgetting that their success reflects on their entire community." (Isabelle Hudon, President and CEO, Board of Trade of Metropolitan Montréal)

We strive to do the right thing, sometimes to a fault. Principle is the foundation that supports our actions, and we invest time and energy in clarifying it. Principle

Illustration 13.1

Canadian Leadership Brand

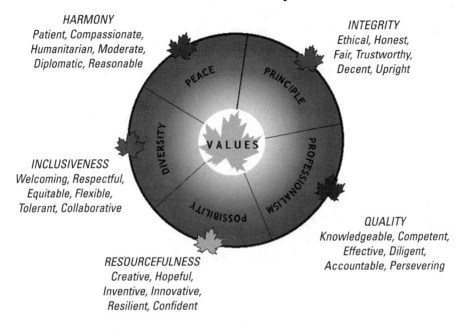

HARMONY
Patient, Compassionate,
Humanitarian, Moderate,
Diplomatic, Reasonable

INTEGRITY
Ethical, Honest,
Fair, Trustworthy,
Decent, Upright

INCLUSIVENESS
Welcoming, Respectful,
Equitable, Flexible,
Tolerant, Collaborative

QUALITY
Knowledgeable, Competent,
Effective, Diligent,
Accountable, Persevering

RESOURCEFULNESS
Creative, Hopeful,
Inventive, Innovative,
Resilient, Confident

develops attributes such as ethical, honest, fair, trustworthy, decent and upright. "The Canadian thing is to be fair, extremely ethical, almost too fair." (David Carey, President, Volleyball Canada)

Internationally, we are viewed as the good guys: modest, decent, fair, the ones who play by the rules. Mostly, it is to our advantage: better to make decisions that you can live with in all conscience than to win on shady moral ground. The bottom line is integrity. "We are uniquely positioned to play a role regarding ethics in the workplace. We could help other countries improve the quality of ethics at work." (Suzanne Blanchet, President and CEO, Cascades Tissue Group)

Principle doesn't guarantee success, but it guarantees reputation. The most gratifying form of success is the one that comes from a combination of creativity, professional standards and strong ethics.

Professionalism

Professionalism is a leadership requirement and it means much more than expertise. It is a combination of *savoir faire*, effectiveness, discipline and appropriate behaviour. Professions in the strictest sense are regulated by codes of conduct and member behaviour is monitored by professional associations.

In Canada, we prize doing a good job; sloppiness and half measures are not our thing. As a result, we take care of upgrading our knowledge. We value education and enjoy accessible and inexpensive education at the primary and secondary levels, as well as an ever-expanding network of colleges and universities. Distance education is becoming increasingly popular, as are workplace training and certification programs of all kinds.

But acting professionally is more than competence; it's about behaving in a manner befitting the role. For instance, judges who have no values lose credibility, and therapists who share their own problems with patients cross the line. Professionalism means playing the part *and* looking the part. It also means having a code of ethics and clarity of purpose: Who are you serving and how? For example, you wouldn't want to be operated on by a surgeon who doesn't value life.

To describe our professionalism, respondents used words like knowledgeable, competent, effective, diligent, accountable and persevering. In many ways we are "'the little engine that could'—lots of determination, heart and energy. Give us a shot and see how well we do." (Bruno Biscaro, COO, Accucaps Industries Limited)

Like our national animal, the beaver, we keep at it until the job is done. "Canadians are very resourceful in difficult situations. We get things done. We look at situations differently and are extremely creative. As a result, we are widely respected." (Mel Benson, Board Member, Suncor Energy Inc.)

Many respondents shared stories like this: "Canada is the third-largest exporter of engineering services in the world. We are recognized worldwide for our competence and perceived as very strong. We easily outrank our competitors in bids because of our inclusive and democratic approach. My successful African experience has helped me understand why we are so sought-after in international projects. I am now opening offices in Asia and South America!" (Kazimir Olechnowicz, President and General Manager, CIMA+)

Possibility

As a young country, we have a sense of the possible. Moreover, history has showed us that people can succeed despite overwhelming odds. We have made remarkable progress since our inception, and generally enjoy prosperity, quality of life and a good reputation. The future looks bright.

Possibility produces attributes such as creative, hopeful, inventive, innovative, resilient and confident. "Out of nothing, we can create something fantastic. We are possibility addicts!" (Cora Tsouflidou, President, Chez Cora/Cora's)

Possibility manifests itself in many ways—innovation, problem-solving, inventiveness—and is displayed in many sectors. From winning literary prizes to organizing award-winning exhibits, we do it all!

Here's an example shared by Clément Guimond, General Coordinator, Caisse d'économie solidaire Desjardins [Credit Union]: "Our organization was born of the desire to shape a better world where everyone can become an actor instead of a spectator, in a more democratic environment, allowing people to realize their ambitions. Over time, we have become the 'banker of dreams.' For instance, we are Cirque du Soleil's financial institution because we agreed to their first loan. Once, they sent a plaque that said, 'Circus or Credit Union, we share a common passion for pushing back the limits of the possible over and over again.'"

Possibility keeps our culture positive and hopeful instead of resigned and bitter. It is a prerequisite for crafting visions and taking risks. Once again, Alberta's pride Paul Brandt sums it up perfectly in his song *Small Towns and Big Dreams*: "That's where I come from, that's who I am. Hard-working and God blessed. Yes Sir! Thank you Ma'am! The best things around that I have ever seen came from small towns and big dreams."

The belief in possibility, along with the accompanying sense of hope, is the seed of greatness. It is where everything starts; without it, people become resigned, paralyzed and cynical. It's up to us to keep the flame of possibility alive. More on that in the next chapter.

Diversity

The ability to productively manage differences is fast becoming a critical success factor in today's global economy. Diversity means creating a large enough container for everyone to participate. When societies choose to exclude some of their citizens based on ethnic background, physical ability, religion, colour, etc., they waste valuable contributions and plant the seed of social unrest and revolution. As history has amply demonstrated, exclusion leads to resentment, outrage and violence. If change cannot happen by *evolution,* the excluded group makes sure it happens through *revolution* and the price to pay is in blood.

Immigration, space, history, values and wise leadership have resulted in Canada's decision to value diversity. It took us decades of groundbreaking legislation and changing attitudes. Because Canada chose the mosaic over the melting pot, our society is a rich, textured and complex tapestry. "We are open to other points of view and cultures. We lead through consensus-building. We don't impose our way." (Stacey Allaster, President, Sony Ericsson WTA [Women's Tennis Association] Tour; Former Vice-President and Tournament Director, Tennis Canada) This decision had a profound effect on our leadership style and produces attributes like welcoming, respectful, equitable, flexible, tolerant and collaborative.

The path to accepting and leveraging differences is paved with tolerance and open-mindedness. At times, it's also liberating and fun. One of the authors recently watched a TV show on Irish dancing in the Prairies, featuring dance competitions, training, costume-making, etc. A striking feature was that a significant number of people involved were not of Irish descent and generally unfamiliar with Irish traditions. For example, many people from Asian and Eastern European backgrounds had won regional dancing championships and were on their way to national and even international competitions. The program showcased interviews with parents and students alike, who saw Irish dancing as an opportunity to broaden their horizons and expand their knowledge base, on top of learning a skill and keeping fit. Witnessing these welcoming attitudes was refreshing and gratifying.

Diversity is hard work, but it brings many joys and enriches our lives and perspectives. One of the authors recently attended a concert featuring the Juno Award-winning band African Guitar Summit, a group composed of musicians from several African countries, performing songs in their native languages and wearing traditional dress. The music was upbeat and positive and the musicians impressive. The packed audience gave them a standing ovation. How fortunate we are to live in a country open to the world and its cultures. Through it, we grow as people and a society.

Peace

As Canadians, we are privileged to enjoy peace and deeply appreciate it. We understand that a bad deal for one of the parties will eventually sour it for all, and therefore we try to find workable solutions, ideally through *consensus*, and, if not, through *compromise*. "War is not our first course of action. We may bicker and debate, but we resolve our issues in a non-violent way" (Suzanne Christie, Project Manager, Peel Mentoring Network; Instructor)

Peace is our *most important* value and also a cornerstone. As such, it is the dominant colour of our Leadership Brand and the key to unlocking our culture. Peace is who we are, what we cherish, what we will put our lives on the line for. At a profound level, we understand that peace is the prerequisite for prosperity, security, justice and well-being. Therefore, we work for it within and outside our borders in official and non-official ways.

Our culture and temperament entice us to seek harmony and cooperation. "We try to find winning solutions using good judgement. We naturally rally people towards a winning position." (Marie-France D'Auray-Boult, General Director,

Performance & Knowledge Management Branch, Canadian International Development Agency [CIDA])

At the simplest level, peace means the absence of war; however, it can also mean fewer conflicts, a culture of collaboration and a space where many divergent beliefs can cohabit without clashing. "We are inclusive, inclined to build bridges to peace and harmony." (Ruth Kelly, President, Venture Publishing Inc.; Publisher and Editor-in-Chief, *Alberta Venture*)

Peace develops attributes such as patient, compassionate, humanitarian, moderate, diplomatic and reasonable. "We are flexible and help knit things together. We are part of solutions." (Dave Mowat, CEO, Vancity Credit Union) This explains our success in peacekeeping, negotiation and conflict resolution. "We love peace and are creative. We are excellent mediators because of our fairness." (Yolande James, MNA for Nelligan, Québec)

How can we leverage our expertise, not just in peacekeeping but in peace making, problem-solving, conflict resolution and mediation? Every Canadian has the potential to become a catalyst for peace—an awesome role, responsibility and expectation. We have a big future in this respect if we make the right moves. More on that in the next chapter.

Levels of Intensity

The attributes derived from the cornerstones can be plotted on a spectrum of intensity: high (at its best), medium (average) and low (poorly actualized).

- 'High' represents the ideal, attained by some, part of the time, but not consistently by everyone.
- 'Medium' is where most people sit, most of the time.
- 'Low' is where all of us fall, some of the time, in our bad moments; where people begin their development; or where those unaware of the attribute or uninterested in it reside permanently.

When a culture is aligned, the majority of people demonstrate the attributes to a medium or high level, with some outliers demonstrating behaviours that clash with the majority. The ideal, of course, is high, and not surprisingly, respondents wished for brand attributes to be displayed more consistently, at a higher level of intensity, by more people.

It's important to set the bar high. Bearing that in mind, there are two dangers:

- **Not doing it:** Behaviours clash with the norm and become dissonant, creating a negative reaction; for instance, an unscrupulous leader in a principled society, a bully in a participatory system, a doomsayer in an ingenious group.

- **Overdoing it:** An overdone strength can become ineffective; for instance, someone who is too trustworthy becomes gullible. When this occurs, it dilutes the brand, produces doubt about the attribute, and starts a quest to restore balance. If diversity is overdone, for example, people worry about diluting the Canadian identity and seek to protect the Canadian core.

Table 13.2

	Characteristics			
Not doing it	**Low**	**Medium**	**High**	**Overdoing it**
PRINCIPLE				
No scruples	Minimum conscience	Above board and correct	Highest possible standards	Don Quixote
PROFESSION-ALISM				
Doesn't have a clue	Barely functional	Fully functional	A true pro	Perfectionism
POSSIBILITY				
Why bother trying?	Let's try	We can do it	We'll find a way no matter what	Champion of lost causes
DIVERSITY				
My way is the best, if not the only way	Accept differences	Value differences	Leverage differences	Chaos: anything goes
PEACE				
I am right and you are wrong	I am open to hearing your point of view	I see both sides	Let's find a solution we can both live with	Gives in at all cost

Medium to high intensities are optimal; low intensity is functional. Not doing it and overdoing it are both ineffective. The trick for Canada and other nations is to maintain ourselves in the 'zone' where we are effective and at the same time express our individuality.

CONCLUSION

The least we can say is that Canada has a good thing going. This research confirmed what our professional practice has shown us: Canadians are sitting on a gold mine and don't know it. Our traditional modesty prevents us from looking at ourselves long enough to see how good we are and how high we could fly. Checking ourselves in the mirror doesn't mean becoming self-absorbed and arrogant; it means doing a reality check. If we don't like something, we can change it. If we really like something, we can make the best of it.

In the next chapter, we will look at how to enhance our leadership impact as a nation, construct our leadership identity and strengthen our brand attributes.

CHAPTER 14

THE SCHOLAR AND THE WARRIOR

Let's take time to talk about our Canadian values. This will help us deal with a lot of issues. Let's unite our collective voice.
Mariette Mulaire, Executive Director
Economic Development Council for Manitoba Bilingual Municipalities

We are fortunate to live in a great country and it should continue to prosper. How to make it better is the important question.
Kevin Cameron
Consultant; Former President, The Halifax Mooseheads Hockey Club

We need to develop a culture of excellence. Competition is fierce at the international level. If we don't stand out, we won't be noticed. Our leadership is understated, efficient and inclusive. It is a process leadership and a great strength to share with others, but we must also expand competence.
Marc Poulin
President Operations, Québec Region, Sobeys Inc.

OUR LEADERSHIP VOICE

One of the authors recently visited the Royal Ontario Museum. In a section, two massive statues, a scholar and a warrior, were guarding a tomb, providing guidance and protection to the soul of the departed. The docent guiding the tour explained that ancients believed these complementary energies were optimal to safeguard souls.

After reflecting on the Canadian leadership brand, the authors concluded that these roles fit our approach, and embody the legacies of Pearson and Trudeau discussed in the previous chapter. The scholar represents wisdom, perceptiveness, diplomacy: Pearson. The warrior represents courage, determination, assertiveness: Trudeau. These two complementary energies convey our nature and aspirations. Interviewees repeatedly stated that the Pearson legacy must be reinforced, a tradition to maintain. Likewise, they advised emulating Trudeau's strength, an aspiration to reach.

The scholar/warrior framework seems suitable for our nature, stature and aspirations. The power generated by this image illustrates how much guidance can be derived from having a clear leadership identity and utilizing our brand attributes. As introduced in the previous chapter, entities such as nations can be viewed as leaders, or not. It depends on how its members experience their collective leadership identity and on their willingness to act. Therefore, how can we go about affirming our leadership identity?

Defining Our Core

In their landmark research *Built to Last* (New York, Harper Business, 1997), James C. Collins and Jerry I. Porras identified what makes the difference between exceptional and successful organizations. They found that the exceptional ones possess a stable core containing ideology and providing guidance that they preserve at all costs. Such organizations also strive for progress and continuous improvement. Having a solid core doesn't mean being stifled and unable to keep with the times. But it does tell you what to change and what to safeguard. These two internal forces (preservation and progress) complement and regulate each other: core provides continuity and drive expands possibilities and potential.

The million-dollar question organizations and nations struggle with is *what to put in the core?* Too much, and the organization becomes unwieldy and difficult to change. Too little, and the organization loses its identity, descending into chaos. Typically, core comprises mission, vision, values. It can also be complemented by elements like code of ethics, guiding principles, promise, etc.

Illustration 14.1

Too Much or Too Little?

TOO MUCH:

Lacks flexibility

Change is slow and difficult

TOO LITTLE:

Identity diluted

Anything goes

As a nation, what should be part of our core? How can we define a core we resonate with and are willing to protect and defend? Just like for organizations, the challenge is to balance stability and drive for continuous improvement. However, the balance imperative can apply to other dimensions, for instance, balancing openness with diversity while safekeeping the Canadian identity; balancing multicultural richness while setting aside what is not in line with our values; balancing economic development with a sustainable environment. "We have a can-do attitude and show tolerance. We need to continue on this path without losing True North. We are modest and must remain so, but must also become more aware of our strengths." (Honourable Herménégilde Chiasson, Lieutenant Governor, New Brunswick)

Defining Our Mission

It starts by defining our mission, which is like looking in the mirror and asking *what are we all about?* Mission speaks to core, essence, and therefore, essentials—deciding what really matters, and ensuring that it survives and thrives.

Natalie MacMaster, our young Cape Breton fiddle sensation, performs Celtic airs inspired by her island's tradition with great passion and reverence. Obviously, this music means a lot to her and she wants to preserve and enhance it. One might think this musical format would be relegated to a niche market, but Natalie, who seems in her thirties, has already released 10 CDs and recently taped a PBS special. This goes to prove that the truer you are to yourself, the more people can 'see' you. This principle applies to people and nations: a clear identity ensures visibility.

We must think strategically about our identity and future. "Take a step back and figure out who we are and what we want to be. We should not just be reacting to situations. Stop reacting and have a plan." (Stuart MacMillan, Founder and Chairman, Ignition Strategies)

Once the mission is in place, the next step is about defining our vision.

Defining Our Vision

Crafting a vision is like looking through a window: Where do we want to go? If mission is about identity, vision is about direction.

Mission ensures you *stay true* to yourself and vision ensures you have *a destination* and a road map so don't get sidetracked by the crisis or opportunity of the day. For example, consider the level of focus, alignment and sustained effort it took Ireland to transform itself into the Silicon Valley of Europe and be called "The Celtic Tiger."

To be productive and satisfied, countries, just like organizations and individuals, must define both their mission and vision. This is the starting point to fulfilling potential. And much like organizations and individuals, countries go through normal phases of growth, plateaus and renewal.

Moreover, a link exists between vision and visibility: Leaders need to have a vision in order to be visible to themselves and others. Expressing a vision shows leadership and inspires confidence. In fact, it represents the first step on the leadership path. Upon reaching the vision or destination, the leader will be hailed as a visionary. Visioning is a *fundamental* leadership act.

Consequently, creating a vision for Canada's future will make us more visible to ourselves and each other. "We are insufficiently aware of who we are and what we have; we don't know ourselves well enough. It's not that there is no identity, but rather that we are unevenly aware of it or don't share the same awareness. We must know who we are in order to protect what matters. We must define our country better." (Marc Mayer, Director, Montréal Museum of Contemporary Art)

This process will also help us appreciate our uniqueness and focus us on expressing our voice instead of comparing it, awakening our passion for Canada along the way. "We need to become overt, not covert, patriots. Stop being modest. Develop pride in our nation. The most important holiday of the year in my family is Canada Day. I want my daughters to grow up proud of their country and capable to help it become even better." (Mark Surrette, President, Robertson Surrette)

To define and affirm our mission and vision, interviewees suggested engaging in a national dialogue. In this day of easy travel and powerful technology, this excellent idea is realistically doable through a combination of interactive citizen forums and surveys, conducted live and via distance technology. Every Canadian could provide input, and the process, while driven by the federal government, could be conducted by a specialized, professional and objective third party to guarantee data integrity.

Once the data is collected, it needs to be analyzed and priorities selected, which would constitute the second round. Once again, citizens could make their choices known through a variety of formats. Finally, the vision and mission could be crafted and options presented for selection. In the end, we would end up with short, condensed and powerful mission and vision statements. For instance, remember NASA's vision in the '60s: "A man on the moon by the end of the decade."? And what about Nike's "Just do it!"? In only three words, Nike manages to convey its philosophy and propel its customers into action.

Every successful organization knows that the mission/vision exercise is a recurrent one; it must be revisited periodically. At the onset of the 21st century, the time has come to search our collective soul and come up with mission and vision appropriate for our times, aspirations and dreams. "Let's go back to basics: What is Canada about? What is our vision, where are we going and how will we get there? How can we work with other nations to learn?" (Joan C. Gibb, President, Canadian Cancer Society, Oakville Unit)

Because of our process expertise and federative structure, we have the skills to devise a good methodology to engage in an effective national dialogue.

EXPRESSING OUR LEADERSHIP VOICE

Once mission and vision are defined, they will act as a guidance system to determine our course of action in key areas, called strategic priorities. Without presuming what those will be, let us share the interviewees' recommendations for asserting our leadership and expanding our capacity to lead in a manner suited to our nature and stature. We have used the scholar/warrior model to organize them.

The Scholar

The scholar is wise, thoughtful and strategic. Here are two avenues that fit into this realm:

Increase Our International Presence

There is an abundance of opportunities to contribute internationally. Where can we add more value? What is the best use of our energies and limited resources?

"We have a lot to offer other countries and to do so, we must avoid self-absorption and be present. It's tempting to concern ourselves only with our own successful world, but the temptation must be resisted." (Louise Pelletier, Regional Director, Mauricie Region, Production of the Cascades, Hydro-Québec)

In order to be effective on the international scene, international knowledge is a must. "To reinforce our presence, Canadians need to be better informed and educated on international affairs. We also have to participate in more international projects, expand our peacekeeping efforts and generally become more proactive." (Pierre David, Executive Director, CMHC International [Canada Mortgage and Housing Corporation])

We could enhance international knowledge by, for instance, focusing on international affairs as early as secondary school, expanding international affairs contents and programming in the media, increasing international exchanges for youth and adults, etc.

Rethink International Aid

As a wealthy and successful nation, we have a responsibility to help those in need. Not only is it the right thing to do from a moral point of view, but in the long run, we stand to benefit. Developing nations need infrastructures and know-how, which we can help implement.

Respondents spoke of the need to become more strategic about international aid while maintaining our capacity to respond to emergencies. Jean-François Bouchard, President, Sid Lee, put forward a valid principle: "We need to do more for fewer, instead of doing little for many: pick our battles. We can't be all to all people. What is our focus? We must define our strategic orientations and priorities instead of diluting our efforts."

Interviewees suggested increasing international aid to at least 1% of gross national product. We are a privileged, rich, value-driven country; we should give and do more in a focused and consistent way. "If we had maintained aid with international countries, they would need less help now. We have failed to keep up with demands over the past 20 years. People used to be able to go to international opportunities volunteering. This has diminished greatly. Fundamental change is required." (Elizabeth O'Neill, Executive Director, Big Brothers Big Sisters, Edmonton and Area)

Respondents also suggested that our guiding principle should be to help countries achieve their potential according to what *they* aspire to. We should not impose our policies and systems on the nations we assist, but use our process skills to help them fashion theirs. "With recent reinvestment of research money, Canada has moved forward. We have the ability to have a huge impact on the international scene. We don't realize how much impact Canada can have, for example, on global health. We underestimate what we can offer—we should be more forthcoming." (Dr. Alan Bernstein, O.C., President, Canadian Institutes of Health Research)

The Warrior

The warrior is assertive, steady and bold. Here are some avenues to explore in this realm.

Define a Framework for Foreign Policy

Daily, many things happen in the world that require a response, but without an overarching framework, it's easy to become reactive and treat incidents in isolation.

To become stronger leaders on the international scene, we need to outline a long-term strategic framework, because social change takes a long time. Such a framework will go beyond terms in office and will guide politicians, regardless of which party is in power, in foreign policy decision-making. "As we are not a big nation, we can strengthen our role by making conscious decisions about foreign policy. We need to find our niche and concentrate on what we can do well." (May Brown, C.M., O.B.C., Former Councillor, City of Vancouver, B.C.)

For example, should we be neutral like Switzerland? What should be our policy regarding refugees or genocides? Since a lot of problems now require global solutions, what is our stance on global issues, like the environment, and on management of global diseases, such as AIDS? Such a framework would determine long-term orientations and criteria for decision-making, providing consistency and preventing reactivity. "We can be vocal on human rights, but these are often forgotten for economic reasons." (Shauna Sylvester, Founding Executive Director, Institute for Media, Policy and Civil Society [IMPACS]) "We have not developed congruent foreign affairs policies. We have not been able to sustain one position and keep working at it." (James [Sa'ke'j] Youngblood Henderson, I.P.C., Research Director, Native Law Centre of Canada; Professor, Aboriginal Law, College of Law, University of Saskatchewan)

Having such a framework would help governments, regardless of who is in office, make consistent decisions that fall within the boundaries of the framework and would reduce the see-saw effect too often witnessed in politics. It would also guide trade policies and partnerships.

Balance Trade

Leadership assumes a position of strength and we can't lead if our economy depends on a limited number of trade partners. Remember the softwood lumber dispute? Mothers used to say *don't put all your eggs in one basket* and they were right. This principle should guide our trade policy. We need to balance trade, expanding and diversifying our reach. This requires making strategic decisions about who we accept as trade partners and establishing a wide variety of partnerships. Having a balanced trade portfolio will also give us the freedom to distance ourselves from trade partners' foreign policies we don't subscribe to, and increase our negotiation power.

In Summary

Much like accidental leaders, we need to commit to leadership and see ourselves as leaders. To do so, we must define grounded motives to lead and put together a construct to guide our leadership efforts, including mission, vision, priorities, strategies and action plan. Leadership effectiveness is the result of consciousness, planning and taking action. We can be both the scholar and the warrior, for their ultimate goal is the triumph of peace: the scholar uses intellectual capital and competence to preserve the wisdom of the past; the warrior creates the conditions for peace and is well-equipped to resolve conflict, make a stand and wage battle if necessary.

Paralympic Athlete and Champion, Chantal Petitclerc, summed it up: "We should not be afraid to assert and express ourselves, and trust in our values. We should select causes to get involved in, choosing quality over quantity. Let's capitalize on our strengths, believe in ourselves and go for it!"

STRENGHTENING OUR LEADERSHIP BRAND

What can we do to strengthen the brand?

Disseminate the Brand

We need to increase our awareness of our own leadership style. In order to do so, respondents put forward a number of ideas:

Make History a National Priority

It starts with education: making history interesting by focusing on patterns, not just events and dates, and linking them to the present. 'History is written by winners,' the saying goes. To counteract this temptation, it's important to offer a variety of perspectives, such as from Aboriginals, women, minorities, immigrants, etc. A dream would be to create a national core curriculum with some room for regional and provincial differences.

Not only does history need to be a priority in education, but also in day-to-day life. Knowledge of history is uneven in the Canadian population and this presents many dangers, from taking for granted institutions hard fought for, to dismissing significant contributors, to misreading current events due to lack of context and misunderstanding regional struggles. There is a core historical knowledge that every Canadian should know, regardless of province and generation.

Publicize Canadian Heroes

We need to be more familiar with our heroes and their deeds, from Tecumseh to Nellie McClung and Jean Lesage. Past leaders should not be forgotten, because they have shaped our country and given it so much. This knowledge encourages pride, fortifies resolve and ensures that their sacrifices and memories are not forgotten. The CBC has been a big help with its stellar series 'Canada: A People's History,' and their miniseries on political leaders such as Pierre Elliott Trudeau or on important pages of our history. These are excellent vehicles, but much more can be done: websites, conferences, educational materials, podcasts, even a national society dedicated to educating the public about heroes of all kinds.

Boost Canadian Pride

Olympic Games and similar events increase national pride but they're not enough. We need infrastructures, programs, events, contests, etc. The federal government is the natural leader in this regard, but multiple stakeholders can intervene.

How many unsung heroes would inspire us if we knew about them? One of our interviewees, Tim Armstrong, Task Force Leader, Vancouver Urban Search and Rescue Team; Canada Task Force 1, went to New Orleans in the wake of Hurricane Katrina with his 46-member group and proceeded to save 119 people. Moreover, Tim, a national expert on search and rescue matters, has helped many large Canadian cities develop their search and rescue strategy. A true hero in more ways than one, not only does he save people (warrior), he develops infrastructures to assist others in doing the same (scholar). We are proud of you, Tim!

Since role models and mentors are considered the number one leadership development vehicles in the country, we need to increase their visibility and, for this, enlist the help of the media.

Strike a New Balance in the Media

Currently the media devotes more attention to problems than solutions, to dramas than success. This has a significant effect on people's consciousness, leading to the belief that the world is a horrible place, failure is everywhere, and the odds of success poor. This constant barrage of negative information erodes the sense of the possible, reduces the 'can-do attitude' and instills a 'why bother?' stance, particularly devastating for young people.

Our media can do better by displaying success and enticing people to dream. Frequently, interviewees expressed the need to see series on community heroes, successful businesses, communities that overcame difficulties and governments that devise wise and innovative policies. The media has the research and communication capability. If we expect more, they will deliver.

LEVERAGING THE BRAND

As we have seen in the previous chapter, our national leadership brand is composed of a value core that forms five cornerstones which materialize into attributes; they, in turn, influence behaviours. Our brand is good. How can we make it stronger?

Reinforce Values

Values are at the heart of the brand. "Our place is to strive to act based on a sense of values, in a consistent way." (Chris Rudge, CEO and Secretary General, Canadian Olympic Committee) Values need to be protected and affirmed. "Fairness and compassion for minorities are essential. We need to maintain a social safety net and a community conscience. Sometimes, I worry they are eroding." (Louis O'Reilly, President, O'Reilly International Entertainment Management)

Canadian values could be taught in schools, reinforced by award programs, immortalized by people who represent them, embedded in national and provincial legislative frameworks, discussed in legislatures, etc.

We need to align our understanding of what our values are, what they mean and how to keep them alive, healthy and strong.

Reinforce Cornerstones

Here are some suggestions from interviewees on how to strengthen each cornerstone:

Principle

Principle anchors the whole edifice.

Ethical Foundation

Interviewees suggested making ethics a national preoccupation, for instance, by adopting, distributing and reinforcing a Canadian code of ethics upon which organizational and personal codes of ethics could be based. This would provide a strong basis for emphasizing what matters, taking action based on principles, standing up on issues, and, ultimately, putting our money where our mouth is.

Respondents also recommended including ethics in the educational curriculum at all levels, starting in elementary school. Ethics help build the fabric of society, so children should be introduced to the topic early on in a practical manner. "Young people today are hardly taught ethics. Where will they get their sense of value? If strong values don't come from them, we will not be a very strong nation." (Doreen McKenzie-Sanders, C.M., Executive Director, Women in the Lead Inc.) If given an ethical grounding in their youth, children would be more inclined, as they grow up, to apply an ethical foundation to their careers, whether in business or elsewhere.

We have the reputation of being the 'good guys.' Let's live up to it by designing and disseminating solid ethical foundations and passing the torch to the next generations through education.

Balanced Rights and Responsibilities

In general, interviewees said we need a better balance between rights and responsibilities. The pendulum is presently on the side of rights and doesn't clearly state citizens and politicians' responsibilities and expected contributions. We have done an admirable job of creating a legislative framework that guarantees rights and freedoms and with defining what the state can do for its citizens. To paraphrase John F. Kennedy, the time has come to define what citizens and politicians must do for their country and what they are accountable for.

For instance, what are the responsibilities of individuals to the community and vice versa? How can we educate youth to assume responsibilities and reinforce them? "We need to add a responsibility section to the Canadian Charter of Rights and Freedoms. It's important that people, particularly youth, understand that it's not a one-way street." (Dr. Cyril Simard, President and CEO, ECONOMUSEUM Network) The state doesn't have only responsibilities, and citizens, only rights. It's time to paint a clear picture on both sides of the fence.

Professionalism

Canada is a knowledge-based economy. In order to succeed now and in the future, we need to be well-educated. Years ago, the Irish government set out to make Ireland the most educated country in the world, with strong and innovative policies. They have now succeeded, proving it can be done. We can do it, too.

It starts with literacy, the gate to knowledge. For too many Canadians, that door is still shut, condemning them to live on the margins of society. To eradicate this problem would require a national and concerted effort, aligning all provinces and territories.

Secondly, we should guarantee that abundant and suitable educational opportunities are available to all Canadians, including immigrants, people living in rural Canada, Aboriginals, disabled people, etc.—smart strategies appropriate to the reality and the culture of each targeted group. One size doesn't fit all, and that includes the gifted and high potentials, as well.

Thirdly, let's create the best possible conditions for our educators, because the future of Canada is in their hands. Let's give them the knowledge and skills they need to perform, and the appreciation they deserve. We should revere them as a national treasure, yet they are often taken for granted and their contribution dismissed. We need to give them the tools to do nothing short of a fantastic job— providing high-quality education.

Fourthly, we need to ensure the educational system better prepares people for the realities of the workplace. Extensive application is required to transform knowledge into know-how. Although co-op programs have proven a winning formula, they are still the exception, not the norm. They need to become more commonplace. Isabelle Courville, President, Hydro-Québec TransÉnergie, made an eloquent case: "We must develop process skills in young people. Currently, there is too much emphasis and activities focused on the contents, not enough on the container. To integrate theory requires practice. That is why I prefer hiring graduates from co-op universities, as they have practical experience."

Finally, expose students to the global context. For example, Queen's University's vision is to "develop exceptional students and scholars for citizenship and leadership in a global society," while Royal Roads University wants to "meet the needs of learners and the requirements of the global marketplace." Exchanges and double degree programs are becoming increasingly popular and soon will be commonplace at the university level. Why not broaden them to the high school level?

"Colleagues in other countries tell me that Canadian leaders have excellent intellectual capacity and ability to find common grounds." (Diane Gorman, Former Assistant Deputy Minister, Health Canada, Governement of Canada) If we want this kind of feedback to continue, we need to heavily invest in education and do so creatively.

Possibility

Believing you can succeed and finding ways to do so is the underpinning of possibility. As a young nation with a successful past and present, we find it easier to have a sense of the possible. "We are a free country, have freedom of expression and demonstrate it in our ability to express creativity. We are not repressed or suppressed and act accordingly. We are also open to the world and have a resourceful and creative workforce." (Suzanne Blanchet, President and CEO, Cascades Tissue Group)

Possibility is also the key to a successful future, for it leads to discoveries, stunning art and ingenious solutions. It requires creativity, which, like leadership, is a skill and can be developed. Therefore, we must equip children and adults with creative thinking capabilities and provide support, acknowledgement and opportunities that will allow creativity to emerge. "We must set up programs for people to innovate and create completely new realities. Maybe prizes or scholarships given to creative people? We must also put in place positive and distinct policies. We must show the way and break new ground in the realm of creativity." (Francine Brousseau, Vice-President Development, Canadian Museum of Civilization Corporation)

One of the most potent demonstrations of possibility is the arts, because they convey meaning, culture and uniqueness. "Canadian artists are a tremendously successful export around the world. They truly symbolize Canada for the world." (Peter Herrndorf, O.C., President and CEO, National Arts Centre) Canadian art organizations and artists are recognized for their excellence all over the world. According to *Canada at a Glance: Arts and Culture* published in 2005 by the Government of Canada, "Canadian culture reaches far beyond the country's borders. Canada is the second largest source of international music talent in the world. Two Canadian novelists, Margaret Atwood and Yann Martel, won the

Booker Prize, one of the most prestigious literary awards in the world in the past five years."

Here's what one of our most revered creators has to say: "Canada is a young country with lots of opportunities to create. Over the years, we have conceived things to help bridge communication and reach out to each other across the size of our country. Abroad, we are perceived as cutting-edge. Cirque du Soleil, for example, knows how to integrate various disciplines from different cultures." (Robert Lepage, President, Robert Lepage Inc.; Stage and Artistic Director, Ex-Machina)

We reach out to each other across our vast landscape via the arts, which have become our 'third official language.' Through the arts, we learn about different sensibilities and perceptions, connect with regional cultures and history, derive meaning, and share of ourselves with the world. "Our distinctive voice is creativity. The proof is in all the cultural products we export with such success. We must continue in the same vein, for we have the opportunity to make a big difference in the life of millions of people." (Richard Blackburn, General and Artistic Director, Théâtre de la Dame de Cœur)

In some cases, our artists are better known abroad than at home. We have to do more, through promotion and education, to publicize our artistic creators' achievements. It is a shame when artists feel they have to go elsewhere to be appreciated. We then lose their brain power and contribution. We must do a better job of acknowledging and supporting our creators and appreciating their impact.

We need to develop a sense of collective responsibility towards our national treasure: creativity. If we want innovation, we have to nurture it. How about developing a national possibility strategy that would invest in and support creativity, innovation, research and entrepreneurship in all its forms?

Diversity

Learning to manage differences has proven a slow, painful and humbling process for humankind. Many bloody wars can trace their origin to an inability to respect and appreciate differences. Today, the world has become too small and weapons too powerful: we need to significantly expand our ability to manage differences worldwide or we could literally all go up in flames. To ensure our survival on earth, managing differences has to become a global priority.

Let's see how the process works:

Illustration 14.2

Managing Differences: from Rejection to Synergy; from Homogeneity to Tapestry

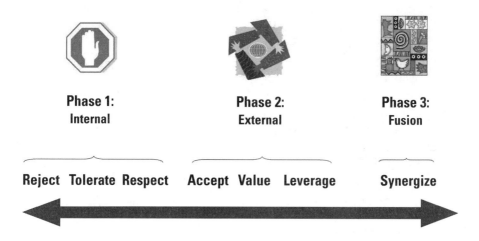

Phase 1:	Phase 2:	Phase 3:
Internal	**External**	**Fusion**

Reject Tolerate Respect   Accept Value Leverage   Synergize

The first phase of this model moves from rejection to respect. Legitimizing the validity of different perspectives, beliefs, traditions, etc., represents a huge shift in consciousness. It has taken centuries to accept that different does not mean wrong, it just means another perspective. It's about appreciating relativity.

The second phase involves accepting and leveraging differences for greater effectiveness. Skill-building occurs, because managing differences is an acquired competency. Diversity becomes a source of enjoyment, learning, and competitive advantage.

The final phase is about synergy. At this point, diversity is viewed as a liberating force: boundaries and limitations disappear and components combine to create new realities. The possibilities are endless and the results magnificent! Our guitar virtuoso Jesse Cook is a prime example of this synergy in the musical realm.

How can we improve? Interviewees made a number of useful suggestions.

Balance

Strike the right balance between protecting core Canadian identity and respecting differences. Sometimes, this means that diversity cannot be accommodated. This was the case in 2005, when the Government of Ontario contemplated introducing the Muslim Sharia system to mediate family disputes. In the end, the government rejected the idea because of the difficulty of protecting women's rights. It also eventually abolished the Jewish and Christian mediation systems and affirmed that the legal system is the only route to resolve family disputes in Ontario. By protecting the rights of women and levelling the playing field for family dispute resolution, the Ontario Government made a leadership decision to 'safeguard the core.'

All across the country, legislators are struggling with similar issues, and the pressure to decide in a fair, equitable and consistent manner is mounting. Decision-making criteria must become more explicit and consistent, not only for legislators but other leaders. For instance, employers need to decide how to treat religious holidays, prayer time at work, dress code issues, etc., in a way that is fair to mainstream and other employees. Leaders always have to consider the greater good of the whole, versus that of a minority or an individual. This is a key leadership responsibility, and to exercise it fairly they need a framework, which at this point is lacking. Let's help our leaders lead by providing them with explicit criteria to make fair and consistent diversity decisions across the nation.

People of First Nations

We also need to improve in addressing the needs of First Nations citizens, who face bigger challenges in accessing education, health care, housing and employment. "We are attempting to assist people in need. We play the role of peacekeeper, but this is in conflict with our approach to Aboriginal people. There are significant issues facing the indigenous people." (Bernd Christmas, Lawyer and Mi'kmaq Leader)

We cannot boast about our diversity expertise if we don't ease these challenges. However, in recent years, political leaders have become more aware of the importance of allowing people of First Nations the space and respect to make decisions about internal community matters. There is hope. "Canada, as a nation of many cultures ... or as a culture of many nations, should assert itself as a world leader. We can all sit at one council fire and each have an equal voice. But first, we must ensure equality and quality here at home and strengthen everyone's self-esteem." (Joseph Paquette, Mixed Blood Elder)

Peace

Through our conciliatory approach, we can stand as the custodians of peace and sound processes, policies and frameworks. For example, we can expand peacekeeping into peace making, using preventive measures and bringing parties to the table to discuss issues *before* major conflicts erupts. Waiting until things boil up to the point of conflict brings out the worst in everyone.

We must commit to our stellar military on a permanent, sustainable basis. To say that we are a peacekeeping nation but not have the resources to support it, creates a credibility gap. "We have to walk the talk and strengthen our developmental as well as our military presence in an unsettled world." (Patrick Reid, O.C., M.C., C.D., Chairman, Rick Hansen Foundation)

Gladys Osmond, Leader of The Granny Brigade, who has corresponded with our militaries for 20 years, and has learned a lot 'straight from the horse's mouth.'

> We are respected because we treat people fairly, even our enemies. For instance, recently, Canadian medical personnel treated a Taliban leader in Afghanistan. The soldiers were asked, "Why did you do this?" They responded, "Because we are Canadians and we treat people with compassion." We are diverse but we all hold core Canadian values true to our heart. Another example was a 12-year-old girl from a village who had been shot in the hip during a crossfire. The Canadian soldier who found her lying on the road, took her to the hospital and visited her every day. He brought her a teddy bear and held her hand, even though they couldn't speak each other's language. One day, the girl's father came to the hospital while the soldier was there and thanked him; they both burst into tears. There are so many stories like these. Our militaries are truly the ambassadors of Canadian values: they act with compassion and kindness.

But peace efforts must go beyond the military. Many civilians could get involved in problem-solving, conflict prevention and resolution through effective facilitation, mediation and arbitration. These roles fit our temperament, expertise and ambition. Why not leverage this natural flow on a large scale? Why not set up a national dispute resolution institute to train competent resources and deploy them for domestic and international projects?

We are like the warrior whose ultimate goal is the triumph of peace, but we can also be the scholar who uses intellectual capital and competence to set up the conditions for peace to emerge and last. Without peace, there is no safety, prosperity or development. Without peace, there is no future. War leaves populations wounded and traumatized and it takes years to recover. War creates victims, not leaders. Wars have an impact on business, not just politics. The devastating effects of war can be felt by the individuals, community, society, and the world.

Ensuring that peace triumphs over war can be viewed as the most crucial form of leadership. We are good process keepers and peace is the ultimate process to keep. So, let us take our best and offer it to the world!

CONCLUSION

To assert our national leadership and increase its impact, we must define our identity as leaders, and determine what we want to provide leadership on (priorities), and how (strategies and action plan). This must to be a conscious effort, agreed to by engaging all Canadians through a national dialogue. In leadership, strategic thinking has to replace improvisation.

CHAPTER 15

PUBLIC LEADERSHIP ISSUES

People go into politics for honourable reasons and often find they are unable to lead as they had envisioned, due to all kinds of constraints. As a result, some very talented people don't offer themselves since it can be a thankless task.

Anne McGuire
President and CEO, IWK Health Centre

Walls between elected officials and their constituents must disappear: less talking and more listening. Question periods are a shame—they are not debating, they are insulting each other. Let the level of debate rise. Let's get on with the business of leadership. Focus on open access to citizens instead of the next election. Follow your heart instead of your political ambition.

Albert Schultz
Founding Artistic Director, Soulpepper Theatre Company

THE STAKEHOLDERS' DANCE

In a democracy, four key stakeholder groups engage in the political arena: elected officials, citizens, public servants and the media. How they act and interact determines the success or failure of public leadership. "Elected officials must understand their own motivations: Why do they want to go into politics? It's important to have projects for society in order to rise above simply winning seats or seeking power. Currently, politics is not very attractive for people of stature. I wonder to what degree the public sector can foster leadership practice and development." (Jocelyn Deschênes, Producer, President, Sphère Média Plus)

The principles that define stakeholder roles and guide their interaction have evolved over time and, according to interviewees, now need to be re-examined and adjusted. For instance,

- The Internet has revolutionized how governments deliver service and increased expectations about speed and accuracy.
- Instant access to information has made citizens better informed and more critical.
- TV has profoundly altered how politicians communicate and how their effectiveness is perceived. We live in the age of televised parliamentary debates, sound bites and spin. Everything is instantaneous and live. Politicians lack the time required to reflect on complex issues and come to meaningful conclusions. "It is difficult to frame complex issues in a short time. They need development and coaching on how to do this effectively." (Bill Hamilton, Executive Coach, W.J.A. Hamilton & Associates; Former Senior Vice-President, BMO and CIBC)

How can we define stakeholder roles and responsibilities more clearly, give people the skills and tools required to play them well, and facilitate stakeholder interaction to increase its effectiveness?

ELECTED OFFICIALS

Elected officials are a cornerstone of democracy. How can we create conditions for their success?

Wanted: Competence, Consistency and Integrity

It is impossible to strengthen Canadian leadership without strengthening leadership in the public sector. And it starts with elected officials who make decisions that affect everyone and influence the future of the country.

Currently, elected officials are set up to fail. Interviewees expressed dissatisfaction with the current state and pessimism about the future, unless *significant* change occurs. A major overhaul, not a simple tune-up, is required to groom the quantity and quality of public leaders the country requires. We need to wake up and take action—Canada cannot afford leadership incompetence or scarcity in public office. "There are not enough great leaders to take us where we want to go. We need to create leadership opportunities for many more people to contribute through traditional and unconventional ways. This will shape the face of leadership, infuse it with social concerns and influence the world. It will create a leadership movement." (Ruth Armstrong, President, Vision Management Services; Governance Professor, York University, Schulich School of Business)

Present conditions have created a crisis of confidence, eroding trust between leaders and their electorate on three levels: competence, consistency and integrity. In his book *Change Leadership: Inform, Involve, Ignite! Tools, Tips and Templates for Succeeding at Organizational Change* (Canadian Society of Association Executives, Toronto, 2007), Robert L. Harris, President of Robert Harris Resources, explains that trust levels are structured like a pyramid: the higher you go, the more trust is precious and fragile:

Competence: People will not follow a leader they view as incompetent, at least not for long. Leaders who don't know what they are doing or where they are going don't exactly inspire confidence. When leaders fail the competency test, the leadership relationship aborts at this early stage.

Consistency: Leaders who veer off course too often, who are inconsistent in their decisions or whose actions clash with their words soon lose the confidence of their followers. Consistency is about focus, strength and steadfastness. Inconsistency translates as betrayal for followers and loyalty subsequently vanishes.

Integrity: Integrity is the zone where leaders ultimately win or lose. Ethics, principles, fairness, honesty and decency are, in the end, more important than results; therefore, sleazy, power-hungry, greedy leaders fall from grace, sometimes violently. A trust rupture at this level creates a lot of damage and is almost impossible to recover from.

This model applies not only to individual leaders, but also to the organizations they represent because they, too, have to behave like leaders as well as supporting and expanding leadership capacity. Applying this trust model to elected officials' current circumstances sheds light on the present crisis of confidence:

Competence: Politics is always a second career. Elected officials come to their new role unprepared because their primary expertise resides elsewhere. So how are the various levels of governments compensating for this knowledge gap? Not sufficiently. As a result, elected officials climb a steep learning curve with minimum support, hampering their ability to perform and meet their electorate's expectations.

Consistency: Currently, elected officials' time horizon is their term in office. Profound social change takes much longer than that. Within the short time frame of office terms, elected leaders can become more preoccupied with re-election and day-to-day issues than engineering social change. As a result, they can make decisions inconsistent with their predecessors', their own platform and often the wishes of their electorate. Inconsistency disenfranchises voters and fractures trust.

Integrity: Integrity breakdowns shatter public trust. Remember the sponsorship scandal? Followers need to trust their representatives, individually and collectively, and have faith in the system's fairness. Transparent, just, and efficient systems with lots of checks and balances ensure probity. After the extensive and thorough inquiry conducted by Judge Gomery into the sponsorship scandal, how many recommendations have been implemented? The scandal was bad enough, but not implementing recommendations is a double blow. Integrity truly holds the power to 'make or break' trust.

As we can see from this brief analysis, there is lots of room for improvement and this means willingness to consider radical change. So, keep an open mind as we examine this in greater detail.

Competence

Leadership is an act of bravery at the best of times, but particularly for elected leaders taking on a daunting role for which they have no formal training, in a complex environment where the learning curve is steep, development is scarce, mistakes are made public and the media relentless. As an illustration, imagine that you have been 'selected' to become a dentist. You know nothing about dentistry but gamely show up at your clinic only to find out you have to perform a tooth extraction … on TV. This is more or less the reality elected officials face every day—not a pretty picture. From this perspective, it's a miracle anyone runs for office.

A significant transformation is involved from being an ordinary citizen to becoming a polished legislator. "When they show up in parliament, they don't have the training to do their job." (Veronica Lacey, President, The Learning Partnership) "Success in any field requires blending competence and values. In terms of competence, public leaders face a steep learning curve upon arrival, as everything is new. Do they get all the development and support required to perform? Regarding values, both individual politicians and political parties need to become more aware of the importance of defining and affirming values." (Michèle Fortin, President and CEO, Télé-Québec)

Maybe in our grandparents' time, people could run for office and 'figure it out' as they went along, but major change is now required. "We have to put in place development infrastructures for elected officials: intensive and ongoing training, peer coaching by experienced parliamentarians for newly elected ones, regular progress reviews, etc. Moreover, we must ensure that backbenchers and senior public servants can play a greater role in drafting legislation." (Françoise David, Co-Spokesperson, Québec Solidaire)

Developing Competence

Our current stance about public leaders' development is naïve and unrealistic. "Elected officials are left to their own devices. As a nation, we totally underestimate what it would take to give these people the tools and support to perform better. They need extensive orientation, induction, development, coaching, handbooks, ethics training, etc., to build bench strength." (Patrick Cuenco, Co-founder, Junior Hong Kong-Canada Business Association)

Strangely enough, development infrastructures for public servants (people who are not elected but employed or appointed), are far more sophisticated, strategic and available than those for public officials. Let's mention the Canada Revenue Agency and CMHC programs, to name a few.

This calibre of *savoir faire* must be transferred to elected officials. "Set up a school for ministers and deputy ministers." (David Levine, President and CEO, Montréal Regional Health Authority)

Does it make sense that a director in a ministry benefits from considerably more development than the minister in charge? "Like any organization, governments should provide development for elected officials. Citizens must feel that politicians are competent. Every profession requires credentials and training. Why not people in office? We have to upgrade the image of politics as a profession." (Françoise Bertrand, President and CEO, Fédération des Chambres de Commerce du Québec [Québec Federation of Chambers of Commerce])

Programs for elected officials have to reach a comparable level to those intended for public servants. "Intensive training is required. Currently, there is too much learning on the job; development must be structured." (Dr. Michel Portmann, Professor, Université du Québec à Montréal [UQAM] [University of Québec in Montréal])

Ensuring Competence

To solve the development problem, we recommend importing the certification best practice from the co-op sector. Recognizing that Board members come from varied backgrounds and possess different types of expertise, co-operatives offer their officers certification programs to align mindsets and even out the playing field. This ensures that Board members acquire a common language, skills and foundations. This improves decision-making because they share a common framework.

Certification programs include modules such as ethics, problem-solving and conflict resolution. They recognize that elected officials have to perform tasks outside of their normal realm of activity, such as public speaking and strategic planning. And to ensure performance, they give them the tools to succeed.

For example, La Coop fédérée, an agricultural co-operative, offers three certification levels leading to credits. Upon accumulating a number of credits, participants move to the next level and take on more responsibilities. The basic level is for members, the second for administrators, and the third for senior officers. For instance, administrators learn about team-building, motivation and public speaking. Meanwhile, senior officers learn about public relations, leadership, meeting facilitation and international trade. Moreover, La Coop fédérée offers credits for co-op activities, which enables members to practise skills and foster alignment and cohesiveness. (Adapted from www.coopfed.qc.ca, January 2007.)

We were overjoyed to discover a model to professionalize leadership, transferable to elected leadership. It's ironic, if not downright strange, to think that people who make such important decisions do not benefit from extensive development and support.

We also suggest that performance in public leadership requires investment. Just like in elite sports, producing athletes who can win Olympic medals requires infrastructures, resources and money; talent alone does not suffice. Citizens will need to view this as a solid investment, not a frivolous expense. In the end, we all have a stake in public leaders' performance. "We must have the courage to invest in people and their development and create environments conducive to professional development." (Mariette Mulaire, Executive Director, Economic Development Council for Manitoba Bilingual Municipalities)

Consistency

Consistency is the by-product of a long-term vision and a clear sense of direction. When these are missing, leaders focus on the day to day, becoming reactive and treating events as incidents instead of viewing them in a larger context.

This is even more important for public than for business leaders, because they preside over the destinies of millions. What is their essential mandate?

Kazimir Olechnowicz, President and General Manager, CIMA+, an international engineering consulting firm, describes politicians' highest calling in eloquent terms: "Public leaders' reason for being is to create a vision for the best possible future of their society and to manage transformation towards it. It's a collective consultation and alignment process where, ultimately, everyone plays a part. Not easy to execute, but that is the mandate. In the past, politicians who succeeded were able to fulfill it."

For instance, Tommy Douglas made an enormous contribution to the country by not only fulfilling this mandate, but going the extra mile. Politicians must accept this mandate and feel comfortable with their role. As a society, what can we do to help them fulfill both mandate and role?

In a democracy, we entrust public leaders to represent us and, with our input, come to conclusions about vision, direction and transformation. It is both their vocation and legacy. When they succeed, like Sir John A. Macdonald, who gave birth to the country and saw to its expansion from coast to coast, their vision lives on for generations. "We should not refrain from talking about visions for our society. Crafting them is public leaders' reason for being and their role; for instance, think of Trudeau's 'just society.' Collectively, we must share common projects, move forward towards a good society and believe in our vision with passion and a twinkle in our eyes. I don't see a lot of passion in public leaders; often they become managers instead of leaders. Is the system geared to produce managers?" (Chantal Petitclerc, Paralympic Athlete and Champion)

Long-Term Focus

Crafting a societal vision requires the ability and the luxury to focus on the long term. "Systemic change is required. Move from an election focus to a long-term view. To develop, you need sustainability across a wide horizon." (Sue Lee, Senior Vice-President, Human Resources and Communications, Suncor Energy Inc.)

But we wonder, does the system allow politicians to cast their gaze towards the future? "The goal of the public sector is to pursue long-term agendas for the greater good of society. This can never be done in a short time. Do elected officials have the possibility to think long-term? Are constraints so important that they prevent public leaders from playing their individual and collective roles?" (Michèle Fortin, President and CEO, Télé-Québec)

Strategic Thinking

Ability to envision a preferred future; not only requires long-term, but strategic thinking. As such, public leaders act like executives. "They should be strategic instead of looking at the trenches; they must articulate and frame a vision and remind their team that everything needs to feed into it." (Valerie Payn, President, Halifax Chamber of Commerce)

Strategic capability is a strange mixture of right- and left-brain attributes: the ability to evoke a vision and fire the imagination, coupled with the ability to analyze and elaborate plans. Many politicians never had to think in such broad terms in their previous careers and now must do so on a wide variety of complex topics like the environment, the economy and health care.

The situation is further complicated by the fact that public leaders must be both responsive to their constituents *and* proactive about the future. If politicians are only reactive, they rob constituents of their future. Likewise, if they lose touch with the needs, views and aspirations of their electors, the visions and strategies they craft will crumble. "Stop relying on polls; that is not leadership. Take on important issues." (Honourable Carole Taylor, O.C., Minister of Finance; M.L.A., Vancouver-Langara, British Columbia Government; Former Chair, CBC/Radio-Canada)

As we said earlier, public officials, like other leaders, must act as helicopters and hover above the landscape to view the total picture, and dive down at times to intervene on specific issues. "The business of health care is very complex. To achieve outcomes, leaders have to see the big picture. This involves looking at the coordination and delivery of care, both from an internal and external perspective. To address the health status of a population, leaders have to envision partnerships with non-health entities, i.e., environment, housing, labour, citizenship, etc." (Bruce Harber, President and CEO, York Central Hospital)

As a society, we need to make sure public leaders *can get* to the big picture. "Part of the problem is politicians are elected for fixed terms. Wanting to get re-elected, they often make the quick-win decisions without enough focus on long-term planning. As a society, we must find a way to encourage them to think beyond their mandate." (Diane Rabbani, Human Resources Consultant; Former Deputy Minister, British Columbia)

Ensuring Consistency

How can we foster a long-term strategic focus? For all levels of government, we suggest creating strategic frameworks, including vision, mission, values, guiding principles, and priorities, run at set intervals and including extensive input from constituencies. These could be conducted through highly interactive open policy forums using live and online methodologies.

Once the strategic framework is crafted, politicians become their custodians, regardless of party allegiance. This would enable all governments in power to strive for a broad, input-loaded vision and to align their decisions accordingly. This would also avoid embarrassing policy flip-flops. "We need to agree on values and principles to work with and stick to them, measure success and report on it. This will require a shift in paradigm and environment. Let's create the conditions to reduce short-sightedness in government." (William Adair, Executive Director, Canadian Paraplegic Association of Ontario)

Suzanne Christie, Project Manager, Peel Mentoring Network; Instructor, summed it up well:

> A process by which people could care beyond their term in office would be the mark of true leadership. Today's decisions will impact our grandchildren. Elected officials' responsibility is to care for what is in their custody and leave it in a better state than they found it. In order to do so, they need to put thought into the process and discuss important issues such as environment, treasury, etc. Part of leadership is also ensuring that the next group of leaders will be prepared and knowledgeable. Trusteeship is the definition of leadership.

In this scenario, public leaders could implement a strategic framework with confidence, knowing it represents what the public wants. This would ensure a long-term horizon, continuity and more satisfying outcomes for everyone.

Integrity

As we have seen earlier, service is the ultimate purpose of leadership; nowhere is it truer than in the public sector. It is not simply about serving customers, but serving public interest in the deepest sense; not just making decisions, but conveying meaning; not only crafting legal frameworks, but affirming values. "We must develop the capacity to serve and help egos take a back seat. The perspective is serving the country, not becoming prime minister. This means that greater good must come first. A focus on greater good will enable leaders to marshal the best of themselves and their talent." (Rémi Tremblay, President, Esse Leadership)

The relationship that binds public leaders and their constituents is based on integrity. Politicians need to generate trust in their persons and the institutions they represent. Ask yourself: as a citizen, am I confident that this candidate can represent my interests, and do I also believe the system to be fair and effective? "Public leaders must be more preoccupied with serving their country than with getting re-elected. Authenticity and credibility are essential for people to trust them." (Pierre Dion, President and CEO, TVA Group Inc.)

A lack of integrity erodes trust, then eradicates leadership. When constituents perceive that their representatives pursue motives other than service, cynicism and disengagement set in. However, power, status, self-interest and greed constitute strong temptations.

How can integrity prevail? It starts with intention. "Politicians need to examine what they do and why they do it and become aware of their responsibilities and impact on the communities they serve. Power is vested in them by their constituencies. If they get disconnected from them, their power dissipates." (François Saillant, Coordinator, Front d'action populaire en réaménagement urbain, FRA-PRU [The Popular Face of Action in Urban Refitting])

Ensuring Integrity

This quest is partly personal: individual leaders must examine their own motivations. On the other side of the coin, public service entities, political parties and Canadian society in general, must breed integrity by creating fair, transparent, equitable systems that encourage above-board conduct, discourage cheating and punish delinquents. Organizations also have a responsibility to communicate integrity expectations. Ethics training, as well as conflict of interest guidelines and consequences for breaching them, should be a priority. "Bring their skills up to date, for instance, how to conduct themselves in public and deal with charity gifts or donations so they do not find themselves in conflict of interest." (Lorna Barr, Former Deputy Chair, British Columbia Utilities Commission)

Integrity materializes through accountabilities and these must be more clearly defined. Right now, the perception is that politicians benefit from impunity. At all levels of government, mandate, expectations and deliverables should be spelled out. If the environment clearly defines accountabilities, measures results and sets consequences to performance, candidates will rise to the challenge and the power or status hungry will eventually drop out. "Public leadership needs to be centred around civic and common good. Leadership is not about manipulation, but spirituality." (Fred Mattocks, Executive Director, Regional Programming, Production and Resources, CBC English Television)

Wanted: A Professional Structure

Public leadership is a *professional* occupation and should be treated as such. A bona fide profession is composed of the following characteristics:

- A distinct body of knowledge differentiating it from other fields.

- Admission criteria and credentials.
- Development programs to prepare for the profession and continuing education to keep skills and knowledge current.
- A code of conduct based on professional ethics.
- Processes to develop and refine professional judgement.
- Avenues for vigorous debate and decision-making about issues facing the field.
- Appeal and discipline infrastructures to deal with complaints, issues of malpractice or unethical conduct.

Injecting these principles into elected leadership would bring structure, standards, rigour and discipline to the field and is eminently doable. Bottom line, we must elevate the field of elected leadership by structuring it like a bona fide profession. Professions are equipped with distinct and relevant bodies of knowledge and extensive systems to impart them and upgrade professionals' skills. Moreover, they are selective as to who enters and stays in the field. A similar mindset needs to be infused in elected leadership and it begins with a comprehensive talent management pipeline

Talent Management

Talent management can be compared to a pipeline distributing the energy required to activate an organization, much like electricity or gas. Therefore, it must be viewed holistically: all components are related and affect each other in a positive or negative way. The following questions are important to consider:

- How can we define public leadership roles, mandates, responsibilities, and accountabilities?
- What are the competencies required to succeed as a public leader?
- How can we best recruit quality candidates?
- On which criteria should selection be based?
- Once public leaders are elected, how can we orient, develop and support them to ensure optimal performance?
- How can we monitor and manage performance?
- How can we recognize and reward good performers? How can we deal with poor performers?

Each step of the talent management pipeline must be carefully designed, planned and executed. Moreover, linkages between steps must be articulated and managed and the whole edifice integrated. Current reality is far from such a comprehensive strategy.

Complaining that there is a lack of good elected leaders is not productive; doing something about it is. For example, in the Québec City area, the sports community set out to produce more elite athletes. A council was established (Conseil du sport de haut niveau de la région de Québec) and it started soliciting funds, building infrastructures and developing coaches. It paid off: Many athletes who ranked fourth and fifth at the Torino Winter Olympics originated from that region. Relate this to politics. If we want outstanding political leaders and statesmen, we have to do something about it. Longing will not conjure them out of thin air.

Interviewees believe that we require a well-conceived talent management blueprint clearly defining all the steps.

Role Definition

People go into politics with good intentions but often with a poor understanding of job realities. There must be more information about what to expect in public office. "It is very empowering to learn, in a non-partisan way, from those who have won and lost in politics. In Nova Scotia, a session was organized for women contemplating politics, where they heard from candidates who ran and were defeated, as well as those who were successful." (Dr. Sheila Brown, Former President and Vice-Chancellor, Mount Saint Vincent University)

Moreover, potential candidates need to know the skills they require to succeed as elected officials and determine if they are suited for the role. Skills include how to communicate effectively, think and act strategically, negotiate, build rapport, consult, dialogue, debate and rally different perspectives.

Respondents suggested structuring a competency system and publicizing it. Information about the role and suitability could be packaged in tool kits available to the public, online and in print. "Work with the public to help them understand what is expected of the role, before they think of getting into politics. Offer courses in schools and provide methods to evaluate capacity to contribute. People need to understand the responsibility and the important role they would be taking on. Too often, newly elected officials are stunned by the amount of work involved." (Judy Rogers, City Manager, Vancouver, British Columbia)

A clearer picture of the public leadership role, lifestyle and profile is required so that individuals considering such a career can make informed decisions.

Attraction

Good leaders gravitate towards gratifying roles. Is public leadership gratifying? "Too often, we underestimate just how demanding the work of a politician can be.

It takes a lot of generosity to use your talents in the service of the public interest. Politicians face a twofold challenge: they must be able to show people just how great the challenges are, while at the same time being persuasive leaders, able to move things along." (Isabelle Hudon, President and CEO, Board of Trade of Metropolitan Montréal)

Competition for leadership talent is fierce. If a role is perceived as thankless, its attraction potential is low. Do present conditions entice established leaders? The answer is a resounding *no*. "Elected officials are poorly compensated, lead crazy lives, are always in the media, mostly in a negative light. Conditions are very difficult. Where are the rewards? The younger generation shows a lack of interest, if not an outright disgust for politics. Who will take over?" (Michèle Fortin, President and CEO, Télé-Québec)

Considerable change must happen in the areas of compensation, development, support, rewards and recognition to make these roles more gratifying. "We must change the perception of public leadership and prepare a solid and relevant succession so the democratic system functions well. Currently, politics doesn't attract the calibre of leaders it used to." (Raymond Côté, President, Sports Québec)

Attracting a large pool of competent candidates will demand fundamental change both in the system and in citizens' attitudes. "We need to do a better job in picking good political leaders. Have more women and established leaders join the ranks. Income is not there, price on family is too high, and personal sacrifices are required. Elevate position and remuneration to attract better leaders. They are crucified in the press. There's no respect for the public leadership role. We don't seem to want to make it easy for them. They are expected to work like a dog and face non-stop criticism. This is not conducive to effective leadership." (Honourable Margaret McCain, O.C., O.N.B., Philanthropist; Former Lieutenant Governor, New Brunswick)

As a society, we need to create conditions for public leaders to succeed. Otherwise, we can kiss talent goodbye and pay a hefty price in our future prospects. A new paradigm and innovative approaches are required. "Look at co-op programs. Government can learn from commercial environments." (Bill Roberts, President and CEO, S-VOX) "Have more secondments from one sector to the next. Share experience across areas. Encourage working for the not-for-profit sector. Meet people on neutral grounds." (James Gray, O.C., A.O.E., Chairman, Canada West Foundation; Founder and Former Chairman, Canadian Hunter Exploration Ltd.)

Selection Criteria

The marketplace increasingly raises the bar of entry requirements to any field. Success requires an ever-expanding mix of ability, knowledge and experience.

Competencies for public leaders should be defined, publicized and developed, and the most important competency is leadership. If established leaders are recruited, the learning curve is less steep and performance higher. "We need to recruit better candidates against pre-determined criteria. Attract already successful people who have proven their value. Set up the system so they can win. Don't corrupt the ones with good intentions." (Peter Herrndorf, O.C., President and CEO, National Arts Centre)

Credentials should also be considered. "Competency criteria are required for any job—why not for public officials, especially ministers? Should we say, at the municipal level, a college degree, and at the provincial and federal levels, a university degree or at a minimum, a significant working experience in fields pertinent to any ministerial responsibilities?" (Joanne Lalumière, Executive Director and Corporate Secretary, Société zoologique de Granby [Granby Zoological Society])

As mentioned earlier, contrary to other jobs, public leaders arrive in their new role with no previous experience; however, this could be compensated through competencies, credentials and extensive development. At this point, none of these systems are in place on a consistent basis across the federal, provincial, regional and municipal levels. This state of affairs would create a public outcry in any professional field, yet we put up with it in public leadership, which has more impact than any other profession. Consider this: "In 2003, a survey of leading historians, political scientists, economists, former senior government officials, authors and journalists named Lester B. Pearson Canada's best prime minister of the last 50 years." (CBC, Greatest Canadian Contest, 2004) Why was Pearson so good? Because his credentials, competencies and experience had superbly prepared him for the role. A career diplomat, he was familiar with the workings of government and had acquired the required skills through practice. Therefore, he succeeded!

Has the time come to define entry-level requirements for office? This would assume ways to evaluate candidates and, to be fair, infrastructures to prepare candidates for selection. For instance, "Queen's University offers a program for parliamentarian training to think of issues in a non-partisan way." (Allan Taylor, O.C. Former Chairman and CEO, Royal Bank of Canada)

Compensation and Benefits

Given that the commitment required of public leaders goes beyond the nine-to-five workday, is the compensation in line with workload and accountabilities? Once again, interviewees said a resounding *no*. "Compensation is often considered a taboo subject but is a problem in the public sector. The sacrifices and opportunity costs are often too great for some natural leaders to bear. Usually the investment in public leaders will pay off." (Jack Graham, Partner, McInnes Cooper)

How much does the CEO of a major organization make? Likewise, how much should the prime minister make? The responsibilities are more than comparable. The prime minister and premiers are like executives who devise strategies for the successful future of the country. They should be compensated accordingly.

As in any organization, job descriptions need to be evaluated, accountabilities and impact measured, and a fair compensation system set up. This shouldn't be the subject of derision for the citizenry but a realistic marketplace comparative examination. "Politics at any level can be very onerous: a huge commitment with minimal financial reward. We need to change the system to attract the brightest and best. Public life should be prestigious. Right now, the value proposition is not there. We need to re-examine the reward structure." (Larry Berg, President and CEO, Vancouver International Airport Authority)

Starting salary is one component; another is setting up a pay-for-performance system. When compensation is tied to meeting and exceeding expectations, individuals are less resistant to public salary increases. "They should be offered bonuses when they meet their objectives." (Suzanne Blanchet, President and CEO, Cascades Tissue Group)

If we want returns, we must first invest. "Pay enough to attract the best minds. Demand competencies and accountability. A major overhaul is required." (Rod Smith, Senior Partner, Focuspoint Strategic Management; Former President, Black Photo Corporation)

Orientation

Good orientation and induction processes can mean the difference between success and failure. And giving people the key to their office and a box of files doesn't constitute effective orientation. "It's important to orient newly elected officials to institutions and their culture in order to help them infuse their actions with meaning. The lack of context often relegates politics to a superficial level. Public leadership is such an important role, yet leaders are inadequately or not prepared for it. They need a structured orientation to their role, function and context, similar to what takes place in large corporations." (Gilles Harvey, Executive Director, Land Register, Ministère de la Justice du Québec [Québec Department of Justice])

Because of the lack of experience, extensive orientation is required on parliamentary procedures, administrative infrastructures, resources, expectations, policies and procedures, etc. "Orientation and training need to be comprehensive and ongoing." (Robbie Shaw, President, IWK Foundation)

"Elected officials must know what they are responsible for as well as the extent of their responsibilities. At the onset, they may have a vague or erroneous perception of their areas of responsibilities. As well, they do not possess all the knowledge they need to perform their new role. Therefore, frequent briefing sessions are required to help them acquire all the knowledge required to govern efficiently." (Donald Dion, Elite Sports Consultant, City of Montréal; Diving Olympic Coach)

What is available in the crucial first months to help newly elected officials find their voice and way as public leaders? Not enough. What should be available? A lot more.

Support

It's lonely at the top, particularly when you are new to the field and have few contacts. Coaching, mentoring, shadowing, sponsorship, buddy systems and other support systems should be in place to support growth. "Effective mentoring programs must be set up where the more experienced mentor supports the 'learner' in a structured model." (Elaine Taranu-Teofilovici, Former CEO, YWCA Canada)

In an age where most executives benefit from personal coaches and seasoned mentors, public leaders should have access to a comparable level of service. "Get them business advisors to offer a different perspective. Tailor developmental plans to their needs." (Sarah Raiss, Executive Vice-President, Corporate Services, Trans-Canada Corporation)

Support will often make the difference between staying on the leadership path or quitting, especially when the going gets tough. "It's important to have coaches and mentors … to have the freedom to fail and make mistakes with a safety net. It impedes learning not to be able to make mistakes." (Rob Dexter, Q.C., Chairman and CEO, Maritime Travel Inc.)

And this should not be a haphazard affair but an integrated, effective system that any MP, MPP or municipal councillor could benefit from. Governments at all levels have the responsibility to put in place infrastructures to give public leaders the tools to succeed. In the end, it boils down to 'who cares for the caregiver?'

Performance Management

Like in any other job, public leaders have to perform. What are the criteria defining good performance? How are performance expectations communicated? How is performance monitored and managed? How are they informed of their results? How are good and poor performers dealt with? "We need to offer opportunities to those who stand out, give them responsibilities to stretch them and development training to help them think. Pick the rare gems and promote them." (Dominique Anglade, Consultant, McKinsey & Company)

Interviewees overwhelmingly agreed that formal performance management systems, such as the ones in place in other sectors, should be set up. The question is, what would they look like? "Define the end state/vision, set the metrics that denote progress to the vision, fuel the team's energy and then provide the means for the team to sharpen their focus." (Bruno Biscaro, COO, Accucaps Industries Limited)

Should there be third parties, like the auditor general, spearheading performance evaluations? Don Yamkowy, Owner, Nishi-Khon/Key West Travel Ltd., made a very interesting suggestion: "Structure a report card. Set up an outside group that reviews quantitative goals and promises, measure results and draft a report on their findings. It will make people accountable."

Performance management systems could include several perspectives, such as constituents, colleagues, bureaucrats and the public at large. "Use 360-degree instrument devices to get real feedback. It is important to provide training and coaching to re-orient where required." (Julia Hill, Director General, Health Canada, Government of Canada)

They could be based on a balanced scorecard composed of metrics like service quality to constituencies, legislature behaviour, initiative and innovation, decision-making, problem-solving, ethics, etc. "Give people wide-ranging experiences to stretch them and provide feedback on their performance." (Christine Hart, President, Accord/hart & associates inc.)

There are many alternatives, but we need something more sophisticated than voting if we want to monitor and evaluate performance. "Elected officials need to be held accountable and punished when guilty. Political leadership has been poor at taking responsibility for actions and errors. I sometimes feel that we have leaders by default." (Michael Philbrick, Branch Manager, GMP Private Client LP; Former CFL player, Hamilton Tiger Cats)

Rewards and Recognition

Often, public leadership ends up being dispiriting. "We have made it a tough job and are fortunate that people run for it. We need to invest this role with a level of respect and responsibility. We need to have compassion for public leaders and cut them some slack." (Mary Hofstetter, President and CEO, The Banff Centre)

Public leaders shouldn't have to wait for death for us to acknowledge their contribution. These men and women work very hard to improve public well-being and should be offered gratitude instead of constant criticism. There should be more awards, prizes and celebrations. Let's find ways to attract, develop and support outstanding political leaders. Let's make public leadership visible and important. "Help them be the best they can be. Create a society that values leadership. Provide time and resources for development." (Elizabeth O'Neill, Executive Director, Big Brothers Big Sisters, Edmonton and Area)

The Buck Stops Here

As Canadian citizens, we are responsible for both problem and solutions. Individually and collectively, it's in our power to take action and strengthen this critical area. "Elected officials determine our collective future. We must redefine their mandate and value their role, invest this denigrated profession with importance, and support those who dare to take it on. A strong sense of duty is required, for it is a difficult path." (Francine Brousseau, Vice-President Development, Canadian Museum of Civilization Corporation)

Upgrading the talent management pipeline doesn't contravene democratic practice—anybody can run. But they should know what they are getting into, have a better idea of the fit, and understand that extensive development will be required and their performance managed. A more professional approach to talent management is urgently required.

Wanted: Effective Leadership Practices

Having adequate development infrastructures and a professional structure for the field of elected leadership, will go a long way towards increasing its efficiency and capacity to serve. Interviewees also shared tips on effective leadership practices:

Stay in Touch with Constituencies

Public leaders represent their constituencies; however, in the whirl and swirl of political life, it's easy to get caught up in parliamentary fever and lose touch with the very people who mandated them. Interviewees' loud and clear message was: find ways to stay in touch with your electorate. "Stay down to earth. Don't lose touch with people. Be present to your constituencies." (Peter Eriksson, Olympic and Paralympic National Coach, Track and Field)

"Vote is based on values. If your values are in line with those of your community, you can be successful. You must understand the current values of your citizens. The democratic process matters." (Doug McCallum, Former Mayor, Surrey, British Columbia)

The bond between citizens and public leaders is a special relationship and needs to be nurtured. "Citizens and politicians need to demonstrate mutual respect. There has to be numerous opportunities for people to participate. Likewise, elected officials need to be involved in the implementation of policies they spearheaded. An emphasis on accountability leads to openness." (Honourable Joseph L. Handley, Premier, Northwest Territories)

It goes beyond presence and connection. Elected officials must avoid becoming 'elitist officials,' jet-setting in a privileged world. "The disconnect between the public and government is part of the problem. We need to work on the nature of that disconnection and generate a greater number of opportunities for politicians to experience people." (Honourable Ken Dryden, MP; Former Minister, Social Development, Government of Canada)

The desired outcome is an environment where citizens and politicians strive to work together in a culture of civic collaboration. "Once elected, some politicians assume they have to dominate the landscape. They are scared because their egos are on the line. This is why they keep talking and tend to control conversations: they are afraid they won't know how to react to a statement. Instead, they should be open-minded and develop their listening skills. This will help to avoid the cocky approach. Listen, ask for opinions; this will help you get adjusted." (Philip Owen, Former Mayor, Vancouver, British Columbia)

Technology is a useful tool for citizen engagement. "Open the process up to grassroots. Have webcast presentations. People could debate issues and input on policies on the Internet. Engage people in the process; there is never too much of it. It is important to have members at large represent different communities affected by policies." (Marion Lay, President, 2010 Legacies Now) Large group intervention techniques also present promising avenues. Citizens want greater involvement in policy-making, and modern tools enable this process.

Politicians also need to interact with other community change agents: individuals and advocacy groups who have expertise and thoughtful perspectives on relevant issues. Most importantly, they should view these as allies, not enemies. "Public leaders have to learn to cooperate with civil society without feeling threatened. Neighbourhood and community groups have a lot to offer; their expertise can enrich public leaders' perspectives and lead to consensus." (Nancy Neamtan, President and Executive Director, Chantier de l'Économie Sociale [Social Economy Working Group])

Participative democracy and civic collaboration are lofty goals and will require a considerable effort to implement. But if we put our minds to it, we can succeed, because these objectives fit our temperament, values and intentions. First, we need to put it to the forefront of our consciousness. Then, plan for action and implement. The rewards will speak for themselves.

Raise Level of Debate

Several interviewees mentioned the necessity of raising the level of debates in both form and substance. "Policy debates have lost quality. Politicians shouldn't scream and yell at each other; it drives the right people out of politics." (Bill Hamilton, Executive Coach, W.J.A. Hamilton & Associates; Former Senior Vice-President, BMO and CIBC)

Debates at all government levels are now televised. By watching, citizens can learn, reflect and make up their own minds about issues. Televised proceedings can be a source of inspiration and pride, but right now it seems elected leaders are missing the mark and doing so very visibly. "Too often, debating in parliament shows lack of respect, civility and decency to one another. Lying, grandstanding, positioning and deceit are all too common." (Paul Henderson, Founder and President, The Leadership Group; Maple Leafs Hockey Alumni)

How can we create a space that allows public officials to deliberate in a productive, apt and creative manner? "We just need to get the parliamentarians to stop fighting like high school kids and behave in an appropriate and inspiring manner. They need to stop finding fault and blaming each other and start acting constructively." (Gladys Osmond, Leader, The Granny Brigade) Perhaps we need to question a fundamental assumption: Is debate the best format?

New Paradigm Required

In fact, the format for political discussion is increasingly viewed as an issue. The *Oxford Dictionary* defines debate as 'discussion in which opposing arguments are presented.' This approach may no longer serve us. It fosters argumentation, bickering and blame, and invariably produces winners and losers, causing loss of face and resentment.

We may need to switch to dialogue. The *Oxford Dictionary* defines dialogue as 'conversation intended to explore a subject or resolve a problem.' It comes across as less confrontational, because it is not based on a win-lose paradigm. Change is required to create an environment where elected officials can interact in a constructive manner to examine and resolve today's complex issues with the depth of analysis and innovative thinking they deserve.

Lorraine Pintal, C.M., General and Artistic Director, Théâtre du Nouveau Monde, had a powerful suggestion: "Public leaders should be trained on mutual gains bargaining to find inclusive solutions that stand a chance to last. They need to acquire better tools to manage dynamics and tensions amongst themselves and with their constituencies."

Mutual gains bargaining opens up a world of possibilities. Based on solutions meeting joint interests, the method is conducive to consensus and promotes collaboration. One of the authors uses this technique in her professional practice and has seen it produce nothing short of miracles: union and management agreeing on every article of a collective agreement and building stronger relationships, and citizen groups and municipal administrations resolving community problems in innovative and satisfying ways. If this method was taught to parliamentarians and municipal councillors, their productivity and effectiveness would double, if not triple. We see this as a promising avenue for the future.

CITIZENS

Let's now move on to our second stakeholder group: citizens.

Rights and Responsibilities

We live in a democracy where citizens have rights and a voice; however, we also have the responsibility to participate in the democratic process. "Responsibility belongs to the citizens and they should hold politicians accountable. They elect them and can fire them when they are not measuring up." (Ruth Kelly, President, Venture Publishing Inc.; Publisher and Editor-in-Chief, *Alberta Venture*)

In the last 20 years, voting rates have decreased in western democracies. Governments are currently studying the causes of this phenomenon. But voting is only the basic requirement of individuals, almost symbolic in nature. In reality, responsibilities must go much further. "Citizens have the responsibility to serve their community, for instance on local councils or through other means. People need to get involved." (Dr. Colin MacDonald, President and CEO, Clearwater Seafood)

Paradoxically, as voting rates decrease, citizens' requests increase for more involvement in policy and decision-making. Therefore, the last 10 years have witnessed an explosion of forums, town hall meetings, Internet surveys, etc. As a result, when participation processes are non-existent or weak, citizens complain bitterly, often to the media.

Likewise, demands for transparency and accountability are on the rise. When decisions are perceived as unfair, rigged or made behind closed doors, the reaction is outrage. Finally, more citizens are taking advantage of redress mechanisms to communicate their displeasure, state their expectations and seek fair and equitable treatment. "If decisions are made by lobbyists unbeknownst to legislators, confidence in the democratic process erodes. Lobbying has a destructive effect on public leadership." (Clément Guimond, General Coordinator, Caisse d'économie solidaire Desjardins [Credit Union])

The price of democracy is constant vigilance, goes the saying. Citizens need to be alert, attentive, careful and vocal. "It is the citizens' responsibility not to take democracy for granted." (Judy Rogers, City Manager, Vancouver, British Columbia) So what can citizens do to enhance the health and effectiveness of the democratic system? In a nutshell, *demand and give more*. "Citizens need to be more responsible; if we demand more, public leaders will have to raise their level of performance. People must elect candidates who assume leadership." (Ève-Lyne Biron, President and General Manager, Laboratoire Médical Biron)

Civic Education

In order to achieve greater citizen engagement, we need to significantly expand and upgrade civic education for students and adults, particularly new immigrants. Our understanding and appreciation of democracy and democratic systems should be more aligned. "Educate people on the role of elected officials in the school system. Courses should not be optional and they should be in-depth." (Shauna Sylvester, Founding Executive Director, Institute for Media, Policy and Civil Society [IMPACS])

Patrick Cuenco, Co-founder, Junior Hong Kong-Canada Business Association, concludes, "We need to educate the public about their rights and responsibilities, raise expectations and deliverables. A good example is Canada 25: Youth leadership groups from all over the world devise policies for government, and present them to parliaments. This gives youth exposure to government and policy-making. We need to teach young people how government works."

PUBLIC SERVANTS

Public servants are the backbone of the Public Sector. Their ability to serve citizens effectively and support elected officials can have a huge impact on how citizens perceive governments.

Continuous Improvement

Recently, the various levels of government have made a substantial effort to improve service quality as well as information access. Tremendous progress has been made and positive changes have occurred. Public servants everywhere have risen to the challenge, increasing system effectiveness and expanding their capacity to serve.

Meanwhile, many Crown and Government Corporations have metamorphosed into model organizations. For instance, the Liquor Control Board of Ontario (LCBO) has become a stellar example of retail excellence. Hydro-Québec is a leader in alternative electricity production. Saskatchewan General Insurance (SGI) boasts record sales. It seems these hybrid organizations have succeeded in blending private and public sector characteristics to a remarkable advantage.

According to interviewees, the next challenge for the public sector is performance management, discussed earlier. Like private sector employees, public servants are responsible to deliver outcomes. "Public servants must be accountable, individually and collectively. This can be accomplished by giving them clear objectives and the leeway to achieve them." (Yolande James, MNA for Nelligan, Québec)

Like other employees, public servants strive to achieve and want recognition for their efforts. "We must redefine roles, reform public service and refuse to accept mediocrity. Human beings are competitive—good performances must be acknowledged." (Suzanne Blanchet, President and CEO, Cascades Tissue Group)

In order to do so, they need space to take calculated risks, innovate and exercise their judgement. Rigid environments are not conducive to excellence, because they kill initiative. "Bureaucracy must be pared down to give public servants the freedom to innovate, instead of limiting their contributions." (Gérald Larose, Professor-Researcher, School of Social Work, Université du Québec à Montréal [UQAM])

Judging by their recent service and technology upgrade, public servants are up to the performance challenge.

Leadership Requirement

Not only must public servants perform and deliver, they must provide solid leadership to changing elected officials. Bureaucrats know how to navigate government infrastructure and can orient politicians to it. "We require great people to run bureaucracies and advise elected officials. Politicians must show leadership, and bureaucrats fuel it by showing them how the nuts and bolts work, not the opposite." (Dave Mowat, CEO, Vancity Credit Union)

They are also responsible for running the government infrastructure efficiently and effectively. Therefore, the quality of decision-making is prime. "We must develop the leadership skills of those working behind the scenes, as they carry out a lot of the work; that is where the money should be spent. The leading role of a great leader is to make more leaders." (John Radford, Former Vice-President, Sales and Marketing, Ford of Canada Motor Company*)*

Another opportunity for enhanced performance is ensuring that the public service remains neutral.

MEDIA

In recent years, experts say that the relationship between media and politicians has deteriorated. According to some, it's now at an all-time low. The old model seems broken and renewal, required. In general, respondents agree with this diagnosis and identified two specific issues to examine and resolve: accountability, and balancing good and bad news.

Accountability

In democracies, an implicit social contract exists between media and society. Media is granted 'freedom of the press' and, in exchange, reports on events and trends according to proper journalistic principles and ethics. We expect it will provide accurate information and, more importantly, help us make sense of it. Ultimately, the media is a meaning-making device.

The nature and environment of the media changed dramatically during the 20th century, prompting the current malaise. For example, technology now provides instant access to worldwide news, speeding up momentum and raising expectations. The proliferation of players makes the field insanely competitive, adding pressure to cut corners. TV has gained prominence and its constraints affect how news is presented and what is valued: image taking precedence over contents, and the need for speed forcing the reduction of intricate information to sound bites, which in turn can easily degenerate into spin. Has the landscape altered enough to warrant a revision of the social contract?

These new conditions are disastrous for politics. Elected officials need time to analyze and synthesize multifaceted issues in order to capture their essence. This demands consultation, research, dialogue, etc., all of which cannot be performed quickly. As a result, public leaders and media are working at cross-purposes. The media wants speed and simple messages delivered by good-looking people and politicians require time to craft complex messages delivered by knowledgeable people regardless of their looks. How can politicians and the media come to a new arrangement that allows both parties to fulfill their mandates?

This issue has the making of a profound society debate: Who is the media responsible to? What is it responsible for? How is its performance monitored and evaluated? Where are the checks and balances? How can it play a useful and appropriate role without becoming a tyranny? "The power of the press now is not healthy, as they don't present all the facts. Separate political from practical motivations and they will become more effective. Thinking through if decisions are prudent is also important." (Dr. Joseph Segal, C.M., O.B.C., O.St.J., President, Kingswood Capital Corp.)

Elected officials live in a fishbowl under the watchful eye of the media. Imagine you are an MP. In your previous life, you watched TV. Now, you are on TV. Mikes are thrown in your face and you have to competently answer questions in 30 seconds or less and do so in a confident and polished manner. You run the risk of embarrassing yourself in front of millions. "It's hard to take risks in public. Public officials are harassed by the media." (Michèle Thibodeau-DeGuire, C.M., C.Q., President and Executive Director, Centraide [United Way] of Greater Montréal)

Moreover, you never know what twist the media will give your message. You might be quoted out of context. Your segment might be contrasted with others and make you look foolish or inept. Your ego wants to hide or run. Is the media on a mission to ensure no one ever runs for office again? "The press is the biggest enemy of politicians and leaders. They are too aggressive in their critique." (Honourable Margaret McCain, O.C., O.N.B., Philanthropist; Former Lieutenant Governor, New Brunswick) "Unbalanced and inaccurate reporting by the media does a serious disservice to leadership, as it discourages open and transparent dialogue as well as access to business leaders." (Joseph Randell, President and CEO, Air Canada Jazz)

Alfred Smithers, O.C., President and CEO, Secunda Group of Companies, summed up the issue well: "People who enter public life risk being demonized by the media and their opponents for the sake of trying to do something good for society. It is easy to sit on the sidelines and expect perfection in an imperfect world. Unfortunately, people in public life are held to an extremely high standard—one that is probably impossible to meet. Society has to gain respect for political institutions and political leaders. Without it, effective leadership is hard to demonstrate and bring to the forefront. People and the media need to be more charitable, understanding and slower to cast judgement on politicians."

As a society, we need to engage in a vigorous dialogue to examine and update the mandate and accountabilities of the media and determine new rules of engagement between media and politicians to better serve the public.

Balancing Good and Bad News

The information we receive has a profound impact on our collective consciousness. An exaggerated focus on the negative creates a gloom and doom atmosphere where problems outweigh solutions, fraud prevails over ethics and incompetence reigns supreme. This is dangerous because it creates resignation and apathy: *Why bother trying? Why vote when they're all crooks anyway? We haven't had good leaders since Trudeau. Nothing ever changes, so why should I get involved?*

As a society, if we lose confidence in our ability to change and hope for the future, we will flounder. In theory, the media is responsible for reporting on what happens. Many good things happen: Problems are solved, progress is made, success is achieved, and people take care of their community and show courage in the face of adversity. Suspiciously, there is very little reporting on 'good news.' The position seems to be 'only sensational news will sell.' This is quite an unfortunate state.

In the course of our research, we had the privilege of speaking with 295 leaders across Canada who greatly impressed us with their projects and accomplishments, and, yet, the likelihood of these inspiring stories making it into the media is slim. Mistakes, mishaps, problems that never got solved receive more attention than the thousands that did. Why this obsession with the negative and the sensational? "Media picks on failures and exceptional behaviours. They need to state what their values are and objectives and report based on them—not on the rhetoric." (Elizabeth Jane Crocker, Author; Co-Owner, Woozles and P'lovers)

A successful model to resolve this issue is the Employment Equity Act. When introduced in 1986, it met with backlash because people worried about their ability to meet quotas and the danger of hiring or promoting incompetents in order to do so. Over time, however, the legislation forced organizations to become more innovative in sourcing qualified candidates and to look beyond appearances. Twenty years later, the workforce composition has been profoundly altered and career opportunities for designated groups have greatly improved. More importantly, the legislation has completely transformed attitudes and HR practices.

A similar system could be used with the media: it would be required to provide a certain percentage of good news as part of its redefined social contract. There would be resentment at first, but it would force the media to pursue different news items and cover news in a more balanced way. Over time, it would transform the information we are exposed to and raise our consciousness of the possible.

Balancing news is not an attempt to gloss over dark realities or dumb down issues, but rather to turn the spotlight in another direction: to people triumphing over difficult circumstances, entrepreneurs building successful businesses, legislators passing progressive laws, etc. For instance, one could envision a series on successful corporations, progressive communities, unsung heroes, innovative legislations and 'against all odds' accomplishments.

These would provide a source of inspiration as well as opportunities to learn and to share best practices across the country, building hope. Budding leaders would not shy away from contributing, but be inspired. A better balance would empower people to dream big, to do and dare more. A consciousness of possibilities is far superior to one of limitations. As a society, which one do we want to cultivate?

CONCLUSION

To improve the quality of public leadership, we have to look at it from a holistic perspective and redefine the roles and accountabilities of the four stakeholders: elected officials, citizens, public servants and media. Doing so will facilitate better interaction and smoother dynamics between the parties.

Of the four stakeholders, elected officials need the most attention. Current reality doesn't meet the needs of the constituencies, which are getting increasingly disenfranchised and cynical. "Is the system set up for performance? Apparently not, for it prevents elected officials from staying close to their electorate and focuses their efforts on re-election instead of on serving their constituencies' interests. Moreover, the system doesn't promote ownership of individual and collective accountabilities. Finally, everything is over-institutionalized and limits citizens' real participation and involvement. This kind of system is not conducive to leadership emergence; it lacks fluidity and erects roadblocks." (Marc Poulin, President Operations, Québec Region, Sobeys Inc.)

A major overhaul is required, including building a solid foundation of competence, consistency and integrity; re-structuring the field as a profession and upgrading all aspects of the talent management pipeline; and changing the format for parliamentary discussions, moving from debate to mutual gains dialogue.

Citizens, for their part, must become more aware of their civic responsibilities, which will require considerable civic education for both adults and children. Public servants' performance and change capacity have tremendously increased in the last 15 years. This trend must continue, and their capacity to lead, expand.

The media and elected officials are now almost unable to meet each other's needs. A new social contract must be defined for the media and new boundaries set up for its relationship with elected officials. Finally, it is important to strike a better balance between good and bad news in the media, in order to maintain a sense of possibility, foster hope and celebrate success.

Profound change is required to improve public leadership. Are we up to the task?

CHAPTER 16

CONCLUSION

THE HERO AND THE GEESE

In recent years, much noise has been made in the media and elsewhere about a 'leadership crisis.' Apparently, a lack of leadership quality and quantity currently prevails, with supply insufficient to meet demand. Although intellectually, we acknowledge this fact, psychologically, we are still operating under an old paradigm: the hero who appears in exceptional circumstances and saves the day. Appealing as this myth might be, it is the stuff of legends, not a useful construct for today's realities.

Many factors have contributed to erode the leader/hero myth: democracy, mass education, technology, population explosion, etc. Most significantly, objective leadership research conducted in the 20th century shifted the focus from *who* leaders are to *what* they do, reducing the importance of external factors such as appearance, gender and physical ability, and increasing the value of effective behaviours and skill deployment.

Still, it's hard to let go of the knight in shining armour, and this prevents us from taking strategic action about leadership development on a large scale. We still hope that enough competent leaders will emerge on their own, and are disappointed when they don't, for under the old paradigm, enough 'natural' leaders would surface to meet society's needs.

Maybe the media barrage will wake us up. We need a reality check comparable to the one experienced by the Canadian Olympic Committee after the 2004 Athens Summer Games. The Committee came up with a plan and it worked. Very simply, if you want 'medal material' athletes or leaders, you have to groom them. Talent alone is not enough.

The time has come to get out of our victim/princess consciousness, pull up our sleeves and save ourselves. The knight in shining armour must be replaced by a critical mass of effective leadership practitioners. Today's paradigm is the Canadian Geese flying in a V formation. Everyone has to 'sail their leadership ship.' The hero has to give way to the geese. But how can we produce the critical mass of leaders we require?

The Quest

Therefore, our research sought to answer these three questions:

1. What are the best ways to develop competent leaders?
2. How can we ensure a reliable supply of capable leaders for the country?
3. How can we strengthen Canadian Leadership?

To find the answers, we interviewed a representative sample of established leaders and qualified professionals. They confirmed what we already suspected intuitively: Success in the global 'Leadership Olympics' means that leadership and its development have to become a national priority. This assumes a considerable investment in financial and human resources, infrastructures, as well as long-term outlook. As financial planners would say, if we want the ROI, let's start investing.

DEVELOPING COMPETENT LEADERS

How to groom the next leadership generation?

What Is the Process?

How does leadership development work?

The Path to Maturity

In order to determine how the process works, we sought first to identify the dynamics of leadership evolution: How is leadership born, and how does it evolve, grow and mature? Are there some common patterns to anticipate on the path to leadership maturity? The answer is yes.

Overall Infrastructure

The axiomatic sequence proceeds in three stages:

- **Immanence:** connecting with the leader within. The possibility for leadership rests in everyone; the question is how to activate it.
- **Emergence:** manifesting leadership. Once leadership potential is activated, how to facilitate its emergence?
- **Transcendence:** transforming reality and self through leadership. How to use leadership as a transformation compound in order to transcend present limitations and ensure the best possible future? How to derive maximum growth from the leadership experience?

Access Routes

Interviewees described two very different access routes for immanence. One is adopted by the majority (two-thirds of respondents) and the other by the minority (one-third of respondents). For the majority, external circumstances trigger the connection with leadership, while a minority feels an intense relationship with the leader within at an early age. We called the first group accidental because they often stumble upon leadership by accident, and the second innate because they exhibit a passion and disposition for leadership in their younger years. These access routes do not impact leadership capability; both types can be very effective.

Innates will invariably show up, because leadership is tied to their identity. But their numbers are insufficient to meet society's needs. Therefore, creating conditions in which accidentals can and are encouraged to lead becomes paramount. To fill the leadership gap, we must co-opt the accidentals.

Stages of Growth

The above structure forms the canvas upon which lies the road map to capacity expansion. It mirrors organic growth, transitioning from seeding (immanence), to growing (emergence), then blossoming and pollinating (transcendence). In this latter phase, the leader transforms the present, is in turn transformed by the experience, and finally 'seeds' other leaders, leaving behind a legacy of leadership descendants. Along the way, emphasis and priorities shift as stages bring up different challenges, but learning is a constant companion and transition must occur to move forward.

The Leadership Ride

As leaders travel along the path, their inner experience is affected by the twists and turns of the road. How is the journey perceived from the inside? Most people experience it like a roller coaster: The highs are high and the lows low, success is intoxicating and failure crushing. It gives and takes large quantities of energy and, to sustain momentum, leaders must find ways to balance its flow and stabilize the pain/gain ratio.

Leadership is a 'peak' experience. It propels you out of the mundane into a realm of possibility where the rapture of life is intensely felt. Respondents stated that leadership made them better people and enabled them to contribute more. Overall, they would not have missed the experience for the world. However, they complained of isolation. What could be done to increase leader support and collegiality? A sense of belonging and a friendly presence would allow more leaders to stay the course and flourish.

To Summarize

Viewing leadership from the inside sheds some light on internal wiring that is generally invisible. We were delighted to find more similarities than differences and even those are not random. 'Looking in' illuminated how to best leverage existing processes and growth stages. It's similar to being aware of developmental phases, such as adolescence or midlife crisis. If you know what lies ahead, you can prepare for it.

How to Optimize the Process?

In leadership, regardless of nature, nurture is required. Even the most talented or proficient can benefit from development. All interviewees stressed its importance; development enables growth in skill and confidence and enhances adaptability. The question becomes *What are the best ways to structure development efforts for maximum results?*

The Apprenticeship Model

The most relevant construct seems to be the apprenticeship model, because it combines theory, practice and coaching, blending art and science. It acknowledges that proficiency doesn't happen overnight, but evolves progressively. It recognizes that development occurs primarily from the 'inside out' with the input of 'outside in' information, such as frameworks, guidance, advice, feedback, etc.

By its very appellation, apprenticeship clearly implies that the objective is mastery: superb execution coupled with a sound instinct and reliable judgement. It's about finding and expanding the flow, not fixing gaps or compensating for deficiencies. The model also stresses the importance of the master-apprentice relationship, which fits the high value placed on mentoring by interviewees.

Program Architecture

Program experts confirmed the apprenticeship model and identified its major components: education, practice, self-discovery, support and community.

Education is useful to acquire frameworks, concepts and a common language, but leadership proficiency requires extensive practice, supported by coaching. Leadership is a process, much like cooking: You have to master techniques and try various recipes to become competent. You also have to sharpen your own instinct about ingredient combination and menu selection. This validates the apprenticeship model. Professionals told us that optimal programs include extensive practice components, both in class where the best learning is experiential, and outside the classroom, through a variety of carefully selected and supervised practicum applications.

But education and practice are not enough. Individuals have to discover their leadership identity and appreciate their impact. This means understanding motivational drivers and identifying strengths and weaknesses for best leverage. When leading, the entire person must be mobilized to serve the role. Therefore, self-discovery is essential, because operating in a blind spot considerably reduces leadership effectiveness.

To alleviate growing pains, developing leaders also need support and guidance. Since mentoring is the most effective leadership development method, it's important to provide coaching, assistance, advice, sponsorship and more. Finally, to minimize isolation and maximize a sense of belonging, leaders need a community to share their learnings, solve problems and network.

When these five components are strategically designed and integrated optimally for each participant, impressive things occur.

Individual Learning Strategy

But programs cannot be responsible for learner development. You can bring a horse to water, but you can't make him drink, says the proverb. Participants are ultimately in charge. And the more aware they are of the process, the more they learn: A sharp consciousness derives meaning and speeds up the process. Second, participants need to quickly access their intuition, a fundamental leadership capability. Nothing fast-tracks leadership proficiency like the development of a reliable instinct.

Likewise, leaving development to chance slows it down. Although opportunities will present themselves, learners have to seek those that best fit their current developmental stage. Therefore, interviewees emphasized the importance of planning, which provides a sense of control and focuses the learning process strategically.

For instance, it's important to determine what to do before, during and after the leadership experience. Before, identify your purpose: Who and what are you serving and how? Next, build your platform: What are your vision, values, principles and ethics—the fundamentals guiding your leadership practice? Preparation is the process of 'going in' to clarify intentions, structure foundations and connect with the leader within. 'During' is the firsthand experience that broadens skills, expands scope and builds resilience to adversity. This phase is about reaching out. Afterwards, analysis fosters learning by extracting maximum juice. It's now time for stepping back.

These in/out/back dynamics are necessary to keep the development process on track. Action without analysis leads to the endless repetition of the same mistakes; likewise, analysis without action leads to paralysis. These dynamics help leaders appreciate their impact and adjust behaviours as they go along.

ENSURING A RELIABLE LEADERSHIP SUPPLY FOR CANADA

How to make sure we have enough leaders to meet our needs?

Organizational Leadership Strategy

Organizations have a major role to play and a big stake in leadership development. They must provide an environment conducive to leadership emergence, practice and development. The more effective they become at structuring their efforts in a strategic and integrated manner, the more leaders will blossom. Our research uncovered that a large number have already embarked on this path and some are very advanced.

To create a leadership-prone environment, organizations must clarify their leadership orientation, and entrench a leadership 'conscience.' In the process, they ponder questions such as *Do our executives model effective leadership behaviours? Have leadership expectations been defined? How do we support and reward good leaders and how do we deal with poor performers? How do we identify and track leadership talent?* Soon, they conclude that, as an entity, they must behave like a leader, not only in their sector but in the community.

Building the Leadership House

In order to answer these questions and others, organizations define their essential beliefs about leadership and its value: a 'platform' that acts as a compass and an anchor, guiding and grounding their activities. Once the platform is in place, it provides a solid foundation.

Next comes the infrastructure, the configuration that enables the free flow of people and ideas required for effective leadership practice. We discovered that optimal structures provide support, reduce obstacles and demand low maintenance. Typically, this means flat, decentralized and participative.

Likewise, 'breeding' leaders calls for vast open spaces and freedom. Structures impact leadership emergence. As Marc Poulin, President Operations, Québec Region, Sobeys Inc., wisely commented, "In order to create a critical mass of leaders, leadership must be awakened and developed in a lot of people. For leadership to thrive, a fluid environment and numerous practice opportunities are required."

Once the house is built, it's ready to be peopled by dedicated and competent employees. The bond between organization and employees affects not only engagement and loyalty, but productivity and innovation. A climate loaded with possibility gives employees the motivation and freedom to act. Therefore, begin with a solid and well-laid-out house and turn it into a home by creating a caring atmosphere brimming with opportunities.

When configured properly, organizations constitute fertile grounds for leadership practice and development. As a result, they achieve their goals and leaders expand their capacity—a win-win proposition.

Leaving leadership emergence to chance is short-sighted and risky. Therefore, a deliberate approach is required. We need to become proactive, devise plans and align our actions.

Best Practices from the Co-op Sector

We discovered many interesting practices applicable to other sectors. The co-op culture is community grounded and therefore, in it for the long haul—democratic, interdependent, holistic and collaborative. The emphasis is on common interests and win-win solutions that have a chance to last.

Co-ops manage their social and economic mandates and aim for the sustainable development zone, where the balanced scorecard reigns and consultation is a way of life. Other sectors are currently trying to acquire this holistic, long-term perspective.

The co-op culture displays a blended leadership style, mixing business, community and democracy, conducive to leadership success. It does so first, because co-ops are aware of the service imperative; second, because they view people as their reason for being and the means to accomplishment; and third, because everyone is expected to provide leadership in some capacity. This no-nonsense expectation, also present in the military, goes a long way to stimulate leadership emergence and the belief in continuous improvement.

Co-ops have access to a large pool of potential leaders at their disposal and use different development strategies depending on the targeted population. For instance, they structure leadership education in layers. It starts with citizen and co-operative education to set the foundations. It then proceeds to organizational and professional training to ensure job competence fits the organization. Finally comes leadership education, the grand finale. The sequence is a smart way to induct leaders to their various roles and responsibilities. Resourcefulness, collaboration and common interests form the fabric of co-operative life. These components could be beneficial for other sectors, as well.

National Leadership Strategy

A national leadership strategy would make leadership and its development a national priority, stressing the importance of capable leadership and the imperative to invest in this crucial resource. The strategy would be crafted through a national dialogue, which would produce a comprehensive plan. Interviewees said the focus should be on three pillars: leadership education, widespread mentoring programs and the establishment of a national leadership institute.

Leadership Education

Leadership is almost invisible as a field of study. Interviewees suggested making the study of it mandatory at all levels and in all provinces, configuring it according to the apprenticeship model and adapting the practicum components to age groups.

Ideally, leadership education should be project driven to enable students to practise skills and gain experience. Kids would select a project to lead, such as a blood drive or a charity fundraising event. As the children grow older, projects would become bigger and more externally driven. If we start now, we might see significant results in 10 to 12 years.

Widespread Access to Mentoring

In order to produce more quality leaders, we need to expose more people to mentoring. This means creating widespread programs for youth and adults, in school and at work. Good programs carefully select mentors according to pre-determined criteria, train mentors, orient those mentored, and monitor relationship progress and outcomes.

National Leadership Institute

Finally, we advocate the creation of a National Leadership Institute to develop a coast-to-coast strategy, keep leadership a priority in our consciousness, and act as a catalyst for information sharing, education and resource development.

Improving Leadership in the Public Sector

It is impossible to strengthen Canadian leadership without improving leadership in the public sector. To do so, the four key stakeholder roles (elected officials, citizens, public servants and the media) must be revised and redefined, as must be the way they interact.

Elected Officials

How can we enhance the quality of elected leadership?

Enhancing Development Infrastructures

Transitioning from an ordinary citizen to a polished legislator is no small feat. Existing systems have proven insufficient to prepare elected officials to play their role. Paradoxically, much better development systems are in place for public servants. The quality and quantity of development systems available to elected officials must rise to a level comparable to what is offered to public servants.

Structuring the Field Like a Profession

The field of elected leadership has to be professionalized. Currently, accountabilities are fuzzy and consequences of poor performance are vague. Much more specificity and rigour have to be injected into the way elected leaders' performance is defined, measured and managed.

Moreover, a formal and integrated talent management infrastructure must be put in place to define and publicize the roles, attract and recruit good candidates based on pre-determined criteria, orient and develop them, manage their performance, reward and recognize them. The current system is at least 30 years behind best practices in the marketplace.

The essential mandate of elected officials is to create a vision for their society and manage the transition towards it. This requires strategic thinking and wide horizons—a difficult focus for officials when they are embroiled in day-to-day issues and crises. To remedy the situation, interviewees suggested holding regular Canada-wide forums to craft the optimal vision and strategies for the future of our country. Once the vision and strategies are crafted, politicians become keepers of the direction and architects of change, regardless of party allegiance.

Finally, debate seems to have run its course. A more productive format is required and interviewees recommended dialogue, coupled with training on interest-based problem solving, so that elected officials can have productive conversations instead of shouting and insulting each other. The container has to be upgraded in order for the quality of the contents to rise.

Citizens

Good leaders are, first and foremost, good citizens. This means being aware of both rights *and* responsibilities and acting on them. "Ask not what your country can do for you—ask what you can do for your country," said John F. Kennedy. Currently, there is too much emphasis on the 'parent state' taking care of the 'child' and not enough on the child giving back.

Interviewees recommended increasing the 'responsibility' component of the Canadian Charter of Rights and Freedoms by defining our duties to society. We must make them specific and include accountability metrics and consequences for not fulfilling them.

Citizens must also take a more active role in democracy, and this requires education to align and motivate. Interviewees recommended enhancing civic education for children, immigrants and adults.

Obviously, citizens and civic leaders must know Canada. This is a challenge because of our size, diversity and bilingualism. Therefore, we need to put extra effort into making future leaders 'Canada savvy.' A wide array of programs is required for adults and children to foster knowledge acquisition, reduce disparities in understanding, and infuse Canadians with a deep love and respect for the country.

Public Servants

Public servants have come a long way. The last decade has seen remarkable changes in terms of responsiveness, transparency, service and innovation. They benefit from more development and it shows. The next challenges, said interviewees, are greater accountability and better performance management, as well as more leadership support for elected officials.

Media

The mandate and responsibilities of the media need to be revised. Who is the media accountable to? What is it accountable for? And, how to rectify the fact that they are working at cross-purposes with elected officials whose needs are profoundly different from theirs? A new 'social contract' must be redefined between those parties, to minimize tension and enable them to work productively.

A better balance between good and bad news also has to be restored; an overemphasis on bad news erodes self-confidence and breeds resignation. People need to hear about success stories—how people solved problems—instead of suffering a constant barrage of disasters and crises.

STRENGHTENING CANADIAN LEADERSHIP

How to expand our leadership capacity and enhance our impact?

Understanding Our Leadership Brand

Inclusion is the first trademark. Our size, political structure, bilingualism, diversity and history combine to make us inclusive. Our reputation, political stability, balanced views and moderate temperament reinforce our inclusive style: We suggest building bridges instead of walls, seek solutions based on common interests instead of seeking to win at all costs. As a result, people are open to our influence.

Because of our penchant for inclusion, we value process skills, our second trademark. We excel at processes such as consensus-building, consulting, project management, mediation, and policy development. Consequently, our contribution and demeanour are prized on the international scene. In the complex world we live in, the future belongs to integrators, not bullies. As Lester B. Pearson said, "The 21st century will belong to Canada." No one suspects us of a domination agenda, so people trust us and look for our expertise, professionalism, and level-headedness under pressure.

Our brand itself rests on the bedrock of Canadian values and is composed of five characteristics that interact and intermingle. The first one is *principle*: the desire to behave in accordance with strong ethical, moral and democratic principles, which we often take for granted. Here's an example: An interviewee from the public sector was presenting at an international conference on his organization's talent management practices. During the presentation, he noticed many puzzled looks. At the end, several participants asked, "Do you mean that in your country people are selected and promoted on the basis of merit?" When he answered in the affirmative, they were shocked.

The second attribute is *professionalism*. We want to do a good job and we care. Canada isn't a place where sleaze prevails. We try to do our best. Like beavers, we labour until we get it right. Here's an example: An interviewee's organization had been awarded a large contract to build a bridge in a developing country. When he asked why his firm had been chosen, the response was "Because you are Canadian. We know you will work hard, won't let us down and will treat us with respect."

The third is *possibility*. As a young and successful nation, we believe in the possible, and to make the possible happen, we demonstrate a flair for treasures of creativity and resourcefulness in everything we do. From the B.C. loggers and environmentalists who joined forces to ecologically operate a forestry business, to RIM, which invented the Blackberry, to Cirque du Soleil's astonishing creativity, we do it all.

The fourth is *diversity*. Managing differences has almost become second nature and we have constructed an impressive legislative framework to do it. We have enough physical and emotional space to allow different perspectives to cohabit, and value the rich tapestry our society has become. Recently, an interviewee was invited for a Mother's Day dinner ... at a Jewish-Italian restaurant. She found the combination of foods and cultures very stimulating!

The fifth and most defining attribute is *peace*. We enjoy peace at home, and through our peace making and keeping efforts, we bring it to the world. Peace is the guiding force behind many Canadian attributes, such as fairness, seeking harmony and win-win solutions, balancing viewpoints, ensuring everyone has a voice, and preventing conflict escalation. More than any other attribute, it shapes our temperament, predisposing us to tolerance and diplomacy.

Respondents with international experience thought we are sitting on a gold mine and don't know it. Becoming more aware of our brand's trademarks and attributes will enable us to leverage them and contribute to shaping our international role and presence.

Strengthening Canadian Leadership

To improve the brand, we need to follow in the footsteps of former prime ministers Pearson and Trudeau. Pearson represents the wisdom and knowledge of the scholar: statesmanship, diplomacy, decency and guidance. He left us with a tradition to maintain. Trudeau represents the assertiveness, courage and force of the warrior: protection, affirmation, confidence and boldness. He left us with something to aspire to. Respondents believed that Pearson and Trudeau's combined influence can preside over the nation's destiny.

Several steps can be taken. First, clarify the 'Canadian core' in order to protect our identity, while remaining open to multiculturalism. Canada is like a big salad where every ingredient retains its uniqueness and flavour, not a stew where everything becomes almost undifferentiated. However, a core Canadian 'dressing' must bind us together. What are the ingredients for the dressing? How can we make sure every citizen is 'coated' with it? How can we ensure it doesn't get diluted or lose its essence?

Second, define a long-term and strategic focus for our international efforts on all fronts. As a nation, our ultimate goal is the triumph of peace, because we know it is a condition for development, education and prosperity. How can we combine the warrior and the scholar energies to achieve this lofty goal?

Third, publicize the brand and reward great Canadian leaders, past and present. A better understanding of our brand will enable us to commit to leadership and select appropriate avenues suited to our skills, temperament and values. We could be the process experts, the fixers, the developers. We don't have to be the imperialists or the bullies.

To reinforce specific attributes, interviewees suggested:

- Crafting a national code of ethics to reinforce *principle*.
- Improving the quality and availability of education to reinforce *professionalism*.

- Expanding orientation programs to immigrants to strengthen *diversity.*
- Balancing the good news/bad news ratio in the media to expand *possibility.*
- Engaging in early conflict detection and resolution to nurture *peace.*

FINAL WORDS

This project took three years of our life and was an incredible adventure. In our minds, we visualize it as a map of Canada with people holding hands across it. We were humbled and awed that all these wonderful leaders and program experts agreed to share their stories with two strangers, just because we asked.

The collective intelligence garnered in this book is their voice: strong, steady and determined. Because of their generosity, we can all learn and see ourselves a bit more clearly. May their wisdom guide us on our path to leadership enlightenment.

PART IV

RESEARCH AND
INTERVIEWEE INFORMATION

APPENDIX I

RESEARCH PROCESS AND STATISTICAL INFORMATION

IN THE BEGINNING...

As Human Resources professionals, we are often asked generic questions like: *How can we find good leaders? How do we develop them? What are the best practices in leadership development in Canada? What can we learn from what others are doing?*

Likewise, people wonder about issues specific to this time and place: *How is Canadian leadership different from leadership in other countries? How effective is the Canadian leadership brand and how can we expand our capacity to lead? How can we ensure Canada has an abundant supply of capable leaders? How can we strengthen our leadership presence and impact, particularly on the international scene?*

Wanting to find answers to these important questions, we did some research and found very little about leadership development based on the experience of successful Canadian leaders and the expertise of Canadian leadership professionals. This came as a surprise, because we've met many exceptional leaders throughout our careers, and have been privileged to learn from their wisdom.

Therefore, in the summer of 2004, we embarked on a research project to discover the best practices in leadership development in Canada.

RESEARCH GROUPS

We decided to interview two key groups likely to have expertise on this topic:

1. Successful leaders in all sectors of the economy.
2. Leadership development professionals involved in designing, delivering and managing programs across the country.

Our goal was to gather a representative sample from all sectors and regions and to portray the diversity of the Canadian population.

We started by designing a structured interview guide for each group and piloting them with leaders and professionals we knew well. Respondents provided useful feedback to simplify and optimize the questionnaires. Pre-set formats helped with consistency in data collection.

Leaders

Our primary goal with this group was to identify the developmental strategies they found most useful. To establish a common ground, we first asked them to define leadership and to identify what they value most in leaders. This was important to establish a common baseline and understand the foundations of their leadership practice, before getting into their leadership development journey, and obtain subsequent advice for developing leaders. Finally, we wanted to get their thoughts on Canadian leadership and their recommendations to strengthen it.

Professionals

From experts, we sought to find out what works best to grow leaders, and how their programs evolved over time to maximize effectiveness. The interview guide dealt with program start-up and evolution, contents, audience, intended and actual outcomes, key learnings, and recommendations.

Co-ops

As data collection evolved, a pattern emerged. Interviewees were consistently saying that the type of leadership poised to succeed in the 21st century is democratic, predicated on influence versus authority, able to rally diverse constituencies in a cohesive and productive manner, concerned with community well-being and seeking to give back. Other critical success factors include a focus on the long term and on sustainable development, and outcome evaluation with integrated metrics going beyond simple numbers.

We realized that this type of leadership is practised in co-operatives through their ideological foundation, governance principles and infrastructure. We therefore decided to include co-op representatives, both leaders and program experts. To reflect co-op realities, a slightly different interview guide was used for program experts. We selected a representative sample of various sizes and types, in many sectors across the country, as well as federations and associations. This yielded specific chapters on best practices in the co-op environment.

REPRESENTATIVE SAMPLE

Canada is a vast and diverse country. It was important to recruit participants mirroring the Canadian population.

Leaders

We decided not to limit our research to the world of business but include all sectors of economic activity. Leaders came from the following sectors:

- Artistic/entertainment/media/communications. We called upon artists, broadcasters, producers, artistic directors, CEOs, etc.
- Business (for profit): small, medium-sized and large corporations. We interviewed CEOs, COOs, vice presidents, directors, board chairs, entrepreneurs, etc. Co-op leaders were included in this section.
- Community (not for profit): charity, advocacy organizations. We listened to executive directors, activists, philanthropists, community workers, advocates, etc.
- Public sector: all levels of government—federal, provincial, regional and municipal; para-public entities—Crown corporations, hospitals, education, social agencies. We talked with senior public servants, politicians, ministers, directors, etc.
- Sports (professional and amateur). We consulted with athletes, Olympians, coaches, administrators, etc.

Professionals

Leadership development professionals came from nine categories where programs are located:

- Community groups
- Consulting firms
- Co-ops
- Corporations (business)
- Institutes
- Public sector entities
- Sports federations and associations
- Universities
- Youth organizations.

Regions

We worked hard to achieve a fair representation from coast to coast that somewhat mirrors the distribution of the overall population. The following regions were represented: Atlantic Canada (Newfoundland, PEI, New Brunswick and Nova Scotia), Québec, Ontario, the Prairies (Saskatchewan, Alberta and Manitoba), British Columbia and the North (Northwest Territories, Yukon, Nunavut).

Diversity

To reflect Canadian diversity, we included people from all regions and sectors, men and women, anglophones and francophones, Aboriginals, representatives from various ethnic backgrounds, visible minorities and people with disabilities. Leaders were of all ages—some in early stages of their career, some in mid-career, and others retired, but still playing an active leadership role in their community.

Candidate Selection

Our goal was to access people who make a significant difference in their field or community, not just the well-known superstars. As a reference, we used the Kotter Model described in Chapter 1 on page 10, because our focus was on leadership in action; in other words, on people who get results through others and realize their vision.

We started with a small nucleus of leaders we knew in each sector. Following a 'web' process, we asked interviewees to suggest other leaders they respected and the web grew. Other leaders were selected because of their national profile. A few came to our attention through the media.

We sought to achieve a balanced representation and a mix of inspiring high profilers and 'local heroes' that readers can identify with, learn from and emulate.

DATA COLLECTION

Candidates were sent an invitation accompanied by the book outline and relevant interview guide for their category. This way, they were able to determine their willingness to participate and, if interested, prepare for the interview.

For the most part, interviews were conducted over the phone, and lasted between 45 and 90 minutes. Notes were taken, compiled by question and analyzed to identify themes and patterns. Subsequently, models were created, and chapters outlined and written. The manuscript is based on the aggregated data as well as the wisdom and expertise we have gained during our professional careers.

It was paramount to maintain the integrity of the information. We solicited and received permission from participants to aggregate their data, list them in the Appendix, and use specific quotes, as well as personal anecdotes. We would have liked to feature many more quotes and additional points; however, we were limited by space constraints. More information is available on our website, www.canada-leadership.com.

STATISTICAL OVERVIEW

Our research is based on input from 295 leaders and 66 program experts. Where appropriate for statistical purposes, we have rounded off percentages.

Some participants were selected for their experience in a sector; for example, former Olympians who speak about their involvement in sports even if they have now moved on to other fields. Likewise, a number of participants have well-rounded lives, exposing them to several sectors, such as leaders who primarily work in business, but are active in the community. In addition, a few leaders have changed roles since the interviews and some have retired. We have used "former" to indicate previous occupations, regardless of movement to another position or stage. Therefore, in Appendix II, we have listed the top sectors that leaders feel they belong to and reflected their former title where relevant for this research.

Similarly, some interviewees have also relocated to another region or their responsibilities have expanded from one region to others. Therefore, in Appendix II, we reflect their most current region; however, for statistical purposes, we have also indicated the region and sector they belonged to at the time of the interview.

A small number of leaders have asked not to be listed, because of personal circumstances. Their contribution, though, is still part of the aggregated and statistical data, even if their names are not listed. Others, due to changes in their work situation, were impossible to reach and therefore are not listed. Should we succeed in reconnecting with them, they will appear in subsequent editions of this book and their information will be added to our website.

STATISTICAL PROFILE

In this section, we will outline various statistical features.

Leaders

The following is the statistical profile of leaders interviewed:

Participation Rate

Approximately 79% of those we reached out to agreed to participate.

Listing

Two hundred ninety-five leaders were interviewed and 286 are listed. Nine people were either unreachable at the time of finalizing the list, or did not want to be listed for personal reasons. However, their data is aggregated with the others.

Sector Representation

In order to reflect employment patterns in the general population, business leaders, including co-operative leaders, constitute the largest group (28.8%), followed by the public sector (23.4%), community (17.6%), sports (15.2%) and arts/entertainment (15%).

Gender Representation

Men represent 55.6% of interviewees, while women represent 44.4%.

Language Representation

Approximately 73% of interviewees are Anglophones, and 27% are Francophones. Francophones outside Québec constitute 2.7% of the total. Ten percent of overall interviewees stated being bilingual. A number of participants speak languages other than English and French.

Distribution

Participants reflect the population density of Canada. Ontario constitutes the largest group (28%), followed by (24.7%) Western Canada (Prairies and B.C.), 19% from Québec, 14.2% from the Atlantic provinces and, finally, 1.4% from the North. About 12.6% were grouped under 'Canada' to reflect their pan-Canadian responsibilities.

Leaders' breakdown by region is from east to west, and by sector, in descending order of the number of contributors:

Table I:1

	Business	Public	Community	Sports	Arts/Enter-tainment
Atlantic	14 (16.5%)	13 (18.8%)	8 (15.4%)	2 (4.4%)	5 (11.4%)
Québec	18 (21.2%)	12 (17.4%)	8 (15.4%)	7 (15.6%)	11 (25%)
Ontario	26 (30.6%)	17 (24.6%)	13 (25%)	8 (17.8%)	19 (43.2%)
Prairies	15 (17.6%)	4 (5.8%)	8 (15.4%)	6 (13.3%)	4 (9%)
B.C.	7 (8.2%)	9 (13%)	9 (17.3%)	8 (17.8%)	3 (6.8%)
North	1 (1.2%)	2 (2.9%)	0 (0%)	0 (0%)	1 (2.3%)
Canada	4 (4.7%)	12 (17.4%)	6 (11.5%)	14 (31.1%)	1 (2.3%)
Total Partici-pants	85	69	52	45	44

Programs

The following is the statistical profile for programs:

Participation Rate

Approximately 89% of program experts contacted agreed to be interviewed.

Listing

Sixty-six programs were interviewed and 64 are listed. Two programs could not be reached at the time of finalizing the list; however, their data is aggregated.

Sector Representation

Co-ops represent 36.4% of participants, universities 13.6%, private sector corporations 12.1%, public sector organizations 10.6%, institutes 6%, sports programs 6%, community programs 6%, youth programs 4.5% and consulting firms 4.5%.

Official Language Representation

Approximately 19.5% provide programs in both official languages, 58.7% offer programs only in English and 21.7% offer programs only in French.

Distribution

The table on the next page provides a breakdown of programs by region from east to west, and by sector, in descending order of the number of contributors.

A number of organizations like consulting firms, universities, institutes, etc., offer programs across Canada; however, for statistical purposes, we have included them in the province where their head office is located.

OTHER SOURCES

This manuscript is the result of data collected from participants and our own knowledge and experience. We have also referred to other books or models that are publicly available. When we have done so, we have mentioned the source.

Table I:2

	Co-ops	University	Private	Public	Institutes	Community	Sports	Consultants	Youth
Atlantic	4 (16.7%)	2 (22.2%)	—	—	1 (25%)	—	—	—	—
Québec	9 (37.5%)	2 (22.2%)	1 (12.5%)	2 (28.6%)	1 (25%)	—	2 (50%)	—	—
Ontario	5 (20.8%)	3 (33.3%)	5 (62.5%)	1 (14.3%)	1 (25%)	1 (25%)	—	2 (66.6%)	—
Prairies	2 (8.3%)	1 (11.1%)	1 (12.5%)	1 (14.3%)	1 (25%)	—	—	—	1 (33.3%)
B.C.	3 (12.5%)	1 (11.1%)	1 (12.5%)	—	—	3 (75%)	—	1 (33.3%)	—
North	1 (4.2%)	—	—	—	—	—	—	—	—
Canada	—	—	—	3 (42.9%)	—	—	2 (50%)	—	2 (66.6%)
Total Programs	24	9	8	7	4	4	4	3	3

CONCLUSION

We believe we have achieved a fairly representative sample across sectors and regions. It was a wonderful adventure to seek out and identify those capable resources.

APPENDIX II

LEADERS INTERVIEWED

Authors' Note:

The list below includes information received from participants and it represents their status as of February 2007. It is organized in alphabetical order and is listed as such: last name, first name, designations, title, sector(s) of involvement and region(s). We have attempted to portray participants' information as accurately as possible; however, with such a large number of people interviewed, mistakes can occur. We apologize if any have.

A number of interviewees have won awards. However, for the sake of the book brevity, these awards have not been listed. For additional information, please consult our website www.leadership-canada.com

In the case of organizations with French names, we have attempted to provide an English equivalent. When this occurs, the English adaptation follows the French in brackets. When the French words resemble the English, we have not provided an equivalent.

A

Abbot-Peter, Marni Marie • Provincial Coach and Player, BC Wheelchair Basketball Society • Sports, Public, Community • British Columbia

Abbott, Janice Marie • Executive Director, Atira Women's Resource Society • Community, Business • British Columbia

Adair, William (Bill) K. • Executive Director, Canadian Paraplegic Association of Ontario • Community • Ontario

Allan, M. Elyse, MBA • President and CEO, GE Canada • Business • Canada

Allaster, Stacey, B.A., MBA • President, Sony Ericsson WTA (Women's Tennis Association) Tour; Former Vice-President and Tournament Director, Tennis Canada • Sports, Community • Ontario

Amyot, Denise • Vice-President, Leadership Network, Public Service Human Resources Agency, Government of Canada • Public • Canada

Anglade, Dominique, P.Eng., MBA • Consultant, McKinsey & Company • Business • Québec

Armstrong, Ruth R., MBA • President, Vision Management Services; Governance Professor, York University, Schulich School of Business • Community, Public • Ontario

Armstrong, Tim • Task Force Leader, Vancouver Urban Search and Rescue Team; Canada Task Force 1 • Public • Canada

Austin, Janet E.M. • CEO, YWCA of Vancouver • Community • British Columbia

B

Babineau, Guy • Director of Wellness, CBC/Radio-Canada • Media • Canada

Bales, John • CEO, Coaching Association of Canada • Sports • Canada

Bardswick, Kathy • President and CEO, The Co-Operators • Business • Ontario

Barr, Lorna R., B.Sc., M.A. • Former Deputy Chair, British Columbia Utilities Commission • Public • British Columbia

Bartels, Kathleen S. • Director, Vancouver Art Gallery • Arts • British Columbia

Bastien, Yvon • Former President and General Manager, Sanofi Synthelabo Canada • Business • Québec, Canada

Bates-Van der Zeijst, Johanna Maria • President, Johanna M. Bates Literary Consultants, Inc. • Communications • Prairies

Bebis, Stephen • CEO, Golf Town • Business • Canada

Béchard, Bruno-Marie, P.Eng. • Rector, Université de Sherbrooke • Public • Québec

Bencz, Marjorie J., C.M. • Executive Director, Edmonton Gleaners Association (Edmonton's Food Bank) • Community • Prairies

Benson, Mel E. • Board Member, Suncor Energy Inc. • Business, Community • Prairies

Berck, Phyllis Etta • Manager, Partnership Development, Toronto Parks, Forestry and Recreation; Former Chair, CAAWS (Canadian Association for the Advancement of Women and Sport) • Public, Community, Sports • Ontario

Berg, Larry • President and CEO, Vancouver International Airport Authority • Public, Community, Business • British Columbia

Bernstein, Dr. Alan, O.C., FRSC • President, Canadian Institutes of Health Research • Public • Canada

Bertrand, Françoise • President and CEO, Fédération des Chambres de Commerce du Québec • Public, Community • Québec

Bird, Robert (Ian) • Senior Leader, Sport Matters Group • Sports, Community • Canada

Biron, Ève-Lyne • President and General Manager, Laboratoire Médical Biron • Business • Québec

Biscaro, Bruno • COO, Accucaps Industries Limited • Business • Ontario

Blackburn, Richard • General and Artistic Director, Théâtre de la Dame de Cœur [Queen of Hearts Theatre] • Arts • Québec

Blanchet, Suzanne • President and CEO, Cascades Tissue Group • Business • Québec

(Boot) Agnew, (Sunni) Sonja • President and CEO, ZenithOptimedia • Communications, Business • Ontario

Bouchard, Jean-François • President, Sid Lee • Communications • Québec

Bowes, Paul Gerard • Head Coach, Men's National Team, Canadian Wheelchair Basketball Association • Sports • Ontario

Brault, Simon, O.C. • Director General, National Theatre School of Canada • Arts • Québec, Canada

Brooks, Dr. Mary R., Ph.D. • William A. Black Chair of Commerce, School of Business Administration, Dalhousie University • Public • Atlantic

Brousseau, Francine, M.A.P. • Vice-President, Development, Canadian Museum of Civilization Corporation • Arts, Public • Canada

Brown, May, C.M., O.B.C., LL.D. (Hon.) • Former Councillor, City of Vancouver, B.C. • Public, Community, Sports • British Columbia

Brown, Dr. Sheila A. • Former President and Vice-Chancellor, Mount Saint Vincent University • Public • Atlantic

Burke, Brian • Executive Vice-President and General Manager, Anaheim Ducks; Former GM, Vancouver Canucks • Sports • British Columbia

C

Cahill, Moya N. • President, Pan Maritime Energy Services Inc. • Business • Atlantic

Cameron, Kevin Gerard • Consultant; Former President, The Halifax Mooseheads Hockey Club • Sports, Business • Atlantic

Cameron, Richard (Ric) • Senior Vice-President, Canadian International Development Agency (CIDA) • Public • Canada

Cardinal, Charles H. • Consultant in Planning, Periodization and LTAD (Long-Term Athlete Development) • Sports • Québec, Canada

Carey, David Scott • President, Volleyball Canada • Sports, Business • Ontario

Carr, Glenna, ICD.D • Corporate Board Director; Former Deputy Minister and Secretary, Management Board of Cabinet, Ontario • Business, Public • Ontario, Canada

Chiasson, Honourable Herménégilde • Lieutenant Governor, New Brunswick • Public, Arts • Atlantic

Choquette, Natalie • Diva • Arts • Québec

Christie, Suzanne Dorothy • Project Manager, Peel Mentoring Network; Instructor • Community • Ontario

Christmas, Bernd • Lawyer and Mi'kmaq Leader • Public, Business • Atlantic

Cimolino, Antoni • General Director, The Stratford Festival of Canada • Arts, Community • Ontario

Cohon, George Alan, O.C., O.Ont. • Founder, McDonald's Restaurants of Canada and McDonald's Restaurants in Russia • Business • Ontario

Cooney, Jane • President, Books for Business • Communications, Business • Ontario

Cooney, Patrick M. • President, Jory Capital Inc. • Business • Prairies

Côté, Raymond • President, Sports-Québec • Sports • Québec

Courville, Isabelle • President, Hydro-Québec TransÉnergie • Public • Québec

Cousineau, Alain • Chairman, President and CEO, Loto-Québec • Public • Québec

Crocker, Elizabeth Jane • Author; Co-Owner, Woozles and P'lovers • Business, Arts, Community • Atlantic

Crombie, Honourable David, P.C., O.C. • President, Canadian Urban Institute; Former Mayor, Toronto • Public • Ontario

Crooks, Charmaine • Track and Field Olympian • Sports, Community, Business • British Columbia

Crosbie, Honourable John C., P.C., O.C., Q.C. • Former Minister, Government of Canada • Public • Atlantic

Cuenco, Patrick Lawrence, B.I.B. • Co-founder, Junior Hong Kong-Canada Business Association • Business, Public, Community • Ontario

D

D'Amours, Alban • President and CEO, Desjardins Group • Business • Canada

Daniels, Lyle W. • Director, Sports, Culture, Youth and Recreation Department, Federation of Saskatchewan Indian Nations • Sports • Prairies

D'Auray-Boult, Marie-France • General Director, Performance & Knowledge Management Branch, Canadian International Development Agency (CIDA) • Public • Canada

David, Françoise • Co-Spokesperson, Québec Solidaire • Public • Québec

David, Pierre • Executive Director, CMHC International (Canada Mortgage and Housing Corporation) • Public • Canada

Davidson, Dr. Valerie J., Ph.D., P.Eng. • NSERC/HP Canada Chair for Women in Science and Engineering, School of Engineering, University of Guelph • Public • Ontario

Davis, Honourable William G., P.C., C.C., Q.C. • Former Premier, Ontario 1971-1985 • Public • Ontario

Dépin, Marc-André • President and CEO, Norampac Inc. • Business • Canada, US, France

Deschênes, Jocelyn, M.A. • Producer, President, Sphère Média Plus • Arts • Québec

Dexter, Rob Paul, Q.C. • Chairman and CEO, Maritime Travel Inc. • Business • Atlantic

Dinter-Gottlieb, Dr. Gail • President and Vice-Chancellor, Acadia University • Public • Atlantic

Dion, Donald Ernest • Elite Sports Consultant, City of Montréal; Diving Olympic Coach • Sports • Québec

Dion, Pierre • President and CEO, TVA Group Inc. • Media • Québec

Dobell, Ken • Former Deputy Minister and Cabinet Secretary, Office of the Premier, British Columbia • Public • British Columbia

Dryden, Honourable Ken • MP; Former Minister, Social Development, Government of Canada • Public • Canada

Duffy, Gerard (Gerry) Francis • Strategic Management Consultant; Former Senior Vice-President, Methanex • Business • British Columbia

DuPont, Bonnie Dianne, CHRP, M.Ed. • Group Vice-President, Corporate Resources, Enbridge Inc. • Business • Canada

E

Eriksson, Peter E., M.Sc. • Olympic and Paralympic National Coach, Track and Field • Sports • Ontario, Canada

F

Filion, Yves, P.Eng. • President, CIGRÉ (Conseil international des grands réseaux électriques) [International Council on Large Electric Systems]; Former President, Hydro-Québec TransÉnergie. • Public • Québec

Fortin, Michèle • President and CEO, Télé-Québec • Arts, Media, Public • Québec

Furlong, John A.F. • CEO, Vancouver 2010 Olympic and Paralympic Winter Games • Sports, Community • British Columbia, Canada

G

Gartner, Max • Chief Athletic Officer, Alpine Canada • Sports • Prairies

Germain, Christiane • Co-President, Groupe Germain Inc. • Business • Québec, Ontario

Gibb, Joan C. • President, Canadian Cancer Society, Oakville Unit • Community • Ontario

Goldbloom, Dr. Ruth M., O.C. • Chair, Pier 21 Foundation • Community • Atlantic

Gonthier, Stéphane • Senior Vice-President, Eastern North America, Alimentation Couche-Tard Inc. • Business • Canada

Gorman, Diane Cheryl • Former Assistant Deputy Minister, Health Canada, Government of Canada • Public • Canada

Graham, John (Jack) • Partner, McInnes Cooper • Business, Community, Sports • Atlantic

Gray, James Kenneth, O.C., A.O.E. • Chairman, Canada West Foundation; Founder and Former Chairman, Canadian Hunter Exploration Ltd. • Business • Prairies

Greenhalgh, Paul • Director, Corcoran Gallery of Art; Former President, NSCAD (Nova Scotia College of Art and Design University) • Arts, Community • Atlantic

Grieve, James (Jim) Patrick, MBA • Director of Education, Peel District School Board • Public • Ontario

Guimond, Clément • General Coordinator, Caisse d'économie solidaire Desjardins [Credit Union] • Business, Community • Québec

Gutman, Dr. Gloria Margaret, Ph.D. • Professor Emerita, Gerontology Department; Director of the Dr. Tong Louie Living Laboratory, Simon Fraser University • Public, Community • British Columbia

H

Hamilton, William (Bill) James • Executive Coach, W.J.A. Hamilton & Associates; Former Senior Vice-President, BMO and CIBC • Business, Public • Ontario

Handley, Honourable Joseph L. • Premier, Northwest Territories • Public • North

Handling, Piers • Director and CEO, Toronto International Film Festival Group • Arts • Ontario

Hansen, Rick, C.C., O.B.C. • President and CEO, Rick Hansen Foundation • Community • Canada

Harber, Bruce William, FCCHSE, MHA • President and CEO, York Central Hospital • Public • Ontario

Hart, Christine E., LL.B. • President, Accord/hart & associates inc. • Business, Public, Community • Ontario

Harvey, Gilles • Executive Director, Land Register, Ministère de la Justice du Québec [Québec Ministry of Justice] • Public • Québec

Haskayne, Richard F., O.C., F.C.A. • Board Chair Emeritus, University of Calgary • Community • Prairies

Hayman, Paul Albert Ward • Executive Vice-President, The Franchise Company • Business • Ontario

Henderson, James (Sa'ke'j) Youngblood, I.P.C. (Indigenous Peoples' Counsel) • Research Director, Native Law Centre of Canada; Professor, Aboriginal Law, College of Law, University of Saskatchewan • Public • Canada

Henderson, Paul G. • Founder and President, The Leadership Group; Maple Leafs Hockey Alumni • Community, Sports • Ontario

Herbert, Dr. Carol Pearl, MD, CCFP, FCFP, FRCP (Glasg), FCAHS • Dean, Schulich School of Medicine & Dentistry, University of Western Ontario • Public • Ontario

Herrndorf, Peter A., O.C. • President and CEO, National Arts Centre • Public, Arts • Canada

Herring, Glen D. • Former Vice-President and General Manager, Polymers, AT Plastics Inc.; Former Canadian Alliance Candidate • Private, Public, Community • Ontario

Hervieux-Payette, Honourable Céline, Q.C., LL.B • Senator; Lawyer, Fasken Martineau DuMoulin • Public, Business, Community • Québec, Canada

Hill, Julia • Corporate Secretary, Citizenship and Immigration Canada, Government of Canada • Public • Canada

Hines, Gregory C., B.Sc., C.I.M • President and CEO, Tm Bioscience Corporation • Business • Canada

Hoag, Glenn A. • Head Coach, Team Canada Men's Volleyball; Head Coach, Men's Volleyball Team Vert & Or [Green and Gold], Université de Sherbrooke • Sports, Public • Québec, Canada

Hofstetter, Mary E. • President and CEO, The Banff Centre • Public, Arts, Community • Prairies

Holloway, Sue • Double Olympic Medalist, Kayak • Sports, Community • Ontario

Houde, Jean • Deputy Minister, Ministère des Finances du Québec [Québec Ministry of Finance] • Public • Québec

House, Jeannie Rosemary, B.A., B.Ed., LL.B. • Director, Advocacy & Information, Newfoundland and Labrador Health Boards Association • Public • Atlantic

Hudon, Isabelle • President and CEO, Board of Trade of Metropolitan Montréal • Public, Community • Québec

I

Istvanffy, Peter E. • President and CEO, Calgary Academy • Public, Community • Prairies

J

Jackson, Marguerite • CEO, Education Quality and Accountability Office (EQAO) • Public • Ontario

Jacobs, Leona Catherine • Grandmother Leona, Ojibwa Elder • Community • Ontario

James, Yolande • MNA for Nelligan, Québec • Public • Québec

Jarvis, Patrick Douglas, B.Ed., C.E.T. • Owner and President, Amarok Training Services Ltd.; Former President, Canadian Paralympic Committee • Sports, Community • Canada

Johnson, Nancy Myers, RN, B.N., M.Ed., CHRP • Director and Vice-President, Huntley Communication Services Inc. • Public, Community • Ontario

Jones, Thomas (Tom) • CEO, Commonwealth Games Canada • Sports, Community • Canada

Jules, Clarence T. (Manny) • Chairman, Indian Taxation Advisory Board • Public • Canada

Juriansz, Honourable Mr. Justice Russell G. • Judge, Court of Appeal for Ontario • Public • Ontario

K

Karetak-Lindell, Nancy • MP, Nunavut • Public • North

Kelly, Ruth • President, Venture Publishing Inc.; Publisher and Editor-in-Chief, Alberta Venture • Business, Communications • Prairies

Kent, Thomas (Tom) W., C.C., M.A., LL.D., D.LITT. • Former Deputy Minister, Government of Canada • Public • Canada

Knebel, John • Co-founder, KWA Canada • Business • Ontario

Knox, Janet Elizabeth, RN, MN, MBA, CHE • President and CEO, Annapolis Valley District Health Authority • Public • Atlantic

Kolida, Robert • Senior Vice-President, Human Resources, HBC Group • Business • Canada

L

Lacey, Veronica S. • President, The Learning Partnership • Public, Community • Canada

Lachance, Victor G. • Consultant; Former President and CEO, Canadian Centre for Ethics in Sport • Community, Sports, Public • Ontario, Canada

Lalumière, Joanne, M.Sc. • Executive Director and Corporate Secretary, Société zoologique de Granby [Granby Zoological Society] • Public, Community • Québec

Lapierre, Yvon • Plant Manager, Owens, Illinois; Former Mayor, Dieppe, New Brunswick • Business, Public • Atlantic, US

LaRosa, Susan Frances • Director of Education, York Catholic District School Board • Public • Ontario

Larose, Gérald • Professor-Researcher, School of Social Work, Université du Québec à Montréal (UQAM) • Public • Québec

Lay, Marion • President, 2010 Legacies Now • Sports, Community, Arts • British Columbia

Lee, Nancy Carolyn • COO, Olympic Broadcast Services; Former Executive Director, CBC TV Sports; Chef de Mission, CBC Olympics • Media, Sports • Ontario, Canada

Lee, Sue • Senior Vice-President, Human Resources and Communications, Suncor Energy Inc. • Business • British Columbia, Prairies and Ontario

Lefebvre, Monique • Executive Director, Défi Sportif and AlterGo, People with Disabilities in Action • Sports, Community, Public • Québec

Lepage, Robert, O.C., O.Q. • President, Robert Lepage Inc.; Stage and Artistic Director, Ex-Machina • Arts • Québec

Levine, David, B.Eng, M.Phil., M.A.S. • President and CEO, Montréal Regional Health Authority • Public • Québec

Lewis, Mary A. • Director, Government Relations and Health Partnerships, Heart and Stroke Foundation of Ontario • Community • Ontario

Lindemann, Barry Thomas • Manager Community Affairs, Canadian Paraplegic Association, Alberta • Community • Prairies

Logan, Scott, M.Sc. • CEO, Halifax 2014 Commonwealth Games, Candidate City • Sports, Public • Atlantic

Losier, Denis • President and CEO, Assumption Life • Business • Atlantic

Lougheed, Honourable Peter, P.C., C.C., Q.C. • Former Premier, Alberta • Public • Prairies

M

Macdonald, Brian • Choreographer and Director • Arts • Ontario

MacDonald, Dr. Colin Edward, LL.B. (Honorary) • President and CEO, Clearwater Seafood • Business, Community • Atlantic

MacDonald, Norine A., Q.C. • President, The Gabriel Foundation, The Senlis Council • Community • Canada

MacGillivray, Frederick R., LL.D. • President and CEO, Trade Centre Limited, Halifax • Public • Atlantic

MacKenzie, Muriel (Ann), CA, CPA, MEC • President and CEO, Nova Scotia Film Development Corporation • Arts, Public • Atlantic

MacMillan, Stuart Alexander • Founder and Chairman, Ignition Strategies • Business • Ontario

MacNeil, Dr. Teresa Sarah, C.M., Ph.D., LID • Director, Extension Department, St. Francis Xavier University • Community, Public • Atlantic

Malcom, John • CEO, Cape Breton District Health Authority • Public • Atlantic

Malone, Doreen E., CA • General Manager, Neptune Theatre • Arts, Community • Atlantic

Marshman, Kevin P. • Vice-President and General Manager, Worldwide Customer Services, NCR Canada Ltd. • Business • Ontario, Canada

Matheson, Dr. Jane Ellen, Ph.D., RSW • CEO, Wood's Homes, Calgary • Community • Prairies

Mattocks, Fred • Executive Director, Regional Programming, Production and Resources, CBC English Television • Media • Canada

Mayer, Marc • Director, Montréal Museum of Contemporary Art • Arts, Community, Public • Québec

McCain, Honourable Margaret, O.C., O.N.B. • Philanthropist; Former Lieutenant Governor, New Brunswick • Community, Public • Ontario, Atlantic

McCallum, Doug W. • Former Mayor, Surrey, British Columbia • Public, Business • British Columbia

McDonald, Bernadette Valerie • Author; Former Vice-President, Mountain Culture, The Banff Centre • Arts, Public • Prairies

McDonough, Alexa • MP; Former Federal NDP Leader, Government of Canada • Public • Atlantic

McEwen, Robert (Rob), MBA • Chairman and CEO, U.S. Gold and Lexam Explorations • Business • Ontario

McGregor, Marg, Eileen Mary Catherine • CEO, Canadian Interuniversity Sport; Chef de mission, Team Canada, Torino Paralympic Games, 2006 • Sports, Community • Canada

McGuire, Anne Isobel, RN, BN, MHSA, CHE • President and CEO, IWK Health Centre • Public • Atlantic

McKenzie-Sanders, Doreen Marion, C.M. • Executive Director, Women in the Lead Inc. • Communications, Community • British Columbia

McKinnon, Becky • Executive Chairman, Timothy's World Coffee • Business • Canada

McPherson, Dr. Gary, C.M., LL.D. (Honorary) • Executive Director, Canadian Centre for Social Entrepreneurship, University of Alberta • Community, Sports, Public • Prairies, Canada

McRae, Judy, B.A., M.Sc. • Athletic Director, University of Waterloo • Public, Community, Sports • Ontario

Merklinger, Anne • Director General, Canoe Kayak Canada • Sports • Canada

Mills, Jim P. • President and CEO, Office Interiors • Business • Atlantic

Milne, Janet Margaret • Former Assistant Deputy Minister, Finance and Administration, Government of Canada • Public • Canada

Milton, Claire, LL.B. • General Counsel and Secretary, High Liner Foods Inc. • Business, Community • Atlantic

Mintz, Dr. Jack M. • Professor, Business Economics; Director, International Tax Program, Institute of International Business, Rotman School of Management; Former President, C.D. Howe Institute • Public • Canada

Mitton, Susan Young • Regional Director, CBC Radio, Maritimes • Communications, Public • Atlantic

Monette, Richard Jean, C.M., DHum, LL.D. • Artistic Director, The Stratford Festival of Canada • Arts, Community • Ontario

Morin, Pierre • Former Director, Parks and Recreation, City of Montréal • Community, Sports • Québec

Morin, Scott • Director and Producer, Universal Jazz • Arts • Ontario

Mowat, David (Dave) • CEO, Vancity Credit Union • Business • British Columbia

Mulaire, Mariette, C.I.M., P.Mgr. • Executive Director, Economic Development Council for Manitoba Bilingual Municipalities • Public, Community, Business • Prairies

Mullen, Cary Lee • Olympian and World Cup Champion; Serial Entrepreneur; Professional Speaker • Sports, Business • Prairies

Murphy, Judy A., CA • COO, Royal Winnipeg Ballet • Arts, Community • Prairies

Mustard, Dr. Fraser, O.C., O.Ont., M.D., Ph.D. • Founding President, The Canadian Institute for Advanced Research • Community • Ontario

N

Nadeau, Luc • Executive Vice-President, Corporate Communications and External Relations, and President of the Luxury Products Division, L'Oréal Canada • Business • Québec

Neamtan, Nancy • President and Executive Director, Chantier de l'Économie Sociale [Social Economy Working Group] • Community • Québec

Nicholson, Suzanne L. • Executive Director, Field Hockey Canada • Sports • Ontario

Niczowski, Susan • President, Summer Fresh Salads Incorporated • Business • Ontario

Nind, Sidney Ben • Artist; Executive and Artistic Director, Northern Arts & Cultural Centre • Arts, Community • North

Novak, Dr. Isaac Michael, B.Sc., DDS • Owner, Novak Dental Office • Business • Ontario

O

Oldfield, Robert (Graydon) • Canadian Downhill and Combined Champion, Canadian Alpine Ski Team Association; Branch Manager and Associate Director, Financial Services ScotiaMcLeod • Sports, Business, Community • Ontario

Olechnowicz, Kazimir, P.Eng. • President and General Manager, CIMA+ • Business • Québec

Olthuis, Clarence • Chairman, United Farmers of Alberta Co-operative Limited (UFA) • Business • Prairies

O'Neill, Elizabeth Anne • Executive Director, Big Brothers Big Sisters, Edmonton and Area • Community • Prairies

O'Neill, Karen M. • Vice-President, External Affairs, Marketing and Communications Rick Hansen Foundation; Former CEO, Commonwealth Games Association • Community, Sports • British Columbia, Canada

O'Reilly, Louis A. • President, O'Reilly International Entertainment Management • Arts • Prairies

Osmond, Gladys Vivian • Leader, The Granny Brigade • Community • Atlantic

Owen, Philip • Former Mayor, Vancouver, British Columbia • Public, Business, Community • British Columbia

P

Paquette, Joseph (Joe) R. • Mixed Blood Elder • Public, Business, Community • Canada

Paquette, Sylvie, FCAS, FCIA • Executive Vice-President, Corporate Development, Desjardins General Insurance Group • Business • Québec, Canada

Paquette, Wendy • Former Senior Vice-President, Aliant Inc. • Business • Atlantic

Parker, Steven B. • Chairman, CCL Group • Business • Atlantic

Parsonson, Laura Collings, B.A., B.Ed. • Head of Library; Assistant Curriculum Leader, Program Support, Martingrove Collegiate Institute • Public, Community • Ontario

Pascoe, Byron Ethan • Business Manager, Let It Out Entertainment Inc. • Arts, Business • Ontario

Patten, Rose M. • Senior Executive Vice-President, Human Resources and Strategic Management, BMO Financial Group • Business • Canada

Payn, Valerie, MBA • President, Halifax Chamber of Commerce • Public, Community • Atlantic

Pelletier, Louise • Regional Director, Mauricie Region, Production of the Cascades, Hydro-Québec • Public • Québec

Peplinski, Jim D. • Chairman, Humberview Group of Companies • Business, Sports • Prairies

Petitclerc, Chantal • Paralympic Athlete and Champion • Sports • Québec, Canada

Peverett, Jane Leslie, FCMA • President and CEO, British Columbia Transmission Corporation • Public, Business • British Columbia

Pfeiffer, Michael L., BS-EE, MBA • President and CEO, QC Data International Inc. • Business • Prairies

Philbrick, Michael Leighton • Branch Manager, GMP Private Client LP; Former CFL player, Hamilton Tiger Cats • Sports, Business • Ontario

Pintal, Lorraine, C.M. • General and Artistic Director, Théâtre du Nouveau Monde [New World Theatre] • Arts • Québec

Porco, Carmela Rosaria • Former Vice-President and COO, Doubleday Canada • Business, Communications • Ontario

Portmann, Dr. Michel, Ph.D. • Professor, Université du Québec à Montréal (UQAM) • Public, Sports • Québec

Poulin, Marc, MBA • President Operations, Québec Region, Sobeys Inc. • Business • Québec

Pringle, Andrew • President, Canadian Foundation for AIDS Research • Community, Business • Canada

R

Rabbani, Diane, B.A, B.Com. • Human Resources Consultant; Former Deputy Minister, British Columbia • Public, Business • British Columbia

Radford, John Douglas • Former Vice-President, Sales and Marketing, Ford of Canada Motor Company • Business • Ontario

Rae, Honourable Robert (Bob), PC, O.C., O.Ont., Q.C. • Former Premier, Ontario • Public, Business • Ontario

Raiss, Sarah E., MBA, ICD.D • Executive Vice-President, Corporate Services, TransCanada Corporation • Business • Canada, United States

Rancourt, Serge • President, Publicis Canada • Communications • Ontario, Québec, British Columbia

Randell, Joseph David • President and CEO, Air Canada Jazz • Public, Business • Atlantic, Canada

Rebello, François • President and CEO, Groupe Investissement Responsable [Responsible Investment Group] • Business • Québec

Reid, Patrick, O.C., M.C., C.D. • Chairman, Rick Hansen Foundation • Public, Community, Business • British Columbia, Canada

Reid, R.T.F. (Bob) • Chairman, British Columbia Transmission Company • Business • British Columbia

Reist, Lorene Janice • Business Director, Western Canada, NYCOMED Pharma Inc. • Business • British Columbia, Prairies

Riley, Dr. Sean E. • President and Vice Chancellor, St. Francis Xavier University • Public • Atlantic

Rivoire, Eleanor Mary Francis, B.Sc. Nursing, M.Sc. Paediatrics • Senior Vice-President, Patient Care Program & Chief Nursing Executive, Kingston General Hospital; Vice-President, Patient Care & Chief Nursing Executive, Quinte Health Care • Public • Ontario

Roberts, William (Bill) Dwight, B.A., M.A., MBA • President and CEO, S-VOX • Arts, Business, Community, Public • Ontario

Robinson, Peter • CEO, Mountain Equipment Co-op • Business • Canada

Rogers, Margaret (Judy), MPA • City Manager, Vancouver, British Columbia • Public • British Columbia

Rudge, Christopher (Chris) • CEO and Secretary General, Canadian Olympic Committee • Sports, Community • Ontario, Canada

S

Saillant, François • Coordinator, Front d'action populaire en réaménagement urbain (FRAPRU) [The Popular Face of Action in Urban Refitting] • Community • Québec

Sanderson, Lyle, B.A.(PE), M.Sc., Chartered Professional Coach • Coach Emeritus, College of Kinesiology, University of Saskatchewan • Sports • Prairies

Schultz, Albert Hamilton • Founding Artistic Director, Soulpepper Theatre Company • Arts, Community • Ontario

Scott, Donna Mae, O.C. • Former Vice-President, Canadian Publishing, Maclean Hunter Ltd. • Business, Arts • Ontario

Scott, Dr. Jacquelyn Thayer, O.C., Ph.D., LL.D. • Past President and Professor, Cape Breton University; Deputy Chair, Prime Minister's Advisory Council on Science and Technology • Public, Business, Community • Atlantic

Segal, Dr. Joseph, C.M., O.B.C., O.St.J., LL.D. (Honours) • President, Kingswood Capital Corp. • Community, Business • British Columbia

Semkiw, Brian William, P.Eng. • Chairman, Rand Worldwide • Business • Ontario

Sharp, Caroline • Director General, Volleyball Canada • Sports, Community • Canada

Shaw, Robbie L. • President, IWK Foundation • Community, Public, Business • Atlantic

Shields, Ken William Daniel, C.M., BA, MPE • Former Head Coach, Canadian National Men's Basketball Team • Sports • British Columbia

Simard, Dr. Cyril, Ph.D. • President and CEO, ECONOMUSEUM Network • Public, Business, Community • Québec, Atlantic, Ontario

Skulsky, Dennis • President, CanWest MediaWorks Publications Inc. • Communications • Canada

Sleeman, John W. • Chairman and CEO, Sleeman Breweries Ltd. • Business • Canada

Smith, Rod • Senior Partner, Focuspoint Strategic Management; Former President, Black Photo Corporation • Business, Community • Canada

Smith, Tricia, B.A., LL.B., LL.D. (Honorary) • Partner, Barnescraig & Associates; 2007, Canada's Chef de Mission, Pan American Games; Rowing Olympian • Sports, Community • Canada

Smithers, Alfred, O.C. • President and CEO, Secunda Group of Companies • Business • Atlantic

Staines, Mavis Avril • Artistic Director, Canada's National Ballet School • Arts, Community • Canada

Steadward, Dr. Robert, O.C., LLD (Hon) • Honorary and Founding President, International Paralympic Committee • Sports • Prairies

Stevenson, Sandra Lee • President and CEO, Sport BC • Sports, Community, Business • British Columbia

Stewart, Nalini, O.Ont. • Chair and Director of numerous community organizations and charities • Community, Public • Ontario

Strauss, Christi • President and CEO, Cereal Partners Worldwide, S.A.; Former President, General Mills, Canada • Business • Ontario

Surrette, Mark James, B.Com, MBA • President, Robertson Surrette • Business • Atlantic

Sylvester, Shauna Marie • Founding Executive Director, Institute for Media, Policy and Civil Society (IMPACS) • Community • British Columbia

Szwarc, David • Chief Administrative Officer, Region of Peel • Public • Ontario

T

Taranu-Teofilovici, Elaine, B.Sp. Ps., M.A. • Former CEO, YWCA Canada • Community • Québec, Ontario

Taylor, Allan Richard, O.C. LL.D. • Former Chairman and CEO, Royal Bank of Canada • Business, Community • Ontario, Canada

Taylor, Honourable Carole, O.C. • Minister of Finance and M.L.A., Vancouver-Langara, British Columbia Government; Former Chair, CBC/Radio-Canada • Public, Communications • British Columbia

Therrien, Joanne • President, Vidacom Inc. • Business, Arts • Prairies

Thibodeau-DeGuire, Michèle, C.M., C.Q., P.Eng. • President and Executive Director, Centraide [United Way] of Greater Montréal • Community • Québec

Thorsell, William • Director and CEO, Royal Ontario Museum • Arts, Community • Ontario

Todd, David B. • General Manager, Shell Canada, Drilling • Business • Prairies

Todd, Murray Blake, P.Eng. • President, Canada Hibernia Holding Corporation • Business, Public • Prairies

Tremblay, Pierre-Marc, MBA • President and CEO, Restaurants Pacini Inc. • Business • Québec

Tremblay, Rémi • President, Esse Leadership • Business • Québec

Treusch, Andrew • Senior Assistant Deputy Minister, Strategic Policy and Planning, Human Resources and Social Development, Government of Canada • Public • Canada

Tsouflidou, Cora • President, Chez Cora/Cora's • Business • Québec

V

Vaccarino, Dr. Franco Joseph • Chair, Psychology Department, University of Toronto • Public • Ontario

van Dyke, Vickie Louise • Midday Host, Smooth Jazz Wave 94.7; Singer and Writer • Arts • Ontario

Verreault, Denise, C.M., C.Q. • President and CEO, Groupe Maritime Verreault Inc. • Business • Québec

W

Walker, Dr. David, FRCPC • Dean, Faculty of Health Sciences, Queen's University • Public • Ontario

Walker, Douglas (Doug) L., P.Eng. • CEO, Noise Solutions Inc. • Business, Community • Prairies

Waridel, Laure • Eco-sociologist; Author; Co-Founder, Équiterre • Community • Québec

Watson, Elizabeth June, LL.B. • Principal, Governance Advisory Services • Public, Private • British Columbia

Watt, Jim • Vice-President, Corporate Affairs and Corporate Secretary, United Farmers of Alberta Co-operative Limited (UFA) • Business • Alberta

Watters, Marge • Co-founder, KWA Canada • Business • Ontario

Weber, Diane E. • Volunteer; Former Vice-President, Bell Canada/CGI • Business, Community • Ontario

White, Shelley • CEO, United Way of Peel • Community • Ontario

Wray, C.E. (Lyn), C.A., M.A., CFP • Division Manager, Financial Planning and Corporate Risk Management, Manitoba Hydro • Public • Prairies

Y

Yamkowy, Don • Owner, Nishi-Khon/Key West Travel Ltd. • Business, Community • North

Z

Zarnke, Paul • Executive Director, Children's Aid Society, Region of Peel • Public, Community • Ontario

APPENDIX III

LEADERSHIP PROGRAMS

Authors' Note:

The list below includes information received from participants. Programs are listed by sector, in alphabetical order. The list appears as such: name of organization, name of program (if available), interviewee(s), region(s), website, if applicable. The list represents program status as of February 2007.

We have attempted to portray participants' information as accurately as possible; however, with such a large number of organizations interviewed, mistakes can occur. We apologize if any have.

For organizations with French names, we have attempted to provide an English equivalent. When this occurs, the English adaptation follows the French in brackets. When the French words resemble the English, we have not provided an equivalent.

COMMUNITY

Action Canada Foundation • Program: Action Canada • Interviewee: Cathy Beehan, CEO • British Columbia, Canada • www.actioncanada.ca

Minerva Foundation for BC Women • Interviewees: Denise Coutts, Executive Director; Nancy McKinstry and Julia Kim, Board members • British Columbia • www.theminervafoundation.com

Peel Leadership • Program: Flexible Thinker • Interviewee: Michael Rosenberg, Founder • Ontario • www.leadershippeel.org

CONSULTING FIRMS

Getting in the Groove • Program: Jazz and the Improvising Organization • Interviewee: Brian Hayman, President • Ontario, Canada • www.gettinginthegroove. com

The Corporate L.I.F.E. Centre Inc. • Program: Developing High Performance Organizations • Interviewee: Mervin Hillier, President • Ontario, Canada • www. corporatelife.ca

The Refinery Leadership Partners Inc. (formerly CEL, Centre for Exceptional Leadership Inc.) • Program: Leadership Development • Interviewees: Dr. Rosie Steeves, President; Barbara Ross-Denroche, Principal • British Columbia and Prairies • www.refineryleadership.com

CO-OPERATIVES

Agropur coopérative • Interviewee: Robert Lavallée, Director, Organizational Development • Retail • Québec • www.agropur.com

Alberta Community and Co-operative Association • Interviewee: Carol Murray, Co-op Resource Specialist • Association • Prairies • www.acca.coop

Arctic Co-operatives Limited • Interviewee: William L. Lyall, President • Retail • North • www.arcticco-op.com

British Columbia Co-operative Association (BCCA) • Interviewee: John Restakis, Executive Director • Association • British Columbia • www.bcca.coop

Co-op Atlantic • Interviewee: Léo LeBlanc, Corporate Secretary and Vice-President, Human Resources & Corporate Affairs • Retail • Atlantic • www. coopatlantic.ca

Coopérative de Développement Régional Outaouais-Laurentides (CDR) [Outaouais-Laurentides Regional Development Co-operative] • Interviewee: Yannick Bouchard, Advisor, Co-operative Development • Services • Québec • www. cdrol.fcdrq.coop

Coopérative des travailleurs forestiers de Sainte-Marguerite (COFOR) [Sainte-Marguerite Forest Workers Co-operative] • Interviewee: Alain Dufour, Executive Director • Forestry • Québec • www.ccfq.qc.ca/coop/cofor.html

Coop Santé Aylmer Health Co-op • Interviewee: Guy Benoît, President • Services • Québec • www.coopsa.org

Co-operators General Insurance Company • Interviewee: Nancy Rooney, Director, Organizational Development • Finance • Ontario • www.cooperators.ca

Coriolis Énergie • Interviewee: Pier-André Bouchard St-Amant, President • Services • Québec

Credit Union Central of Canada • Interviewee: Cheryl Byrne, Vice-President, Knowledge Services • Finance • Ontario • www.cucentral.ca

Envision Financial • Interviewee: Barry Delaney, Senior Vice-President, Governance and Strategy • Finance • British Columbia • www.envisionfinancial.ca

Fédération des caisses populaires acadiennes [Federation of Acadian Credit Unions] • Interviewee: René Legacy, Vice-President, Communications and Strategy • Finance • Atlantic • www.acadie.com

Fédération des coopératives funéraires du Québec [Québec Federation of Funeral Co-operatives] • Interviewee: Alain Leclerc, Executive Director • Services • Québec • www.fcfq.qc.ca

Fédération québécoise des coopératives forestières [Québec Federation of Forestry Co-operatives] • Interviewee: Jocelyn Lessard, Executive Director • Forestry • Québec • www.ccfq.qc.ca

Gay Lea Foods Co-operative Limited • Interviewee: Michael Barrett, Vice-President, Human Resources and Corporate Secretary • Retail • Ontario • www.gaylea.com

Growmark Inc. • Interviewee: Claude Gauthier, Director of Operations • Retail • Ontario • www.growmark.com

Institut Coopératif Desjardins • Interviewees: Jacques Couture, Director and Diane Séguin, Consultant, Program Development • Finance • Québec • www.desjardins.com

La Coop fédérée • Interviewee: Ernest Desrosiers, Former Chef de l'Exploitation [COO] • Retail • Québec • www.coopfed.qc.ca

Newfoundland and Labrador Federation of Co-operatives • Interviewees: Glen Fitzpatrick, Managing Director; Beverley Rose, Former Project Co-ordinator, Co-operative Development • Association • Atlantic • www.nlfc.coop

Nova Scotia Co-operative Council • Interviewee: Dianne Kelderman, Chief Executive Officer • Association • Atlantic • www.nsco-opcouncil.ca

Ontario Co-operative Association • Interviewee: Denyse Guy, Executive Director • Association • Ontario • www.ontario.coop

SaskCentral • Interviewee: Sid Bildfell, CEO • Finance • Prairies • www.saskcentral.com

Vancity Credit Union • Interviewee: Grace Pulver, Vice- President, Human Resources • Finance • British Columbia • www.vancity.com

INSTITUTES

Centre international de recherche et d'études en management (CIREM) [International Center for Research and Studies in Management] • Program: CIREM-HEC Development for Senior Managers • Interviewee: Georges Bourelle, President and CEO • Québec • www.cirem.ca

Niagara Institute • Interviewees: John Rankin, Executive Director; Donna Porter, Lead Facilitator • Ontario, Québec • www.niagarainstitute.com

The Banff Centre • Program: Leadership Development • Interviewees: Lisa Jackson, Associate Director of Operations; Andre Mamprin, Former Director • Prairies • www.banffcentre.ca

The Shambhala Institute for Authentic Leadership • Program: Authentic Leadership Summer Program • Interviewee: Susan Szpakowski, Executive Director • Atlantic • www.shambhalainstitute.org

PRIVATE SECTOR

BMO Financial Group Institute for Learning • Interviewee: Corey Jack, Executive Head • Ontario, Canada

Cirque du Soleil • Program: Leadership Development • Interviewee: France Dufresne, Director, Organizational Development and Training • Québec

HBC Group • Program: Talent Management Strategy • Interviewee: Christine Brown, General Manager, Human Resources, HBC Stores and Specialty • Ontario, Canada

Maple Leaf Foods Inc. • Program: Maple Leaf/Ivey Leadership Academy • Interviewee: Dr. Robert W. Hedley, Vice-President, Leadership • Ontario

Shell Canada Limited • Interviewee: Mona Jasinski, Manager, Learning and Development • Prairies

Telus Corporation • Program: Leadership Now • Interviewee: Josh Blair, Senior Vice-President, Human Resources Strategy and Business Support • British Columbia, Canada

The Franchise Company • Program: The Leadership Development Program • Interviewees: Tim Clark, Vice-President, Human Resources Development; Beth Shearer, General Manager • Ontario, British Columbia, Prairies

PUBLIC SECTOR

Canada Mortgage and Housing Corporation (CMHC) • Program: Fundamentals of Effective Leadership • Interviewee: Jean-François Pinsonnault, Consultant, Learning and Development, Human Resources • Canada

Canada Revenue Agency • Programs: Management Development • Interviewee: Richard Bégin, Director • Canada

Canadian Forces
- **Royal Military College (Kingston)** • Program: Military Psychology and Leadership • Interviewee: Captain (N) Alan Okros, Professor; Former Director, Canadian Forces Leadership Institute • Canada
- **Canadian Forces College (Toronto)** • Program: Department of Command, Leadership and Management • Interviewee: Commander Gregg Hannah, Senior Staff Officer • Canada

Centre Québécois de Leadership [Québec Centre for Leadership] • Interviewee: Gilles Harvey, Former Director • Québec

Humber Institute of Technology and Advanced Learning • Interviewee: Dr. Patricia Hedley, Director of Professional Development • Ontario

SaskEnergy • Program: Leadership Development • Interviewees: Barb Tchozewski, Organizational Effectiveness Coordinator; Tracy Singer, Former Organizational Effectiveness Coordinator • Prairies

Université de Sherbrooke • Program: Micro-diplôme de deuxième cycle en leadership dans le domaine public [Graduate Micro Diploma in Public Leadership] • Interviewees: Pierre Binette and Jean-Herman Guay, Professors, Faculté d'histoire et sciences politiques [Faculty of History and Political Sciences] • Québec

SPORTS

CAAWS (Canadian Association for the Advancement of Women and Sport) • Program: CAAWS Women and Leadership • Interviewee: Karin Lofstrom, Executive Director • Ontario, Canada • www.caaws.ca

Coaching Association of Canada • Program: National Coaching Certification • Interviewees: John Bales, CEO; Dr. Jean-Pierre Brunelle, Professor, Faculty of Physical and Sports Education, Université de Sherbrooke; Lead, Francophone Program, Leadership and Ethics Module, Montréal National Coaching Institute • Canada • www.coach.ca

Conseil du sport de haut niveau de Québec [High-level Sports Council, Québec City Region] • Interviewee: Jacques Loiselle, Former President • Québec • www.cshnq.org

Fédération de hockey sur glace du Québec Inc. [Québec Ice Hockey Federation] • Program: Integrated Structure for Player Development • Interviewee: Sylvain B. Lalonde, Executive Director • Québec • www.hockey.qc.ca

UNIVERSITIES

Queen's University, School of Business • Program: International Exchange • Interviewee: Angela L. James, Director, Centre for International Management • Ontario • www.business.queensu.ca

Royal Roads University • Program: Masters of Arts Leadership (Health, Justice & Public Safety) and MBA Leadership Programs, School of Leadership Studies • Interviewees: Dr. Nancy Greer, Acting Director, Professor and Academic Lead; Dr. Gerry Nixon, Acting Director, School of Leadership Studies; Dr. Doug Hamilton, Chair, Faculty Development • British Columbia • www.royalroads.ca

Schulich School of Business, York University

- **Schulich Executive Education Centre (SEEC)** • Interviewee: Dr. Alan C. Middleton, Executive Director • Ontario, Canada • www.seec.schulich.yorku.ca
- **MBA Program, Skills for Leadership and Governance** • Interviewee: Dr. Patricia Bradshaw, Associate Professor, Organizational Behaviour • Ontario, Canada • www.schulich.yorku.ca

Université de Moncton • Program: Institut de Leadership • Interviewee: Dr. Jean-Guy Vienneau, Professeur, École de Kinésiologie et de Récréologie, [Professor, Kinesiology and Recreology School] • Atlantic • www.umoncton.ca

Université de Sherbrooke Département de Management, Faculté d'Administration, [Department of Management, Faculty of Administration] • Program: Développement du leadership, Centre d'Entreprises [Centre for Business] • Interviewee: Dr. Mario Roy, Chair, Organization of Work Studies, • Québec • www.usherbrooke.ca/vers/ceot

Université Laval, Département de Management • Program: Complexité, Conscience et Gestion [Complexity, Conscience and Management] • Interviewees: Dr. Mario Cayer and Dr. Marie-Éve Marchand, Professors • Québec • http://www5.fsa.ulaval.ca

University of Alberta, School of Business, Executive Education and Lifelong Learning • Program: Leadership Development • Interviewee: Linda Arnoldussen, Director, Learning and Operational Excellence • Prairies • http://execed.bus.ualberta.ca

University of Guelph, Centre for Studies in Leadership • Program: M.A. (Leadership) • Interviewees: Dr. Brian Earn, Director; Dr. Michael Cox, Associate Director • Ontario • www.leadership.uoguelph.ca

University of New Brunswick, Renaissance College • Program: Bachelor of Philosophy in Interdisciplinary Leadership Studies • Interviewee: Dr. Pierre Zundel, Dean • Atlantic • www.unb.ca

YOUTH PROGRAMS

ESTEEM Team Association • Interviewees: Sandra Gage, Executive Director, Partnership Development; Shelly O'Brien, Executive Director, Programs • Ontario, Canada • www.esteemteam.com

Rotary International • Program: Rotary Youth Leadership Awards • Interviewee: Theresa (Therri) Papp, Consultant • Prairies • www.rotary.org

The Duke of Edinburgh's Award, Ontario Division • Interviewee: Jill Hermant, Executive Director • Ontario, Canada • www.dukeofed.org

BIBLIOGRAPHY

Bill C-38, Civil Marriage Act 2005. c. 33 of the Statutes of Canada. 38th Parliament—1st Session.

Bruce, Harry. *Never Content*. Toronto: Key Porter Books, 2002.

Cameron, Julia. *The Artist's Way*. New York: Tarcher, 2002.

Campbell, Joseph. *The Hero's Journey: Joseph Campbell on His Life and Work*. New York: Harper and Row, 1990.

'Canada at a Glance: Arts & Culture,' Spring 2005, Government of Canada, High Commission of Canada, http://www.dfait.gc.ca/canada-europa/united_kingdom/pdf/CultureRGB.pdf

Canada Council for the Arts, *Annual Report 2004/05*, http://www.canadacouncil.ca/aboutus/organization/annualreports/cp127707515975214586.htm?subsiteurl=%2fcanadacouncil%2farchives%2fcouncil%2fannualreports%2f2004-2005%2ffoundations.asp

Canadian Charter of Rights and Freedoms, Schedule B, Constitution Act 1982, Part I, http://laws.justice.gc.ca/en/charter/index.html

Canadian Forces Leadership Institute, *Duty with Honour: The Profession of Arms in Canada*. Published under the auspices of the Chief of the Defence Staff by the Canadian Defence Academy, Canadian Forces Leadership Institute, 2003.

Canadian Multiculturalism Act, R.S. 1985, c. 24 (4th Supp), http://www.pch.gc.ca/progs/multi/policy/act_e.cfm

Canadian Race Relations Foundation Act, 1991, c.8, Assented February 1991.

Citizenship and Immigration Canada. *Forging Our Legacy: Canadian Citizenship and Immigration, 1900-1977*. Chapter 6: Trail-Blazing Initiatives, http://www.cic.gc.ca/english/department/legacy/chap-6.html#top

Cohon, George. *To Russia with Fries*. Toronto: McClelland and Stewart, 1997.

Collins, James C. and Jerry I. Porras. *Built to Last*. New York: Harper Business, 1997.

Covey, Stephen. *The 7 Habits of Highly Effective People*. New York: Simon and Schuster, 1989.

DePree, Max. *Leadership Is an Art*. New York: Doubleday, 1989.

Drucker, Peter F. *The Effective Executive*. New York: Harper & Row, 1985.

Dryden, Ken. *The Game*. Toronto: John Wiley & Sons Canada, 2005.

Employment Equity Act, 1995, c.44. Assented December 15, 1995, http://laws.justice.gc.ca/en/E-5.401/238505.html#top

France 2.fr, *Pourquoi le Canada fait-il rêver?* (*Why Canada makes us dream*) Monday, March 20, 2006, http://info.france2.fr/encadres/21696886-fr.php

Goleman, Daniel. *Emotional Intelligence*. New York: Bantam Books, 1995.

Greenleaf, Robert K. *Servant Leadership*. New Jersey: Paulist Press, 1977.

Harris, Robert L. *Change Leadership: Inform, Involve, Ignite! Tools, Tips and Templates for Succeeding at Organizational Change*. Toronto: Canadian Society of Association Executives, 2007.

Howell, WC and Fleishman, EA (eds.). *Human Performance and Productivity*. Vol. 2: Information Processing and Decision Making. Hillsdale, NJ: Erlbum, 1982.

Kirkpartrick, Donald. *Evaluating Training Programs: The Four Levels*. San Francisco, CA: San Diego State University, Educational Technology, 1994.

Kotter, John P. *John P. Kotter On What Leaders Really Do*. Watertown, MA: Harvard Business School Press, 1999.

Official Languages Act R.S. 1985, c.31 (4th Supp) http://laws.justice.gc.ca/en/O-3.01/253512.html

Rae, Bob. *From Protest to Power*. Toronto: Viking, 1996.

Robbins, Anthony. *Unlimited Power*. New York: Simon & Schuster, 1986.

Stephen Lewis Foundation, The Directors, http://www.stephenlewisfoundation.org/about_who.htm

Women in the Lead, Women in the Lead Incorporated, McKenzie-Sanders, Doreen (editor). Vancouver, British Columbia, 2004.

INDEX

A

Abbot-Peter, Marni, 19
ability, 53
Aboriginal community
    leaders, 15, 21, 25, 74, 85, 99, 153, 207, 247
    needs of, 256
    spirituality, 55
    strategies including, 197
Acadia University, 211
access routes, 69–73, 289
accidental leaders
    access routes, 69, 71–73
    advantages and disadvantages, 68
    characteristics of, 62–63
    identity, 67
    impetus for leadership, 64–65
    maturity, 73–75
    motivation, 66
    ratio of, 60–61
Accord/hart & associates inc., 275
accountability, 5, 14, 282–285
Accucaps Industries Limited, 30, 44, 57, 158, 234, 275
achievement, 17
acting, 18, 20–21
action, 15, 20–21, 85–86
Action Canada Foundation, 119, 122, 131, 134

action leaders, 17
activities, 37
Adair, William
    national leadership style, 228
    public leadership, 267
adversity, 21, 86, 157
African Guitar Summit, 236
Agropur coopérative, 167, 169, 177, 186, 189
Air Canada Jazz, 154, 198, 220, 283
Alberta Community and Co-operative
    Association, 180
Alberta Venture, 207, 209, 237, 279
alignment of words and actions, 15
Alimentation Couche-Tard Inc., 13, 57, 89, 201, 220
Allaster, Stacey, 235
AlterGo, 17, 25, 59
Amarok Training Services Ltd., 83
Amyot, Denise
    apprenticeship model, 103
    characteristics of leadership, 20
    development strategy, 79
    national leadership style, 222
Anglade, Dominique
    apprenticeship model, 106
    process of leadership, 42
    public leadership, 275
Annapolis Valley District Health Authority, 26, 106

appreciation by organization, 157–158
apprenticeship model
    development and, 107–108, 117
    evolution in, 4
    in leadership education, 198, 199, 290–
        291, 295
    mastery and, 102–105
    mentors, 99–100
    structure, 97–98
    support in, 124
Arctic Co-operatives Limited, 176–177, 180,
    182, 184, 187
Armstrong, Ruth, 261
Armstrong, Tim, 249
Arnoldussen, Linda
    development program architecture, 114,
        115
    effective program structure, 138
The Artist's Way (Cameron), 78
Assumption Life, 103, 199
Atlantic Canada, 12
attitude, 14–16
Atwood, Margaret, 253–254
Austin, Janet
    national leadership style, 228
    process of leadership, 49
authenticity, 54
authority, 53

B

Babineau, Guy
    the call to leadership, 60
    development strategy, 83
    journey of leadership, 32
baby boomers, 210
balance, 190, 255–256
Bales, John
    effective program structure, 138, 139
    leadership education, 203
    process of leadership, 43
The Banff Centre, 51, 66, 99, 114, 124, 131,
    152, 157, 275
Bardswick, Kathy, 169, 170, 194
Barr, Lorna, 268
Barrett, Michael, 161, 169, 177–178, 188, 189
Bartels, Kathleen
    characteristics of leadership, 20

development strategy, 82
    leadership education, 204
Bastien, Yvon
    apprenticeship model, 108
    the call to leadership, 63, 66
    characteristics of leadership, 14
    development strategy, 88
    environment of organization, 156
    journey of leadership, 26
    leadership education, 200
Bates-Van der Zeijst, Johanna Maria
    development strategy, 81
    environment of organization, 155
BC Wheelchair Basketball Society, 19
Béchard, Bruno-Marie
    the call to leadership, 67
    characteristics of leadership, 17
    co-operatives, 163, 172, 178
Beehan, Cathy
    development program architecture, 119,
        122
    effective program structure, 131, 134
Bégin, Richard
    development program architecture, 112,
        122
    effective program structure, 130, 135
behaviour, 11
believing, 18, 19–20
bench strength, 14
Bencz, Marjorie, 61
benefits, value of, 32
Benoît, Guy, 179, 182, 188
Benson, Mel
    the call to leadership, 58
    characteristics of leadership, 21
    national leadership style, 234
    process of leadership, 52
Berg, Larry
    development strategy, 80
    public leadership, 273
Bernstein, Alan
    apprenticeship model, 99
    the call to leadership, 64
    leadership education, 209
    leadership identity, 247
Bertrand, Françoise
    leadership education, 202

public leadership, 263
best practices, 10–11, 190–192
Big Brothers Big Sisters, 246, 276
Bildfell, Sid, 170, 172, 176, 185, 187, 193
Biron, Ève-Lynne
  leadership education, 198
  public leadership, 280
Biscaro, Bruno
  the call to leadership, 57
  environment of organization, 158
  journey of leadership, 30
  national leadership style, 234
  process of leadership, 44
  public leadership, 275
Black Photo Corporation, 212, 273
Blackburn, Richard
  the call to leadership, 74
  characteristics of leadership, 18, 21
  development strategy, 82
  journey of leadership, 28
  leadership identity, 254
  national leadership style, 220
Blair, Josh
  development program architecture, 116,
    119
  effective program structure, 129, 136, 139
Blanchet, Suzanne
  apprenticeship model, 99
  development strategy, 86
  leadership identity, 253
  national leadership style, 233
  public leadership, 273, 281
blind spots, 69
blooming stage, 47–48, 51, 53–54
Blueprint, 58, 69, 71–73
BMO, 24, 58, 145, 228, 260, 278
BMO Financial Group, 50, 65
BMO Financial Group Institute for Learning,
  109, 113, 125
board members, 180–181, 192, 264
Board of Trade of Metropolitan Montréal, 81,
  232, 271
Boisaco Inc., 173
Bono, 230
Booker Prize, 253–254
Books for Business, 49
Boot, Sunni, 43

Bouchard, Jean-François
  development program architecture, 124
  leadership identity, 246
Bourelle, Georges, 114
Bowes, Paul, 65
Bradshaw, Patricia
  development program architecture, 120
  effective program structure, 134
brand
  of Canadian leadership, 229–238, 297–
    299
  cornerstones, 231–239
  leveraging, 250–257
  strengthening, 248–250
Brandt, Paul, 231, 235
Brault, Simon
  the call to leadership, 58
  environment of organization, 152
British Columbia Co-operative Association,
  165, 178, 185
British Columbia, Government of, 69, 94, 96,
  152, 153, 195, 196, 266
British Columbia Transmission Corporation,
  24
British Columbia Utilities Commission, 268
Brooks, Mary, 103
Brousseau, Francine
  characteristics of leadership, 15
  environment of organization, 156
  leadership identity, 253
  public leadership, 276
Brown, Christine
  development program architecture, 119
  effective program structure, 135
Brown, May
  characteristics of leadership, 18
  leadership identity, 247
Brown, Sheila, 270
Brunelle, Jean-Pierre, 138–139
Bublé, Michael, 29
Bucket, Hyacinth, 89
Built to Last (Collins, Porras), 242
Byrne, Cheryl, 171, 173, 186

C
Caisse d'économie solidaire Desjardins, 9, 54,
  153, 235, 280

Calgary Academy, 155

Cameron, Julia, 78

Cameron, Kevin
  characteristics of leadership, 18
  leadership identity, 241

Cameron, Richard, 87

Campbell, Joseph, 26

Canada, Government of, 20, 33, 41, 42, 64, 65, 67, 79, 83, 102, 103, 150, 209, 213, 221, 222, 253, 275, 277

Canada at a Glance: Arts and Culture (Government of Canada), 253

Canada Hibernia Holding Company, 106

Canada Mortgage and Housing Corporation (CMHC), 113, 117

Canada Mortgage and Housing Corporation International, 158, 223, 230, 246

Canada Revenue Agency, 112, 121, 130, 135, 263

Canada Task Force 1, 249

Canada West Foundation, 203, 271

Canada's National Ballet School, 21, 102

Canada-wide knowledge, 202–204

Canadian Alpine Ski Team Association, 52, 155

Canadian Association for the Advancement of Women and Sport (CAAWS), 112, 114, 138

Canadian Cancer Society, 53, 65, 245

Canadian Centre for Ethics in Sport, 64, 195, 230

Canadian Charter of Rights and Freedoms, 296

Canadian Co-operative Association (CCA), 162, 169

Canadian Forces, 10, 100, 110–111, 230, 257

Canadian Forces College, 10, 115, 133

Canadian Hunter Exploration Ltd., 203, 271

Canadian Institute for Advanced Research, 67

Canadian Institutes of Health Research, 64, 99, 209, 247

Canadian International Development Agency (CIDA), 43, 87, 236

Canadian Interuniversity Sport, 46, 105, 158, 212

Canadian Museum of Civilization

Corporation, 15, 156, 253, 276

Canadian National Men's Basketball Team, 205

Canadian Olympic Committee, 17, 75, 225, 250

Canadian Paralympic Committee, 83

Canadian Paraplegic Association, 14

Canadian Paraplegic Association of Ontario, 228, 267

Canadian Wheelchair Basketball Association, 65

Canadian Worker Co-operative Federation (CWCF), 167

CanWest MediaWorks Publications Inc., 150, 208

Cape Breton University, 82, 157, 199

Cardinal, Charles
  journey of leadership, 30
  process of leadership, 43

Carey, David
  development strategy, 86
  environment of organization, 146
  national leadership style, 233

caring atmosphere of organization, 147, 155–158

Carr, Glenna, 211

Cascades Tissue Group, 86, 99, 233, 253, 273, 281

Cayer, Mario, 127

CBC English Television, 51, 78, 148, 202, 268

CBC Olympics, 84

CBC Radio, Maritimes, 71, 221

CBC/Radio-Canada, 32, 60, 69, 83, 152, 266

CBC-TV Sports, 84

CCL Group, 84

C.D. Howe Institute, 222

Centraide (United Way), 30, 283

Centre for Exceptional Leadership Inc. *See* The Refinery Leadership Partners Inc.

Centre international de recherche et d'études en management (CIREM), 114

Centre Québécois de Leadership, 105, 120, 137

certitude, 15

challenges, 37, 73

Chantier de l'Économie Sociale, 277

character, 14, 48

Charles, Gregory, 4
Chez Cora/Cora's, 12–13, 33, 103, 220, 234
Chiasson, Herménégilde
  characteristics of leadership, 13
  environment of organization, 158
  leadership identity, 243
  national leadership style, 221, 223
Children's Aid Society, 17, 51, 71
Choquette, Natalie
  apprenticeship model, 97
  the call to leadership, 65, 70
  development strategy, 90
  environment of organization, 156
  journey of leadership, 26
Christie, Suzanne
  environment of organization, 158
  national leadership style, 236
  public leadership, 267
Christmas, Bernd
  apprenticeship model, 99
  leadership education, 207
  leadership identity, 256
Churchill, Winston, 3
CIBC, 24, 58, 145, 228, 260, 278
CIMA+, 46, 234, 265
Cimolino, Antoni
  the call to leadership, 67, 74
  characteristics of leadership, 13, 22
  journey of leadership, 25
  process of leadership, 50, 54
Circle K, 201
Cirque du Soleil, 112, 114, 133, 235
citizens, 279–280, 296–297
civic education, 280
civic responsibility, 202
Clark, Tim
  development program architecture, 113,
    119
  effective program structure, 132
Clearwater Seafood, 9, 26, 50, 65, 80, 279
climate of organization, 147, 158–159
coaching, 54, 126, 274
Coaching Association of Canada, 43, 138,
  139, 203
cognition, 78
Cohon, George
  environment of organization, 152
  national leadership style, 228

collaboration, 16–18
Collins, James C., 242
communication, 17, 208–209
communities of practice, 127–128
community
  in co-operatives, 189
  in development programs, 118
  as early influence, 60
  leadership process stages, 47–48, 51–54
  values, 231
community service, 150
compensation for elected officials, 272–273
competence, 14, 261–264
configuration of organization, 147, 150–155
conscience of organization, 147–150
Conseil du sport de haut niveau de Québec,
  113, 140, 270
Conseil international des grands réseaux
  électriques (CIGRÉ), 59, 201
consistency, elected officials and, 261, 262,
  264–267
Cooney, Jane, 49
Co-op Atlantic, 166, 180
Co-op Cofor, 173
Coop Santé Aylmer Health Co-op, 179, 182,
  188
co-operatives
  best practices, 190–192, 294
  community, 189
  continual improvement, 180–183
  definition of, 162–164
  education, 183–186, 264
  evolution of, 168–170
  expectations in, 177–178
  formation of, 164–165
  function of, 165–167
  infrastructure, 176–177
  leadership style, 170–174
  organization of, 167
  resourcefulness, 173–174, 191
  staff, 182–183
  stakeholder alignment, 179
  succession planning, 186–187
  support, 188–189
The Co-Operators, 169, 170, 194
Co-operators General Insurance Company,
  177, 178, 182, 183, 192
Corcoran Gallery of Art, 102

cornerstones of leadership brand, 231–239, 251–257
The Corporate L.I.F.E. Centre Inc., 122, 132, 136, 139
cost, 30, 34
Côté, Raymond
    environment of organization, 150
    public leadership, 271
Courville, Isabelle
    leadership education, 198
    leadership identity, 252
    process of leadership, 47
Cousineau, Alain
    leadership education, 206
    process of leadership, 46
Coutts, Denise
    development program architecture, 114
    effective program structure, 132, 138
Covey, Stephen, 168, 199
creativity, 15, 173–174, 191
credibility, 87
Credit Union Central of Canada, 171, 173, 185, 186
credit unions. See co-operatives
Crocker, Elizabeth Jane, 284
Crosbie, John C.
    characteristics of leadership, 20
    journey of leadership, 33
Cuenco, Patrick
    apprenticeship model, 102
    development strategy, 81
    leadership education, 199
    national leadership style, 219
    process of leadership, 45, 48–49
    public leadership, 263, 280
culture education, 204
CUSOURCE, 185

D

Dalhousie University, 103
Dallaire, Roméo, 11, 228
D'Amours, Alban
    characteristics of leadership, 19
    co-operatives, 165, 170, 194
    development strategy, 89
    environment of organization, 153
    leadership education, 203

    on leadership issues, x
D'Auray-Boult, Marie-France
    national leadership style, 236
    process of leadership, 43
David, Françoise
    process of leadership, 52
    public leadership, 263
David, Pierre
    environment of organization, 158
    leadership identity, 246
    national leadership style, 223, 230
Davidson, Valerie, 231
Davis, William G.
    characteristics of leadership, 18
    development strategy, 85
    national leadership style, 227–228
debate, 278–279, 296
decentralized organizational structure, 151–152
decision making, 37
Défi Sportif, 17, 25, 59
Delaney, Barry, 175, 178, 179, 180, 181, 182, 185
demand for leaders, 2
Dépin, Marc-André, 51
DePree, Max, 12
Deschênes, Jocelyn
    environment of organization, 151
    public leadership, 260
Desjardins, Alphonse, x, 164–165
Desjardins Cooperative Institute, 120, 186
Desjardins General Insurance Group, 59, 78
Desjardins Group, x, 19, 89, 153, 164–165, 170, 181, 185, 194, 203
Desrosiers, Ernest, 172, 179, 186, 192
determination leaders, 17
development
    apprenticeship model, 4, 97–100, 197–198
    environment of organization and, 153–155
    leadership emergence and, 62
    mentoring, 209–211
    need for, 287–288
    of new leaders, 52
    ongoing, 192
    organization strategies, 292–293
    phases, 44–55

process, 78–79, 288–292
program experts, 2
of public leaders, 5
strategy, 78–94
of team members, 18
See also education; programs
Dexter, Rob
leadership education, 200
public leadership, 274
Dinter-Gottlieb, Gail, 211
Dion, Céline, 29
Dion, Donald
characteristics of leadership, 15
process of leadership, 42
public leadership, 274
Dion, Pierre
co-operatives, 171
journey of leadership, 29
public leadership, 267
discipline, 37
discovery, 36
diversity, 235–236, 238, 254–256, 298, 300
Dobell, Ken
apprenticeship model, 96
leadership education, 196
Doubleday, Canada, 71
Douglas, Tommy, 105, 218–219, 265
Dryden, Ken
development strategy, 83
national leadership style, 221
public leadership, 277
Duffy, Gerry
environment of organization, 157
national leadership style, 223, 227
Dufour, Alain, 173
Dufresne, France
development program architecture, 112,
114
effective program structure, 133
The Duke of Edinburgh's Award, 129, 138,
140
DuPont, Bonnie Dianne
apprenticeship model, 96
the call to leadership, 67
environment of organization, 150
duty, 74–75
dynamics, 33–38

E
Earn, Brian
development program architecture, 115
effective program structure, 134
Economic Development Council for
Manitoba Bilingual Municipalities, 241, 264
ECONOMUSEUM Network, 252
Edmonton Gleaners Association, 61
education
of citizens, 297
civic, 280
in co-operatives, 183–186, 191–192
in development programs, 118
in leadership strategy, 5
mastery and, 96
mentoring outreach, 209–211
national strategy, 196–199
in school system, 199–209, 294–295
See also development; program
architecture; programs
effectiveness, 62
ego, 13
elected officials
effective leadership practices, 276–279
media and, 282–285
as professional occupation, 268–276,
295–296
trust model, 261–268
See also public leadership
emergence, 44–46, 47–55, 289
emotions, 19–20, 35
Employment Equity Act, 284
empowering organizational structure,
152–153
Enbridge Inc., 67, 96, 132, 150
energy, 15, 24, 27–29
Enron, 13
entertainment industry, 29
entrepreneurs
in co-operatives, 184
environment for, 151, 157
experience and, 207
in school system, 198, 202, 203
strategies for, 254
as vehicle for leadership, 201
environment of organization, 146–160
Envision Financial, 174, 178, 179, 180, 181,
182, 185

Equiterre, 202
Eriksson, Peter
    characteristics of leadership, 14
    public leadership, 276
Esse Leadership, 224, 267
ESTEEM Team Association, 109
ethics, 85, 172
Evangeline Community Health Services Co-
    op, 174
execution, 100–105
Ex-Machina, 203, 254
expectations, 177–178
experience
    development and, 103–104
    of leadership, 290
    in leadership education, 207–208
    learning from, 80, 87
    personal, 24–29
external landscape, 19
eyes, 18, 19

F
facilitation, 50
fairness, 85
faith, 19–20
family influences, 58–59, 60
Fasken Martineau DuMoulin, 41, 83
Fédération de hockey sur glace du Québec
    Inc., 116, 128, 139, 140
Fédération des caisses populaires acadiennes,
    180, 181, 182, 187, 188, 193
Fédération des Chambres de Commerce du
    Québec, 202, 263
Fédération des coopératives funéraires du
    Québec, 171, 173, 189
Federation of Acadian Credit Unions, 180,
    181, 182, 187, 188, 193
Fédération québécoise des coopératives
    forestières, 181
feedback, 88–93, 123–124
field-specific programs, 119
Filion, Yves
    the call to leadership, 59
    leadership education, 201
first filters, 59–60
First Nations people. See Aboriginal
    community

Fitzpatrick, Glen, 171, 184, 189, 193
flat organizational structure, 151
focus, 37, 53, 72
Focuspoint Strategic Management, 212, 273
the Force, 58, 69–70, 72–73
Ford of Canada Motor Company, 282
foreign policy, 247–248
Fortin, Michèle
    development strategy, 84
    leadership education, 207
    public leadership, 263, 265, 271
Foster, David, 101
foundation, building, 81–85, 190, 192–193
foundations of practice, 14
Fox, Quintin, 169
France 2 TV network, 225
The Franchise Company, 29, 113, 119, 132
Front d'action populaire en réaménagement
    urbain (FRAPRU), 159, 268
Fruits & Passion, 201
Furlong, John
    development strategy, 77, 83
    national leadership style, 217

G
Gage, Sandra, 109
gain (pain/gain dynamics), 30–38
Gandhi, Mohandas, 10
Gauthier, Claude, 181, 182
Gay Lea Foods Co-operative Limited, 161,
    169, 178, 188, 189
gender issues, 63
Germain, Christiane, 65
Getting in the Groove, 113, 131, 137
Gibb, Joan C.
    the call to leadership, 65
    leadership identity, 245
    process of leadership, 53
Globe & Mail, 179
GMP Private Client LP, 275
goals, 81
going in, 79, 80–85
Goldbloom, Ruth M., 82
Gonthier, Stéphane
    the call to leadership, 57
    characteristics of leadership, 13
    development strategy, 89

national leadership style, 220
Gorman, Diane
    apprenticeship model, 102
    leadership identity, 253
Governance Advisory Services, 197
Graham, Jack
    leadership education, 207
    process of leadership, 49
    public leadership, 272
Granby Zoological Society, 210, 272
Granny Brigade, 12, 89, 208, 257, 278
Gray, James
    leadership education, 203
    public leadership, 271
greed, 13
Greenhalgh, Paul, 102
Greenleaf, Robert K., 12
Greer, Nancy
    development program architecture, 115,
        121, 126
    effective program structure, 132, 136
Greiner, L.E., 168
Groban, Josh, 101
Groupe Germaine Inc., 65
Groupe Investissement Responsable, 154
Groupe Maritime Verreault Inc., 20, 81, 97
growing stage, 47–48, 50–51, 53–54, 289
Growmark Inc., 181, 182
Guimond, Clément
    characteristics of leadership, 9
    environment of organization, 153
    national leadership style, 235
    process of leadership, 54
    public leadership, 280
Gutman, Gloria, 18
Guy, Denyse, 166, 181, 186

H
Halifax Chamber of Commerce, 79, 266
Halifax Mooseheads Hockey Club, 18, 241
Halifax 2014 Commonwealth Games,
    Candidate City, 87
Hamilton, Bill
    the call to leadership, 58
    environment of organization, 145
    journey of leadership, 24
    national leadership style, 228

public leadership, 260, 278
Hamilton Tiger-Cats, 275
Handley, Joseph L.
    development strategy, 78
    leadership education, 208
    public leadership, 277
Handling, Piers
    the call to leadership, 59, 70
    leadership education, 209
hands, 18, 20–21
Hannah, Gregg
    characteristics of leadership, 10
    development program architecture, 115
    effective program structure, 133
Hansen, Rick, 77
Harber, Bruce
    development strategy, 78
    environment of organization, 153
    public leadership, 266
Harris, Robert L., 261
Harrop-Procter Community Co-operative,
    164
Hart, Christine, 275
Harvey, Gilles
    apprenticeship model, 105
    development program architecture, 120
    development strategy, 86
    effective program structure, 137
    journey of leadership, 39
    public leadership, 273
Hayman, Brian
    development program architecture, 113
    effective program structure, 131, 137
Hayman, Paul, 29
HBC Group, 59, 134
HBC Stores and Specialty, 119, 135
health risks, 36
heart, 18, 19–20
Hedley, Patricia, 136
Hedley, Robert W., 130
Henderson, James (Sa'ke'j) Youngblood
    characteristics of leadership, 15
    journey of leadership, 25
    leadership identity, 247
Henderson, Paul
    the call to leadership, 71
    environment of organization, 159

public leadership, 278
Herbert, Carol
  the call to leadership, 68
  characteristics of leadership, 18
Hermant, Jill, 129, 137–138, 140
hero myth, 4, 11, 287
heroes, 249
The Hero's Journey (Campbell), 26
Herrndorf, Peter
  development strategy, 82
  leadership identity, 253
  process of leadership, 42
  public leadership, 272
Hervieux-Payette, Céline
  development strategy, 83
  process of leadership, 41
Hill, Julia, 275
Hillier, Mervin
  development program architecture, 122
  effective program structure, 132, 136, 139
Hillier, Rick, 12
Hines, Gregory
  apprenticeship model, 97
  development strategy, 92
  environment of organization, 146
history, 225, 235, 249
Hitler, Adolf, 3
Hoag, Glenn, 88
Hofstetter, Mary
  apprenticeship model, 99
  environment of organization, 157
  process of leadership, 51
  public leadership, 275
Holloway, Sue
  apprenticeship model, 104
  environment of organization, 159
honesty, 85
Houde, Jean
  journey of leadership, 33
  national leadership style, 231
House, Jeannie, 49
Howell, W.C., 100
Hudon, Isabelle
  development strategy, 81
  national leadership style, 232
  public leadership, 271
the Hugger Busker, 126

Humber Institute of Technology and
  Advanced Learning, 136
humour, 15
Huntley Communication Services Inc., 95
Hydro-Québec, 32, 102, 156, 246, 281
Hydro-Québec TransÉnergie, 47, 59, 198,
  201, 252

I

identity
  accidental/innate dynamics, 67–68
  authenticity and, 54
  defining core, 242–258, 299
  development and, 48, 78, 79
  focus on, 10
  loss of, 36
Ignition Strategies, 244
immanence, 44, 47–55, 58, 289
immigration, 225–226, 235
impact
  assessment of, 87–93
  dynamics of, 33, 38
  national, 218
  understanding, 80
impetus for leadership, 64–66
improvement, 112
inclusion, 18, 220–222, 297–298
Indian Taxation Advisory Board, 52
individual stage, 47–49, 53–54
individual values, 231
influences
  early, 58–60
  in leadership education, 208–209
  leadership trademark and, 223–229
initiative, 201
innate leaders
  access routes, 69–70, 72–73
  characteristics of, 62–63
  identity, 68
  impetus for leadership, 65–66
  maturity, 73–75
  motivation, 66–67
  ratio of, 61
innovation, 113–114
inspiration, 19–20
inspiration leaders, 17
Institute for Media Policy and Civil Society

(IMPACS), 247, 280
integrity, 84, 261, 262, 267–268
intention, 82–83
interdependence, 168
interest, 13
internal landscape, 19
international aid, 246–247
International Center for Research Studies in Management (CIREM), 114
International Council on Large Electric Systems, 59, 201
intuition, 78
isolation, 28, 36, 127, 290
Istvanffy, Peter, 155
IWK Foundation, 64, 160, 273
IWK Health Centre, 67, 154, 259

J

Jack, Corey, 109, 113, 125
Jackson, Lisa
    development program architecture, 114, 124
    effective program structure, 131
James, Angela L.
    development program architecture, 125
    effective program structure, 134
James, Yolande
    development strategy, 91
    national leadership style, 237
    public leadership, 281
Jarvis, Patrick, 83
Jasinski, Mona
    development program architecture, 116
    effective program structure, 134
Jean Coutu, 201
Johanna M. Bates Literary Consultants Inc., 81, 155
Johnson, Nancy Myers, 95
journey of leadership
    dynamics, 33–38
    rewards and costs, 30–33
    uniqueness of, 23–29
Jules, C.T., 52
Junior Hong Kong-Canada Business Association, 45, 48, 81, 102, 199, 219, 263, 280

K

Karetak-Lindell, Nancy
    apprenticeship model, 99
    national leadership style, 225
Keeping Up Appearances, 89
Kelderman, Dianne, 167, 169, 174, 181, 185, 193
Kelly, Ruth
    leadership education, 207, 209
    national leadership style, 237
    public leadership, 279
Kennedy, John F., 251, 296
Kim, Julia
    development program architecture, 114
    effective program structure, 132, 138
King, Martin Luther, 10
Kingston General Hospital, 11, 46, 83
Kingswood Capital Corp., 17, 66, 283
Kirkpatrick, Donald, 136
Knebel, John, 15
Knox, Janet
    apprenticeship model, 106
    journey of leadership, 26
Kolida, Robert, 59
Kotter, John, 10
Kouzes, James M., 10
KWA Canada, 15, 17

L

La Coop fédérée, 172, 179, 186, 189, 192, 264
Laboratoire Médical Biron, 198, 280
Lacey, Veronica
    the call to leadership, 65
    public leadership, 262
Lachance, Victor
    the call to leadership, 64
    leadership education, 195
    national leadership style, 230
Lalonde, Sylvain B.
    development program architecture, 116, 128
    effective program structure, 139, 140
Lalumière, Joanne
    leadership education, 210
    public leadership, 272
landscape, 19
language education, 204

LaRosa, Susan
  development strategy, 83, 86
  national leadership style, 220
Larose, Gérald
  environment of organization, 151
  leadership education, 202
  public leadership, 281
Lavallée, Robert, 169, 177, 185–186
Lay, Marion, 277
leadership
  characteristics of, 10
  demand for, 2
  international appeal of, 5, 220–223
  motives for, 66–67
  supply of, 5, 292–297
The Leadership Challenge (Kouzes, Posner),
  10
leadership education. See development;
  education; programs
The Leadership Group, 71, 159, 278
Leadership Is an Art (DePree), 12
leading by example, 75
learning
  assistance, 125
  stages, 53
  strategy, 78–79, 291–292
The Learning Partnership, 65, 262
LeBlanc, Léo, 166, 180
Leclerc, Alain, 171, 189
Lee, Nancy, 84
Lee, Sue
  the call to leadership, 71
  development strategy, 78
  leadership education, 210
  public leadership, 265
Lefebvre, Monique
  the call to leadership, 59
  characteristics of leadership, 17
  journey of leadership, 25
legacies, 21, 51–53, 81, 289
Legacy, René, 180, 181, 182, 187, 193
legislation, leadership trademark and,
  226–227
Leonardo da Vinci, 97
Lepage, Robert
  leadership education, 203
  leadership identity, 254

Lesage, Jean, 249
Lessard, Jocelyn, 181
Let It Out Entertainment Inc., 52, 64, 75
Levine, David
  process of leadership, 43
  public leadership, 263
Lewis, Stephen, 228
Lexam Explorations Inc., 14, 207
Lindemann, Barry, 14
Liquor Control Board of Ontario (LCBO),
  281
literacy, 252
The Little Prince (Saint-Exupéry), 105
Lofstrom, Karin
  development program architecture, 112,
    114
  effective program structure, 138
Logan, Scott, 87
Loiselle, Jacques
  development program architecture, 113
  effective program structure, 140
London Philharmonic, 164
London Symphony Orchestra, 164
L'Oréal Canada, 12, 23, 79, 208
Losier, Denis
  apprenticeship model, 103
  leadership education, 199
Loto-Québec, 46, 206
loyalty, 17
Lyall, William, 180, 182, 187

M

MacDonald, Colin
  the call to leadership, 65
  characteristics of leadership, 9
  development strategy, 80
  journey of leadership, 26
  process of leadership, 50
  public leadership, 279
Macdonald, John A., 265
MacGillivray, Frederick, 145, 157
MacKenzie, Ann, 71
Maclean Hunter Ltd., 23, 63, 79
Maclean's magazine, 178, 221
MacMaster, Natalie, 243
MacMillan, Stuart, 244
MacNeil, Teresa, 49

Mac's, 201
Malone, Doreen, 47
Manitoba Hydro, 19, 70, 79
Maple Leaf Foods Inc., 130
Maple Leafs Hockey, 71, 159, 278
Marchand, Marie-Éve, 127
Maritime Travel Inc., 200, 274
Marshman, Kevin
  development strategy, 92
  journey of leadership, 27
Martel, Yann, 253–254
Martingrove Collegiate Institute, 43, 66, 210
mastery, 100–105, 117
Mattocks, Fred
  development strategy, 78
  environment of organization, 148
  leadership education, 202
  process of leadership, 51
  public leadership, 268
maturity, 42–43, 54, 73–75
Mayer, Marc
  the call to leadership, 75
  characteristics of leadership, 16–17, 21
  leadership identity, 244
McCain, Margaret, 271, 283
McCallum, Doug
  the call to leadership, 66
  national leadership style, 222
  public leadership, 276
McClung, Nellie, 10, 249
McDonald, Bernadette
  the call to leadership, 66
  environment of organization, 152
McDonald's Restaurants, 152, 228
McDonough, Alexa
  the call to leadership, 64
  environment of organization, 150
  leadership education, 213
McEwen, Rob
  characteristics of leadership, 14
  leadership education, 207
McGregor, Marg
  apprenticeship model, 105
  environment of organization, 158
  leadership education, 212
  process of leadership, 46–47
McGuire, Anne

the call to leadership, 67
environment of organization, 154
public leadership, 259
McInnes Cooper, 49, 207, 272
McKenzie-Sanders, Doreen
  journey of leadership, 26
  leadership identity, 251
McKinnon, Becky
  the call to leadership, 62
  leadership education, 198
McKinsey & Company, 42, 106, 275
McKinstry, Nancy
  development program architecture, 114
  effective program structure, 132, 138
McPherson, Gary
  the call to leadership, 74
  national leadership style, 231
  process of leadership, 55
meaning, 37
media, 250, 282–285, 297
mentoring
  apprenticeship model and, 99–100
  in development programs, 125, 126
  for elected officials, 274
  expansion of, 198–199
  in leadership process, 52
  in leadership strategy, 5
  outreach program, 209–211, 295
metamorphosis, 25–26
Methanex, 157, 223, 227
methodology, process as, 18–21
Middleton, Alan C.
  development program architecture, 116
  effective program structure, 133, 139
Mi'kmaq, 99, 207, 256
military, 10, 100, 110–111, 230, 257
Mills, Jim
  development strategy, 84
  environment of organization, 154
Milne, Janet
  the call to leadership, 65, 67
  leadership education, 209
  process of leadership, 42
Minerva Foundation for BC Women, 114, 132, 138
Mintz, Jack, 222
mission, 81, 242, 243–244

mistakes, 157
Mistry, Rohinton, 204
Mitton, Susan
   the call to leadership, 71
   national leadership style, 221
Mixed Blood, 21, 25, 55, 74, 85, 153, 256
models. *See* role models
Monette, Richard
   apprenticeship model, 98, 101–102, 104
   leadership education, 200
Montréal, City of, 15, 29, 42, 61, 223, 274
Montréal Museum of Contemporary Art, 17, 21, 75, 244
Montréal Regional Health Authority, 43, 263
Morin, Pierre
   the call to leadership, 61
   journey of leadership, 29
   national leadership style, 223
motivation
   exploring, 79
   success as, 29
   of team members, 17–18
   vision and, 28
motives for leadership, 66–67
Mount Saint Vincent University, 270
Mountain Equipment Co-op, 84, 168, 193
Mowat, Dave
   apprenticeship model, 102, 106
   the call to leadership, 67
   co-operatives, 172, 193
   national leadership style, 237
   public leadership, 281
Mulaire, Mariette
   leadership identity, 241
   public leadership, 264
Mullen, Cary
   development strategy, 84
   leadership education, 199
Multi-Cultural Health Brokers Co-operative, 173
multiculturalism, 299
Murphy, Judy
   the call to leadership, 68
   characteristics of leadership, 19
   development strategy, 87
   journey of leadership, 32
Murray, Carol, 180
Mustard, Fraser, 67

N

Nadeau, Luc
   characteristics of leadership, 12
   development strategy, 79
   journey of leadership, 23
   leadership education, 208
National Arts Centre, 42, 82, 253, 272
National Leadership Institute, 199, 211–213, 295
national leadership strategy, 5, 196–199, 294–295
national leadership style, 218–239
National Theatre School of Canada, 58, 152
Native Law Centre of Canada, 15, 25, 247
NCR Canada Ltd., 27, 92
Neamtan, Nancy, 277
Nelson, Horatio, 208
Neptune Theatre, 47
Neufeld, Martin, 126
New Brunswick, Government of, 13, 158, 221, 223, 243, 271, 283
New Brunswick University, 119, 122, 135
Newfoundland and Labrador Federation of Co-operatives, 171, 184, 189, 193
Newfoundland and Labrador Health Boards Association, 49
Newfoundland Filmmakers Co-operative, 178
Niagara Institute, 113, 121, 185–186
Nike, 245
Nind, Ben
   apprenticeship model, 95
   the call to leadership, 66
   environment of organization, 160
Nishi-Khon/Key West Travel Ltd., 53, 69, 275
Noise Solutions Inc., 63
Norampac, 51
Northern Arts & Cultural Centre, 66, 95, 160
Northwest Territories, Government of, 78, 208, 277
Nova Scotia College of Art and Design University, 102
Nova Scotia Co-operative Council, 167, 169, 174, 181, 185, 193
Nova Scotia Film Development Corporation, 71
Nunavut, Government of, 99, 225
NYCOMED Pharma Inc., 146, 209

O

O'Brien, Shelly, 109
observation, 102
Office Interiors, 84, 154
Okros, Alan
  characteristics of leadership, 10
  development program architecture, 111
  effective program structure, 131, 133
  leadership education, 200, 211
Oldfield, Graydon
  environment of organization, 155
  process of leadership, 52
Olechnowicz, Kazimir
  national leadership style, 234
  process of leadership, 46
  public leadership, 265
Olthuis, Clarence, 194
Olympic athletes, 84, 104, 159, 199
Olympic Broadcast Services, 84
Olympic coaches, 14, 42, 274, 276
Olympic Games, 11
Ondaatje, Michael, 204
O'Neill, Elizabeth
  leadership identity, 246
  public leadership, 276
Ontario, Government of, 18, 85, 105, 206, 211, 228, 256
Ontario Co-operative Association, 166, 181, 186
Ontario Trillium Foundation, 132
opponents, 91
optimism, 14–15
O'Reilly, Louis
  the call to leadership, 61, 68, 70, 74
  leadership identity, 250
O'Reilly International Entertainment Management, 61, 68, 70, 74, 250
organization
  atmosphere of, 155–158
  climate of, 158–159
  configuration of, 150–155
  conscience of, 147–150
  environment of, 146–147, 160
  importance of leaders, 3
  leadership development, 292–293
  leadership process stages, 47–48, 51, 53–54

programs, 119
orientation, 273–274
Osmond, Gladys
  development strategy, 89
  leadership education, 207–208
  leadership identity, 257
  public leadership, 278
  service, 12
outlooks, 14–16
Owen, Philip
  leadership education, 210
  national leadership style, 226
  public leadership, 277

P

pain/gain dynamics, 30–38
Papp, Theresa
  development program architecture, 121
  effective program structure, 132
Paquette, Joseph
  the call to leadership, 74
  characteristics of leadership, 21
  development strategy, 85
  environment of organization, 153
  journey of leadership, 25
  leadership identity, 256
  process of leadership, 55
Paquette, Sylvie
  the call to leadership, 59
  development strategy, 78
Paralympic athletes, 15, 88, 248, 265
Paralympic coaches, 14, 276
parental influences, 58–59, 60
Parker, Steven, 84
Parsonson, Laura Collings
  the call to leadership, 66
  leadership education, 209
  process of leadership, 43
participative organizational structure, 152
partnerships, 16–18, 21, 22
Pascoe, Byron
  the call to leadership, 64, 75
  process of leadership, 52
passion, 19–20, 27
Patten, Rose
  the call to leadership, 65
  process of leadership, 50

Payn, Valerie
  development strategy, 79
  public leadership, 266
peace, 236–237, 238, 256–257, 298, 300
peaceful leaders, 17
Pearson, Lester B., 227–228, 229, 242, 272, 298, 299
Peel, Region of, 154
Peel Leadership Program, 132, 137, 138, 140
Peel Mentoring Network, 158, 236, 267
Pelletier, Louise
  apprenticeship model, 102
  environment of organization, 155–156
  journey of leadership, 32
  leadership identity, 246
people, dynamics of, 33, 35–36
People's Car Co-operative, 173
perceptions, 42–43
performance appraisals, 91–92
personality traits, 10, 63
Petitclerc, Chantal
  characteristics of leadership, 15
  development strategy, 88
  leadership identity, 248
  perception of, 25
  public leadership, 265
Peverett, Jane, 24
Pfeiffer, Michael, 157
phases of becoming a leader, 44–55
Philbrick, Michael, 275
Pier 21 Foundation, 82
Pinsonnault, Jean-François, 113, 117
Pintal, Lorraine
  characteristics of leadership, 16
  leadership education, 206
  national leadership style, 219
  public leadership, 278
platform
  building, 14, 79, 80–85
  in co-operatives, 193
  of organization, 148–150
political leadership. See public leadership
pollinating stage, 47–48, 51–54
The Popular Face of Action in Urban
  Refitting, 159, 268
Porco, Carmela, 71
Porras, Jerry I., 242

Porter, Donna, 121
Portmann, Michel, 263
Posner, Barry Z., 10
possibility, 234–235, 238, 253–254, 298, 300
Poulin, Marc
  apprenticeship model, 99
  development program architecture, 293
  development strategy, 81, 92
  environment of organization, 151
  journey of leadership, 27
  leadership identity, 241
  process of leadership, 44
  public leadership, 285
Pourquoi le Canada Fait-il rêver?, 225
power, 54
practice
  in co-operatives, 187–188
  in development programs, 118, 121–122
practices
  best, 10–11, 190–192
  foundations of, 14
pride in country, 249
Prime Minister's Advisory Council on
  Science and Technology, 82, 157, 199
principle, 232–233, 238, 251–252, 298, 299
problem solving, 54
process
  in access routes, 72
  dynamics of, 33
  in maturation process, 43–44
  as methodology, 18–21
  pain/gain dynamics, 36–37
  perception of, 24–29
process expertise, 222–223
process skills, 47, 120, 205–206, 222–223, 246, 298
professionalism, 233–234, 238, 252–253, 296, 298, 299
program architecture
  components, 117–128
  defining program, 110–112
  design, 114–115, 130–133, 291
programs
  evaluation, 135–140
  motivations for, 112–114
  participant selection, 133–135
  structured learning, 105–107

target audiences, 115–116
psychometric instruments, 123, 124
public leadership
    citizens and, 279–280, 296–297
    co-operative model, 180–181, 192
    development strategy, 5
    effective leadership practices, 276–279
    elected officials, 260–279, 295–296
    enhancement of, 295–297
    leadership trademark and, 227–229
    media and, 282–285
    performance management, 274–275
    as a professional occupation, 268–269
    public servants, 263, 280–282, 295–296,
        297
    stakeholders, 260
    talent management, 269–276
public programs, 119
public servants, 263, 280–282, 295–296, 297
Publicis Canada, 23
Pulver, Grace, 161, 186, 188
purpose
    clarification of, 80–81
    dynamics of, 33
    pain/gain dynamics, 36–37
    perception of, 24–29
    service as, 12–13, 21–22, 171–172
pyramid structure, 162

Q
QC Data International Inc., 157
qualities acquired, 36
Québec, Government of, 33, 39, 86, 91, 231,
    237, 273, 281
Québec Centre for Leadership, 105, 120, 137
Québec Federation of Chambers of
    Commerce, 202, 263
Québec Federation of Forestry Co-
    operatives, 181
Québec Federation of Funeral Co-operatives,
    171, 173, 189
Québec Ice Hockey Federation, 116, 128,
    139, 140
Québec Solidaire, 52, 263
Queen's University, 5, 16, 25, 46, 61, 93, 99,
    125, 134, 196, 252–253
Quinte Health Care, 11, 46, 83

R
Rabbani, Diane
    development strategy, 94
    environment of organization, 153
    leadership education, 195
    public leadership, 266
Radford, John, 282
Rae, Bob
    apprenticeship model, 105
    leadership education, 206
Raiss, Sarah
    apprenticeship model, 102
    characteristics of leadership, 13
    process of leadership, 51
    public leadership, 274
Rancourt, Serge, 23
Rand Worldwide, 64
Randell, Joseph
    environment of organization, 154
    leadership education, 198
    national leadership style, 220
    public leadership, 283
Rankin, John, 113
rapport, 17
reaching out, 80, 85–86
reality, 19
Rebello, François, 154
The Refinery Leadership Partners Inc., 113,
    120, 131, 136, 137
reflection, 78, 87–93, 104
Reid, Patrick
    apprenticeship model, 103
    environment of organization, 155
    leadership education, 211
    leadership identity, 257
Reist, Lorene
    environment of organization, 146
    leadership education, 209
relationships, 16–18, 35, 208–209
research, participation in, 2–3, 303–312
resilience of organization, 156–157
resourcefulness, 173–174, 191
respect, 84
responsibility
    of citizens, 279–280, 296
    of media, 297
    reinforcement of, 251–252

self and, 36
   service and, 14
Responsible Investment Group, 154
Restakis, John, 165, 178, 185
Restaurants Pacini Inc., 33, 45, 105
results, dynamics of, 33, 38
rewards, 30, 34, 275–276
Rick Hansen Foundation, 77, 103, 155, 211, 257
rights, 251–252, 279–280, 296
Riley, Sean, 32
risk, 27, 33
Rivoire, Eleanor
   characteristics of leadership, 11
   development strategy, 83
   process of leadership, 46
Robbins, Anthony, 201
Robert Harris Resources, 261
Robert Lepage Inc., 203, 254
Roberts, Bill, 271
Robertson Surrette, 39, 85, 158, 217, 244
Robinson, Peter
   co-operatives, 168, 193
   development strategy, 84
Rogers, Judy
   apprenticeship model, 99
   public leadership, 270, 280
role models, 63, 99–100
roles, 73, 96–97, 270
roller coaster, 24, 26–27
RONA, 201
Rooney, Nancy, 177, 178, 182, 183, 192
Rosenberg, Michael, 132, 137, 138, 140
Ross-Denroche, Barbara
   development program architecture, 113, 120
   effective program structure, 131, 135–136, 137
Rotary International, 121, 132
Rotman School of Management, 222
Roy, Mario, 124
Royal Bank of Canada, 82, 150, 272
Royal Military College, 10, 111, 131, 133, 200, 211
Royal Ontario Museum, 242
Royal Roads University, 115, 121, 126, 132, 136, 253

Royal Winnipeg Ballet, 19, 32, 68, 87
Rudge, Chris
   the call to leadership, 75
   characteristics of leadership, 17
   leadership identity, 250
   national leadership style, 225

S
Saillant, François
   environment of organization, 159
   public leadership, 268
Saint-Exupéry, Antoine de, 105
Sanofi Synthelabo Canada, 14, 26, 63, 66, 88, 108, 156, 200
Saskatchewan, 197
Saskatchewan General Insurance (SGI), 281
SaskCentral, 166, 170, 172, 176, 185, 187, 193
SaskEnergy, 116, 117, 126, 130, 139, 263
scholar model, 242, 245–247, 299
Schultz, Albert
   environment of organization, 159
   journey of leadership, 25
   national leadership style, 219
   public leadership, 259
ScotiaMcLeod, 52, 155
Scott, Donna
   the call to leadership, 63
   development strategy, 79
   journey of leadership, 23
Scott, Jacquelyn Thayer
   development strategy, 82
   environment of organization, 157
   leadership education, 199
Secunda Group of Companies, 220, 283
seeding stage, 47–48, 53–54
seeing, 18, 19
Segal, Joseph
   the call to leadership, 66
   characteristics of leadership, 17
   public leadership, 283
self
   dynamics of, 33
   pain/gain dynamics, 35–36
   requirements of, 49
   view of, 69
self-actualization, 34
self-discovery, 119, 122–124

self-service, 13
Semkiw, Brian, 64
service
  accidental/innate dynamics, 66–67
  in leadership process, 51–53
  pain/gain dynamics, 37
  as purpose, 12–13, 21–22, 171–172
  responsibility of, 14
The 7 Habits of Highly Effective People
  (Covey), 168, 199
Shakespeare, William, 122
The Shambhala Institute for Authentic
  Leadership, 131, 137
Shaw, Robbie
  the call to leadership, 64
  environment of organization, 160
  public leadership, 273
Shearer, Beth
  development program architecture, 113,
    119
  effective program structure, 132
Shell Canada, Drilling, 13, 77
Shell Canada Limited, 116, 134
Shields, Ken, 205
Sid Lee, 125, 246
Simard, Cyril, 252
Simon Fraser University, 18
skill building, 48, 193
skills, 14
Skulsky, Dennis
  environment of organization, 150
  leadership education, 208
Sleeman, John, 78
Sleeman Breweries Ltd., 78
Smith, Rod
  leadership education, 212
  public leadership, 273
Smithers, Alfred
  national leadership style, 220
  public leadership, 283
Smooth Jazz Wave 94.7, 41, 52, 91, 210
Sobeys Inc., 27, 44, 81, 92, 99, 151, 241, 285
social conscience, 13
Social Economy Working Group, 277
Société zoologique de Granby, 210, 272
Sony Ericsson Women's Tennis Association
  Tour, 235

Soulpepper Theatre Company, 25, 159, 219,
  259
space
  diversity and, 235
  in leadership education, 208
  leadership trademark and, 223–224
Sphère Média Plus, 151, 260
spirituality, 54–55, 74
sponsorship, 126, 274
Sport BC, 84, 153
sports, as early influence, 59–60
Sports Québec, 150, 271
St. Francis Xavier University, 32, 49
St. Mary's University, 185
staff, 182–183
stages
  of leadership phases, 47–55
  of maturity, 42–43
Staines, Mavis
  apprenticeship model, 102
  characteristics of leadership, 21
Steeves, Rosie
  development program architecture, 113,
    120
  effective program structure, 131, 135–136,
    137
stepping back, 80, 87–93
Stevenson, Sandra
  development strategy, 84
  environment of organization, 153
Stewart, Nalini
  leadership education, 203
  process of leadership, 49
stimulation, 37
strategic thinking, 265–266
Stratford Festival of Canada, 13, 22, 25, 50,
  54, 67, 74, 98, 101, 104, 200
strength, 14
structure of organization, 147, 150–155
structured learning, 105–107, 128
style
  balance of, 16–17
  brand, 229–238
  of Canadian leaders, 218–220
  in co-operatives, 170–174
  influences on, 223–229
  international appeal of, 5, 220–223

success, 27, 29
succession planning, 186–187
Sullivan, Sam, 11
Suncor Energy Inc., 21, 52, 58, 71, 78, 210,
    234, 265
supply of leaders, 5, 292–297
support
    in co-operatives, 188–189
    development and, 104–105
    in development programs, 118, 124–126
    for elected officials, 274
    as source of energy, 27, 28–29
supporters, 91
Surrette, Mark
    development strategy, 85
    environment of organization, 158
    journey of leadership, 39
    leadership identity, 244
    national leadership style, 217
Surrey, city council, 66, 222, 276
surveys, 91–92
sustainability, 27
S-VOX, 271
Sylvester, Shauna
    leadership identity, 247
    public leadership, 280
Szpakowski, Susan, 131, 137
Szwarc, David, 154

T
Taranu-Teofilovici, Elaine
    development strategy, 88
    public leadership, 274
Taylor, Allan
    development strategy, 82
    environment of organization, 150
    public leadership, 272
Taylor, Carole
    the call to leadership, 69
    environment of organization, 152
    public leadership, 266
Tchozewski, Barb
    development program architecture, 116,
        117
    effective program structure, 130, 139
team
    in co-operatives, 182–183

    dynamics of, 33, 35–36
    leader impact and, 88–93
    leadership process stages, 47–48, 50–51,
        53–54
    motivation of, 17–18
    relationship with, 208
Team Canada Men's Volleyball, 88
Tech Co-op, 164
Tecumseh, 249
Télé-Québec, 84, 207, 263, 265, 271
Telus Corporation, 116, 119, 129, 136, 139
Tennis Canada, 235
Teresa, Mother, 10
theatre, 96–97
Théâtre de la Dame de Cœur, 18, 21, 28, 74,
    82, 220, 254
Théâtre du Nouveau Monde, 16, 206, 219,
    278
themes of experience, 24–29
Thibodeau-DeGuire, Michèle
    journey of leadership, 30
    public leadership, 283
Thierren, Joanne, 67
360-degree assessments, 91–92, 123, 124
time, 35
Time Magazine, 228
Timothy's World Coffee, 62, 198
Tm Bioscience Corporation, 92, 97, 146
Toastmasters Club, 80
Todd, David
    characteristics of leadership, 13
    development strategy, 77
Todd, Murray, 106
Toronto International Film Festival Group,
    59, 70, 209
trade, 248
Trade Centre Limited, 145, 157
trademarks of Canadian leadership, 220–223,
    297–299
TransCanada Corporation, 13, 51, 102, 274
transcendence, 44, 46, 47–55, 289
transformation, 15, 24, 25–26
Tremblay, Pierre-Marc
    apprenticeship model, 105
    journey of leadership, 33
    process of leadership, 45
Tremblay, Rémi

national leadership style, 224
public leadership, 267
Trudeau, Pierre Elliott, 227–228, 242, 249,
  265, 299
trust, 4
Tsouflidou, Cora
  apprenticeship model, 103
  characteristics of leadership, 12–13
  journey of leadership, 33
  national leadership style, 220, 234
TVA Group Inc, 29, 171, 267
Twain, Shania, 29
2010 Legacies Now, 277

U
uncertainty, 15
United Farmers of Alberta Co-operative
  Limited, 165, 194
United Way, 30, 222, 283
United Way Campaign, 80, 150
Université de Moncton, 177
Université de Sherbrooke, 17, 67, 88, 124,
  139, 163, 172, 178
Université du Québec à Montréal, 151, 202,
  263, 281
Université Laval, 127
University of Alberta, 55, 74, 114, 115, 138,
  231
University of Bologna, 185
University of Guelph, 115, 126, 134, 231
University of Saskatchewan, 15, 25, 247
University of Toronto, 230
University of Western Ontario, 18, 68
Unlimited Power (Robbins), 201
U.S. Gold Corporation, 14, 207

V
Vaccarino, Franco, 230
values
  in co-operatives, 172
  defining core, 242
  diversity and, 235
  foundation building and, 81, 84–86
  leadership brand, 230–231, 298
  reinforcement of, 250
van Dyke, Vickie
  development strategy, 91

leadership education, 210
process of leadership, 41, 52
Vancity Credit Union, 67, 102, 106, 161, 172,
  186, 188, 193, 237, 281
Vancouver, city council, 11, 18, 210, 226, 247,
  277
Vancouver, City of, 99, 270, 280
Vancouver Art Gallery, 20, 82, 204
Vancouver International Airport Authority,
  80, 273
Vancouver 2010 Olympic and Paralympic
  Winter Games, 77, 83, 217
Vancouver Urban Search and Rescue Team,
  249
Venture Publishing Inc., 207, 209, 237, 279
Verreault, Denise
  apprenticeship model, 97
  characteristics of leadership, 20
  development strategy, 81
Vidacom Inc., 67
Vienneau, Guy, 177
visibility, 36
vision
  defining core, 242, 244–245
  as foundation, 81, 83
  leadership process stages, 53
  in the process, 18
  as source of energy, 27, 28
visionary leaders, 17
visioning, 19
vocation, 24, 25
voice, 245–248
Volleyball Canada, 86, 146, 233

W
Walker, David
  apprenticeship model, 99
  the call to leadership, 61
  characteristics of leadership, 16
  development strategy, 93
  journey of leadership, 25
  leadership education, 196
  leadership style, 5
  process of leadership, 46
Walker, Doug, 63
Waridel, Laure, 202
warrior model, 242, 247–248, 299

Watson, Elizabeth, 197
Watters, Marge, 17
West, Mae, 63
White, Shelley, 222
W.J.A. Hamilton & Associates, 24, 58, 145,
   228, 260, 278
Women in the Lead Inc., 26, 251
Woozles and P'lovers, 284
words and actions, alignment of, 15
workshops, 105–107, 128
World Cup athletes, 84, 199
worth, 35
Wray, Lyn
   the call to leadership, 70
   characteristics of leadership, 19
   development strategy, 79

Y

Yamkowy, Don
   the call to leadership, 69
   process of leadership, 53

public leadership, 275
yin and yang, 20
York Catholic District School Board, 83, 86,
   220
York Central Hospital, 78, 153, 266
York University, 116, 120, 133, 134, 139, 261
Young Presidents' Association, 29
youth, 5
YWCA, 49, 88, 228, 274

Z

Zarnke, Paul
   the call to leadership, 71
   characteristics of leadership, 17
   process of leadership, 51
ZenithOptimedia, 43
Zundel, Pierre
   development program architecture, 119,
   122
   effective program structure, 135